P9-EDF-344

Trade Secret Theft, Industrial Espionage, and the China Threat

Trade Secret Theft, Industrial Espionage, and the China Threat

Carl Roper

CRC Press is an imprint of the
Taylor & Francis Group, an **Informa** business

CRC Press
Taylor & Francis Group
6000 Broken Sound Parkway NW, Suite 300
Boca Raton, FL 33487-2742

Printed on acid-free paper
Version Date: 20131017

International Standard Book Number-13: 978-1-4398-9938-0 (Hardback)

Visit the Taylor & Francis Web site at
http://www.taylorandfrancis.com

and the CRC Press Web site at
http://www.crcpress.com

Contents

About the Author

Carl A. Roper is a retired government official who—as a Security Specialist with the Department of Defense Security Institute (DoDSI)—was a lead instructor providing general and specialized security training across the spectrum of government agencies and industry. He developed the DoDSI Risk Management course and was instrumental in enhancing other courses. Mr. Roper is also a retired U.S. Army Counterintelligence Special Agent. As a professional author, he has written numerous magazine articles and security books. He holds a BA from The American University, Washington, D.C., and an MSA from Central Michigan University, and is currently a Security Consultant and Trainer.

He lives in Richmond, Virginia.

Introduction

> [W]e're going to aggressively protect our intellectual property. Our single greatest asset is the innovation and ingenuity and creativity of the American people. It is essential to our prosperity and it will only become more so in this century.

President Barack Obama[1]
March 11, 2010

This book is the product of hundreds and hundreds of hours of research, with material, both primary and secondary, reviewed, studied, and gleaned from numerous sources, including White House documentation, the US Congress, various other government agencies, many web searches for specific and general information, certain web blogs that are concerned with China's growing economic influence, and then the analysis of the accumulated information. This book is based on known facts, facts that most Americans have never seen, probably due to the massive amount of information with which all people are inundated with each and every day; it's just too much for most. As such, the development did not take on a typical "easy read and enjoyment," but perhaps more of a dry, college textbook (you remember those!) that is concerned with facts and substance, not that of pure enjoyment. To some, parts may seem like a fiction novel, but it is all true. Finally, this is not the final word on this very important subject of intellectual property, economic espionage, and national secrets being stolen by China, as the subject area is always increasing day by day with the finding of new facts, conjectures, and opinions on the subject. No one person, this author included, will ever be the "authority" on the subject as it is just too large to encompass.

The threat from China and the continuing loss of intellectual property and trade secrets in their varied forms, from the United States and also from other countries throughout our world, are ever-increasing as China attempts to gain a firmer control on the world economy and leverage its way to the top of the pile, controlling as much as possible, obtaining as much information as possible, and converting such information for its own use and purposes, be they short- or long-term.

Within this book, you will learn of the many methods and techniques used to obtain information, see a bit of history over centuries where espionage has played a role in the economy of various countries, view some cases that have come to light when individuals were caught, and also come to understand how the economy of a nation can increase or decrease, depending upon whether that nation is protecting its intellectual property or not, or whether it is stealing such property for its own use.

China is not alone in collecting information for its own economic and military expansion. To some extent, every country seeks out information on other nations. In this instance, though, China has become more aggressive than even the old Soviet Union in collecting information. When the USSR was still in existence, information collected was more of military and political in nature. Since its demise, more theft has occurred, with China being the culprit this time—in both volume and specificity—and it is not just military or political, but runs the entire gamut of just about every area you could think of.

China has made great strides over the past several decades and can be considered the number one perpetrator in the world for the collection of intellectual property, inventions, patents, and trade secrets. And China's biggest target is the United States, because it is more innovative, has a higher level of technology than other nations, and makes greater strides in science, technology, agriculture, and medicine. Theft reduces economic, military, and political power. Vice versa, it provides the country committing the theft with a much greater ability to increase its own political, military, and economic power, expanding it beyond anything that we could ever imagine.

Unfortunately, as of this writing, the US economy is not as great as it once was, and this can be laid directly at the doorstep of those individuals who choose to ignore proper procedures to protect the information, limit access to it, or look the other way for the purpose of making a few extra dollars at the expense our nation's security.

Insofar as possible, the author has created each chapter as a stand-alone chapter, in that each could be used wholly separate from the rest of the book. Those individuals that perform specific security functions, perform research on various topics, require specifics for the protection of their information, or desire to know what the Chinese are doing and how they do it need only to go to a specific chapter without the rest of the book encumbering them, in order to obtain the details. Even then, each chapter will provide you with a greater insight and knowledge of the ongoing Chinese threat.

From the time the draft of this book is completed until publication, about a dozen more espionage cases will probably come to public light. Unless it is a major case that will garner a fair amount of headlines, you might not hear about some of them. It could take at least a few seconds of airtime on television or it could be a very small article in the newspaper, but know that each one is another step in the continuing theft of America's economic secrets that can benefit China. In March 2012, a new case came to light, as the Chinese government, using a front company called Pangang Group Co., Ltd, was identified in court papers in the San Francisco federal court of using economic espionage to steal trade secrets. The individuals involved were of Chinese ethnicity and former DuPont scientists. Regretfully, they were successful in their endeavor to obtain what the Chinese government wanted. In addition to specific trade secrets, the Chinese used a stolen DuPont instruction manual—labeled Confidential—and were able to build a Chinese factory to produce a much sought after product. In a $17 billion-a-year industry, the Chinese are now able to compete, at a lower cost, and able to sell the product for less than DuPont. The author will follow this case closely.

In May 2012, the FBI launched a new campaign targeting corporate espionage. They pointed out that American industry and private-sector businesses are the choice target of foreign intelligence agencies, criminals, and industry spies and are costing America over $13 billion a year! Anywhere there is a concentration of high-tech research and development companies, laboratories, major industries, and national defense contractors, thieves are at work. They are looking to steal information and communications technology, which form the backbone of nearly every other technology; business information that pertains to supplies of scarce natural resources or that provides global actors an edge in negotiations with US businesses or the US government; military technologies, particularly marine systems, unmanned aerial vehicles, and other aerospace/aeronautic technologies; and civilian and dual-use technologies in fast-growing sectors like clean energy, health care/pharmaceuticals, and agricultural technology.

Finally, cases and public information data from the past few years have been included in the book. All these were put together to provide you a greater appreciation of why America needs to develop and implement greater and more sophisticated levels of security protection to ensure that our greatest economic secrets are not stolen in the future.

REFERENCE

1. President Barack Obama, remarks by the President speaking before the Export-Import Bank's Annual Conference, Washington, D.C., March 11, 2010 [can be seen at: www.whitehouse.gov/omb/intellectualproperty/quotes].

Carl A. Roper
Richmond, Virginia
May 2013

1 China: The Red Dragon of Economic Espionage

There is no nation that engages in surreptitious illegal technology acquisition for purposes of both commercial piracy and military advancement on a scale that approaches that of the People's Republic of China.

John N. Hostettler, Indiana
Chairman, Subcommittee on Immigration, Border Security, and Claims[1]

People ran into the streets, shouted, and partied all night: The Wall Had Fallen! The world was free of Communism, and the Soviet Union was no more. The downfall created a number of new, little nations. The world was safe... or so we all assumed. Nobody had much thought for China, the last refuge of Stalinist hard line Communism. Since 1949, the People's Republic of China under Mao had become a communist nation in the Far East. Now, it was the newest threat to freedom-loving people around the world; only we didn't necessarily recognize that fact.

China is the Red Dragon, like the cute pictures you see in books and on postcards—or marching in parades (Figure 1.1). It looks harmless, just a caricature of some imaginary mythical creature of old. Unfortunately, and most regretfully, it is real. Like the words in a well-known movie title, China is a crouching tiger waiting to pounce, a hidden dragon of great fire awaiting its chance to charge forward, spitting out dangerous fire and devour everything in sight.

Today's China is far different from its characterized mythical past. It is, in essence, a quiet, stealthy tiger sneaking around, sometimes in plain view, at other times hidden among the forest of trees, always seeking and taking, then slinking away with no one the wiser until later. And like the big red dragon, it is slowly raising its monstrous head, but, in this case, roaring with fire by shooting out the flames of an increased economy, to take advantage of the rest of the world.

The dragon we see as a constant flow of products with the "Made in China" tag that crosses every border in the world, with products of questionable origin, products based on stolen technology, based on stolen or reverse-engineered methods, and even products that look the same and operate the same, except they are being made—in many cases—with our own designs.

China, then, is a dangerous country with its sharpened claws reaching out across the world, both to sell their products and to obtain our secrets that allow them to make those products and more products for a fraction of the investment cost.

In a Congressional Research Service report to Congress of 1999, entitled *China: Suspected Acquisition of U.S. Nuclear Weapons Secrets*, which was updated in February 2006—but also confirmed by an article by Jonathan Weisman in the *Baltimore Sun*, Baltimore, Maryland, on May 22, 1999—a representative of the Intelligence Community reported that in an Intelligence Community's damage assessment, "China obtained by espionage classified US nuclear weapons information that probably accelerated its program to develop future nuclear weapons."[2]

The assessment also revealed that China obtained information on "several" US nuclear reentry vehicles, including the Trident II submarine-launched missile that delivers the W88 nuclear warhead as well as "a variety of" design concepts and weaponization features, including those of the neutron bomb.

FIGURE 1.1 Do not underestimate the power and reach of the red dragon! A dancing dragon from a Chinese New Year festival. (Courtesy of Shutterstock/Christophe Testi.)

In 2000, Federal Bureau of Investigation (FBI) Director Louis Freeh briefed the Senate Intelligence Committee on what he called a "very serious" espionage threat from China.[3]

In 2005, David Szady, Assistant Director of the FBI's Counterintelligence Division claimed that "China is the biggest (espionage) threat to the U.S. today."[4]

In 2011, an FBI representative stated that China is *the* major electronic espionage threat. And, again, in 2011, in an Alexandria VA court, Assistant US Attorney Ken Sorenson presented a brief in which he said that "China aggressively seeks U.S. defense technologies, and the People's Liberation Army are now shown to have been actively working on stealth aircraft designs…."[5,6]

But, while these identified China as targeting the United States, we were not alone in China's quest for secrets. In England, MI5 had said that the Chinese government represents "one of the most significant espionage threats to the UK."[7]

To the north of the United States, Canada's intelligence service has, for a number of years, been greatly concerned about China's growing economic threat. The Canadian Security and Intelligence Service over a period of years have released a number of reports detailing the threat and the various economic targets throughout the nation. In those reports, China has been dramatically highlighted as the major threat to Canada's economic security and well-being.[8]

Canada also sees China as using their nation as a doorstep to enter America.

At the 5th Annual IT Security Conference in 2010, Kevin Cearlock of the Houston, Texas FBI office gave a presentation to IT businesses and other professionals. Upon reviewing his presentation, several items really jumped out, not that they were unknown, but that they never really seemed of such great interest before the presentation was given. During the presentation, Special Agent Cearlock said that "China is the most aggressive country conducting espionage against the United States and U.S. interests world-wide," and that collection efforts against "the U.S. has roughly doubled since the end of the Cold War." He went on, further telling his most interested audience that the main focus for all foreign intelligence, which had been military secrets, had shifted to "critical technology and U.S. proprietary economic information."[9]

The previous examples are but a small sampling of US, Canada, and UK concerns over Chinese espionage activities. But it goes back much further than Americans might imagine.

Up until the fall of the Berlin wall and the breakup of the Soviet Union, the greatest concern about espionage activities came from the Soviet Union. Probably about 95% of all activity was targeted at the military, political, and industrial bases. But, unfortunately, forgotten was the sleeping giant called China, who had been very quietly making great inroads. They, too, were targeting the United States, in addition to just about every other country wherein they could gain some sort of foothold in order to obtain intellectual, scientific, research and development (R&D), military, and political secrets or any other information to better boost their nation at all levels.

Over the past five decades, the world has watched China evolve from a peasant nation to one of large factories of all types, high educational standards, a standing military that is the equivalent of that for all of Europe and, most importantly—and disturbingly—a deep-rooted desire to be the number one producer of consumer goods worldwide (Figure 1.2). Whether this is for good or bad must be based in many instances upon the acquisition of foreign data and technology in its many forms. This data and technology is necessary to advance their own production and economy, create more jobs and factories, and bring in many more foreign dollars to the already bulging monetary system. All of this for the ever-increasing economic power they wish to exert throughout the world.

Every country, of course, has a knowledge base of qualified intellectuals in many different fields. From these individuals, new products and ventures evolve and the economy rises, perhaps even significantly where the proper inroads of technology and consumerism are successfully targeted.

But, when the acquisition of economic information comes from other countries, and those various enterprises are supported by the government, either directly or otherwise, the question arises as to the true intent of that country. The acquisition of such information must be wholly legal and proper if the country is to continue to be successful, admired, and respected throughout the world for its endeavors. In a situation like this, though, China's worldwide acquisition of intellectual property (IP) by theft is just plain greed, and while the world recognizes the fact of the thefts and greed, the Chinese economy continues to grow, and that is at the expense of the entire world. Further, the majority of their targets are in the United States.

As the United States has, for over a century and more, been considered the focal point for technology advancement, economic growth and strength, and the ability to take an idea and grow it into a profitable product or enterprise, the nation has been the central target for IP theft. This is unfortunate because, as a leader, everyone wants to emulate this nation, and they have a desire to meet or exceed our economic development and, in doing so, use any means necessary to achieve such goals. In this regard, China stands at the forefront of such information acquisition.

FIGURE 1.2 As a leading producer of consumer goods worldwide, the People's Republic of China's "Made in China" label has become ubiquitous in manufactured goods.

As then FBI Director Louis J. Freeh stated at the Hearings on Economic Espionage before the House Judiciary Committee way back in 1996:

> The development and production of proprietary economic information is an integral part of virtually every aspect of United States trade, via its commerce and business and, hence, is essential to maintaining the health and competitiveness of critical segments of the United States economy. This in addition to ensuring a strong military through the products of commerce that benefit and support the military might of the United States. The theft, misappropriation, wrongful receipt, transfer, and use of United States proprietary economic information, particularly by foreign governments and their agents and instrumentalities—but also from domestic malefactors—directly threatens the development and production of that information and, as a result, directly imperils the health and competitiveness of a great nation. The ever-increasing value of proprietary economic information in the global and domestic marketplaces, and the corresponding spread of the latest technologies, are now effectively intertwined to significantly increase both the opportunities and motives from China for conducting economic espionage. The targets of economic espionage are varied ... but high-technology and defense-related industries remain the primary targets of foreign economic intelligence collection operations.
>
> Many U.S. high-tech industrial sectors are targeted by the Chinese. The industries which are immediately targeted include biotechnology; aerospace; telecommunications, including the technology to build the National Information Infrastructure; computer software and hardware; advanced transportation and engine technology; advanced materials and coatings, especially those that include "stealth" technologies; energy research; defense and armaments technology; manufacturing processes; and semiconductors.[10]

Further, from the non-creative side of commerce is all the supporting supplemental proprietary business information, that is, bid data, contracts, and customer and strategy information in these sectors, which are aggressively targeted. Collectors for this "supplemental" information have also shown great interest in government and corporate financial and trade data that would allow their continuing commerce and business infrastructure to determine specific and future pricing development as well as being able to better sell any commercially viable product for a lesser price due to the fact that the various costs of developing and manufacturing the product is well below what a US manufacturer would have to pay.[10]

Freeh goes on to say that all these industries of commerce "are of strategic interest to the United States on three different levels as:

1. They produce classified defense products for the government.
2. They produce dual-use technology which can be used in both the public and private sectors.
3. They are responsible for the latest R&D, all of which results in the creation of leading-edge technologies critical to maintaining US economic security.

Losses at or within any of these levels could easily affect US international competitiveness and national security" at any given time.[10]

In addition to technological information, there is the continued Chinese collection of intelligence data on US government plans and policies with regard to trade and industry. The collection of sensitive foreign economic intelligence frequently enhances a nation's military, as well as economic capabilities. Likewise, the line separating purely economic intelligence from political intelligence is as difficult to draw as that between technical and military intelligence.

In the Foreign Intelligence Collection report of 2011, the Office of the National Counterintelligence Executive stated that China is a very persistent collector. It said that "Chinese leaders consider the first two decades of the 21st century to be a window of strategic opportunity for their country to focus on economic growth, independent innovation, scientific and technical advancement, and growth of the renewable energy sector."[11] Hence, the time is now for America to take a really hard look at what IP must be protected, and do it. There can be no slacking in this regard or China will definitely move to the very forefront as the world's economic leader.

The impact of such Chinese espionage targeting is not lost on the US Intelligence Community. Neither the Intelligence Community as a whole nor the FBI specifically has ever systematically evaluated the costs of economic espionage. The time, personnel, and monetary effort that must be put into such an evaluation would take years and thousands of man-hours, which would take away from other efforts, but would also—by necessity—become a continuing effort to update the conclusions since so much espionage is being conducted and not necessarily known. The US private sector has made some efforts to estimate its losses to economic espionage and other foreign economic intelligence operations; however, to date, these cost estimates have generally been based upon small, unrepresentative samples of the US business community and have tended to emphasize companies with holdings in the United States rather than overseas.

The FBI, on its official web site, discusses economic espionage, noting that the Cold War is not over. Rather, it states that "it has merely moved into a new arena: the global marketplace." The FBI has estimated that, every year, *billions* of US dollars are lost to foreign and domestic competitors. These competitors are those who will deliberately target economic intelligence in the myriad of flourishing US industries and technologies, taking their time to cull intelligence out of shelved technologies by exploiting open source information and company trade secrets.

A proper comprehensive evaluation and up-to-date analysis of what is being stolen must, by necessity, include all US commerce manufacturing and production that is also being performed outside the physical United States. Understandably, US industry across the board would be quite reluctant to publicize such occurrences of economic espionage. Such publicity would quickly and easily adversely affect and shake up their stock values, their potential and current customers' confidence, and, ultimately, the various industries' competitiveness and market share across the board with known US and other foreign competitors. Nevertheless, in the last few years, there have been a number of studies and estimates that have attempted to quantify the scope and impact of economic espionage.[10]

The history of collecting data on these types of theft is slowly growing, reaching back for several decades. For a number of years into the present, the American Society for Industrial Security (ASIS), now known as ASIS International, has had an annual survey report produced.[12] Going back to when the survey first started, it found that all types of commercial espionage during 1991–1992 resulted in major losses to US firms in the following areas: pricing data ($1 billion), product development and specification data ($597 million), and manufacturing process information ($110 million). Since that time, ASIS has produced more reports of this nature. Each one continues to indicate an ever-growing espionage effort aimed at the United States and its commercial entities. The ASIS studies have been referred to in various Congressional and other government reports, indicating the true worth of their accuracy and concern by the security industry.

As early as 1982, the US International Trade Commission (ITC) estimated that piracy of US IP rights in a number of selected industrial sectors have cost the nation's business $6 billion to $8 billion in annual sales and cost US citizens around 131,000 jobs.[13]

In 1987, the ITC estimated the losses to all US industries at $23.8 billion. (Using the 1982 average loss ratio of $7 billion = 130,000 jobs, this would constitute a loss of approximately 450,000 US jobs.)[13] This is a very rapid growth for losses in such a short amount of time.

Depending upon which of the various other reports you might also view, the losses attributed to economic espionage can range upward of $300 billion, or possibly beyond. It's difficult to equate since some companies will never reveal that they have been successfully targeted. In other instances, some companies may not yet know how much was stolen or the true value of the stolen information.

Over the years, though, China's industrial espionage efforts have been caught red-handed, with their hands deep in our cookie jar, pulling out as many secrets as they can grasp at one time. And it has happened over and over. China's ongoing and coordinated industrial espionage attack within the United States has threatened the economic and national security, and one doesn't need to look very far to find scary examples. According to the non-profit Alliance for American Manufacturing, one interested case involved two engineers who worked at a Goodyear tire manufacturing facility at Tennessee.

> The Chinese tire manufacturer paid the two thieves … to enter a Goodyear facility under false pretences and use cell phones to photograph processes and technology that it could then use to make similar tires without going through product development. In a year of huge layoffs in our manufacturing sector, this scheme could easily lead to Goodyear having to unfairly compete with a knock-off of its own proprietary design. Stuff is really cheap when you steal it, and it appears that the Chinese have decided not to waste years and millions—or even billions—of dollars on research and development when they can pay far less obtaining critical product information from spying and theft. American consumers are familiar with China's designer knock-offs and pirated DVDs, but its industrial espionage goes beyond breaking intellectual property laws on consumer goods. Indeed, China's plan to steal propriety information is organized, strategic and a danger to US interests. China's wide-reaching and aggressive industrial espionage is not just about tires, handbags or movies; it is an enormous threat to our national and economic security.[14]

Fortunately, the thieves were caught. Note here that nowhere was the Chinese government involved or ever linked to the incident. This is very typical. There are no direct links that a person could find that would prove beyond doubt that the Chinese government had a hand in the espionage attempt to steal trade secrets. This seems to always be the case with China. That said, China does nothing without approval "from above," be that approval from "on high," from the military, or from a government committee that supports rapid economic growth. Knowing, though, and proving it are a different matter entirely.

Other cases that come to light from time to time include government defense and technology contractors, private industries, and even agents operating within our military itself. Chinese nationals (especially those who become naturalized citizens), over time, will rise to hold sensitive positions in many of our organizations and also in our government contractor facilities, and these naturalized citizens are in an excellent position to obtain it and have the information exploited back in China.

In recent years, China has increasingly encouraged American companies to relocate their manufacturing facilities and capabilities to China, which they have been more than willing to do. This, of course, is very strategic on China's part. Once a company is located in China, the product can then be "reverse engineered." A critical concern here is that once the product is in China, the Chinese workers take advantage of the manufacturing process to learn as much as possible about it. Essentially, the American company will most assuredly find it necessary to share the many individual parts or even all of its technology and numerous manufacturing methods with the workers. This would be under the guise of the many workers learning how to better perform their daily jobs properly. As they do so, they pick up and learn just about everything necessary so that in a short time, the Chinese can set up their own company and make and market the same product at a much lower price. Whether it is patented would not be a concern in China, and even if the product is patented in the United States, it is not patented in China, and under Chinese law, it is legal for a Chinese firm to patent and make the product and sell it, using China's "first to patent" in China law, which is to their advantage, and to the disadvantage of the rest of the world.[15]

In the case of stolen patent designs, the Alliance for American Manufacturing states: "Chinese companies are not even required to prove that designs which they present for patent protection are their own. American law enforcement and security agencies need to pay closer attention to this activity and more aggressively and publicly pursue prosecution of these high level bandits. American companies and our military must scrutinize more carefully any Chinese nationals involved in technology or product development."[15] At this point also, US interests should override the need to have the product and its technology and IP information moved to China. If this is not accomplished, either by law or by self-imposed controls of the private sector commerce community, America can only look forward to having its economic and national security interests stolen from right under everyone's collective noses.

Since such actions are now not in place, it currently allows China to take the information, techniques, and other items of value and start or expand a separate business venture to directly compete with the United States for the same product, except they will produce and sell it at a much lower price.

The United States, being a great benefactor to the world, encourages the free exchange of most scientific and technical information and has many government programs to support the exchange of technology to facilitate economic development in a wide variety of foreign countries. However, the United States must draw a very clear line to protect information that is classified, concerns militarily critical technologies, is subject to export controls, or is proprietary information that is the IP of a specific firm or individual. This is especially critical when such information is crucial to the US national security and economic sectors in terms of ultimate superiority in the product development and also when the information has a valid national defense basis for withholding it from a foreign nation that is willing to take it and directly compete against US interests.[16]

Global economic competition has, to a large extent, replaced the Cold War political and military competition between East and West. As a result, friends and allies, as well as less friendly countries, now pursue their national interests through espionage against the United States. Their goal is to develop a competitive edge in the global market place or boost military readiness, while drastically reducing their own R&D costs. China is, and will continue into the foreseeable future, to be at the forefront in this regard.

PROTECTING US INTELLECTUAL PROPERTY OVERSEAS

A few years ago, the US House of Representatives held a series of sessions on "Protecting U.S. Intellectual Property Overseas: The Joint Strategic Plan and Beyond." One very important aspect of the hearings was to highlight the important role US Immigration and Customs Enforcement (ICE) plays in combating IP theft in today's global economy.

According to ICE Director John Morton, in his opening statement before the US House of Representatives, Committee of Foreign Affairs, Hearing on Protecting US Intellectual Property Overseas: The Joint Strategic Plan and Beyond in July of 2010:

> Simply put, American business is threatened by those who pirate copyrighted material and produce counterfeit trademarked goods. Criminals are attempting to steal American ideas and products and sell them over the Internet, in flea markets, in legitimate retail outlets and elsewhere. From counterfeit pharmaceuticals and electronics to pirated movies, music, and software, IP thieves undermine the U.S. economy and jeopardize public safety. American jobs are being lost, American innovation is being diluted and the public health and safety of Americans is at risk—and organized criminal enterprises are profiting from their increasing involvement in IP theft.[17]

These items are not just stolen in the United States, but anywhere in the world where US companies set up R&D facilities and manufacturing plants, because the security protection safeguards and lax security personnel protection are much looser in overseas environments.

The government is responding to this organized criminal activity through a first-of-its-kind, aggressive, coordinated, and strategic offensive that is designed to target those counterfeiters and also those who pirate the copyrighted material for monetary gain.[17]

BACKGROUND OF THE PROBLEM

Again, in this regard, Congress did its own research, although not very much of their results were seen, read, and understood by the American public and the appropriate manufacturers. The US House of Representatives Committee on Foreign Affairs, hearings on "Protecting U.S. Intellectual Property Overseas: The Joint Strategic Plan and Beyond" (July 21, 2001), highlighted the very important role played by the ICE in combating IP theft. The following is excerpted from their report:

> America's entrepreneurial spirit and integrity are embodied by the creativity and resourcefulness of our workforce. Intellectual property rights and the ability to enforce those rights encourage American companies to continue the tradition of American innovation and develop products, ideas, and merchandise. This tradition of innovation and productivity has given America an advantage in the global economy.

> Intellectual property rights are intended to discourage thieves from selling cheap imitations of products, which are often far less safe or reliable than the original products. More importantly, intellectual property rights protect our nation by preventing the proliferation of counterfeit pharmaceuticals, preserving national and economic security, and ensuring consumer safety. Violators depress investment in technologies needed to meet global challenges and also put consumers, families, and communities at risk. They unfairly devalue America's contributions, hinder our ability to grow our economy, and compromise American jobs.
>
> Intellectual property rights protect consumer trust and safety, as counterfeit "products pose significant risks to: our communities by threatening public health through the introduction of substandard or unapproved products meant for public use or consumption; our military members through untested and ineffective components; our transit systems through auto parts of unknown quality that play critical roles in security passengers; and our health care systems through suspect pharmaceuticals and semiconductors used in life-saving defibrillators. Intellectual property rights also protect the actor, director, writer, musician and artist from having a movie, manuscript, song or design illegally sold by someone who had no part in the artistry of creating it."[18]

The report also was concerned with the foreign ownership aspect of businesses, when it said:

> As foreign corporate ownership becomes widespread, as multinationals expand, as nation-states dissolve into regions and coalesce into supranational states – the classic, exclusionary, and dichotomous view of the world ("we" versus "they") will fade. But the notion of "proprietary information" is here to stay. And theft will never cease as long as there is profit to be had.[19]

Since assuming office, President Obama ordered a review of our nation's cyber security. "The national security and economic health of the United States depend on the security, stability and integrity of our nation's cyberspace, both in the public and private sectors," said John Brennan, Obama's top adviser for counterterrorism and homeland security. "The president is confident that we can protect our nation's critical cyber infrastructure while at the same time adhering to the rule of law and safeguarding privacy rights and civil liberties."[20]

This review may well have been predicated on the 2008 US–China Economic and Security Review Commission's Annual Report to Congress that argued for tighter computer security measures to prevent data loss or corruption, where it was stated that "China is targeting US government and commercial computers for espionage."

At another hearing, this one held by the House Permanent Select Committee on Intelligence, cyber defense experts testified that government agencies are insufficiently coordinated to handle an attack and that efforts to build a top-notch IT defense have not adequately addressed issues in the private sector. This is an ongoing concern and can be shown frequently by the various newspaper and television reports of attacks on computer systems in both the government and private sectors.

"Our current information infrastructure is riddled with holes, unknown backdoors, and is extremely difficult to protect in the face of increasingly sophisticated adversaries," said Paul Kurtz, a partner with Good Harbor Consulting and a consulting member of the CSIS Commission on Cybersecurity.[21]

In 2008, the theft of IP from US companies was occurring, at a minimum, of approximately $200 billion a year. Others have put the cost at perhaps $300 billion. Nobody really knows, but the guesswork involved in making such numerical predictions is typically based on a wide-ranging analysis of many various business and financial indicators from around the world and also the publicized espionage cases that reach the public media. In some cases, manufacturers themselves report estimated losses, but keep their names very quiet when reporting such activities. When information is supplied for the annual ASIS report on IP theft, the manufacturers know that the information supplied is being reported anonymously to the ASIS, and their companies will not be identified in any way. There are a lot of new products out there and they cost a lot of money to develop. American industry and the US government spend, as Paul Kurtz put it, "billions of dollars to develop new products and technology that are being stolen at little to no cost by our adversaries. Nothing is off limits—pharmaceuticals, biotech, IT, engine design, weapons design."[22] This last statement is aptly put, as China is the greatest economic threat to the United States and the world!

Espionage and the theft of IP require people to obtain the data. Thousands of business people enter the United States every year, and when they are Chinese, be assured that they are targeting each and every business wherein they can learn something to take back and apply to the Chinese economy. Now, imagine 200,000 Chinese college students attending our various colleges and universities, taking basic and advanced courses that will allow them to learn our latest business, electrical, and mechanical technologies. Science and technology (S&T) are wonderful fields of endeavor, and hold much promise for the future. China realizes this much more than we do. Taking courses is just one aspect of their information-gathering process. They intend, and do, take every advanced course possible. Then, watch these students take "part-time" intern or summer jobs with every possible company wherein they can further their knowledge and obtain hands-on experience with the latest machines and technology.

These students will graduate with advanced degrees and obtain full-time jobs with our Fortune 500 companies, new startups in Silicon Valley in California and, in the Midwest, they will study and apply agricultural knowledge in order to gain further knowledge. They will help shape how we do business by helping us in every way possible.

At the same time, what they gain will be filed away in their brains, the documents they read or review may be copied, the company files—especially R&D, designs, equipment, methodologies, new patent developing offerings, crucial processes and formulas—will be acquired, and, when feasible, all of it will be downloaded from the company web site, or internal company computer systems, put onto disks or perhaps just e-mailed back home to China. Every student will have his or her own method of obtaining the information, saving it, and either storing it locally on disks, e-mailing it home, or copying the documents and carrying them out to where they live, slowly accumulating the data, then at a later date, moved back to China.

All of the above in furtherance of an unofficial and unwritten China policy of grand economic growth, no matter how such growth is achieved. The information may be used to start their own business, assist a current business enterprise for it to expand and grow more rapidly than is feasible, and share it with various other Chinese-approved companies, to think tanks, to the military, and also to those government organs that can also benefit from the information.

Remember the thousands of Chinese that visit the United States every year. The Chinese people, government, businesses, and just plain individuals are great collectors of information (Figure 1.3).

FIGURE 1.3 As an open society, the United States welcomes visitors and students from all over the world. Many are legitimate students and people just wanting to enjoy our country, but others … what information have you inadvertently told an otherwise innocent-looking person?

When they return to China, they may be interviewed by government agents to assess what has been learned. Also, business enterprises and specialists may well further inquire, and then once all the information has been collected and assembled, numerous experts and specialists from a wide array of business enterprises will pour over the gained information and determine its value. That value is then assigned to those companies, research and think tanks, and individuals who can best use the information to develop, increase, expand, or create new products and ventures. The information could have general commercial value or, sometimes, it will have specific military and intelligence value. All this is to their gain, and to the detriment of the United States.

In a US Senate Select Committee on Intelligence report submitted to Congress on economic espionage by China, it was found that with respect to satellite and missile technology, the information that was obtained "enabled China to improve its present and future space launch vehicles and ICBMs. Because such analyses and methodologies are also applicable to the development of other missile systems, China can use the information to improve its short and intermediate range ballistic missiles, and other related technology."[23–25] (Note that these missiles could threaten US forces stationed in Japan and Korea, as well as other allies in the region.)

The House of Representatives Select Committee on US National Security and Military/Commercial Concerns with the People's Republic of China, chaired by Rep. Cox, set about determining what secrets China had stolen in the recent past. They determined that China (a) had nuclear weapons, (b) had missile and space technology, and (c) was working diligently to acquire military technology.[26]

> **Nuclear Weapons** "The People's Republic of China (PRC) has stolen design information from the United States' most advanced thermonuclear weapons." (Referring to alleged spying and computer data leaks at Los Alamos, Lawrence, Livermore, Oak Ridge, and Sandia National Labs.) "The Select Committee judges that the PRC's next generation of thermonuclear weapons, currently under development will exploit elements of stolen U.S. design information." And the "PRC penetration of our national weapons laboratories spans at least the past several decades and almost certainly continues today."[26]

Table 1.1 lists what has been targeted in terms of technologies that have shown up in the news or other places in just a two-year period.

TABLE 1.1
Technology-Targeted Items in a 24-Month Period

2008	Carbon fiber material with rocket and spacecraft applications to China
2008	Military accelerometers to China
2008	Space launch technical data and services
2008	Military technical data on unmanned aerial vehicles
2008	Military aircraft components
2008	Thermal imaging cameras
2008	Military laser aiming devices and fighter pilot cueing systems
2008	US military source code and trade secrets
2008	Controlled amplifiers
2008	Amplifiers/missile target acquisition technology
2008	Trade secrets (not further identified)
2008	US naval warship data
2008	Theft of trade secrets on US space shuttle
2007	Military night vision technology
2007	US stealth missile data and military secrets
2007	Economic espionage and theft of trade secrets
2007	Restricted technology
2007	Illegal exports of military night vision technology
2006	Industrial furnace to the Chinese Army Missile Institute

Keep in mind that this is just what we know about. Imagine what else might be "missing" from our intellectual base.

From the sampling of economic espionage cases worked by the FBI, the majority of individuals pleaded guilty, affirming in the view of many that they were being directed. There is no way that such a collection of educated specialists in science and engineering could or would have performed these acts of their own volition.

Nevertheless, China's responses to any "allegations" of espionage are enlightening, as illustrated by the comments to follow. China has always been in denial for any actions, since they would not consider espionage—that is, espionage that is in their best interests—a crime and thus something to attempt to defend or even acknowledge:

- At a press conference, when questioned by a reporter about an investigator's charges, China's Foreign Spokesman responded that "We do not conduct espionage in this country and the accusations are totally groundless."[27]
- In response to a question regarding a specific case of espionage, a spokesman for the Chinese Foreign Minister Ma Zhaoxu said that "This is not the first time we have heard these kinds of accusations. The so-called espionage activities conducted by China in the United States, are inventions fabricated to suit a particular agenda."[28]
- He then added that as Chinese, "We urge the US to abandon its Cold War mindset, (and to) stop making groundless accusations against China, and do more to improve mutual trust between the two nations and friendship between the two peoples."[28]
- For years, veteran Chinese Intelligence Officer Li Fengzhi, who had worked in the Chinese Ministry of State Security for quite a few years, then defected several years ago and made some very strong statements about the amount and level of espionage that was being conducted by China. He wasn't shy about telling about China's spy agency and its focus not only on sending spies to infiltrate the US intelligence community but also on collecting secrets and technology from the United States. "China spends a tremendous effort to send out spies to important countries like the US to collect information," Mr. Li said.[29]
- In Washington, D.C., Wang Baodong, the Chinese Embassy spokesman, did not address Mr. Li's comments directly, but he did repeat past Chinese government statements regarding its intelligence activities. He said that "Allegations of China conducting spying activities against the United States are groundless and unwarranted." He further commented that "China never engages itself in activities that will harm other countries' national interests."[30]

Canada, a very strong ally of the United States, is not immune to espionage either. When defectors pointed out that China has hundreds of people in Canada conducting espionage, the Foreign Affairs Minister Peter MacKay said that Canada was "very concerned about economic espionage."[31]

China, of course, has always been quick to refute any possible ideas about espionage being conducted by their government. Even China's ambassador to Canada (as others have done around the world) has rejected claims that Chinese spies are stealing Canada's industrial and high-tech secrets. In an interview with CTV News, Ambassador Lu Shumin declared: "There is no Chinese espionage in Canada." He further stated that, "We express our grave concerns about this and, as Chinese ambassador, I can see the so-called Chinese espionage against Canada does not hold water."[31]

The United States, in addition to the rest of the world, is a target of China's growing thirst for economic, military, and political information and technology. And all of it can be applied to their ever-growing military and economic base, helping their economy, strengthening the military, and making for a much more growing power-hungry government that wants to involve itself into every country throughout the world where they can be effective to their own self-benefit.

LONDON SPEAKS OUT

In a June 2011 issue of their paper, *The Telegraph*,[32] published in London, England, it prominently ran an article on China's latest effort to rack up its intelligence abilities by opening a string of spy schools.

China's purpose in setting up the spy schools was to significantly increase the training and recruitment of agents. They would receive and develop in the classroom (and presumably also through practical training exercises) the methodology for intelligence collection and acquisition via a formal college-level training program for future agents—spies, if you will. All the selected students, 30 or 50 or so for each program (the author reads "program" as a given "class" of students), would receive extensive background training in the art of intelligence, espionage, various tradecraft techniques, and the most up-to-date data collection and analysis techniques.

In this day and age, it is a far cry from where, in the past, China has relied mostly on students or academics, in addition to the hundreds of business people and other "visitors" in various countries. This is also a far cry from China's statements that they don't spy on others.

This announcement came about as China opened its eighth National Intelligence College (NIC) according to the article. The latest NIC was located on the campus of Hunan University, in Changsha. Other schools that have already opened are located in Beijing, Nanjing, one in the southern province of Guangdong, and others at Shanghai's Fudan University, Xian, Qindgao, and Harbin.

"The establishment of Intelligence Colleges are in response to the urgent need for special skills to conduct intelligence work in the modern era," said a spokesman for Shanghai's Fudan University. "The college will use Fudan's existing computer science, law, management, journalism and sociology resources and then carry out special intelligence training," he added.[32]

However, not disclosed was the exact location of the new spy school on the various campuses, as other students at Fudan University were being kept largely in the dark about its existence and location.

This author went on the web and researched the various Chinese schools, their curriculums, and various departments. Nowhere could anything about these internal Intelligence Colleges or specific courses to be taught be found. China, then, is keeping them very secret, hiding them in plain sight, so only those students who actually attend these specialized colleges know about it; the other students on any given campus are wholly in the dark. Be this as it may, some people associated with these colleges have spoken out, but somewhat carefully, and we in the West were quick to pick up on it.

"China does not have the talents and skills it needs in its intelligence departments," said Cao Shujin, a deputy dean at the Zhongshan National Intelligence College, where he is also a professor of information management. "We needed to set up specific degree courses to fill those requirements," he added.[32]

Once the selected students have spent years studying information management, "they can elect to switch to the Intelligence College. We have not decided the exact screening process yet." "Elect" to switch? This would sound like a student's choice to move to another field, but if the students have already been selected, they could only "elect" if they knew about the Intelligence College. It seems even the Chinese can't keep their statements and thoughts in good order, like even admitting they have set up Intelligence Colleges. Cao said the new colleges were "nothing for the West to worry about. This is nothing like the changes going on in the People's Liberation Army; we are just trying to provide the right sort of skills for our requirements. Some of our graduates will probably go into the government's intelligence departments, but maybe not all of them."[32]

WHAT DOES CHINA DESIRE TO BE?

A short distance from Richmond, Virginia, is the city of Ashland, which touts itself—rather proudly—as "The Middle of the Universe," and its citizens are justifiably proud of that description.

A world away, China believes itself to be "THE center of the universe," on the assumption that the world will one day look to China for everything.

Why? Fifty years ago, a mere droplet in the bucket of time for history, China had started to emerge from its shadow of self-reliance and started to develop a better economy. It has always been a proud nation, bowing to no one, believing they are always right, can do no wrong, and standing on such principles as "we are right," "we will survive and grow stronger," and "we will lead the world!"

A century ago, nobody would ever believe this, but in the past half-century, using its massive population base, a thirst for education and knowledge, and the newer and newer technologies being developed around the world (mostly in the United States), China has stretched its tentacles far beyond the Great Wall and now touches every part of the world.

During the past five decades, the world has seen China evolve from a peasant nation to one having the largest collection of manufacturing facilities of all types, major medical research facilities, higher education standards, a standing military that is the equivalent of that for all of Europe, and, most importantly—and disturbing—a deep-rooted desire to be the number one producer of consumer goods, which, for good or bad, is based in many instances upon the acquisition of foreign data and technology in its many and varied forms. All of this for China's development as a major economic power throughout the world.

In doing so, China has also amassed a virtual king's ransom of property, stocks, bonds, and businesses of all types throughout the world in addition to untold millions and millions of dollars ready to be spent. So much, in fact, that they can afford to spend recklessly and with abandon in searching out and obtaining newer technologies, trade secrets, inventions, new innovations, chemical and pharmaceuticals formulas, and IP, no matter what the cost.

THE US STAND ON THE NATION'S ECONOMY

As stated in the original proposal for the Economic Espionage and Protection of Proprietary Economic Information Act of 1996:

> The development and production of proprietary economic information is an integral part of virtually every aspect of United States trade, commerce, and business ... the theft, misappropriation, and wrongful receipt, transfer, and use of proprietary economic information belonging to the United States Government and United States firms, businesses, and industry by foreign governments and their agents or instrumentalities directly and substantially threatens the health and competitiveness of critical segments of the United States economy and, consequently, the Nation's security.[33]

All this is very essential to ensure we can maintain a viable health and competitiveness within the critical segments of the economy. Proprietary information, also referred to as trade secrets, has a continually increasing value in the US marketplace. Thus, when this information is tied to the corresponding spread of technology, it will create a significant increase for both opportunities and motives for individuals to conduct economic espionage. As Sherlock Holmes would say, "the game's afoot!" when any foreign government, especially China, actively targets US individuals, businesses, industries, and the US government itself and tries to steal or wrongfully acquire critical technologies, data, and other information. This overall economic and political design is aimed at advancing China's military and industrial sectors with a superior competitive edge. Likewise, the theft of this proprietary information from within the United States has also increased to the detriment of one company and the benefit of another, allowing China to further prosper as the United States slowly loses its economic edge.

Whether you wish to call it economic espionage, research, intelligence gathering, trade development strategies, R&D research, competitive intelligence, or whatever, the acquisition of trade secrets, inventions, and the like means that such information gathering being directed against US economic interests is neither unusual nor unprecedented. The United States and other major industrial countries have been targets of economic espionage for decades, but it has been increasing several-fold over the past few years.

CHINA'S INDUSTRIAL ESPIONAGE

China's ongoing and coordinated industrial espionage in the United States is threatening our economic and national security. One does not have to look too far to find examples.

At a time where we have huge layoffs and massive unemployment, knockoffs of products are seen daily. Where else can you get a $200 pair of fancy shoes for less than $50? Where else can you get a watch that looks like a $2000 Swiss timepiece for around $50? Where but on the streets of the good ol' USA! Flea markets, "sales" stores, tailgate sales, and street vendors have just about any product you want, and they are cheap. The majority are knockoffs—counterfeit versions of the actual products—created with cheap labor and then shipped to the United States and sold for whatever the market will bear. Unless you look closely, they look like the real thing, but they are cheap imitations. And they are costing jobs, profits, and success in the market economy.

This begs the question of why the Chinese would go through the process of product development when they can just steal the designs, blueprints, formula, or the actual product and remake it...and, oh, so much more cheaply? China doesn't want to waste years and untold millions of dollars to develop and then manufacture the product. All those R&D dollars are saved when they can pay far less to obtain critical product information from spying or plain outright theft.

As a consumer, you are very familiar with China's designer knockoffs and pirated DVDs, cut-rate designer clothes, and other products you use or wear daily, but the greater threat to the US economy is China's massive economic and industrial espionage base that lies within their overall plan to steal propriety information of all types. This systematic collection is carefully organized using every possible conceivable means available, in order to obtain valuable information. And this, then, becomes a great danger to US interests.

The following sections have been excerpted and analyzed from information contained in the Chinese government's Ministry of Science and Technology (MOST) website.[34] By studying their plans and directions, one can see where they will be looking for a competitive economic advantage that could only be obtained through a variety of espionage activities to obtain the types and levels of information required. Unfortunately, in some cases, they have already obtained the information and are using it to their benefit, and probably to our detriment.

PROJECT 863

In the mid-1980s, China began a plan that it called "Project 863." This plan came under the auspices of the MOST. MOST had various committees and advisors to make up a very talented pool of people in the science, technology, and manufacturing sectors. Overall, MOST took the lead in drawing up S&T development plans and policies; drafted related laws, regulations, and department rules; and guaranteed their implementation. They were also responsible for drafting the National Basic Research Program, the National High-Tech R&D Program, and the S&T Enabling Program. MOST coordinated basic research, frontier technology research, key technology, and common technology.[34] All of this took time, but remember that these people were specialists in their fields, so it was sort of like several people with similar-type backgrounds sitting down to write a short list of what should be done and how one would go about it. They had the background and the abilities to quickly formulate all these programs. Additionally, they had hundreds upon hundreds of academics and industry specialists who could add to their list of findings and the various procedural elements that would be required to implement the programs successfully.

Whenever appropriate, MOST teams would work closely with other government organizations and their private sector businesses in various scheme demonstrations, assessment, acceptance, and policy making endeavors for the major S&T special projects. Their specialists would also provide advice on any major changes that might or should occur. It also compiled and implemented the various plans for national laboratories, innovative bases, national S&T programs, and research conditions so as to promote a better infrastructure construction and resource sharing.[34]

China has always made a big deal of the "fact" that it is a developing nation not only with a large population but also with limited resources. Looking at the current amount of technology and innovations and joint ventures currently going on in China, that is very hard to believe.

Strengthening China's cooperation with other nations in the fields of S&T and economy has become exceptionally urgent and important. While China emphasizes that they are there to work with developing nations, it is believed that they are going full bore to gain and then maintain any possible regional controls in terms of information and products.

The Chinese government has always paid great attention to S&T exchanges and cooperation programs among developing nations. Under the guise and principle of equality and mutual benefits that would emanate from various shared projects, and results sharing and intellectual properties protection, the Chinese government would be willing to let you be aware of these technologies through selected seminars so as to promote a common development platform in the fields of S&T and economy.[35]

In 2004, for example, China planned to launch 31 international seminars dedicated to developing nations, covering a variety of topics such as agriculture, energy, environment protection, and medicine. Naturally, only the best and brightest Chinese would work the seminars, and those individuals from various countries that were invited, encouraged, or informed about the seminar would be specialists on the various seminar topics and have the ability to provide much needed and desired information valuable to China. Whenever possible, selected individuals who were extremely knowledgeable in a subject would be invited to be premier speakers, with all expenses paid, of course.

All of these programs, initiatives, and ventures are under MOST and came out of their Key Technologies R&D Program.

The Key Technologies R&D Program was the first national S&T program in China and addressed major S&T issues in national economic construction and social development. The program was initiated in 1982 and then implemented through a number of continuing Five-Year Plans. The Program made remarkable contributions to the technical renovation and upgrading of traditional industries and the formation of new industries within China. All the successes would boost the sustainable development of Chinese society and further enhance the national S&T strength and innovation capacity.[34] If you study the business and world sections of a newspaper, or go on the web and look for Chinese agricultural and engineering projects around the world, you will note that a fair number are in developing countries, or at least countries where the influx of Chinese workers and technicians would be appreciated, either because they have abilities not available locally, or they are willing to "assist" in the building of new factories or otherwise expand the economic base. In essence, though, the Chinese are gaining a toehold, and then, after a while, the Chinese workers are not really noticed so greatly as when they first started. Then, the Chinese start opening businesses, getting into current businesses and industries, and learning things they didn't know before. So they provided assistance, but that was to allow China to provide a reasonable explanation for a large influx of their citizens into the local economy from where they will gain further valuable information.

The major overarching goal of the Program is to address pressing major S&T issues in national economic and social development. The program primarily focuses on the R&D of key and common technologies that drive the technical upgrading and restructuring of industries and provides advanced and applicable new technologies, materials, techniques, and equipment to industrial and agricultural production while facilitating the application and industrialization of high-tech achievements to enhance the international competitiveness of key industries and human welfare. It also aims to cultivate an elite group involved in key technology R&D and establish a number of internationally recognized technical innovation bases.[34]

GUIDANCE PROJECTS

At a local level, S&T authorities will manage and supervise various projects, ensuring the goal of optimizing R&D resources distribution and promoting the efficient utilization of the R&D budget.

To facilitate China's Western Development Strategy, the Western Development Project (another program) created several priority projects for the protection and improvement of regional ecology and environment, among other things. This project, when first set up, was expected to enhance S&T innovation capacity, accelerate industrial restructuring and upgrading, and facilitate the fast development of industries.[34] Exactly how well the program has been doing is left to conjecture as China does not reveal all, especially to Western nations.

> Priority tasks for the project includes the ability to: optimize, restructure, and establish a number of S&T innovation bases, including R&D centers, project demonstration, and incubators; to develop, integrate and demonstrate key technologies that serve the ecological and environment construction, and conversion and value addition of local featured resources; to create new patterns for high-tech industrial development in selected areas of the western region; and to conduct S&T training covering different levels and involving extensive domains in order to build up a high caliber S&T contingent; preliminary establish a sound mechanism for east–west cooperation based on the supplementing and joint development of mutual strengths.[34]

This is a very long sentence, but one that covers hundreds upon hundreds of technologies, methods, techniques, and knowledge bases in many different fields of endeavor when one considers how China will use the gathered information across the board of its industrial manufacturing base to expand its growing economy.

The 863 Program itself organizes and implements the many key projects to meet the national *strategic* needs. Strategic is almost like a military marching order, with specific steps being taken, in a very ordered manner, to ensure success. Even their phraseology seems military in its presentation, such as "The strategic objective of the program is to mobilize China's scientific talents in conducting innovative research on major scientific issues in agriculture, energy, information, resources and environment, population and health, materials, and related areas. This is in accordance with the objectives and tasks of China's economic, social, and S&T development goals leading up to 2010 and into the mid-21st century. The Program is built upon a solid S&T foundation for the sustainable socio-economic development for China."[34] Since the program has been around for a while, and by reading news reports and studies of China's growing technological, agricultural, energy, and medical areas, you can easily discern that all this massive growth is not to be seen as solely individual innovation within China, but must be supplemented, if not wholly subsidized, through information and resources obtained outside of China.

NATIONAL HIGH-TECH R&D PROGRAM

Going back a quarter century—in 1986—to meet the global challenges of new technology revolution and competition, four Chinese scientists, Wang Daheng, Wang Ganchang, Yang Jia Chik, and Chen Fangyun, jointly proposed to accelerate China's high-tech development. The late Chinese leader Deng Xiaoping "personally approved the National High-Tech R&D Program," namely, the 863 Program. The Program was implemented almost immediately and since then has boosted China's overall high-tech development and its R&D capacity, expanded its socioeconomic development, and greatly supported objectives related to national security. In April 2001, the Chinese State Council approved the continued implementation of the R&D program. As one of the national S&T programs' trilogy in the 10th Five-Year Plan, the 863 Program continues to play a very important role.[34]

The program objectives have changed and are now aimed at boosting innovation capacity in high-tech sectors, particularly in strategic high-tech fields, in order to gain a foothold in the world arena, to strive to achieve breakthroughs in key technical fields that concern the national economic lifeline and national security, and to achieve great advancement ("leapfrog") in key high-tech fields where China could enjoy a greater relative advantage (over other nations) or where it could take strategic positions in order to provide high-tech support to fulfill strategic objectives in the implementation of the third step of their overall modernization process, one that would allow them to jump with great might into the lead for technology in various fields.[34]

For the immediate future, the program will continue to be at the forefront of world technology (acquisition and development), intensifying its innovation efforts that will allow China to realize its strategic transition from simply pacing with the current technological frontrunners to (again) focusing on leapfrog development. The program, in the long run, can only enhance China's high-tech innovation capacity in selected fields and improve its international competitiveness among various major industries. By building up their mastery of a number of technologies with industrial potential and proprietary IP, which we can somewhat credibly assume they have stolen, China gains the ability to "nurture" and expand a greater number of high-tech industrial growth sources that will ultimately optimize and upgrade its industrial structure. In this way, it will also be fostering both the individual and overall strength of high-tech industries. In doing so, China can also develop innovative and enterprising talents for high-tech R&D and industrialization.[34]

Of the major tasks within the 863 Project, the program addresses a number of cutting-edge high-tech issues of strategic importance, including the following:

1. Developing key technologies for the construction of China's information infrastructure.
2. Developing key biological, agricultural, and pharmaceutical technologies to improve the welfare of the Chinese people.
3. Mastering key new materials and advanced manufacturing technologies to boost industrial competitiveness.
4. Achieving breakthroughs in key technologies for environmental protection, resources, and energy development to serve the sustainable development of their society.[34]

Getting the Data

This is all well and good, at least for China. But a country can't simply state goals and expect the populace to move forward without the appropriate technologies; they must come from somewhere. Unfortunately, these technologies, innovations, patents, trade secrets, and so on, all reside outside Chinese borders. To obtain them quickly, and thus to avoid years and years of R&D and spending untold millions of dollars, the information must be obtained by other means.

Economic Collection and Industrial Espionage

To understand the motives of China is one thing, but to realize that we actually, though somewhat naively, indirectly and unsuspectingly help them to get the data is the real tragedy. The United States encourages the free exchange of most scientific and technical information. Many government programs support the exchange of technology to facilitate economic development in a wide variety of foreign countries. However, a clear line must be drawn to protect information that is classified, concerns militarily critical technologies, is subject to export controls, or is proprietary information that is the IP of a specific firm or individual.

Global economic competition has, to a large extent, replaced the Cold War political and military competition between East and West. As a result, friends and allies, as well as less friendly countries, now pursue their national interests through espionage against the United States. Their goal is to develop a competitive edge in the global marketplace or boost military readiness, while drastically reducing their own R&D costs.

A US VIEW—BACKGROUND OF THE PROBLEM

As we discussed earlier in the chapter, citing John Morton's testimony in 2010 before the House Committee on Foreign Affairs, America has always had a great entrepreneurial spirit and integrity, and they are embodied by the creativity and resourcefulness of the American workers. When these workers see a problem, or the lack of a viable product that would bring change, enhance productivity, or develop something that is needed within the public or private sector, then they go and develop it. IP rights and the ability to enforce those rights had continually encouraged American individuals and companies to continue the tradition of American innovation and the development of new products, ideas, and merchandise. This tradition of innovation and productivity has given America an advantage in the global economy.[19]

These IP rights have been intended to discourage others from selling imitations of the products, almost all of which are often far less safe or reliable than the original products. More importantly, and of concern here, is that such IP rights can protect our nation by preventing the unauthorized proliferation of counterfeit pharmaceuticals, preserving national and economic security, and ensuring consumer safety. When China violates these rights, the violation correlates directly into depressing investment in the technologies needed to meet global challenges. Second, it puts consumers, families, and communities at risk. These gross violations of IP rights also unfairly devalue America's contributions and hinder the ability of the economy to provide continued growth, which then compromise American jobs.[19]

As foreign corporate ownership becomes more widespread, as multinationals expand, and as nation-states dissolve into regions and coalesce into supranational states, the so-called classic, exclusionary, and dichotomous view of the world (the "we" vs. "they" mentality) will fade, which reduces national borders in terms of economic security. But the notion of "proprietary information" is here to stay. Unfortunately, the "notion" is only as good as a nation respects it, and because of this, the theft and creation of illegal products will never cease as long as there is profit to be had.

The Chinese people—government, business, and individual—are pretty much the greatest of all the collectors of information. Using all this initially collected data, individuals and businesses are targeted to gain further information that can't be obtain otherwise, or might be more time-consuming. But the information is there, and they will attempt to gather it, to their benefit, and to the rest of the world's detriment.

The phrase "China is the greatest economic threat to the United States and the world," in one form or another, has been echoed over and over during the past few decades. And not a lot of people are really listening and taking it to heart.

We may have mentioned but not talked a bit about all those visitors from China that visit America each year. They are high school students coming on mini-exchange programs, visiting our high schools for a few weeks and then moving on, and then there are the tourists that you seem to run into everywhere. They're taking pictures of anything and everything. Not just touristy type pictures, but pictures of factories, new products, and so on. They are also engaging in conversations with everyone, learning what you do, where you go, and exchanging business cards... ever wonder why?

Two examples come to mind.

The first example comes, not from the college sector, but from the high school level of temporary visitors to the United States. We can easily understand the fact that the Far East is sending students to the United States so they can "see a part of the world different from their own," observe and partake a little bit in our educational environment, but have you ever considered what they can learn and possibly access in terms of our technology and economic secrets? These seemingly innocent students can play a great threat in collecting information.

Richmond, Virginia, is home to a number of Fortune 500 companies. All are very successful and expanding with new products, techniques, and so on. An exchange student from overseas stays at my house. Like other students from Asia, I find out that he wants to see America and learn, and learn he does. The students are taken on "field trips" to visit various factories and manufacturing sites because we want to show them how successful America is.

Now, remember they are "just high school students," so we show them a lot of stuff. And they learn from these experiences.

Just before he gets ready to go on the next leg of his trip, in this case to southern California where he will be for several more weeks, he asks if I could send some stuff he has back home because there is no space left in his luggage. Sounds reasonable? But I, being somewhat nosey, check out his luggage, and at the bottom of it are papers, more papers, flyers, handouts, company reports, and a few items that look like they had been taken down off a company bulletin board.

I was amazed and almost impressed. I talked with a couple other families who had students staying with them. Calls back told me that those students also had information in their suitcases.

Now, surely, not all of them would need the information.

Next, the thought occurs to me. The students came to Virginia from New York, where they were also feted with tours and inside looks at various businesses. They went from Virginia to southern California, home of Silicon Valley. I suspect they got a lot more information there, in fact, more than enough to fill their suitcases.

Just imagine, high school students in our high-tech facilities, our latest businesses, taking pictures, scarfing up as much information as possible, and we just let them walk out the door, after nicely inviting them in to see the "wonders of American manufacturing and technology." How much did they learn? How much did they take away with them? How much that we don't know did they take away? We may *never* know.

The second example comes from a vacation trip across America. At a national park and again in a couple of cities, I noticed, as you probably have, that many from the Far East come and travel in groups. Perhaps "packs" might be the better term for them. Very seldom is English spoken, but I am sure the majority of them could understand the language and probably speak it to some extent.

Here I am, taking in the sights, looking around, and one Chinese woman approaches and in a reasonable, but somewhat broken, passing English asks if I could take a couple of pictures of them, and of the group, in front of this building. No problem? They line up, I take pictures, then they regroup for more pictures, at different angles, shooting different portions of the building and surrounding area. As they get ready for each picture, simple conversation ensures: "where you from?" "what you do?" and so on. I don't know them, so I lied and said I worked at a random company. After a half-dozen minutes or so, the pictures are over, then a young man, perhaps 30 or 35, comes over and in very good English thanks me for taking the pictures. He is very nice, very polite. "I heard you tell (the lady) what you do. Well, I work in that area, too." Amazing, I thought. Then, "It's like lunch time, let me treat you and your wife to lunch for your taking the pictures." Sorry, I had to run. So, "here's my card, you got one?" Sorry, no card. As I walk away, I turn back looking at something in the distance. He's writing on the card, and another person is taking my picture. Outside of my picture and a name, he really knows nothing about me. I have his card, and perhaps the information on it is correct; I don't know, and I don't intend to find out.

This, then, is China. The United States, in addition to the rest of the world, is a targets of China's growing thirst for military and economic information and the latest technology, all of which can be applied to their ever-growing economic base, helping the economy directly, strengthening the military, and making for a much growing power-hungry government that wants to involve itself into every country where they can further their own self-interests. But while many other nations may have something of interest to China, the United States stands at the forefront of having the most superior R&D facilities, the highest scientific and technology base, and a fantastic ability to develop something where nothing existed before. No wonder China wants what we have… and we may well be giving a way the farm, or at least allowing them to pass through the door without proper protective measures in place.

Thus, here is our current and future threat. This book will discuss past attempts, successes, and failures; identify where the United States stands in terms of countering economic espionage; and also take a quick look at espionage around the world. Also, in future chapters, we will look into the various aspects of the Chinese economic espionage threat and provide a bit of history of economic espionage. After all, China may not have invented it, but China has certainly taken it to a new and higher level in their never-ending struggle to become "top dog" in controlling the world's economy.

REFERENCES

1. Hostettler, John N., Sources and Methods of Foreign Nationals Engaged in Economic and Military Espionage. Hearing before the Subcommittee on Immigration, Border Security, and Claims of the Committee on the Judiciary, House of Representatives, One Hundred Ninth Congress, First Session, Washington, D.C., September 15, 2005.
2. Kan, Shirley A., China: suspected acquisition of U.S. nuclear weapon secrets, Congressional Research Services, December 20, 2000.
3. CNN Staff Reports, FBI director says China poses very serious espionage threat, March 9, 2000, http://archives.cnn.com/2000/US/03/08/freeh.spy/index.html.
4. Smith, Charles R., Chinese cold war on America and its allies, Newsmax.com, *Thursday, Oct. 27, 2005.*
5. Arrillaga, Pauline, AP National Writer (Alexandria, VA), *The Seattle Times*, AP IMPACT: China's spying seeks secret US info, seattletimes.nwsource.com May 7, 2011.
6. *The Guardian*, London, England, AP foreign edition, May 8, 2011.
7. Gardham, Duncan, security correspondent, China and Britain locked in cyber war, *The Telegraph*, London, England, June 24, 2011 (Mr. Gardham was referring to a 14 page document, marked "restricted" from MI5's Centre for the Protection of National Infrastructure (CPNI)).
8. Canadian Security and Intelligence Service (CSIS), Ottawa, Ontario, Canada; Commentary document No. 89: China and the Internet, 2006; No 32: Economic Espionage, 1993; No. 46: Economic Espionage (II); (The Commentary reports are published by the CSIS Intelligence Assessments Branch (IAB) and provides unclassified information on current topics related to the security of Canada, and is written by strategic analysts and subject experts in the security intelligence field. These and other intelligence and security reports can be accessed at their web site, CSIS.-SCRS.gc.ca).
9. Cearlock, Kevin, Special Agent, FBI, 5th Annual IT Conference; Safeguarding American innovation; American Petroleum Institute (API), *5th Annual IT Conference*, Houston, TX, November 11, 2010.
10. Hearings on economic espionage before the House Judiciary Committee, Subcommittee on Crime, Washington, D.C., May 9, 1996.
11. Office of the National Counterintelligence Executive, Foreign spies stealing US economic secrets in cyberspace: report to Congress on foreign economic collection and industrial espionage, 2009–2011, October 2011, http://www.ncix.gov/publications/reports/fecie_all/Foreign_Economic_Collection_2011.pdf.
12. Hefferman, Richard J., CPP, CISM, Chair, ASIS Trends in Proprietary Information Loss Survey; Trends in intellectual property loss, American Society for Industrial Security, Alexandria, VA.
13. Cooper, B., Intelligent essays, Economic Counterintelligence (a personal collection of various essays); found at: intelligentessays.blogspot.com/2008/04/economic-counterintelligence.html.
14. Espinel, Victoria A., US Intellectual Property Coordinator, Intellectual property spotlight, December 2010/January 2011 edition, found at: whitehouse.gov.
15. Caught red-handed: China's industrial espionage, found at: Americanmanufacturing.org/blog?p = 1020; posted by admin, March 19, 2009.
16. United States Department of Agriculture, Personnel and Document Security Division, Economic collection and industrial espionage, Washington, D.C., found at: http://www.dm.usda.gov/ocpm/Security%20Guide/T1threat/Economic.htm.
17. US House of Representatives, Committee on Foreign Affairs, Hearings on Protecting US Intellectual Property Overseas: The Joint Strategic Plan and Beyond, No. 111-111, Washington, D.C., July 21, 2010.
18. Morton, John, Assistant Secretary, US Immigration and Customs Enforcement, Department of Homeland Security, statement before the U. S. House of Representatives, Committee of Foreign Affairs, Hearing on Protecting US Intellectual Property Overseas: The Joint Strategic Plan and Beyond, Washington, D.C., July 21, 2010.
19. Vaknin, Sam, PhD., Center for Strategic and International Studies (CSIS) Commission on Cybersecurity, Washington, D.C. See also *The Industrious Spies: Industrial Espionage in the Digital Age*. Other pertinent reference books of Dr. Vaknin on related topics can be found at samvak.tripod.com/pp144.html.
20. Office of the Press Secretary, President Obama directs the National Security and Homeland Security Advisors to conduct immediate cyber security review, White House, Washington, D.C., February 9, 2009.

21. House of Representatives, Permanent Committee on Intelligence, remarks before the Committee, Washington, D.C., September 19, 2008.
22. Kurtz, Paul, Good Harbor Consulting and a member of the Center for Strategic and Intelligence Studies Commission on Cybersecurity, Washington, D.C., as related on Richard Bejtlich's blog on digital security and the practices of network security monitoring, intrusion detection, and incident response, September 19, 2008 "Cost of Intellectual Property Theft," found at: http://www.taosecurity.blogspot.com/2008/09/cost-of-intellectual-property-theft.html.
23. Senate Select Committee on Intelligence, May 7, 1999, US Senate Select Committee on Intelligence (SSCI) submitted to the Congress on August 3, 2001, a special report on its activities during the period from January 6, 1999, to December 15, 2000 Report 107-51. One of the interim Committee Reports approved on May 5, 1999, found at: intelligence.senate.gov/docs.
24. Schmitt, Eric, Lax monitoring let China improve missiles, panel says, *New York Times*, May 7, 1999.
25. South Asia Analysis Group, Chinese espionage in U.S., found at: southasiaanalysis.org, paper 300, August 2001.
26. House Report 105-85; Report of the Select Committee on U.S. National Security and Military/Commercial Concerns with the People's Republic of China, (also known as Cox Report), Washington, D.C., January 3, 1999.
27. Sinodefenseforum.com, China is the Biggest Espionage Threat to the U.S.: CUS Fears Chinese Industrial Spies; a web site discussing China defense and military forum, as referring to a BBC news article on the BBC web site: news.bbc.co.uk/2/hi/programmes/newsnight/5102358.htm; June 21, 2006.
28. China.org.cn/international, Espionage accusations against China groundless, May 15, 2009.
29. Gertz, Bill, Chinese spy who defected tells all, *The Washington Times*, March 19, 2009.
30. Naskashima, Ellen, Lawmaker calls for international pressure to stop China's cyber-espionage, *The Washington Post*, Washington, D.C., October 4, 2011.
31. CTV.ca, by news staff, Chinese Ambassador rejects espionage claims, April 20, 2006.
32. China opens string of spy schools, Malcolm Moore, *The Telegraph*, London, UK, January 24, 2011.
33. S. 1525 (104th): Economic Espionage and Protection of Proprietary Economic Information Act of 1995, 104th Congress, 1995–1996. Text as of January 25, 1996.
34. Ministry of Science and Technology (MOST) of the People's Republic of China, found at: http://www.most.gov.cn.
35. Institute of Biophysics, Chinese Academy of Sciences, Grants/Fellowships/Awards for International Scientific Exchange and Cooperation, Beijing, China.

2 We Are Not Alone
Economic Espionage and the World

While Chapter 1 highlighted some of China's targeting of the United States—and our own concerns because of China's voracious and unbridled lust for technical secrets—all companies and even individuals must be very aware that China doesn't just target the United States, but other nations as well. Additionally, these other nations, allies and enemies alike, also target everyone else in their quest for economic and military information. As such, we are not alone in being mined for our information. China may target a specific company, a branch of an American company in another country, or a wholly owned company in another country that may or may not use a US product, technique, have patent rights to produce the product in their country, or even have "leased" intellectual property rights for a product. In some instances, it is easier to obtain the same or similar information from another country where protective security measures are not as tight. In such cases, it is easier to target the same information in the foreign country because the company holding the information has different standards of security.

Further, targeted nations, corporations, and individuals, because they are not necessarily American, have Americans working alongside local factory workers, or even being on-site to guide a product process; they just do not maintain the same level of security awareness, company loyalty, or patriotism in terms of protecting such information. In addition to this, it must be considered that the Chinese will also have people working in the company, as long-term "loyal" employees, as college students performing intern work, taking factory tours, and the like. The bottom line, essentially, is that people from competing companies within or from nearby countries, visiting business people, or anyone else will, in one way or another, try to obtain information on everyone else when such information is beneficial to their country, to their business or corporation, or to themselves personally.

The laws made by any nation anywhere for protecting information are just that: laws. And such laws may look great on the books of a given nation, but it doesn't mean that adequate enforcement is performed or even possible. Further, keep in mind that while information is transferred from one country to another, certain protocols are given and received, usually in the form of agreements that the information will not be further shared. Unfortunately, that is most definitely not the case. When it may be to a recipient country's advantage, it might totally disregard any contract protocols for information protection and use it as they so desire, or perhaps quietly pass on the information without notifying the country/company that initially provided the information.

We also must consider multinational corporations that have many offices and business concerns around the world. These companies may pass the information between various offices, branches, and even subsidiaries, or, perhaps, other contracted companies in order to receive favor or minor product parts. But, for the most part, everyone sort of assumes the information will be protected, not passed on or stolen, and that it will stay within the company wherein it has been given. Regretfully, once transmitted to another place, it may be and usually is much easier for an unauthorized person to obtain it.

One of the great things about our society is that while we tend to think of the best in people, we cannot forget that people are not perfect and, as such, will do what is necessary to succeed. For over a half-century, America seemed to be at war with the Soviet Union in protecting our vital national secrets from theft. When the Communist empire fell, everyone assumed the best would come from it. Not necessarily. The fallacy of this assumption has been proven a number of times. Everyone assumed, initially, that the Russians would stop, not just targeting the United States, but other nations for their secrets. It just didn't happen. The political structure changed, but the search for secrets of all types continued unabated, sometimes with government approval, and other times with former intelligence people working for themselves or other commercial entities to obtain the information.

In Tokyo, police were suspicious of a former Nikon Corporation employee. He became involved in the theft of a very high-tech device, and he proceeded to pass it on to a Russian trade official. The device, a variable optical attenuator, at the time of the theft, was still in the development stage. Its designated purpose was to help stabilize optical transmissions in long-distance fiber optic communications. After the person's arrest, an official of the Russian Trade Representation would not comment on the case.[1,2]

This was the sixth case over the past 20 years where the Japanese needed to open an investigation of possible espionage by the local Russian trade office. Only months before this incident, another person within the trade office was accused of buying trade secrets from a subsidiary of the Toshiba company. In this instance, the secrets were sold relatively cheap: for only a million yen. Not a bad deal. The Kyodo News Service reported that the secrets were related to semiconductor technology. In public statements, Toshiba stated that the information could only be used for digital cameras and mobile phones and had no military applications. Other uses of the technology could be in the military sector, making it dual use, which for any country would want it well protected.[1,2] The technology could be used in military submarines, fighter aircraft, or missile guidance systems. So, if you were Toshiba, would you readily admit the numerous potential applications of the stolen data?

But economic espionage and theft do not have to be considered with such high-technology items. Think soccer. The Manchester United team learned that its dressing rooms—where discussions, team meetings, and other team tactics are held during matches—were being bugged during a crucial match. Supposedly, the audio tapes of the talks were even offered to the *Sun* tabloid newspaper.[3] The *Sun*, of course, has been in the news in recent years for, more or less, confirmed allegations of wiretapping, bugging, telephone intercepts, and the like. From that, a number of *Sun* employees have been arrested and are currently awaiting trial on numerous charges.

As Rhymer Rigby reports in his 2006 article "Industrial Espionage Made Easy," "eavesdropping on businesses has become much, much easier with the availability of more powerful, smaller and cheaper recording devices being used. A small MP3 player can record hours upon hours of conversations."[3] There are also fake smoke detectors, bedside radios, and wall-mounted pictures in tastefully created wooden frames that conceal microphones. In addition to miniature microphones, think of cameras being concealed in ventilation systems, knickknacks, pottery, table lamps, and pieces of furniture, or just about anything you can imagine. With the advent of micro-miniature video and audio systems, who knows what item might contain monitoring devices.

Let us traipse through and highlight some of the various economic espionage cases that have taken place around the work, involving a number of countries. From these, you can understand the considerations and concerns that will help you understand and further maintain a critical and supportive view of why economic information must be protected.

At the forefront, understand that China will go to just about any lengths to obtain any type of desired information. For at least a decade or more, it is believed that China has invested in and developed a very heavy espionage presence throughout Europe. Long-term placed individuals working at all levels of light and heavy key industries, including aerospace, chemistry, medicine, heavy industry, communications, and where possible, national defense, are uniquely positioned to know what is going on, understand how the information could help China, and, at the opportune time, use their position or access to obtain the information and pass it on to China.[4]

A few years ago, a senior Chinese spy who was placed in Europe on a long-term espionage mission defected in Belgium. From various interviews and statements, he exposed the Chinese plan to obtain advanced industrial information. A number of news articles throughout Europe detailed many of his allegations. What makes it very credible is that he was in a position to know exactly what was happening. Since the time of his defection, he has provided individual names of hundreds of other spies operating in Europe and related many details of their various activities to authorities.[4]

The desire to get temporary or full-time employees with the appropriate background for numerous job positions, especially when they will be paid less than other employees or are unpaid interns, sets up the use of college and graduate students. The Chinese Students and Scholars Association (CSSA) is prominent in many countries throughout Europe. The CSSA helps students where they are located in various countries studying. One thing they can do is to be a go-between with the students and companies looking for talented students. This Chinese defector was a member of the CSSA in Leuven, Belgium.[4] He had contacts with many students and also contacts with a variety of companies where the students could further learn and work at part- and sometimes full-time jobs. Thus, once placed, students could be "asked" to help China by looking out for information of value that would help China to further grow economically. It wasn't only Belgium, but the entire area of Europe where such activities are taking place. As you read this, the CSSA is still active. So, be assured they are also considering the collection of information for China. Knowing and proving such activities though are, again, difficult.

China's vast network of non-professional intelligence-gathering individuals and organizations seems to act outside the normal channels of professional intelligence gathering, but this is probably not the case. All these non-intelligence organizations and private companies and individuals, while they look to be wholly uncoordinated in their collection activities, are probably directed by "friends" wanting their assistance back in China. China has a long history of using Chinese students studying abroad to collect information. Those in US graduate schools are in excellent positions to make contacts, work for specific companies of interest, and collect open-source information as well as company proprietary and other sensitive information. Long-term students may also become citizens, have dual citizenship, and then work themselves into programs where sensitive and classified government defense information is available.

The actual loss from economic espionage is truly unknown, but the estimates of billions of dollars in losses seem very realistic. As early as 1992, the heads of the Federal Bureau of Investigation and the Central Intelligence Agency in a joint address to Congress indicated that some 20 countries were seriously engaged in espionage, the top ones being Russia, China, North Korea, and Vietnam.[5]

Look north to our neighbor Canada; they can't be left out. Canada is a close second behind the United States in many technology fields. Aerospace, biotechnology, communications, nuclear, oil and gas, environmental technology, information technology, and chemical are the key industrial sectors of the Canadian economy. These companies are targeted for economic and commercial advantage. When such happens, just like in the United States, the damage comes in the form of lost jobs, lost markets, lost contracts, and reduced competitive advantage.

In one instance, a company's technology was compromised when, as it prepared to secure a very lucrative contract from a foreign government, the company allowed an individual to work on a sensitive leading-edge technology project. It would be natural for side-by-side work with the current company and the prospective company to ensure everyone had a firm grasp on the technology that would be used. After all, they wouldn't be competitors, but partners. The foreign government then proceeded to duplicate the technology using the information obtained via direct access by their agent during his time with the Canadian company.[6]

When the potential gains are significant enough, any method or combination of methods will be used to acquire the desired information or technology. Since the end of World War II, the Japanese manufacturing, electronics and technology sectors have gained world presence. It continues to do so, despite the gains being made by China. Some of its companies engage in industrial espionage to get ahead of their competitors. This is what developing countries do, and Chinese companies are doing this for the same reason: it's faster and cheaper than developing the technology themselves.

Chen Yonglin, first secretary of the Chinese Consulate General in Sydney, Australia, defected in June 2005. After his defection, he reportedly said that there were more than 1000 Chinese spies and informants in Australia. The claims were further mirrored in Canada in July 2005, when a former Public Security Bureau individual (who defected in 2001) said that China manages informants in Canada's Chinese community and gathers key economic intelligence.[7,8]

On March 20, 2012, The AP's Louise Watt wrote a lengthy article noting that thousands of Chinese, by learning French and having a good command of the language, were being taken in by the Province of Quebec. These Chinese transplants will have language skills and, most probably, engineering or other skills that are of value. Interestingly, Quebec has its own immigration setup. There is no cap or backlog of applications as there is in Canada's national immigration program. Many of the people coming to Quebec are middle-class professionals, just what Quebec would want, and since they speak very good French, they are welcome. And this is an excellent method for China to move people into Canada; in fact, they encourage people to learn French and then to immigrate. Once in Canada, they can easily move about the country, and soon would be able to set their sights on the United States.[9]

During the period 2001 to 2009, China sent 30,000 immigrants to Australia. How many of them were potential spies? Once they receive their Australian citizenship, they now have a much easier route to getting into the United States, going around US immigration policies relative to the limitations placed on other Chinese who want to get into the United States legally.

A goal common to most countries is to obtain information to support that country's defense industries. Countries seek US defense technologies to incorporate into domestically produced system. By obtaining the technology from the United States, a country can have a cutting-edge system without the cost of research and development (R&D). The technologies not only provide superior systems for a country's own use but also make these products more marketable for exports.

Another country used classic Cold War recruitment and technical operations. It didn't target defense areas specifically, but rather technology itself. The country didn't need our defense data, but for its own national security to be self-sufficient in manufacturing armaments, it would export arms. By obtaining the technology from the United States, it could have cutting-edge weapons systems without the R&D costs and then they would make these products available for export, thus competing with US armaments in the international arms market.

All countries look at the United States with envy when it comes to technological and scientific advancements. The United States continues to be the preeminent world power, with China attempting to become a close second and, eventually in their own eyes, number one economically.

With vital economic interests in addition to military responsibilities throughout the world, where service men and women serve in the cause of peace, a lot of the technology is also spread about the world. The protection of information, critical technologies, and proprietary information becomes difficult at times. *In attempts to maintain the US economic competitiveness, all foreign threats must be treated as direct threats to the United States' economic well-being.* So, at this time, and into the near-term future for the present, economic security is directly tied to—and must be inseparable—from national security.

We are not alone in this practice. Various countries, including allies of varying degrees, continue in their attempts to collect information not only from the United States but also from other countries wherein information may be easier to obtain. Dual-use technology, partnerships, and military trade policies, in addition to many companies becoming conglomerates with a myriad of offices, research, and manufacturing based in many other countries, mean that the technological base will become fragmented when it comes to the vital issue of maximum protection from economic theft.

The targeted technologies and manufacturing bases have not changed, but only the targeting site, which, in this case, is in any country wherein the security level is not as great, which means that information is probably easier to obtain.

Throughout the world, the modernization of a given country's military forces and their desire to upgrade and expand the economy—and also the desire to develop more commercial modernization—will certainly drive the economic intelligence effort. Any idea, be it an invention, a patent, a technological process, a medical breakthrough, or an improved technique that will make money, increase military prowess, and gain favor with another ally in terms of political gain, makes it a given target and a very desirable one. Thus, any such facility or office anywhere in the world that would have economic secrets will be closely studied and evaluated for the potential to obtain the secrets held within its doors.

While traditional collection efforts will always be available to a given country or one of its industrial or business entities, as indicated earlier, much of the collection will come through legal and open means, that is, the use of open-source information. Open-source collection is but a precursor to full-blown economic espionage to gain your secrets.

The Russian Federation that rose after the demise of the Soviet Union is largely unregulated, and laws are not really enforced when it comes to economic espionage against other countries, in addition to their outright theft of products that can be counterfeited and sold worldwide at much lower prices. They are especially heavy into intellectual property rights, such as optical disks (CDs and DVDs).

Now, let's go back to China. In terms of outright piracy, according to Howard L. Berman and his testimony to the House Subcommittee on Courts, the Internet, and Intellectual Property:

> From almost the beginning of recorded history, China has served as a provider of desired goods. Marco Polo traveled the world to bring back goods made in the Orient. Today, China's economy has growth to include the manufacture of many different products, including clothes, purses, software, computers, and movies.
>
> While just as desired as the goods of Marco Polo's day, these modern goods are often not the legitimate product of the original sources. Instead, these goods are copied, reverse engineered and, with limited investment and no payment to the creator, sold for a negligible price for China's 1.3 billion citizens, and exported in massive quantities to other countries, including America.
>
> These cheaper products can then, it is argued, provide the Chinese population with the luxury items they desire but may not be able to afford. I have heard some in the Chinese Government assert that the pirates are merely providing items by functioning as "Robin Hoods" for these goods. Yet this argument holds little credence when those goods are openly exported around the world, disrupting existing markets for legitimate products."[10]

Guansheng Han, a security official who defected from China, spoke out stating that Beijing cultivates sources in the Canadian Chinese community as a way of gleaning intelligence on key economic sectors, including the biopharmaceutical industry.[11,12]

In 2007, the Canadian Security Intelligence Service revealed that China was implicated in about half of the ongoing counter-espionage cases, with some 1500 spies involved.[13,14] Canada allegedly believes that there may be as many as 15 countries involved in various types of espionage operations, and that these may also include such "friendly" nations as France and Israel. No matter, all of them represent a serious risk to Canadian security and economic interests.

Canada also provides an excellent jumping-off point for the United States because of our somewhat lax border controls for people moving back and forth. While the United States requires proof of citizenship, passports, and the like from foreigners, the Chinese will go to great lengths to obtain Canadian citizenship (giving such people dual citizenship since they also maintain their Chinese citizenship) or another form of identification to indicate they are permanent residents of Canada. They can then "visit" the United States at every possible opportunity. Additionally, the use of Canadian identification gets them into the United States. They can then go job hunting where it will do the most good for China. Also, Canada becomes an excellent place from which China can plan and monitor the US economy and then make opportunistic forays to seek out desired items of information. As long as the planners are outside US jurisdiction, it is difficult to determine exactly what they are doing; what companies, products, or individuals are being targeted; and who might be making forays into the United States to obtain the desired secrets.

A few cases involving China and other US allies are of note:

- There are some stories out of the United Kingdom that make claims involving a middle-eastern power and a multi-billion dollar arms deal the United Kingdom was bidding on.[15]
- China has made a great effort to warn its own people about "foreigners" seeking economic intelligence.[15] (In one particular case, the government felt 1000-year-old remedies and ancient healing techniques required protection.)
- Russia accused Asian countries, especially China and North Korea, of economic espionage. It is believed that the theft of technological and commercial secrets from Russia was exacerbated by Russian economic conditions.[15]
- Even French newspapers were able to assemble a major story that is translated as "The Pillage of France," detailing how its national economic interests were injured by spies directed or facilitated by foreign governments.[15]

EXAMPLES OF ATTEMPTS TO OBTAIN ECONOMIC INFORMATION

Every country that can obtain and exploit knowledge of another country will do so. Here are a few examples from around the world:[5]

- China consistently uses members of visiting delegations and exchanges (both students, scientists, engineers, and the like) to conduct economic espionage in the United States, Canada, and other developed countries.
- In Canada, phony work record papers from "sympathetic companies" are used to gain employment at targeted Canadian companies.
- In 1991, the West German intelligence service, so it was claimed, intercepted a foreign company's telecommunications and then proceeded to pass the information to the company's German competitors.
- A General Electric employee was paid about 1 million a year by a South Korean company. The GE employee was to obtain and pass on GE trade secrets concerning synthetic diamond production.
- In the 1980s, Japanese intelligence agents working with various multinational companies were suspected of running secret operations against high-tech firms in California's Silicon Valley.
- The following are three Chinese examples from senior fellow and director of the Technology and Public Policy Program at the Center for Strategic & International Studies, in his January 26, 2011, piece entitled "Does China's New J-20 Stealth Fighter Have American Technology?":

> China specifically denies that it obtained pieces of an USAF F-117 Stealth aircraft shot down by the Serbs in 1999. This denial is specious. The Serbs retained large portions of the aircraft. China was aiding Serbia in the conflict (it has a signals intelligence unit in Belgrade collecting NATO radio traffic). What better way to repay a friend than by sharing the windfall. It is also likely the Serbs offered aircraft remnants to the Russians, and they may even have been willing to sell it on the black market. This sort of sharing would not be unusual.
>
> We know from an earlier incident when a Chinese rocket carrying a US satellite exploded on launch, that the Chinese deployed hundreds of people to creep around the crash site to pick up pieces of the launcher and the satellite. This too is normal practice, an effort to determine what went wrong with the launch, but the Chinese collected pieces of the American satellite as well and subjected them to various tests in an effort to understand how they worked.
>
> China's aircraft industry has benefited from its commercial ties to the West. When McDonnell Douglas assembled passenger aircraft in Shanghai in the early 1990s, the Chinese learned how to improve in two ways. First, when the plant was unoccupied, Chinese personnel

photographed and measured all the manufacturing equipment. Second, just by working in a US plant, individual Chinese learned advanced practices and skills that they could then transfer to their own companies. This learning process continues in the joint aircraft ventures Western firms have in China, and the quality of Chinese aircraft manufacturing has improved rapidly because of this technology transfer.[16]

- In Belgium, Justice Minister Jo Vandeurzen accused the Chinese of hacking his ministries' computers. Since Belgium hosts the North Atlantic Treaty Organization (NATO) headquarters, and also that of the European Union, such espionage would be of extremely great political value to China.[17]
- Germany suspected China in the theft of billions of euros worth of business secrets. This emanated from Berthold Stoppelkamp, head of the ASW (Association for Economic Security). Various firms were targeted and electronics and individuals were used to collect the secrets. Also, Chinese hackers were suspected of infiltrating various government computers and installing Trojan horse spyware on various government computers.[18,19]
- Stefan Zielonka, a Polish cipher officer working for the Polish Military Information Services, vanished in 2009. He was suspected of providing the Chinese government with Polish and NATO cryptography information.[20]
- In Russia, the Chief Executive of Tsniimash-Export, Igor Reshetin and three of his researchers were sentenced to prison for passing dual-purpose technology to China. The technology would allow China to further develop improved missiles, thus accelerating their space program.[21] Since it was dual use, the advantages of further developing the commercial sector electronics also holds true.
- In 2010, the Russian Federal Security Service detained two scientists who worked at the Saint Petersburg Baltic State Technical University for passing classified information to China.[22]
- China had offered Great Britain £50 million to provide a massive mobile communications network to support the 2012 Olympic Games. One can see China here as a great benefactor helping to support the "peaceful" games, but China's other hand may be much more subtle and dangerous. Officials, including experts at its MI5 intelligence agency, fear that China could shut down businesses in the nation with cyber attacks and spy equipment that would be embedded in computer and telecommunications equipment.[23] Since the equipment would stay in Great Britain, who knows where it might end up and when China might activate any spy technology that is embedded in the equipment.
- India recently informed various companies throughout the nation to avoid using Chinese-made telecommunications equipment because of the belief that such equipment can have spy capabilities embedded in the equipment. India's intelligence service also thinks that China is using dozens of "study centers" set up in Nepal near the Indian border for the purposes of spying on India.[24]
- The People's Republic of China and Taiwan regularly accuse each other of spying. In this case, it is pretty much political and military data. In was determined in 2009 that Taiwanese Presidential aide Wang Jen-ping sold nearly 100 confidential documents to China. Also, Maj. Gen. LoHsien-che, the electronic communications and information bureau chief during the administration of former President Chen Shui-bian, was suspected of selling military secrets.[25]

There is an intelligence gathering technique being used for industrial secrets to benefit China. It is called "lamprey" and involves, essentially, for a company to put out a tender or offer to several companies to encourage them to compete for a given contract.[26] When such companies respond, which is very likely when an extremely lucrative contract is possible, in order to get to the top of the pile, they end up providing a great amount of the company's technical information. If they don't reveal it in their package of presentation material, they will not be seriously considered for the contact. Once enough information is revealed, any and all companies that put forth bids are then notified that the project has been "shelved," for one reason or another. In many cases, no reason is given. No contract is ever made. In these cases, a contract was never expected to be made, but the desired technical information has now been obtained, and at a very, very minimal cost. Using the information received, China can then proceed to develop its own products, avoiding the time and cost-consuming R&D, since the technical know-how has already been obtained.

There is also a documented case of a French pharmaceutical company who set up a booth at a convention that was attended by thousands of people. Unfortunately, the company representatives left the booth unattended for a short period. Also left unattended was a sample of a patented liquid. A member of a Chinese delegation touring the convention hall, and realizing what the liquid might reveal, dipped his tie in the liquid for analyzing and copying later. Simple and effective, and cheap!

At one point, China was looking to develop a high-speed rail system. France, which developed high-speed train technology and was at the forefront of Europe's rail system technology, jumped at the chance to land the contract because it had the potential for millions and millions of euros in profit. They even went so far as to offer a six-month training course for Chinese engineers who would have to work on and maintain the train once it was running. After the training period, in which we can assume the engineers received and viewed—and possibly copied or were given copies of the technical specifications—the engineers went home and no contract was ever signed. Sometime later, China unveiled its very own high-speed train that was "remarkably similar" to France's (Figure 2.1).[26]

Another technique that the French bought into was the "mushroom factory." Here, French companies would enter into joint ventures. This is not uncommon, as they tend to make a lot of money and also obtain other technology data that would be useful down the road. Joint ventures are not new and, in fact, both parties usually profit handsomely from them. In this case, however, the joint venture was with the Chinese. Later on, as with the high-speed train situation, the French learned that the shared technology was used to recreate an identical and competing product.[26] To pour more salt on the wound, it was run by the very same individuals who headed the joint venture.

FIGURE 2.1 Shanghai's modern high-speed train.

Then, we have the case of the French company Schneider Electric, which is the most insidious. Schneider Electric had patented a device in 1996 and, after going into a venture with a Chinese company, learned that the same device was being built and sold by the Chinese company. Sue? Sure; of course. But in this instance, it was the Chinese who sued the French company, claiming that Schneider Electric had stolen *their* idea. Schneider lost, to the tune of 330 million yuan.[26] What Schneider failed to reckon with was the Chinese and their "first to patent" laws, which, in effect, says that who first patents [or invents it] in China is the owner. Had Schneider patented it, they might have had only competition as the Chinese would surely have created and made the product anyway. But now, they also had lost a large sum of money.

These examples are but the tip of an iceberg, and such activities or like-type activities can apply to all industrialized countries. Just perhaps, this is a major reason why China is willing to provide technical expertise and engage in major contract negotiations (with some strings attached), and also why China has become so powerful economically.

With all these examples, the reader must remember that China is also a country where the buyer (and seller) should beware. Conventional rules of business and ethical behavior have different meanings to the Beijing regime.

RENEWED FOCUS ON CHINA

While we have illustrated that theft of trade secrets and corporate and economic espionage are global problems perpetrated by numerous countries and governments, the US government has increased its focus on the threat posed by China.

The Obama administration released *The Administration Strategy on Mitigating the Theft of Trade Secrets* in February 2013, a report that highlights numerous cases of trade secret theft. A recent flurry of national stories of purported Chinese espionage—in addition to cyber attacks on major news agencies such as the *New York Times* and others—has forced the administration to redouble efforts to combat the ever-increasing threat. Recent high-profile incidents—apart from the major media agencies—include a growing number of cases of military and corporate trade secret theft. Such examples include household brands like Google, RSA Security, Lockheed Martin, Nortel Networks, defense contractor L-3 Communications, Dupont, and General Motors. The aim of the strategy document: to exert increased pressure on countries, particularly China, that regularly engage in corporate espionage against US businesses. Sixteen of the nineteen cases cited in the report pertain to China, and examples of the country or individuals to acquire information and technology.[27,28]

REFERENCES

1. The Associated Press, Japan Opens Investigation of Industrial Espionage at Nikon, *The St. Petersburg Times*, St. Petersburg, Russia, August 15, 2006.
2. Tscmvideo.com/news/industrial-espionage, *St. Petersburg Times*, Russia.
3. Rhymer Rigby; Industrial Espionage Made Easy, *Financial Times*; London, UK, June 2, 2006.
4. Zhenzhen, Huang for *The Central News Agency*, Chinese spy exposes CCP espionage network in Europe; *The Epoch Times*, July 5, 2005.
5. Porteous, Samuel, Commentary No. 32: Economic Espionage, May 1993; Analysis and Production Branch of the Canadian Security and Intelligence Service, Ottawa, Canada.
6. Backgrounder No. 6—Economic Security, National Coordinator, Economic and Information Security, Canadian Security and Intelligence Service, Ottawa, Canada; February 2004.
7. Hill, John, Defections reveal extent of China's espionage operations, Jane's intelligence review, vol 17, no. 11.
8. *Free Republic*, Fresno, California, web site: freerepublic.com/focus/f-news/1502969/posts; October 11, 2005.
9. Watt, Louise, Chinese seeking to live in Canada, Learning French, Associated Press, March 19, 2012, found at: http://www.kjonline.com/news/chinese-ticket-to-canada-learning-french_2012-03-19.html?pagenum=full.

10. U.S. Congress, House of Representatives, Hearings before the Subcommittee on Courts, the Internet, and Intellectual Property of the Committee on the Judiciary, 1st Session, May 17, 2005, Washington, D.C.
11. Rogers Broadcasting Ltd., Jim Bronskill, *Foreign Spies Target Canada's Natural Resource Sector, CSIS Says*, June 22, 2006; London Free Press, London, UK.
12. Spies now focus on labs and boardrooms, not military HQs, by CP, found at: intelligencesearch.com/ia/127.html, 2006.
13. de Pierrebourg, Fabrice and Juneau-Katsuya, Michael, *Nest of Spies: The Startling Truth About Foreign Agents At Work Within Canada's Borders*; HarperCollins Canada, publishers, 2009.
14. MacLeod, Ian, The spies who love us, The Ottawa Citizen, Ottawa, Canada, September 12, 2009, found at intellibriefs.blogspot.com.
15. Porteous, Samuel, Commentary No. 46: Economic Espionage (II), Analysis and Production Branch of the Canadian Security and Intelligence Service, Ottawa, Canada, July 1994.
16. Lewis, James A., Does China's new J-20 stealth fighter have American technology?, Center for Strategic and International Studies (CSIS), Washington, D.C., January 26, 2011.
17. Sophos Belgium accuses Chinese government of cyber-espionage, May 7, 2008, found at: sophos.com/pressoffice/news/articles.
18. The Local, Russia and China spying on German firms, found at: thelocal.de/money/20090520-19399.html, May 20, 2009; Spiegel.de/international/germany/0,1518,663090,00.html.
19. Chinese spying on German government computers, IRNA—*Islamic Republic News Agency*, Berlin, FRG, August 25, 2007.
20. Polish cipher officer worked for Chinese intelligence?, Polskie Radio. December 22, 2009. Retrieved April 4, 2013.
21. RIA Novisti, Reshetin sentenced to 11.5 years for passing technology to China, December 3, 2007, found at: rapinews.com.
22. Taranova, Alexandra, Two scientists held in Murky spy case, *The St. Petersburg Times*, St. Petersburg, Russia, September 24, 2010.
23. Ashton, James, China gives £50m aid for Olympics, *The Sunday Times*, London, UK, February 20, 2011.
24. Parashar, Sachin, China using Nepal study centres for spying?, *The Times of India*, October 1, 2009.
25. Low, Y. F., United Daily News: The lost military soul, Focus Taiwan News Channel, February 11, 2011.
26. frumforum.com, Peter Worthington, China's Boom: Fueled by Spies?, February 10, 2011.
27. Siohban, Gorman and Jared A. Favole, U.S. ups the ante for spying on firms. China, others are threatened with new penalties, *The Wall Street Journal*, February 21, 2013.
28. The White House, The Administration Strategy on Mitigating the Theft of Trade Secrets, February 2013, Washington, D.C., February 2013, found at: http://www.whitehouse.gov/sites/default/files/omb/IPEC/admin_strategy_on_mitigating_the_theft_of_u.s._trade_secrets.pdf.

3 The Background of Economic Espionage

Over the past three decades, and more so in the past few years, numerous media reports and continuing arrests and trials have demonstrated China's growing economic espionage prowess. The percentage rise seems small when compared to all the espionage that goes on all over the world, but China was far from being the first to engage in economic espionage for its own benefit as a growing nation.

There is nothing really recorded about China engaging in economic espionage a thousand years ago, but China's desire for a continuous growing economy was seen by people from Western Europe as early as the 17th century. French missionary Louis Le Comte, in his memoirs, indicated that economic growth was of primary importance to China. He said that trade and commerce "is the soul of the people." He noted that the Chinese had devoted their work efforts on the use of dishonest "business practices and counterfeit" products, essentially anything and everything that could be made and sold. And that remains so, so true in today's economic business climate.[1]

Nationalistic politics and patriotism are indirectly tied to espionage where one nation excels over another, or can take control of a given environment, and that is the point when the power of economics can become the rule in terms of a nation's economic superiority. Up until the mid-17th century, national loyalty was weak, and the economic prowess of a nation was really regional within each country, depending upon what could be created and sold. Thus, valued product sales only benefited each region—not the country as a whole.[2]

So, let's go back in time for a few centuries and imagine a scenario wherein economic espionage plays a role in nation building and politics at the same time.

Obtaining political secrets was relatively easy. And since political secrets at the time could give great meaning to a nation's desires, any potential future actions or potential military designs were of vital importance to everyone else, especially for those nations that were not necessarily in favor at the time. Consider also that for the average person, and their small-time business, money was just about everything. People earned very little and thus had very little to spend to purchase items that might well be out of their reach. No one really looked out for the Lord of the Manor, or the King, or whomever, but only for themselves. Their lives revolved from day to day about obtaining food and shelter. And all these took money, very little, but little was all they had. Thus, when money was offered for something as insignificant as a bit of information, it was easily obtained.

A person slighted in his quest for a higher government position, or one having divided loyalties, becomes a person of interest to the opposition. Since familial connections could extend to two or more countries, it meant that people were willing to pass on political information in return for favor, or pass on false information to help one side more than another. After all, those friendships made in high political and court circles usually continued on no matter who was in higher leadership positions.

At these levels, a political secret could have long-term economic ramifications as well. The opportunity to recruit lower-level people for espionage was becoming established. Courtiers, secretaries, tradesmen, and specialized builders had access to vast (during those times) amount of information.[2] Since they were not wealthy, the extra income was always welcome.

Control of the high seas meant control of the economy between nations. The Spanish government started building their great armada fleet to control the seas and thus international commerce.[2]

Plans were drawn up and since many sets of plans were required for numerous shipbuilders, it took but a short time before at least one set—or possibly more—was obtained by England.

Since a ship or, more importantly, an armada of ships requires a massive amount of lumber, and workers to be hired, once built, hundreds upon hundreds of sailors must be hired to man the vessels. All this could not be done overnight or in total secrecy. Recruitment of people meant that a secret armada could not be hidden away, but it would be quite well known. From the merchant class, everything in terms of information would be available. Typically, you could expect it to remain within the merchant class, but that could never be, because too many people would have to be curious as to why so much lumber is necessary and why so many people need to be hired all at once, and thus advertising of positions and job recruitment became necessary on a massive scale. Even at this point, ships' stores were starting to be ordered months in advance. The requisitioned stores would ultimately have been transported to given port cities or nearby, then after the ships were completed, the stores would be put on board each ship very shortly before it would sail. Knowledge of the amount of stores, the exact amounts tagged by the number of ships in each port, the loading schedule dates, and then the approximate sailing dates could never be kept secret.[3–5]

There was just too much information floating around, and there were no procedures in place to assure the information remained where it should: closely held. Even with procedures, so much information could not be protected since the business of commerce had to be transmitted either verbally or in writing. And then merchants would keep copies of documents and throw them away when their usefulness seemed over.

Unfortunately, with so much information available to so many people in so many places, it must have been expected that it would leak out, probably sooner than later. England quickly learned of the armada and when it would sail. There were far too many people, especially among the merchant class, hoteliers, and families, who had information. The merchants were the most important and probably the most talkative. Merchants of a given class level worked together to maintain their class status. They talked to each other and passed on business details between themselves and also among merchants in other countries with which they had business on a continuing basis.

Wars, even minor ones, of this period might slow but would not stop the continuing commerce between nations. It was too vital to everyone. Merchants, then, could pass on ship and troop movements (planned or starting to take place), amounts of support equipment necessary because the ships' stores and various pieces of equipment would have to be quickly replaced, sometimes from a neighbor or opposing country. Business was business, and patriotism came after successful business ventures.

When the troops moved toward or into a neighboring country, the use of guides and smugglers in remote areas became a real necessity. Low-paid they were, but even they knew the information could be sold to others, such as merchants in the neighboring country who would then use the information to sell new supplies and equipment to the troops who had used up their own. Resupply was big business!

Troops needed the supplies quickly, so the information that was being sold had good value for everyone concerned, except for the troop's paymaster who would probably be paying inflated prices for the desired supplies.

Thus, during those times, economic espionage was a big business, especially when the economy of a given business or town was at stake.

ESPIONAGE AS A MEANS OF NATION BUILDING

Espionage flourished, though not on the scale of today. Attempts by a government to get closely guarded political, economic, or military information about another nation, especially one that was hostile, were typical of the day. In a more general sense, espionage meant any kind of spying—by a business competitor, a political group, the forces of justice, or a private individual.

Espionage agents were then, as now, usually called secret agents or spies, and they relied as much on bribery, impersonation, blackmail, or theft as they did on secret observation. Their only mission was to get information, not to evaluate it. Some spies were double agents, working for two rival nations. Though not called as such, counterspies tried to prevent espionage; their mission became one of counterespionage, or counterintelligence.[6]

HISTORY

Ancient empires had well-developed espionage networks, and the Old Testament mentions the use of spies by Moses and others. Spying is called the second oldest profession and is shown in the Old Testament no less. When the children of Israel were preparing to enter the Promised Land, the Bible tells us that spies were sent out. "Joshua son of Nun sent two spies out from Shittim secretly with orders to reconnoiter the country. The two men came to Jericho and went to the house of a prostitute named Rahab...."[7]

Rahab, of course, was engaged in the world's oldest profession. Joshua's example has been followed ever since. In our time, the bugging of embassies has been especially popular.

Some economic espionage history can easily be dated back to the 6th century. China had a monopoly in silk production. The Byzantine emperor, Emperor Justinian, around 552 AD, wanting to learn about how silk was produced, proceeded to send two monks into China to gain understanding about silk production and bring back to him the secret of silk. The monks, after a lengthy trip and quite a bit of time in China, succeeded in smuggling some silkworm eggs and mulberry seeds out of China inside their bamboo walking sticks. Mulberry was grown, the eggs hatched, and after a few years or so, the Byzantine Empire started to replace China as a major (and later on as the largest) silk producer.[8,9]

Going back further in China and its control of the silk trade, history tells us that around 2700 BC, the Chinese began making silk. Depending on which you read and believe, emperor Huangdi invented the method for raising silkworms and spinning silk thread. Tradition also credits his wife with discovering silk-making itself, and also the weaving of silk thread into fabric.[10]

The story goes that his wife had accidentally dropped a cocoon into her tea, after trying to pick up several from a mulberry trip in her garden. As she removed the cocoon, the result became one long filament. The emperor built upon this discovery and developed a method to replicate this process, thereby "domesticating" the silkworm. The Chinese were able to keep this process a secret from the world for over 2000 years. By keeping the process a secret, the Chinese crated and held a firm world monopoly on the production of silk fabric. The secret of silk was one of the most zealously guarded secrets in China. So much, in fact, that anyone found guilty of smuggling silkworm eggs, cocoons, or mulberry seeds out of China was put to death.[11]

About 400 AD, another Chinese princess was slated to be married to a prince in India. Ingeniously, she intentionally smuggled mulberry seeds, and the accompanying silkworm eggs, in her headdress. She wanted her soon-to-be new homeland to be capable of producing silk. Gradually, awareness traveled globally, and a few centuries after this, Byzantium—and then other countries such as Italy, Spain, and France a hundred years later—had developed similar capabilities.[10,12]

In the 7th century, the Arabs got around to conquering the Persians and, in doing so, captured their magnificent silks in the process. They then helped to spread sericulture and silk weaving as they swept victoriously through Africa, Sicily, and Spain.[9]

In Western Europe during the 18th century, France sent spies to steal Great Britain's industrial secrets. And in another hundred years,[13] the power loom plans were to be stolen by Americans from England.

Essentially, then, the protection of economic secrets dates back a long ways. General evidence of the planning and activities against unprotected items were not the best. There was a certain amount of "security education" in the past, but when a nation, industry, possible industry, or just plain greed is at stake, then mankind will go to many extremes to obtain the desired information. The sensitive information that was obtained over time would provide adversaries with insight into critical secrets that would include and unlock the secrets of various industrial activities. Simple items such as parts ordering, obtaining primary or subcontractor communications, tests and evaluation, and shipping of deliverables would have been of great interest, and following the thread of such activities would lead to further eye-opening pieces of information that would assist in ferreting out a given industrial secret, process, methodology, or plan.

During the 1200s and 1300s, the Mongols relied heavily on espionage in their conquests throughout Asia and Europe.[14]

Espionage rapidly evolved in Western Europe in the 1700s and 1800s. Under Napoleon and under Prussian leaders Frederick the Great and Otto von Bismark, it flourished.

The Chinese manufactured porcelain that was outstandingly hard, and had been produced as early as the 7th century. Porcelain reached Europe by the end of the 13th century and then rapidly spread in the centuries to come without anyone knowing the secret of its production, only that it came from China.[15]

Fancy porcelain vases could be seen decorating the tables of sovereigns, princes, and noblemen because they were the only ones who could afford to purchase such luxury items (Figure 3.1).

The Chinese created a great mystery around the porcelain manufacturing process and its secret was that of legend and myth. Since China enjoyed a virtual monopoly in its manufacture, the cost for it was very high. It would take several more centuries for the mystery of its manufacturing was uncovered in Europe in the early 1700s.[16]

The secret reached Paris with the assistance of a Catholic Jesuit priest, Francois Xavier d'Entrecolles, who had served as a missionary in China. During his time in China, he paid a visit to the center of the royal porcelain manufacture where he carefully observed everything, then passed on his information to Europe in the form of letters. He gave very detailed accounts of his visit. He even went so far as to describe the location of the city (Jingdezhen), the daily life of the potter families living there, and the security measures introduced to protect the porcelain process. He spent a fair amount of time observing the process of porcelain production in order to capture every little detail. Despite the distrust from Chinese authorities and the stringent security measures, he was even able to obtain and send a sample of China clay to Europe.[17] Porcelain was finally in Western Europe, but China still had another great secret that it held.

FIGURE 3.1 Ancient Chinese porcelains. The porcelain manufacturing process was a closely guarded secret for centuries.

By the early 1800s, England had an unquenchable thirst for tea. Indirectly, this problem helped the East India Company to prosper greatly in the 1800s. Great Britain's problem was that tea was only found in China, which—like porcelain—is monopolized and controlled by China. The British government and the East India Company (documents vary on who actually hired him, but both were probably closely involved) proceeded to hire Robert Fortune, a Scottish horticulturist with the Royal Horticultural Society and somewhat of an adventurer, to go to China and, if possible, steal the secret of their tea production (Figure 3.2). He was to obtain and smuggle tea plants, seeds, and any other secrets out of China and into British-ruled India, where the British could then start producing their own tea.[18,19]

Fortune disguised himself as a Chinese merchant in order to do this enormous and dangerous task. In the end, he succeeded and, within his lifetime, the production of tea in India surpassed China's.

The venture took Fortune several years. He arrived in China in 1843, but didn't know the language. He returned again in 1848 and, appropriately disguised, pretended to be a Chinese peasant and over time was able to obtain and smuggle the tea plants from China into India.

Other documentations show Fortune in disguise as a Chinese Mandarin, and using a local guide, he was able to obtain a tour of a Chinese tea factory, where he meticulously recorded every detail. He also learned a very important fact: green tea and black tea come from the same plant.[19,20] Which of these are the most accurate and true is really immaterial, but the fact that he returned home with a wealth of knowledge about tea, and a generous supply of plants and seeds, is historical truth and another example of economic espionage and what made Great Britain a true believer in the power of spying in order to learn secrets.

The United States was far behind Great Britain and France in the economic technologies of the time, falling behind both nations in terms of economic prosperity. But such people as Samuel Slater, who left England in disguise after holding a position as an apprentice at a state-of-the-art (during those times) cotton mill, became a boon for America. He memorized the cotton mill designs and kick-started America's industrial revolution.[21]

FIGURE 3.2 A portrait of Robert Fortune. (Author unknown, copyright 1900—expired. Illustration in the public domain.)

Francis Cabot Lowell from Massachusetts traveled to England in 1810. He visited a number of various textile mills in both England and Scotland. Evidentially, the British were so proud of their textile mills that he was able to obtain free access. Lowell saw the new power looms that were used for weaving cloth. The looms were much more advanced than those currently in use in New England. He recognized the fact that America must have this loom technology in order to prosper economically and also to cut down the cost of having to buy English textiles. Knowing that Great Britain had made it illegal to let the loom technology out of the country, he carefully memorized the design, so that when he returned home in 1812, he was able to duplicate the new loom. Today, the city of Lowell, Massachusetts, is so named in his honor. The city of Lowell would become the center for America's booming cotton industry, and within a few decades, over 40,000 workers were to be employed in 10 mills.[22–24]

For businesses, owners, or entrepreneurs, to develop their products, by necessity, they had to learn everything about real or potentially real competition; thus, they also had to learn everything of value and importance to gain an upper hand and one way was to spy upon competitors. As such, the use of economic espionage continues today, except that it is more sophisticated and energetic. This is especially true of those new formed companies, those start-ups, those with a new idea or way of doing something. And someone is out there looking for just that item that can be stolen and used in China for their own material gain.

In a way, it starts with what we would call "Market Research." Any company, newly established, with small domestic concerns or large multinational conglomerates having far-flung realizations and greater concerns engage in market research.

As the name implies, it is research, that which is wholly legitimate, to see where the company stands with respect to another company in terms of products in the market, newer products, those under development, or just emerging ideas. This is completely legal and expected by all companies.

For small family-run organizations, this research may be little more than a handful of friends supporting the idea of a local restaurant or specialty store. For large companies, market research can include formal and informal focus groups, statistical analysis of financial information, and even industrial espionage. In general, though, market research takes two forms, primary (direct from individuals within the market) and secondary (using resources such as reports prepared by third parties), and there are many consulting firms that specialize in particular industries or markets.

However, there are particular challenges that all these companies face, and the biggest of these challenges is from China. They could call it market research in their search for the next product, but in reality, we would not see it as such, but rather as just plain outright theft, another name for economic espionage.

So, then, it started more than 2000 years ago as Europeans searched for the secret behind porcelain, then later, silk, and then tea. America obtained technological secrets from England. But now, it is the Chinese who are making inroads. So, history is, in a sense, repeating itself.

REFERENCES

1. Slate, Robert C., Competing with intelligence: new directions in China's quest for intangible property and implications for homeland security; National Intellectual Property Rights Coordination Center; November 2011.
2. Gale Group, *Encyclopedia of the Early Modern World*, Espionage, Copyright © 2004 by The Gale Group, Inc.
3. History Learning Site, The Spanish Armada, found at: HistoryLearningSite.co.uk.
4. The "Invincible" Armada, found at: tudorplace.com.
5. Lee, Robert E., *Introduction to Geography 100: Spanish Armada Overview II*, Green River. Seattle Central Community Colleges, found at: faculty.washington.edu/rel2/geog100-UW.
6. *Espionage*, found at: science.howstuffworks.com/espionage-info.htm.
7. *King James Bible*, Book of Joshua.

8. Sharma, Sameer, Corporate espionage, a presentation manuscript to accompany a slide show, found at: slideshare.net/skyinc/corporateespionage, no date.
9. Silk Association of Great Britain, History of silk, found at: silk.org.uk/history.php.
10. Chinese Empress discovers silk-making, Lei-tzu or Si Ling-chi, By Jone Johnson Lewis, found at: womenshistory.about.com.
11. Silk fabric, History of silk, found at: textilefabrics.org.
12. Connecting women to the silk road: the princess and the silkworm head dress, found at: womeninworld history.com.
13. Sharma, Sameer, PowerPoint slide presentation, Corporate espionage, found at: slideshare.net/skyinc/corporateespionage.
14. What is the history of espionage?, found at: answers.yahoo.com/questions/index.
15. Bata, Tomas, Security against industrial spying, Bachelor Thesis, Faculty of Applied Informatics, University in Zlín, Czech, May 25, 2009.
16. A brief history of Meissen porcelain, found at: antique-china-porcelain-collectibles.com/meissen_history.htm.
17. Harris, John R., Industrial espionage and technology transfer: Britain and France in the eighteenth century, as found in Kevin's Security Scrapbook, found at: archive.feedblitz.com/601361/~3874851.
18. Rose, Sarah, For all the tea in China: how England stole the world's favorite drink and changed history, Hutchinson, 2009.
19. Robert Fortune, found at: explorersgarden.com/explorers-garden/plant-hunter-biogs/robert-fortune.html.
20. Fortune Hunter, May 2011, Cup of Tea blog, located at: http://www.cupoftea.uk.com/news/fortune-hunter-part-ii/68.
21. Cotton Times, U. S. History, Industrial Revolution – Samuel Slater, found at: cottontimes.co.uk/slater.htm.
22. PBS, Who made America, Francis Cabot Lowell, Consolidated Manufacturing, found at: pbs.org/wgbh/theymadeamerica/whomade/lowell_hi.html.
23. The Market Revolution, found at: shmoop.com/market-revolution/timeline.html.
24. Answers.com web site article: The first textile mill was started by who?, found at: History, Politics and Society, located at: wiki.answers.com/Q.

4 PRC Acquisition of US Technology*

An Overview and Short History

The reader needs to understand, even at a somewhat basic level, the methods by which the People's Republic of China (PRC) attempts to acquire US technology. The types of technology and information that the PRC and individual PRC nationals are attempting to acquire through espionage, however, are far broader. The PRC seemingly appears to try to acquire information and technology on just about anything of value. Not all of it, by any means, presents national security or law enforcement concerns, but these other areas of their endeavors are directly related to America's economic status. Economically, the collection effort must be considered extensive and very staggering in the amount of data they desire to obtain by any means.

The PRC's appetite for information and technology is virtually insatiable, and the amount of resources and energy devoted to the task of information collection is constantly expanding to meet its growing appetite. Only a portion of the PRC's overall technology collection activities targeted at the United States is of national security concern, but the impact on our national security could be huge. Given the size and variety of their overall effort, and when taken into consideration the limited available US resources and attention devoted to understanding and countering the PRC's plainly unlawful and threatening elements, both government and citizenry should see a clear cause for concern, and this with the knowledge that other serious economic losses will occur in the future.

It is extremely difficult for the United States to meet the challenge from the PRC's technology acquisition efforts because of the level and amount of traditional counterintelligence techniques that were previously applied to the former Soviet Union. Whereas the Russians were severely restricted in their ability to enter the United States or to travel within it because of State Department requirements and Federal Bureau of Investigation (FBI) surveillance, among other things, the numerous visiting PRC nationals, many of whom come to the United States to pursue purely lawful objectives, are not so restricted. And yet, the PRC employs all types of people, organizations, and collection operations to acquire our sensitive technology. These threats to America's national security concerns have and will probably continue to come from PRC scientists, students, business people, or bureaucrats, in addition to those professional civilian and PRC military intelligence personnel engaged in formalized intelligence operations.

In light of the many interactions that are continually taking place between PRC and US citizens and organizations over the last decade as trade and other legitimate forms of cooperation have blossomed, the opportunities for the PRC to attempt to acquire varying general information and, in particular, technology information, which would include American-sensitive national security secrets, are immense. Moreover, the PRC historically and traditionally normally does not rely on any continued specific oversight and centralized control or coordination in its technology acquisition

* Much of the information for this chapter, in some cases extensive verbatim excerpts, originates from House Report 105-851, Report of the Select Committee on US National Security and Military/Commercial Concerns with the People's Republic of China, US House of Representatives Select Committee, submitted by Rep. Christopher Cox of California, January 3, 1999. The report is also referred to in some web sites as the "Cox Report" and also as the "PRC Acquisition of US Technology." The report that is available to the general public was heavily redacted due to the amount of sensitive classified information that it contained.

efforts, rendering the traditional law enforcement, intelligence, and counterintelligence approaches greatly inadequate. This inadequacy by the United States can be taken by the Chinese as a lack of resources, and without these resources, China has taken a bold effort to overwhelm the protective resources with more than the usual number of espionage activities to gain technological superiority. While it is certainly true that not all of the PRC's technology acquisition efforts are a threat to US national security, that very fact makes it quite a challenge to identify those that are.

As America's concerns grow, it behooves everyone within the government and the private sector to really understand the full range of the PRC's technology acquisition efforts and, thus, to discern its truly frightening and threatening aspects.

THE PRC GOVERNMENT STRUCTURE

The political, governmental, military, and commercial activities of the PRC are controlled directly by three overlapping (some could say overarching because of their approach) bureaucracies: the Communist Party, the State, and the People's Liberation Army (PLA). Foremost of these, and in ultimate control of all these activities in the PRC, is the Chinese Communist Party (CCP). The Communist Party Secretary, Jiang Zemin, has a very powerful dual role, chairing both the Politburo and its powerful executive group, the Politburo Standing Committee. The Politburo, in turn, is supported by the CCP Secretariat, another very large bureaucratic system, which would include more checks and balances than could be imagined, in order to assure the continued control over the populace in addition to guiding the nation's upward mobility toward a supremacy unheard of 30 or 40 years ago.

The State governmental apparatus is under the direct control of the Communist Party Secretary, who in his role as President serves as the official head of the State as well. Subordinate to the CCP Secretary in state affairs is the State Council.

The PLA is also directly under the control of the Communist Party. The top level of PLA authority is the CCP's Central Military Commission (CMC), of which the CCP Secretary is also the Chairman. The CMC's routine work is directed by two Vice-Chairmen who are army generals.

The 24-member CCP Politburo, which ultimately controls the PRC's political, military, governmental, and commercial activities, does not usually conduct its business as a whole. Rather, because of its unwieldy size and membership consisting of persons from outside Beijing, the Politburo acts through its powerful seven-member Standing Committee. Involvement by the entire Politburo occurs when specific decisions are required for major policy shifts, when there are crises that need to be addressed, or when a formal legitimization of a particular policy becomes necessary.

In contrast to the Politburo actions, the seven most senior members of the Communist Party Politburo, which make up the Politburo Standing Committee, meet frequently. The CCP Politburo Standing Committee actually wields the real decision-making power, and the Communist Party Secretariat officially serves as the staff support to the Politburo and oversees the implementation of Politburo decisions by the various State bureaucracies.

The Secretariat is composed of seven members of the Politburo and is more of an executive rather than a decision-making body.

The CCP State Council, the very top level of the governmental apparatus, consists of the Premier, several Vice Premiers, State Councilors, and Secretary and Deputy Secretaries General. It directs the activities of all State ministries, commissions, and offices.

There also exists an eight-member CMC that heads up the PLA. This includes the PRC army, navy, and air force, as well as various espionage operations that are conducted through the Second Department of the PLA. The CMC, then, has a powerful bureaucratic status that is roughly comparable to that of the Politburo Standing Committee and the State Council. It meets regularly to address administrative matters and to formulate future military policy and strategy.

In addition to their policy- and decision-making roles in the CMC, key members of that body—by virtue of their top posts in the CCP—also serve a bridging function between the CCP, the State, and the PLA.

The CMC, a Communist Party body, has no equivalent in the State sector. The State CMC, an organization within the State bureaucracy, is *theoretically* a separate decision-making body, but in reality, it has no unique powers because its membership generally mirrors that of the Party's CMC. Whether or not this mirroring is just a check-and-balances setup or whether it merely rubber stamps and carries out the directions of the CMC is not totally known, but the author surmises it is the latter, functioning in a manner that provides a sense of independence to those beneath them. The Chinese Ministry of Defense, the principal State bureaucracy for dealing with military affairs, is likewise composed of Communist Party CMC members, and its role is primarily a ceremonial one. The domination and control of the PLA by the Communist Party is thus complete.

COSTIND: The CCP's Use of Corporations for Military Aims

The State Council controls the PRC's military–industrial organizations through the State Commission of Science, Technology and Industry for National Defense (COSTIND). The State Council has a decisive and final arbitrator type role in the Communist Party policy because of its function as interpreter, implementer, and overseer of broadly worded and often ambiguous Politburo policy goals. In a way, this is sort of like the old Soviet union, where a policy could be laid out and, no matter how the actual implementation turned out, somebody would be held accountable, especially if the results did not meet expectations. Here, then, the politics of the nation are closely tied to the actual practices of commerce.

Created in 1982, COSTIND was originally intended to eliminate the various conflicts that always arose between the military research and development (R&D) sector and the military production sector by combining them under one organization. But its role was soon broadened to include the integration of civilian research, development, and production efforts into the military. This is a direct reflection of the 16-character policy in which the military (and thus the State) reigns supreme in ensuring the continuation of the CCP.

COSTIND has a heavy bureaucracy in order to preside over a vast, interlocking network of institutions that are dedicated to the specification, appraisal, and application of advanced technologies to meet the PRC's military aims. The largest of these institutions are styled as corporations, notwithstanding the fact that they are directly tied into the service of the CCP, the PLA, and the State. These corporations are well known in many sectors of the world because of their economic value to China. They include the following:

- China Aerospace Corporation (CASC)
- China National Nuclear Corporation (CNNC)
- China North Industries Group (NORINCO)
- Aviation Industries Corporation of China (AVIC)
- China State Shipbuilding Corporation (CSSC)

Until 1998, COSTIND was controlled directly by both the CMC and the State Council. Come March 1998, the COSTIND was "civilianized" and now only has to report to the State Council. With this change also came a new entity, the General Armament Department (GAD). It was created simultaneously under the CMC and assumed responsibility for weapons system management and R&D. By revising the COSTIND, China again expanded its bureaucracy, adding yet another layer of government and, by extension, the amount of "red" tape the bureaucrats would go through to accomplish a project or mission.

CCP SUPREMACY OVER THE STATE, THE PLA, AND THE ECONOMY

The PRC Constitution plainly asserts the supremacy of the Communist Party over all other government, military, and civilian entities. But the CCP also relies on other, more pragmatic methods to ensure its primacy. To ensure control, all State government bodies have senior CCP members in control.

The best and most obvious example of this is the CCP Secretary's simultaneous service as State President and CCP CMC Chairman, which means he has the ultimate control of both the State and the PLA. Other examples of the close-knit controls include one of the two vice-chairmen's simultaneous service as a Politburo Standing Committee member and as a Premier of the State Council, and the second general's dual roles as Politburo member and Vice-Premier of the State Council. Close-knit controls by these three individuals provide the ultimate controls over everything to ensure a continuing power structure for the CCP.

In addition to the CCP Politburo's control of the PRC government and military, throughout the entire country, which can be broken down into various provinces and regions, there are hundreds of similar connections between lower-level Communist Party officials and the State, military, and commercial bureaucracies in the PRC. For example, of the 29 Ministers, 25 of them are in charge of Ministries and Commissions under the State Council, and they are also members of the CCP Central Committee.

Nowhere is the supremacy of the Communist Party more clearly enunciated than with the PLA. This CCP supremacy is explicitly set forth in the PRC Constitution. Additionally, as with the State government, it is not just law but a common control factor that guarantees PLA compliance with the Communist Party's whims and dictates.

The most obvious example of Communist Party control of the PLA can be shown by the position of Chairman of the CMC and, thus, the entire CMC's direct control of the PLA. As the acknowledged leader of the nation and the military, the Communist Party Secretary enforces complete CCP control over the military by never appointing military officers to the powerful CCP Politburo Standing Committee, notwithstanding that there are two officers in the Politburo.

The slogan "the Party controls the gun" is often repeated in speeches by both CCP and PLA officials. This phrase also serves as a constant reminder of CCP supremacy over the military. An article in the official PLA newspaper, published in celebration of Army Day, provides a typical example:

> The Western hostile forces... have never given up their plot to Westernize and disintegrate our country, and they always try to infiltrate and corrode us by advocating the fallacies of de-partyization of the army... in a vain attempt to make our army shake off the Party's absolute leadership and change its nature.

DEVELOPMENT OF THE CCP'S TECHNOLOGY POLICIES

The Politburo addresses broad technology matters through the Science and Technology Leading Group. This group is headed up by the Premier and also includes the Chairman of the State Science and Technology Commission and the Minister of COSTIND. Notice that all in these positions will have close political ties to the CCP Secretary who appoints them, assuring their complete subservience in terms of political survival.

All the technology policy directives will tend to be broad, originating initially from the upper levels of the Communist Party hierarchy. Once they have been created and approved, it suddenly becomes the responsibility of the State Council and its various finite organs to fine-tune and implement them. In addition, the State government, like the CCP itself, also has a number of Leading Groups, including a Science and Technology Leading Group that will also provide expertise and recommendations to the State Council and its organs. There exists a committee of approximately 50 R&D experts that meets annually in order to determine and then provide policy planning and any other required technical advice to the Minister of COSTIND. COSTIND also has the ability and power to further call upon the many academies and institutes under its direction for further clarification of policy implementation or further technical advice.

Within the State Council, the many varied subunits are also the consumers of military research conducted by the military's research bureaucracy, which is composed of numerous think tanks that are scattered throughout commerce and academia. They can provide analysis on a wide range of matters. All of the military research is channeled through a State Council unit known as the International Studies Research Center. The Center acts as a conduit and is a centralized transmission point to channel all relevant intelligence, research reports, and policy documents to the top Communist Party leadership.

THE 863 AND SUPER 863 PROGRAMS: IMPORTING TECHNOLOGIES FOR MILITARY USE

In 1986, CCP "Paramount Leader" Deng Xiaoping adopted a totally new and major initiative, the 863 Program, which was designed to accelerate the acquisition and development of science and technology in the PRC. Deng directed 200 scientists to develop science and technology goals that would include the immediate and long-range future of China. China claimed that the 863 Program produced almost 1500 research achievements by 1996 and was supported by nearly 30,000 scientific and technical personnel who worked to advance the Chinese "economy and... national defense construction." As of 2013, we can only guess the numbers of people and levels of achievements that have been made, in addition to how many more people are involved in the 863 Program.

As another demonstration of the civilian sector supporting the military (and thus the CCP way of life), the most senior engineers behind the 863 Program started out by being involved in strategic military programs such as space tracking, nuclear energy, and satellites. Under COSTIND's management, the 863 Program aimed to narrow the gap between the PRC and the West by the year 2000 in key science and technology sectors, including the following military technology areas:

- Astronautics
- Information technology
- Laser technology
- Automation technology
- Energy technology
- New materials

The 863 Program's large budget was split between military and civilian projects, thus insuring that it focused on both the military and civilian science and technology. Key areas of concern and thus their focus for the military included the following:

- Biological Warfare. In the mid-1990s, the 863 Program unveiled a plan for gene research that could have biological warfare applications.
- Space Technology. PRC planning focused on the development of satellites with remote sensing capabilities, which could be used for military reconnaissance, as well as space launch vehicles. As of 2012, their space ventures now include the moon in the next decade.
- Military Information Technology. The development of intelligent computers, optoelectronics, and image processing for weather forecasting, and the production of submicron integrated circuits on 8-inch silicon wafers are at the forefront of planning for the immediate future. These programs can then lead to the development of advanced military communications systems; command, control, communications, and intelligence systems; and advances in information technology applications for military software development.
- Laser Weapons. China looks to include the development of pulse-power techniques, plasma technology, and laser spectroscopy, all of which are useful in the development of laser weapons.
- Automation Technology. This area of the 863 Program, which includes the development of computer-integrated manufacturing systems and robotics for increased production capability, is focused in the areas of electronics, machinery, space, chemistry, and telecommunications, and could standardize and improve the PRC's military production.

- Nuclear Weapons. Qinghua University Nuclear Research Institute has claimed success in the development of high-temperature, gas-cooled reactors, projects that could aid in the development of nuclear weapons.
- Exotic Materials. The 863 Program areas include optoelectronic information materials, structural materials, special function materials, composites, rare-earth metals, new energy compound materials, and high-capacity engineering plastics. These projects could advance the PRC's development of materials, such as composites, for military aircraft and other weapons.

Thirteen years later after the program was initially announced, China announced a "Super 863 Program." This was a follow-up to the initial program and provided planning technology development through 2010. Even after 2010, the "Super 863 Program" continues the research agenda of the initial 863 Program, which apparently failed to meet the expectations.

This new program called for the continued acquisition and development of technology in a number of areas of military concern, which included machine tools, electronics, petrochemicals, electronic information, bioengineering, exotic materials, nuclear research, aviation, space, and marine technology. Nothing really changed, except the new program continued the old program without anyone being publicly censured for its initial failure to achieve desired results. COSTIND and the Ministry of Science and Technology jointly manage the Super 863 Program, with the Ministry of Science and Technology focusing on biotechnology, information technology, automation, nuclear research, and exotic materials, while COSTIND oversees the laser and space technology fields.

COSTIND, since its inceptions, has and continues to closely monitor any and all foreign technologies, including all those imported into the PRC through joint ventures with the United States and other Western countries. These efforts can be seen as direct evidence that the PRC engages in extensive oversight of imported dual-use technology. At the same time, the PRC also works to translate all foreign technical data, analyze it, and assimilate it for PLA military programs.

The continuation of the 863 Programs only increases the PRC's desire and ability to understand, assimilate, and transfer imported civil technologies to their military programs. More than ever, the Super 863 Program initiatives allow an increasingly greater focus on the development of technologies for military applications. To maximize their efforts, the PRC program managers for the past decade have been emphasizing projects that will attract US researchers. Since the early 1990s, China and particularly the military has been increasingly focused on acquiring US and foreign technology and equipment, especially those including any dual-use technologies that can be integrated into their military and industrial bases.

THE 16-CHARACTER POLICY: "GIVE PRIORITY TO MILITARY PRODUCTS"

In 1997, the CCP formally codified the 16-Character Policy. The "16-Character Policy" provides a unique status as the CCP's overall direction, but carefully provides a unique blurring of the lines between State and commercial entities, and military and commercial interests (see Figure 4.1).

The 16 characters literally mean:

- *Jun-min jiehe* (combine the military and civil)
- *Ping-zhan jiehe* (combine peace and war)
- *Jun-pin youxian* (give priority to military products)
- *Yi min yan jun* (let the civil support the military)

This policy codification was a carefully crafted reaffirmation of Deng Xiaoping's 1978 pronouncement, which holds that military development is the object of all general economic modernization and that the CCP's main aim for the civilian economy is to support the building of modern military weapons and to support the aims of the PLA (Figure 4.2). The 16-Character Policy could

軍民結合
平戰結合
軍品優先
以民養軍

FIGURE 4.1 The PRC's 16-Character Policy.

FIGURE 4.2 Deng Xiaoping, leader of the Communist Party of China circa 1998. (Courtesy of YANGCHAO/Shutterstock.com.)

be interpreted, in light of other policy pronouncements that military modernization is subordinate to general economic modernization, to mean a short-term strategy to use defense conversion proceeds for immediate military modernization.

It provides a way for the military to maintain a firm grasp over the Chinese people, keep the Party in power, and advance its long-range military agenda. It could also mean a long-term strategy to build a civilian economy that will, in the future, continue to advance and further support the building of modern military goods. In practice, however, the policy appears to have meant a little of both approaches, but that could change if China leaps ahead through the use of stolen technologies that can advance both the economic and military sectors.

The CCP's official policy on military modernization, as publicly announced since the late 1970s by then "Paramount Leader" Deng Xiaoping, stated that the PRC is devoting its resources to economic development, and that military development is subordinate to and serves that goal. Unfortunately, this is not the case, as the military continues to expand in both number and types of advanced equipment that have been built upon stolen technologies.

Former Vice-Chairman General Liuy Huaqing, who was part of the CMC and also a member of both the Politburo and the Standing Committee, said in 1992 that economic modernization was dependent not only on "advanced science and technology" but also on "people armed with it." Anything else was "empty talk."

Some of this is evidenced by China as they have used profits from its burgeoning commercial economy to purchase several advanced weapons systems. The most notable of which was the purchase from Russia of 50 Sukhoi Su-27 jet fighters and then the production rights for 200 more, the purchasing of two Kilo attack submarines, and two Sovremenniy missile destroyers.

The PRC also used its excess money to purchase weapons systems or at least their component parts from Israel, France, Britain, and the United States, including air-to-air missiles, air-refueling technology, global positioning system technology, helicopter parts, and assorted avionics.

In addition to providing funds for the purchase of these US and foreign weapons systems, the implementation of the 16-Character Policy serves the PLA in other ways. Among these are the following:

- Funding military R&D efforts
- Providing civilian cover for military industrial companies to acquire dual-use technology through purchase or joint venture business dealings
- Modernizing an industrial base that can, in time of hostility, be turned toward military production

In this manner, as far back as the 1980s, significant portions of the PRC military industry have diversified into civilian production, which would bring in many more foreign dollars and also contacts and businesses that could support the PRC military. The production of profit-producing civilian goods helps keep military–industrial companies in the PRC financially stable, providing for PRC the ability to expand, and helps PRC purchase other military-related items.

The majority of the military-related companies have operated "in the red" for years, bolstered only by extremely generous and forgiving loan arrangements from the PRC's central banks. In the past decade, the author believes, the military have ramped up sales of small weapons around the world, thus obtaining enough money to pull themselves into the "black" and the extra money for purchasing commodities they require.

The blurred lines between military and commercial technology that are the hallmarks of the 16-Character Policy have also created some problems for the PRC, though it is suspected that many will deny this fact. An official of the State Planning Commission, about 15 years ago, had criticized the 16-Character Policy for an insufficient focus on the most advanced military technologies, particularly in aerospace, aviation, nuclear power, and ship building. At the same time, though, the official acknowledged, military industries have been reluctant to share economically valuable technologies with civilian enterprises.

Pursuant to the 16-Character Policy, the PRC has provided more emphasis on the acquisition and development of military technology that must be closely related to its interest in science and technology for economic development. There are times that this has been reflected in tension between the modernization of the PLA and continued development of the economy. The PRC's approach to resolving this internal conflict has been to seek "comprehensive national power," in which high-technology industries, economic growth, and military modernization are all interrelated.

Despite all PRC's public claims, it was estimated that the actual military spending was anywhere between four to seven times greater than official figures would provide. During the 1990s, no other part of the PRC's budget was increasing at the rate of military spending. A large portion of this budget was devoted to military research. Since 2000, it can be surmised that this is still the case, and perhaps the level of spending is possibly upward of 10%, especially with the PRC's desire to move further into space with their rocketry and possible Moon landing in the coming decade.

The success achieved by the United States through the use of high-technology weapons in the 1990 Gulf War led PLA leaders to call for a re-emphasis on military development. PLA leaders began to call for military preparedness to fight "limited war under high-tech conditions."

The PLA has called for more attention to be given to the military aims, and this seems to have had some impact. Li Peng, the second-ranking member of the CCP Politburo, then Prime Minister, and currently in the National People's Congress, said in a speech delivered at the Fourth Session of the Eighth National People's Congress:

> "We should attach great importance to strengthening the army through technology, enhance research in defense-related science, ... give priority to developing arms needed for defense under high-tech conditions, and lay stress on developing new types of weapons."

Communist Party Secretary Jiang Zemin, in March 1997, publicly called for an "extensive, thorough-going and sustained upsurge" in the PLA's acquisition of high technology. The following year, the PRC's 1998 Defense White Paper pointedly stated that "no effort will be spared to improve the modernization level of weaponry."

The modernization of the PLA has placed priority on the development of the following:

- Battlefield communications
- Reconnaissance
- Space-based weapons
- Mobile nuclear weapons
- Attack submarines
- Fighter aircraft
- Precision-guided weapons
- Training rapid-reaction ground forces

These actions are all supported by the PRC's overall economic growth and will continue to improve the PLA's military capabilities in ways that enable the PRC to broaden its geographic focus beyond its national boundaries. Concurrently, during this period of the mid- to late 1990s, the PRC has shifted its military strategy toward rapid-reaction mobility and regional, versus global, armed conflict. Under this framework, the PRC's avowed military strategy became one of "active defense," a "capability for power projection to defend the PRC's territorial ambitions, which extend to not only Taiwan, but also the Senkaku Islands in the East China Sea, and the Spratly and Paracel Islands in the South China Sea."

THE PRC'S USE OF INTELLIGENCE SERVICES TO ACQUIRE US MILITARY TECHNOLOGY

The primary professional PRC intelligence services that are involved in technology acquisition for the greater good of China include the Ministry of State Security (MSS) and the PLA General Staff's Military Intelligence Department (MID).

In addition to, but separate from, these services, the PRC maintains a growing non-professional technology-collection effort by many other PRC government-controlled interests, such as research institutes and growing PRC military–industrial companies. The most egregious losses of US technology in the past have resulted not from professional operations under the control or direction of the MSS or MID, but as part of the continuing commercial, scientific, and academic interactions between the United States and the PRC.

Professional intelligence agents from the MSS and MID account for a relatively small share of the PRC's foreign science and technology collection. The bulk of such information is gathered by various non-professionals, including PRC students, scientists, researchers, and other visitors to the West. It can be surmised that these individuals sometimes are working at the behest of the MSS or MID, but often they really represent other PRC-controlled research organizations—scientific bureaus, commissions, research institutes, and the usual commercial business enterprises.

Anyone unfamiliar with the PRC's intelligence practices often conclude that, because intelligence services conduct clandestine operations, all clandestine operations are directed by intelligence agencies. In the case of the PRC, this is seldom a rule that can be followed with any true accuracy since facts learned from previous espionage cases support the view that it is more than likely a non-professional that is engaged in espionage activities.

Much of the PRC's intelligence collection is independent of MSS direction. For example, a government scientific institute may work on its own to acquire some general or specific information that could relate to one or more projects they are working on, or might be of use for a project currently on the drawing board and planned for the near-term future.

The MSS is headed by a very high-ranking Minister who is a member of the CCP Central Committee. The MSS reports to the Premier and the State Council. Its overall activities are ultimately overseen by the CCP Political Science and Law Commission. It is not unusual for senior members of the CCP's top leadership to be interested in the planning of PRC military acquisitions.

The MSS conducts science and technology collection as part of the PRC's overall efforts in this area, with those most often supporting the goals of specific PRC technology acquisition programs. Nevertheless, the MSS will take advantage of any opportunity to acquire military technology that presents itself.

The MSS relies very heavily upon a network of non-professional individuals and organizations that act outside the direct control of the intelligence services, including scientific delegations and PRC nationals that are working abroad to collect the vast majority of the information that the MSS seeks.

The PLA's MID, also known as the Second Department of the PLA General Staff, is responsible for military intelligence. One of the MID's substantial roles is military-related science and technology collection.

OVERVIEW OF METHODS USED BY THE PRC TO ACQUIRE ADVANCED US MILITARY TECHNOLOGY

The PRC uses a variety of approaches to acquire military technology. These include the following:

- Relying on "princelings" (which are family members and close relatives of high-ranking leaders that have a certain amount of authority and prestige) who can exploit their military, commercial, and political connections with high-ranking CCP and PLA leaders to buy military technology from abroad
- The illegal transfer of US military technology from third countries from which the technology was legally transferred
- Applying pressure on US commercial companies to transfer licensable technology illegally where such technology relates to joint ventures
- Exploiting various dual-use products and services for China's military advantage
- Illegally diverting licensable dual-use technology to military purposes
- Using front companies that are set up within the United States and other nations to illegally acquire technology
- Using commercially viable enterprises and other organizations as cover for technology acquisition
- Acquiring a major interest in US technology companies (sometimes as little as 5%–10%) or attempting to purchase the entire company or enough to officially have a "controlling interest"
- Covertly conducting espionage by personnel from government ministries, commissions, institutes, and military industries independently of the PRC intelligence services

The last is thought to be the main method of PRC intelligence activity in the United States, although during the past decade, the level of intelligence activity publicly acknowledged is from "non-professionals."

The PRC also identifies ethnic Chinese in the United States who have access to sensitive information; sometimes, the PRC is able to enlist their cooperation in illegal technology or information transfers. Finally, the PRC has been able to exploit various weaknesses, gaps, or lapses in the US system for monitoring the sale and export of surplus military technology and industrial auctions.

The PRC is striving to acquire advanced technology of any sort, whether for military or civilian purposes, as part of its program to improve its entire economic infrastructure.

This broad targeting permits the effective use of a wide variety of means to access technology. In addition, the PRC's diffuse and multi-pronged technology acquisition effort presents unique difficulties for US intelligence and law enforcement agencies, because the same set of mechanisms and organizations used to collect technology in general can be used and are used to collect military technology.

The PRC uses a careful blending of intelligence and non-intelligence assets and the reliance on different collection methods, which in the long run presents numerous challenges to the US agencies attempting to meet the PRC threat.

In short, as James R. Lilley, former US Ambassador to the PRC says, "US agencies are 'going nuts' trying to find numerous MSS and MID links to the PRC's military science and technology collection, when such links are buried beneath layers of bureaucracy or do not exist at all."

China Aerospace International Holdings, as an example, is a firm that specializes in foreign technology and military sales. As a Hong Kong subsidiary of CASC, it manages the PRC's missile and space industry. Both organizations mutually benefit from the export of missile or satellite-related technologies and components from the United States, as does the China Great Wall Industry Corporation, also a subsidiary of CASC, which provides commercial space launch services to American satellite manufacturers. As you can see, there is no direct link to the upper echelons of the Chinese government, but rest assured, close contacts are maintained.

CASC is also a substantial shareholder in both the Apstar and APMT projects that work to import US satellites to the PRC for launch by China Great Wall Industry Corporation.

A Chinese–American, Johnny Chung, during the course of plea negotiations for economic espionage, disclosed that during a trip to Hong Kong in the summer of 1996, he met with the head of the MID, Gen. Ji Shengde. Within a month after the meeting, Chung formed Marswell Investment, Inc., possibly capitalizing the new company with some of the $300,000 he had received. The company was based in Torrance, California, a prime location where the China Great Wall Industry Corporation also maintains its US subsidiary. The very close continuing ties between the two companies are highly suspect (though not proven yet).

ACQUISITION OF MILITARY TECHNOLOGY FROM OTHER GOVERNMENTS

To fill its short-term technological needs in military equipment, the PRC has made numerous purchases of foreign military systems. The chief source for these systems is Russia, but the PRC has acquired military technology from other countries as well.

In the past, Israel offered significant technology cooperation to the PRC, especially within the areas of aircraft and missile development. Israel provided both weapons and technology to the PRC, with the most notable being assisting the PRC in developing its F-10 fighter and airborne early-warning aircraft.

From the United States, the PRC has stolen military technology, but until recently, the United States has lawfully transferred little to the PLA. This has been due, in part, to sanctions imposed by the United States in response to both the 1989 Tiananmen Square massacre and to the PRC's 1993 transfer of missile technology to Pakistan.

During the Cold War era, the United States had assisted the PRC in avionics modernization for its jet fighters under the US Peace Pearl program.

Even with this being accomplished, the illegal transfers of US technology from the United States to the PRC have been significant. Significant transfers of US military technology had taken place in the mid-1990s via the re-export by Israel of advanced technology transferred to it by the United States, including avionics and missile guidance useful for the PLA's F-10 fighter. The US Congress and several executive agencies have also investigated allegations that Israel has provided United States–originated cruise, air-to-air, and ground-to-air missile technology to the PRC.

JOINT VENTURES WITH US COMPANIES

Over the years, various pressures have been brought to bear on US companies linked with militarily sensitive technology attempting to do business with the PRC. Such past pressures provided examples of US companies conspiring to evade export control laws in pursuit of joint ventures.

Be that as it may, the Cox Report noted that "the vast majority of commercial business activity between the United States and the PRC does not present a threat to national security," but the report also noted that additional scrutiny, discipline, and an awareness of the various risks involved are necessary with respect to joint ventures with the PRC wherein the potential exists for the transfer of militarily sensitive US technology. This, the author surmises, will continue to present a constant problem that has vexed the nation for years and will continue to do so into the future.

The US National Science and Technology Strategy stated that "Sales and contracts with foreign buyers imposing conditions leading to technology transfer, joint ventures with foreign partners involving technology sharing and next generation development, and foreign investments in US industry create technology transfer opportunities that may raise either economic or national security concerns."

The behavior of the PRC government and the numerous PRC-controlled businesses that deal with US companies that are involved with militarily related sensitive technologies can confirm that these concerns are valid and growing. The expanding number of joint ventures that call for technology transfers between the PRC and US firms is expected to provide the PRC with a continuing access to American dual-use technologies that will provide the PRC with military and commercial advantages.

Technology transfer requirements in joint ventures often take the form of side agreements (sometimes referred to as offset agreements) requiring both that the US firm transfer technology to the PRC partner and that all transferred technology will eventually become the property of the PRC partner. In essence, these requirements mean that the current technologies the PRC desires are being handed to them with little or no recourse about what their eventual and final use will be, whether it be for the military or commercial fields, or both.

While many countries require technology transfers when they do business with US firms, no country makes such demands across as wide a variety of industries as does the PRC. Despite the PRC's rapid economic liberalization over the past three decades, the PRC continues to implement its explicitly designed goals and policies to restrict and manage foreign investment so as to bolster the PRC's military and commercial industries through acquisition of American technology.

The CCP has long believed that forcing technology from foreign firms not only is critical to the PRC but also is a cost that foreign firms will bear in order to obtain PRC market entry. In no other world nation are such practices taken to such extremes, and for the commercial ventures wishing to enter China, it may well be considered as "the cost of doing business."

In the past, the PRC has favored joint ventures with US high-technology companies for several reasons:

- The United States excels in many areas of technology that are of special interest to the PLA and to PRC-controlled firms.
- Many PRC scientists were educated in the United States and retain valuable contacts in the US research and business community who can be exploited for technology transfer.
- Many other countries are more reluctant than the United States to give up technology.

The PRC has dedicated increasing resources to identifying US high-technology firms as potential likely targets for joint venture overtures. Science and technology representatives in PRC embassies abroad are used to assist in this targeting of technology and to encourage collaboration with US firms for this purpose. A soft-sell opening can be expected in these cases since businesses wish to expand into China for the potential sales and profits, but the Chinese experience will, eventually, leave such ventures lopsided as China takes control of the technology for itself.

Unless they are briefed by the FBI pursuant to its National Security Threat List program, US companies are unaware of the extent of the PRC's espionage directed against US technology and thus—at least from the US national security standpoint—are generally unprepared for the reality of doing business in the PRC. US companies lack the knowledge of the interconnections that are held between the CCP, the PLA, the State, and the PRC-controlled companies with which they deal directly in the negotiating process. These interconnections really bind the Chinese state together as they develop newer methods to draw unsuspecting American companies into their technology collection net.

The US General Accounting Office (GAO) found that US businesses have significant concerns about arbitrary licensing requirements in the PRC, because they often call for increased technology transfer. The GAO also found that transparency was the most frequent concern to be reported by US companies. Because of the lack of transparency in the PRC's laws, rules, and regulations that govern business alliances, and the dearth of accessible, understandable sources of regulatory information, US businesses suddenly find themselves being subjected to various technology transfer requirements that are never found in any written documentation or are contained in "secret" rules that only the PRC insiders know about.

Because of the PRC's massive potential consumer market, it becomes a key factor behind the willingness of some US businesses to take unprecedented risks and a willingness to tolerate technology transfers. Some of these transfers could impair US national security, as in the cases of the Loral and Hughes corporations. The obvious potential of the PRC market has increasingly enabled the PRC to place technology-transfer demands on its US trading partners. Without these demands, the companies would be shut out of China for all intents and purposes, losing a potential foothold to another company that is willing to share technology secrets.

Many US businesses believe that they must be in the PRC, lest a competitor get a foothold first. Many high-technology firms believe that it is more important to establish the foothold than to attempt to make profits immediately or gain any more than limited access to the largest potential market in the world for their products. The Cox Report noted that some of the PRC's trading partners have focused more on increased technology transfers in order to raise the attractiveness of their bids.

In addition to traditional types of technology transfer, many US high-technology investments in the PRC will purposely include agreements establishing joint R&D centers or projects. This type of agreement represents a new trend in US investment in the PRC and is a potentially significant development. US companies are not aware of what is really happening.

US companies involved in joint ventures may be willing to transfer technology since they believe that the only risk being taken is a business one, that is, that the transfers may eventually hurt them in terms of market share or competition. The businesses are wholly unaware that any of their technologies that are transferred to a PRC partner will likely be shared within the PRC's industrial networks and with the PLA, or that joint ventures may be used in some instances as cover to acquire critical technology for the military. In essence, then, the technology shared with an individual partner is suddenly available throughout the PRC industrial and military base, and the company that provided it has no idea of its true value across the spectrum of potential uses.

Since COSTIND controls the PRC's military–industrial organizations, it most likely attempts to monitor technologies through these joint ventures. In addition, US businesses will be unaware that joint-venture operations are also vulnerable to penetration by official PRC intelligence agencies, such as the MSS. The joint venture will include the hiring of many Chinese personnel, some of which are most certainly working for or tied to the PRC intelligence agencies. This would allow for the on-site collection of technology during the work day and also during off-hours when no workers are normally present. As such, the Chinese ability to spend time searching through company files for other data that would not be found on the "factory floor" presents the PRC with a tremendous potential to glean information that is normally held and used by only the most senior members of the US company.

In a case from the early 1990s, a US high-technology company and its PRC partner used a joint venture to avoid US export control laws and make a very lucrative sale of controlled equipment to the PRC. When the export license was denied, the US company went so far as to attempt to form a joint venture, under which the technology would then be transferred. What was found out is that the joint venture was controlled by a PRC entity that had been included on the US Commerce Department's Entity List. Its inclusion on the list meant that it presented an unacceptable risk for the diversion of the technology for the development of weapons of mass destruction.

ACQUISITION AND EXPLOITATION OF DUAL-USE TECHNOLOGIES

The acquisition of advanced dual-use technology represents just one of many other methods by which the PRC will attempt to gain advanced technologies for its military modernization from American companies. China's continued military modernization drive includes a well-crafted policy for acquiring dual-use technologies. It seeks civil technology in part in the hopes of being able to adapt the technology to military applications. This has been referred to by some analysts as "spinning on."

There is a strategy that was developed in 1995 that called for the acquisition of dual-use technologies with civil and military applications and then the transfer of R&D achievements in civil technology to the research and production of weapons.

The PRC has collected military-related science and technology information from openly available US and Western sources and military researchers over many years. This collection effort was designed to accelerate the PLA's military technology development by permitting it to follow proven development options already undertaken.

PRC procurement agents would approach US firms to gain an understanding of the uses of available technology and subtly determine if it has dual-use capabilities. At the same time, they wanted to evaluate the possibility for China to purchase the dual-use technology under the guise of civil programs while maintaining its sale within the constraints of US export controls. The PRC has also attempted to acquire information from the United States and other countries about the design and manufacturing of military helicopters. The PRC could also use this approach to acquire chemical and biological weapons technology.

The key organizations in the PRC's drive to acquire dual-use technology include the following:

- COSTIND, which acquires dual-use technology for PRC institutes and manufacturers by assuring foreign suppliers that the technology will be used for civil production. COSTIND uses overseas companies to target US firms for acquisition of dual-use technology for the military.
- The Ministry of Electronics Industry, which is responsible for developing the PRC's military electronics industry. Among other things, the Ministry approves and prioritizes R&D and the importation of electronics technologies that can be used to speed up the PRC's indigenous production capabilities.
- The Ministry of Post and Telecommunications, which is acquiring asynchronous transfer mode switches that could be used for military purposes by the PLA.
- PLA-operated import–export companies, which also import dual-use technologies for military modernization. Polytechnologies, a company attached to the General Staff Department of the PLA, plays a major role in this effort, especially in negotiating foreign weapons purchases.

- The AVIC and its subsidiary, China National Aero-Technology Import–Export Corporation (CATIC), which have sent visitors to US firms to discuss manufacturing agreements for commercial systems that could be used to produce military aircraft for the PLA.

AVIC is one of five PRC state-owned conglomerates that operate as "commercial businesses" under the direct control of the State Council and COSTIND. There have been a number of incidents that highlight CATIC's direct role in the acquisition of controlled US technology. One clear example was CATIC's role as the lead PRC representative in the 1994 purchase of advanced machine tools from McDonnell Douglas.

Another example was their exploitation of civilian end use as a means of obtaining controlled technology. CATIC's 1983 purchase of two US-originated CFM-56 jet engines that was based on the pretext that the engines would be used to re-engine commercial aircraft. Although the CFM-56 is a commercial engine, its core section is the same as the core of the General Electric F-101 engine that is used in the US B-1 bomber. Because of this, restrictions were placed on the export license.

However, the PRC may have exploited the technology of the CFM-56. When the US government subsequently requested access to the engines, the PRC claimed they had been destroyed in a fire. This comes down to "he said, she said." Without the engines, the United States could prove nothing. But China, having the engines, could carefully take them apart, determine the core matter technologies, and then use their aircraft industries and engineering personnel to carefully craft a duplicate engine. China saved thousands of man-hours and development costs, and the end result was a better and faster Chinese military aircraft.

CATIC has also on several occasions misrepresented the proposed uses of militarily useful US technology. The Clinton administration looked into this and determined that the specific facts in these cases could not be publicly disclosed. Thus, the American public and numerous manufacturers are kept in the dark about what really happened and how the Chinese have taken advantage of our secrecy to gain inroads into their level of technology.

The CATIC is a wholly owned PRC business that is under the control of the State COSTIND. CATIC's office in California has played a direct role in obtaining controlled technology from US companies.

Fifteen years ago, AVIC, which is CATIC's parent company, attempted to use a Canadian intermediary to hire some former Pratt & Whitney engineers in the United States to assist in the development of an indigenous PRC jet engine. AVIC's initial approach came under the guise of a civilian project. The engineers were never told that they would be working on a military engine, an engine that would be designed and installed on China's newest fighter jet until negotiations had progressed substantially. Once they learned what China's true intentions were, the engineers pulled out of the project.

The degree of diversion to military programs by the PRC of commercially acquired technologies is unclear, since the Chinese parallel civil–military industrial complex blurs the true end use of technology that has been acquired. Because of this blurring, it is assumed that there are probably many, many more uses being made of US dual-use technology for military production than can be determined.

FRONT COMPANIES

China also acquires US technology through the use of front companies, in which it has been stated by some as being about 3000 or possibly more. The term *front company* has been used in a variety of ways in numerous public reports and academic studies in different contexts and can include many different corporations set up outside China. They can include the following:

- US subsidiaries of PRC military–industrial corporations
- US subsidiaries of PLA-owned and -operated corporations

- Corporations set up by PRC nationals overseas to conduct technology acquisition and transfer
- Corporations set up to covertly acquire technology for an intelligence service, corporation, or institute
- Corporations set up by a PRC intelligence service, corporation, or institute solely to give cover to professional or non-professional agents who enter the United States to gather technology or for other purposes
- Corporations set up by a PRC intelligence service to launder money
- Corporations set up by a PRC intelligence service to raise capital to fund intelligence operations
- Corporations set up by a PRC individual to hide, accumulate, or raise money for personal use
- Corporations set up by organs of the PRC government to funnel money to key US leaders for the purpose of garnering favor and influencing the US political process and US government decision-making

There are differing meanings attached to the term front companies by different US agencies, and this has led to confusion, particularly because many of these front companies fall into several different categories, at the outset or at different times during their existence.

Those US agencies that are responsible for different aspects of national security, law enforcement, and Sino–US relations often do not share even basic data concerning PRC espionage in the United States, and this is a loss for America.

It may also partly explain why, for example, in a Senate testimony on the same day during a hearing, the State Department said it could identify only two PLA companies that were doing business in the United States. The American Federation of Labor and Congress of Industrial Organizations identified at least 12, and a Washington-based think tank identified 20 to 30 such companies. All three figures given were far below the true figure.

It was determined that there were more than 3000 PRC corporations in the United States, some with links to the PLA and a State intelligence service and some with technology targeting and acquisition roles. This is probably a deliberate blurring of "commercial" and "intelligence" operations, which presented greater challenges to any US efforts to monitor technology transfers for national security purposes.

Another complicating factor that has arisen and must be noted is the evolution of the names used by PRC-controlled corporations. Some corporations such as NORINCO and Polytechnologies were easily recognizable as subsidiaries of PRC corporations. Recent changes, however, have made it more difficult to recognize PRC corporations.

Some people have noted that US-based subsidiaries of PLA-owned companies in particular have stopped naming themselves after their parent corporation. This move was probably affected at least in part by criminal indictments and negative media reports that have been generated in connection with their espionage activities in the United States. Many of these companies simply ceased to exist, a phenomenon that would reflect these factors as well as the fact that PRC-controlled companies often do not make enough money to survive as a viable business venture.

However, the PRC intelligence services continue to use their numerous front companies for espionage. These front companies may include branches of the large ministerial corporations as well as small one- and two-person establishments. Front companies, no matter their size, may have positions for PRC intelligence service officers. A good front company should be in a moneymaking business as it will better provide a more legitimate cover for intelligence personnel. It is also noted that some of the PRC front companies would be used to sponsor visits to the United States by delegations that include PRC intelligence operatives.

There have been increasing PRC espionage through front companies during the 1990s and into the new century. The significant number of front companies with ties to PRC intelligence services that were in operation in the United States has probably continued to increase in number, but this cannot be verified with any open source data.

Similar to the old Soviet Union, China also takes advantage of the state-controlled "news" media organizations to gain political influence and gather political intelligence. Well-placed radio and television crews, in addition to the standard newspaper/magazine reports, are in an excellent position to openly probe, question, and attend many meetings and symposia, in addition to Congressional hearings in order to obtain specific information, to identify knowledgeable people in specific fields, and also to gain access to various manufacturing companies to gain information. One of the best areas for scouting out potential targets is the US government. The annual budget hearings provide data on who is spending money on new projects and sometimes the names of the companies involved. The Government Printing Office provides thousands of publications on just about every subject, and these also have references and notes that can be tied to various businesses and individuals of interest, and the cost for such publications is very low.

Back in the 1990s, the PRC also attempted to use front companies to acquire sensitive information on restricted military technologies, including the Aegis combat system. The Aegis combat system used the AN/SPY-1 phased array radar to detect and track over 100 targets simultaneously and a computer-based command and decision system allowing for simultaneous operations against air, surface, and submarine threats. From a military standpoint, this would be a terrific espionage coup if it was successful. It would have provided the Chinese military a greater advantage over the entire Southeast Asia region.

DIRECT COLLECTION OF TECHNOLOGY BY NON-INTELLIGENCE AGENCIES AND INDIVIDUALS

PRC intelligence agencies operate in the Unites States as commercial ventures using the business environment by having entities set up by other PRC government and commercial organizations instead of creating their own fronts. PLA military intelligence officers would, however, operate directly in the United States, posing as military attaches at the PRC Embassy in Washington, D.C., and at the United Nations in New York.

Most PRC covert collection of restricted technology in the United States is accomplished by individuals attached to PRC government and commercial organizations that are unaffiliated with official PRC intelligence services. These organizations collect their own technology from the United States, rather than rely on the PRC intelligence agencies to do it for them. This collection effort would also produce dual collection activities, since neither would know exactly what the other was collecting. Dual collection activities could also ensure that the materials would get to a greater number of potential users, but it can also be used for one to verify the accuracy of the other's collection effort down the road when, for example, a company would receive the same information from two different sources, thus being assured of its accuracy and viability for use within a current or emerging Chinese technology.

It is very possible that the MSS is allowing other PRC government entities to use MSS assets to fulfill their intelligence collection needs. Such findings would further illustrate that Chinese intelligence operations are not necessarily conducted by what are traditionally thought of as "intelligence" agencies.

The main intelligence activity within the United States is not represented by PLA intelligence organizations, but rather by the PRC's military industries and regular components of the PLA. Although military–industrial corporations are not PLA owned, they are deeply involved in arms production and acquisition of military technology.

The activities of CATIC and its US subsidiaries would also further exemplify the activities carried out by the military–industrial companies. Other companies, such as China Great Wall Industry Corporation, will collect technology for their own use, but it may also be used as cover by active intelligence personnel.

Technology acquisition in the United States is also being carried out by various science and technology commissions and organizations. COSTIND, for example, has no official US subsidiary, but it is the primary coordinating authority over the military–industrial corporations that collect technology. COSTIND also uses the "front company" device to procure high-technology products.

The PRC State Science and Technology Commission largely oversees civilian science and technology collection. This Commission also uses the diplomats located in various parts of the United States as key collection tools. In the past, it has provided funding to a PRC scientist to establish various commercial enterprises in the United States as a means of collecting technology information for distribution in the PRC.

The Commission was involved in efforts to elicit nuclear weapons information from a Chinese–American scientist. Their offices in the PRC's seven diplomatic agencies in the United States are tasked to carry out a substantial portion of technology acquisition. The primary role of these offices is to arrange contacts between PRC scientists and their American counterparts.

Various "liaison groups" constitute another collection vehicle. The primary official liaison organization is the China Association for International Exchange of Personnel (CAIEP). CAIEP operates seven "liaison organization" offices in the United States, including one in Washington, D.C., and one in San Francisco. It is one of several organizations set up by the PRC to illegally acquire technology through contacts with Western scientists and engineers.

Other liaison groups include a purported technology company and a PRC State agency. A significant source of their technology collection efforts outside of its formal intelligence agencies comes from Chinese business representatives loyal to the CCP who immigrate to the United States. These individuals pursue commercial interests independent of direct PRC government control. Their primary motive is personal financial gain, and they will sell their efforts and opportunities to any willing consumer. When asked to do so, they collect and pass on US technology back to China. It is believed that the use of this technique has proliferated in recent years.

They also acquire advanced technology through outright information theft. The PRC has used Chinese nationals hired by US firms for this purpose. Supporting this would be PRC's heavy reliance on professional scientific visits, delegations, and exchanges to gather sensitive technology.

As the PRC government has increasingly participated in the global commercial and capital markets, the number of PRC representatives entering the United States has increased dramatically. One estimate is that in one year alone, more than 80,000 Chinese nationals visited the United States as part of 23,000 delegations. Almost every PRC citizen who is allowed to go to the United States as part of these delegations most likely receives some type of collection requirement, according to official sources.

Scientific delegations from the PRC are a typical method used to begin the process of locating a joint venture partner. Delegations have been known to go through the motions of establishing a joint venture to garner as much information as possible from the US partner, only to pull out at the last minute. For a small- or medium-size business, the possibility that real money is almost in their grasp and that the Chinese will fall over backward to broker a deal probably gets the business people more excited than usual. At this point, negotiations may start to really look good; the possibility of a really big return blinds them to what is actually about to happen and the dollar signs are so big that they provide technical information that should not have been passed to the Chinese, and then, once the information and anything else of value has been garnered, the Chinese step back and the deal falls through. The Chinese have obtained what they started out for, and the American company is left with the knowledge that many of their corporate secrets have just been handed over to the Chinese.

Scientific visits and exchanges by PRC scientists and engineers with their US counterparts had always created several risks to US national security. This has been a particular concern in recent years regarding foreign visitors to the Department of Energy's national weapons laboratories.

A risk inherent in scientific exchanges is that US scientists who are in the PRC are prime targets for approaches by professional and non-professional organizations that would like to co-opt them into providing assistance. In many cases, they were able to identify scientists whose views might support the PRC and whose knowledge would be of value to PRC programs.

ILLEGAL EXPORT OF MILITARY TECHNOLOGY PURCHASED IN THE UNITED STATES

The PRC has also been taking advantage of the ongoing US military downsizing. In particular, PRC representatives and their companies in the United States pursue the purchase of high-technology military surplus goods. In a single operation, the Los Angeles office of the US Customs Service seized over $36 million in excess military property that was being shipped overseas illegally. Among the seized US military surplus equipment on its way to the PRC and Hong Kong were the following:

- Thirty-seven inertial navigation systems for the US F-117 and FB-111 aircraft
- Thousands of computers and computer disks containing classified top secret and higher information
- Patriot missile parts
- Five hundred electron tubes used in the US F-14 fighter
- Tank and howitzer parts
- Twenty-six thousand encryption devices

PRC representatives tend to be the biggest buyers of sensitive electronic surplus material. Department of Defense investigators have noticed a trend among the buyers of this equipment: many had worked for high-technology companies in China or for PRC government science and technology organizations.

They have been able to purchase these surplus materials because, in its rush to dispose of excess property, the Defense Department failed to code properly or to disable large amounts of advanced military equipment. These mistakes allowed Chinese buyers to pay for and take immediate possession of functional high-technology equipment. Oftentimes, this equipment was purchased as "scrap," for which the buyers paid pennies on the dollar.

According to one industrial auctioneer, representatives frequent industrial auctions because they offer accurate, well-maintained equipment at bargain prices and with quick delivery. In some cases, once purchased, the buyer can move out the equipment the same day on their own trucks. Moreover, once the PRC obtains this equipment, there are ample resources available in the United States to upgrade the equipment to more modern standards that are acceptable to the Chinese and the equipment can then be put to immediate use.

One California company specializing in refurbishing machine tools, as an example, was approached by representatives from CATIC's El Monte, California, office. The representatives reportedly inquired about the scope of the company's refurbishment capability, including whether it could train CATIC people to rebuild and maintain the machines and whether the company would be willing to assemble the machines in the PRC. The CATIC personnel also reportedly asked if the company could convert a three-axis machine tool to a five-axis machine tool.

For the uninitiated in airplane construction and flight technology, a multi-axis machine tool profiler is designed to build wing spans for the US F-14 fighter. The equipment originally costs over $3 million but was purchased by the PRC for under $25,000 (Figure 4.3).

The representatives were told that the conversion was possible for some machines and very often only requires replacing one computer controller with another.

The US company noted, however, that such a converted machine would require an export license. The CATIC response was rather emphatic, and that they would have "no problem" with the export. The CATIC inquiries came at about the same time CATIC was negotiating the purchase of machine tools from the McDonnell Douglas Columbus, Ohio, plant.

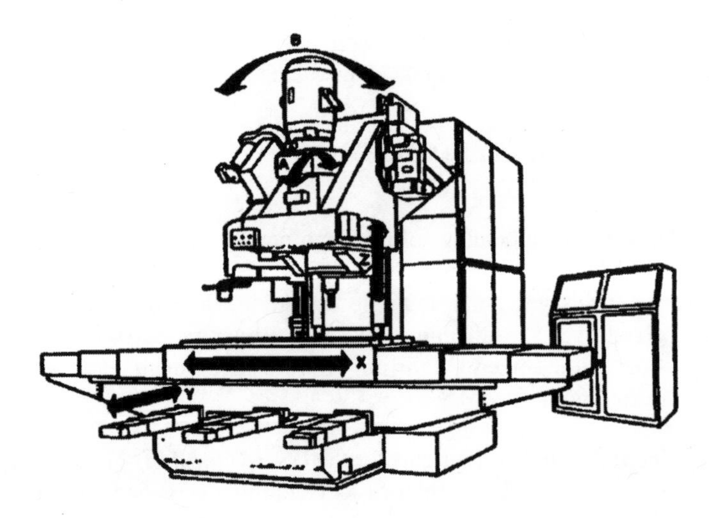

FIGURE 4.3 Multi-axis machine tool profiler designed to build wing spans for the US F-14 fighter purchased by the PRC for under $25,000.

The use of diplomatic pouches and traveling PRC diplomats offers yet another avenue for the illegal export of technology. Almost every PRC government commercial and diplomatic institution in the United States has personnel that facilitate science and technology acquisitions.

The more relaxed controls on the export of militarily sensitive technology to Hong Kong have been allowed to remain in place even though Hong Kong was absorbed by the PRC and PLA garrisons took control of the region on July 1, 1997.

US trade officials have reported that no inspections by the Hong Kong regional government or by any other government, including the United States, are permitted when PLA vehicles cross the Hong Kong border. This provides a wide-open road for which the PRC takes advantage of transporting the technology without any customs checks.

PRC INCENTIVES FOR US COMPANIES TO ADVOCATE RELAXATION OF EXPORT CONTROLS

Every company is eager to expand its business base through joint ventures or sales, especially in markets previously unopened to them. Those US companies in the high-technology sector are very eager to access the PRC market since the sales potential can go through the roof if the right deal is brokered. The PRC often requires these US firms to transfer technologies to the PRC as a precondition to market access. US export regulations can be seen as an impediment to commercial opportunities.

Those US executives desiring to do business in the PRC must share a mutual commercial interest with the PRC in minimizing any export controls on dual-use and military-related commodities.

For a number of years, the PRC has been determined to reduce the restrictions on the export of US communications satellites for launch in the PRC. Provision of such launch services creates a unique opportunity to consult with US satellite manufacturers, access information regarding US satellite technology, and obtain resources to modernize their rockets. US satellite manufacturers are, in turn, very anxious to access the potentially lucrative PRC market and realize that launching in China is a potential condition for obtaining market access.

CHINA'S EFFORTS TO ASSIMILATE ADVANCED US MILITARY TECHNOLOGY

China's approach to US technology firms proceeds from the premise that foreign firms should be allowed access to the PRC market only because such access will enable the PRC to assimilate technology and eventually to compete with or even overtake US technology. As such, the PRC views foreign firms as a short-term means to acquire technology.

In theory, while the PRC is increasingly able to develop its own technology, it will need less and less foreign assistance. In practice, however, China faces numerous challenges for the integration of foreign technology for both its civilian and military industrial bases.

Among the areas where China is particularly dependent upon American technology are computer hardware and microelectronics fields, telecommunications, commercial aircraft, and machine tools. The PRC must continue to rely heavily on joint ventures with foreign firms to provide advanced technology in these areas. Once the technologies are firmly embedded in China, the joint ventures will vanish, and China will have the technology and also the experienced workers who are knowledgeable because they worked for extended periods on the joint venture.

There are several reasons that the PRC has absorbed and assimilated only some, and not other, US military and civilian technologies:

- The PRC's funding of technology development, especially in applied sciences, conflicts with other priorities, including supporting PRC state-owned enterprises as they restructure.
- While the PRC has targeted very sophisticated US military technology, including aerospace and electronics technology, it has not achieved the levels of training and maintenance necessary to absorb.
- The PRC has a reputation for violating intellectual property rights, making some foreign investors hesitant to transfer their most advanced technology.
- There is a tendency for CCP and PLA officials to look toward their personal gain and aggrandizement first, before using State assets for the benefit of the PRC.

The PRC has continually reaped the benefits from advanced US and Western military technology in several areas, including ground force weapons, communications, remote sensing, and tactical and strategic systems. A study by the US Office of Technology Assessment found that joint ventures with the United States in commercial aircraft production appear to have enabled the PLA to machine smoother skins on its fighter aircraft. Other PRC military products, such as air-to-air and surface-to-air missiles, submarines, and short-range ballistic missiles, also appear to have benefited because of technical assistance arising from joint ventures.

The PRC has also succeeded in reverse engineering military hardware acquired from the United States and other countries, thereby defraying the high cost of weapons development. The following are examples:

- During the 1980s and 1990s, the PRC is believed to have diverted US military technology through its civilian programs. In 1983, the PRC is thought to have exploited the CFM-56 jet engine technology from a civilian program. The CFM-56 contains the same core section as the engine used in the B-1B bomber.
- The PRC developed its Z-11 helicopter by reverse engineering the French Aerospatiale AS-350 Ecureuil helicopter.
- The PRC's C-801 anti-ship cruise missile is believed to be a copy of the French Exocet anti-ship cruise missile.

Their scientists have been pressured to reverse engineer US high technology rather than purchase it, even though this means that it may be difficult to maintain because of the lack of service, training, and documentation. It's like having the newest car on the market, but you don't have the skills, equipment, and repair manuals when the car breaks down; the hands-on skills and knowledge are lacking for any significant repair.

For example, the PRC was able to reverse engineer a high-performance computer and produce a copy for far less than the US equipment would have cost. By the time they achieved this success, however, a commercially available desktop computer with the same power could have been purchased for a small fraction of their costs in time, money, and effort. They have the available cash to reverse engineer a product and are willing to pay the cost in order to avoid any long-term dependence on US technology.

As a concluding note to this chapter, at least some of the PRC's statements about its technical progress are distorted so as to increase the PRC's ability to gain access to foreign technology. By claiming substantial indigenous progress in areas ranging from supercomputers to stealth technology, the PRC desires to allay any foreign fears that providing it with advanced technology will improve the PRC's capabilities. It is believed that this tactic was used to overcome US and Western objections to transfer some high-performance computers to the PRC. As the knowledge spreads that China is not so necessarily behind in various fields, it is possible that American and other manufacturers and companies will wise up to China's gambits and refuse to sell products, step away from any joint ventures, and withhold these critical technologies that China is attempting to obtain. Also, the knowledge of the lengths China will go to in order to obtain technological secrets should be a clear warning bell that their espionage efforts will only increase; thus, more limited access and greater security are required to protect against China's efforts.

5 Chinese Product Piracy and Counterfeiting*

From almost the beginning of recorded history, China has served as a provider of desired goods. Marco Polo traveled the world to bring back goods made in the Orient. Today, China's economy has grown to include the manufacture of many different products, including clothing, purses, software, computers, and movies. While just as desired as the goods of Marco Polo's day, these modern goods often are not the legitimate product of the original source; instead, these are goods that are copied, reverse engineered and—with limited investment and no payment to the creator—sold for a negligible price to China's 1.3 billion citizens and also exported in massive quantities to many, many other countries, including America.

The impact of counterfeiting and piracy on American innovators and the general public is impossible to quantify with precision. Pharmaceutical researchers that invest in the development of drugs lose the ability to control the safety of their products. Film studios that produce movies are unable to realize the full measure of profit from their creations. Car manufacturers cannot control the quality of their parts. But perhaps most egregious is that because of piracy, American jobs are lost and American creators lose the benefits of their contributions to the world of creativity.

The Chinese government and some Chinese companies appear to have an interesting philosophy about piracy. They point to their robust laws on intellectual property (IP), show you attempts at enforcement with a televised raid of a market stall, and describe their involvement in the issue by lending you educational materials for high schools on the importance of respecting IP. Piracy, they claim, is not to be tolerated.

Yet the reality is that not only is piracy tolerated, but the government typically turns a blind eye to allow the benefits of piracy to accrue to Chinese consumers. These cheaper products, it is argued, provide the Chinese population with the luxury items they desire, but may not be able to afford. I have heard that some people in the Chinese government assert that the pirates are merely providing cheaper products for those who cannot afford to buy bread, in essence functioning as "Robin Hoods" for these goods. Yet this argument holds little credence when those goods are openly exported around the world, disrupting existing markets for the legitimate product. As noted by the Chamber of Commerce, the value of Chinese counterfeits coming into US markets seized by the United States increases annually.

Rampant piracy has enabled the Chinese economy to move forward rapidly in the race of technology by building off the innovation of others without investing the initial time and capital in development of the product. Their goal of being a dominant market power is no longer in the distant future, but is becoming a reality now in part as a result of pilfering the fruit of many American ideas.

China has been in the news over the past decades for counterfeiting such items, especially movies, presenting a real challenge for the United States. The failure (intended or not) of China to adequately protect and enforce IP rights (IPR) may be systemic and deliberate, rather than mere "growing pains" associated with the development of large-scale market economies. The credibility of China, for one, and its seriousness to enforce legitimate IPR of US companies, is questionable when copyright piracy levels can be as high as 70% to 80% or even as high as 90%, and the

* Much of the information for this chapter, in some cases extensive verbatim excerpts, originates from the Hearing before the Subcommittee on Courts, The Internet, and Intellectual Property, of the Committee on the Judiciary, House of Representative, One Hundred Ninth Congress, First Session in 2005.

government refuses to police even their own businesses that engage in such practices—except for a few "show" raids and trials on smaller factories that are turning out counterfeit copies of IP items. There may be laws, but then such laws, especially in China, would be viewed at a more regional or local level as "what's good for us" instead of "what's legal for everyone."

If China really and sincerely wanted to stop such piracy and massive counterfeiting, it could, because they have. Clearly, when it hurts Chinese interests, the government has been motivated to step in. When T-shirt knockoffs of the Beijing 2008 summer games were being sold, the government quickly closed down the shops and fined the counterfeiters. In 2001, the government tore down almost 700 billboards that illegally associated products with the event, and ripped fake Olympic emblems off some 67,000 taxis. When they want to enforce the laws, they can!

Estimates of copyright piracy, for example, from the copyright software and music industries are illustrative of the scope of the problem, with reports that 90% of all software installed on computers and over 90% of the market for sound recordings in China, for the year 2003 as an example, were pirated.

There is a major challenge with China. The US–China trade deficit runs into the untold billions. Contributing to that deficit is the knowledge that the Chinese do not always play by the rules. Copyright piracy estimates, for example, from the computer software and music industries are illustrative of the problem's scope.

The United States Trade Representative produces a report referred to as Special 301 reviews. These are out-of-cycle reviews and one on the IP situation in China concluded that while China has undertaken a number of efforts at the national level to address the theft epidemic, by amending laws and increasing raids against those selling pirated and counterfeit goods and operating illegal product facilities, China is still not deterring rampant piracy and counterfeiting. Those rates continue to grow, a situation that is hitting small- and medium-size businesses the hardest.

The more China grows, the richer its people get, the more global its industries grow, and the more difficult it is to enforce IP, because there'll be more people willing to pay for pirated goods and more businesses open to sell such goods. This is part of China's low-cost manufacturing machine and part of its overall industrial growth.

In truth, for the last 20-plus years, there has been no true enforcement of IPR in China. And yet, China has still attracted about a trillion dollars in foreign direct investment, mostly due to low wages paid and the costs of raw materials.

It has not been a disincentive for foreign investment to date. In fact, if anything, it's been an incentive, because when the world's manufacturers move to China, they also take advantage of factories that work on machines that are created on pirated platforms, on computer-aided design workstations that run on pirated platforms, on virtually everything inside a factory that is protected by some IP somewhere else. Thus, China incurs no true investment cost, and this foreign investment becomes an essential part of how China produces goods for the world at low prices.

If you want to assert an IP protection regime in China, you're going to have to drive a wedge in between the interest in keeping China the world's low-cost manufacturing center and the interest in keeping the United States a vital knowledge economy in which innovation is primary.

And when you assert an IP regime in China, you're going to see prices go up, and it's going to be the consumer that pays the price. But you're also going to have a conflict of interest among those who buy those goods in the United States. Any time you walk into a big-box store, such as a large discounter, what you are seeing is at least 9 out of 10 of the goods on those shelves coming from China. Often, those goods are made on entire production lines that are created with pirated IP. It is simply a fact. It is a component of the Chinese economy.

And China has very strong interests in not strengthening its IP.

That is the choice that the Chinese regime has made. And reversing that choice, or stopping that choice, requires an extreme willingness on the part of the United States to form a consensus on China, to drive a wedge between those strong interests that deliver wealth to the Chinese people. In the area of pharmaceuticals, it delivers better health to the Chinese people, and in the area of education, it delivers the most advanced technological products available in the world. That is a strong interest to overcome.

China's loose IP regime allows the government to pass on to its citizens goods that make the Chinese people richer, smarter, and healthier. They have solid reasons for doing business the way they do, and many of us would act in much the same way were we in the position the Chinese now find themselves in.

Do a thought experiment. You are the leader of 1.3 to 1.6 billion people who were mostly desperately poor and modestly educated, so you want to help them rise above their current station in life.

Now, you want to build up the nation. To do so, you will have to increase the business sector for greater profits, allowing for an increase in wages. At the same time, you need to keep costs low so people can afford what the businesses produce. At the same time, education enhancement becomes necessary, so you will be in need of the world's best educational resources, in addition to the world's best technology. It costs a lot of money to do this, so you want to grant them this technology and all its benefits either for free, or at least at the most minimal cost possible and without consequence.

You want to transfer to your people the jewels of the world's advanced industrialized nations, paying nothing for much of it, or perhaps only pennies on the dollar, so that your people could become bigger, stronger, and wealthier and have a better life. Suppose, in other words, you could steal the best technology, copyrighted materials, brand names, and top entertainment for your wanting people. And imagine further that you had little expectation of being held to account for that theft. To the contrary, you would be rewarded for it. In fact, that theft would make your country an ever-more desirable home for the very international fashion, technology, and knowledge enterprises you were so liberally borrowing from.

Anyone would make that choice—the choice that the Chinese government and people have made and still do make every day. One of the precepts of good leadership is to make one's people prosperous and capable, and the Chinese practices have followed that hands down. The Chinese are indisputably richer today than ever before; the use of personal computers is widespread and Chinese factories routinely run on the very same software that their competitors in America use. In all, China's creation of an extremely loose IP regime has paid off handsomely. It is now time that we exercise what means we have to enforce global rules that will also serve the American economy.

THE FILM INDUSTRY AND PIRATED DVDS

Hollywood, Bollywood, and even French, Italian, and Russian cinema are available for a pittance on the streets of China. Everyone knows about DVD pirating, but how many have seen how the markets work in the streets of China? One soon sees why there are only a handful of movie theaters in China. Imagine you are at a crowded Shanghai subway stop or a bus station. There stands one or more women (depending on the amount of pedestrian traffic) with a large gym bag. As you pass by, she quickly flips open the bag to reveal hundreds of DVDs, all with different titles. Of course, you stop and browse. You can now peruse the latest American hit movies. Other commuters come by and stop. The weekend will be used up with you, and others, watching the latest movies, and each one for less than a dollar. Walking on down the street, you pass an open alley. A man with a crate of DVDs stands ready to sell you other DVDs. Small stores pop up everywhere, perhaps the back of a truck (a "tailgate" sale), again more DVDs. Isn't it wonderful that all these entrepreneurs are helping the economy? You purchase one or more DVDs from each of them. You may or may not know that these are pirated, but you don't care because the price is so cheap.

The government is slow to crack down on the piracy of entertainment products because these serve a very large social agenda. The two most cited examples of China's disregard for IP are movies sold on pirated DVDs and software copied and sold at low cost in Chinese shops. Nearly every movie and every piece of software in China (except those used by multinational companies operating in China) is somehow stolen.

It is right to criticize these practices, but there must also be an acknowledgement of how we are complicit in them. Anyone who has shopped for a DVD player in an American store in the last few years knows that prices have dropped dramatically. During their first few years on the market,

DVD players were manufactured by a handful of large global consumer electronics companies, and the technology that went into them was protected by patents held by a few of the companies. Any company that wanted to make a DVD player had to pay the consortium that held the patent rights a license fee. Then, "presto," Chinese manufacturers began to make players without paying the license fees. They simply copied the technology and assembled the machines. In fact, they added functions to the players that made them better than any others on the market. One of those functions was the ability to read poor-quality DVD disks, the kind that you have just purchased on your way home from work.

The original intent of the Chinese makers was to sell to Chinese consumers, who pretty much make up the largest group of consumers of recorded entertainment in the world. Soon, instead of five or six foreign companies making and licensing DVD players, there were hundreds of Chinese manufacturers turning them out. Prices dropped from nearly $1000 to around $50. Of course, the players did not stay in China. Today, you can purchase a DVD player for less than $50 at any number of America's big-box stores. That is roughly the price of just a few movie tickets. The chipset and license fee for a DVD player costs about $11. When one sees a Chinese-made player on the shelves of a discount store, it is worth wondering how it could get there unless there were winks and nudges from American retailers who insist on ever-lower prices from their Chinese suppliers, but do not always insist that the goods they buy have the proper IP bona fides.

The motion picture industry and the American software industry suffer in China. It is almost impossible to get the average American to feel pity for Hollywood or for software giants like Microsoft. Or even for big pharmaceutical companies that face their own problems regarding China. There is a group, though, that deserves lots of sympathy: American manufacturers who face intense competition from China's low-cost manufacturing machine. And it is this group that may suffer the most from China's lax IP regime.

American companies are not just creators of IP, they are buyers of it. It can cost millions, or tens of millions of dollars to purchase and service the software to run an American company. Yet, Chinese competitors often pay nothing for the same technology, because it is simply stolen. Walk into the vast majority of Chinese firms that run computers and one will see one workstation after another stuffed with $2 version of software that will cost a Western competitor hundreds of dollars. Go into any company that designs and manufactures highly engineered parts. A metal caster that has built a reputation for making precision parts—the kind that American companies excel at—typically designs its parts at engineering workstations manned by highly trained engineers who run proprietary software that can cost $50,000 to $60,000 a year to run. It is likely to have several such workstations, perhaps dozens or hundreds. Chinese competitors run the same software, but they are unlikely to have paid anything for it. It is easy to understand how low-cost labor contributes to China's low-cost manufacturing. So far, the low cost of technology has been entirely overlooked.

As to the numbers of the total cost of this mismatch, it is unknown, but it is an essential part of the business dynamic that drives manufacturing to China. The cost would almost certainly dwarf the losses in sales suffered by Hollywood or the software industry.

CHINA'S LOOSE IP PROTECTION CONCERNS

As China moves up the economic feeding chain, this level of piracy will play against American companies more and more. Our economic health demands that we address this. One place to look is toward American companies that bring in Chinese-made goods that are made on pirated platforms. That's a daunting task, because nearly everything America buys from China achieves some of its cost competitiveness from China's loose IP regime.

China's loose IP rules also transfer to the Chinese industry valuable intellectual assets that can take American companies years and cost significant sums to develop. American automobile makers can spend half a billion dollars developing and building a new car, and take two years to do it. As soon as the car hits the market, Chinese manufacturers study it and look at how to copy it.

Chery Motors, a company that has been around since 1997, build and ship their automobiles around the world. Chery has been accused by General Motors (GM) of pirating an entire GM car and beating GM to the market with the Chery copy. It is not unusual (probably more the norm) for whole assembly lines to get duplicated in China, where the companies and their copiers need not worry about the cost of developing and designing the lines. In this regard, note that big businesses in the United States are vulnerable, but so are the smaller firms where often one good idea, patented or kept proprietary in some other fashion, is the only truly valuable asset the firm has.

China's failure to police its IP rules often looks less like ineffective government than a conscious policy to shift the highest value goods from other economies into the country. It is, in essence, the largest industrial subsidy in the world, and brilliantly, it costs the Chinese next to nothing.

In 2005, China was identified as the world's third-largest trading nation, and Chinese counterfeiters gave the country's ever-increasing number of globally competitive companies the means to compete against powerful foreign rivals that pay for their use of proprietary technologies. In the overall broader geopolitical context, China's counterfeiters have denied the rest of the world's advanced economies—especially the United States and Japan—the opportunity to sell to China the valuable designs, trademarked goods, advanced technology, and popular entertainment that the Chinese urgently desire but cannot yet produce on their own.

For the United States, this mismatch has become particularly punishing economically. Japan and Germany, which also suffer from China's policies, do not have the huge trade deficits with China that the United States does. One reason is that our export economy is far more dependent on the sale of highly valuable, intangible, and easily copied goods. Japan and Germany make the machines China needs to run. America makes the software that runs those machines. It is far more difficult for US companies to be paid by Chinese users for what we make, though most of the rest of the world pays handsomely for it. Until the United States can determine a method to get paid for what is made and the Chinese use, our deficits will worsen, not improve. Say, for example, that the value of the dollar drops against the Chinese yuan. Economists predict that our trade situation will level out, but they do not take into account that no matter what our goods cost, the Chinese will most likely continue to pay nothing for some of the most useful goods we make. And, as a result, their factories will continue to be able to beat even the most efficient American factories on price.

IP THEFT

IP theft will continue to be rampant without a concerted effort on the part of business and government. About a decade ago, a three-part strategy aimed at mobilizing business and government to fight against counterfeiting and piracy was launched. As part of these efforts, country-specific IPR initiatives that targeted China, Brazil, Russia, India, and Korea, where the problems are particularly acute for American companies, were launched.

So, in early 2004, China's government modestly improved its regulatory environment for IPR protection and carried out what could be called a number of limited raids and other enforcement actions at the central, local, and provincial levels. Fortunately, to prove their point about cutting down on piracy and counterfeiting, they just "happened" to have photographers available and then wasted no time in quickly distributing pictures to shown their concern over this rampant counterfeiting. The pictures, posted on Chinese web sites, only showed a few hundred miscellaneous counterfeited goods found in a storefront, or a several dozen boxes in a small factory, or several thousand counterfeit items being taken out into the street and run over by a steamroller to be destroyed. The number of items seized and documented for the world to see was less than what any small company could turn out in less than a day.

Within a day or so, the company could be back at work; the company happy, the police happy, the government happy, and many around the world happy because China was "cracking down" on the piracy and the counterfeiting of stolen goods. Unfortunately, that is about as far as it went. Until something else pops up to make it a real issue in the news, don't count on too many more raids or pictures becoming available.

Administrative penalties, however, in these cases, are mainly limited to fines and confiscation of fake products. The penalties remain too small to create any form of deterrence for the counterfeiters. It must be noted, though, that there were some signs that new efforts were underway in as recently as 2005 but, in reality, China has not significantly reduced IPR infringement levels and the possibility remains that they never intend to take enforcement seriously.

IP RIGHTS

Upon its accession to the World Trade Organization, China agreed to fully comply with Trade Related Aspects of Intellectual Property Rights (TRIPS) Agreement obligations. Yet, it is clear that the protection that China is actually providing fails to meet the standards of "effectiveness" and "deterrence" set out in TRIPS. IPR violations severely affect virtually all industries, from consumer and industrial goods—including medicines, automobiles and automobile parts, food and beverages, and cosmetics—to copyright works, including entertainment and business software, movies, music, and books. The scope of counterfeiting and copyright piracy in China has worsened and is reaching epidemic proportions.

Over and over in press reports, Congressional hearings, and otherwise, China is found to be the single largest source of counterfeit and pirated products worldwide. Failure to control exports of these products is eroding US companies' profit margins, diminishing brand value, and, in many cases, endangering public safety. US Customs statistics showed an increase of 47% in the market value of counterfeit goods seized in 2004 (up until October 31). Statistics compiled for 2004 by other governments are expected to reflect a similar trend.

Increasingly, counterfeiting in China is harming small- and medium-size US enterprises. Many of these small- and medium-size enterprises do not have operations in China and confront a flood of Chinese knockoffs in the US market or in third-country markets where they export. Smaller companies clearly have fewer resources to deal with investigations and legal action against pirates in China and their middlemen in other countries. Thus, the need for more convincing and proactive government intervention is becoming increasingly apparent.

THE PLIGHT OF THE COPYRIGHT INDUSTRIES DUE TO PIRACY IN CHINA

The Business Software Industry

The plight of the business software industry—one of our nation's most productive and important creative sectors—will be discussed first. The software industry faces piracy rates in China of 90%, one of the highest in the world for that industry. China leads the world in the production and export of counterfeit software—software packages that are purposely designed to replicate the original legitimate product. Losses to US software publishers are estimated to be at least $1.50 billion. China is at least the 6th largest market in the world for personal computers, but about 25th or so on the scale in legitimate software sales. This increasing disparity not only damages the US industry but hurts Chinese software developers as well.

China has failed to criminalize the most damaging type of piracy to the business software industry—the unauthorized use of software within businesses and government institutions. This is a violation of the TRIPS Agreement. Combined with the total absence of a criminal remedy is the absence of all but a few administrative actions against this type of piracy with woefully low and non-deterrent fines. As a consequence, piracy rates continue to remain at staggering levels.

To make matters worse, China is on the verge of shutting down access for US and other foreign companies to the largest purchaser of software in China: the Chinese government. It can accomplish this by adopting draft government procurement regulations that would expressly favor Chinese software only. In short, the situation for this critical copyright sector is truly dire in China with no significant improvement in sight.

The Motion Picture Industry

The US motion picture industry in 2005 faced a 95% piracy rate in China (the highest in the Asia Pacific region, and among the highest in the world), which represented a worsening of the situation from the previous year. Losses to just the motion picture industry, from 1998 through 2004, are estimated at more than $1 billion (not including losses from Internet piracy, which are growing alarmingly). While raids and seizures have increased somewhat following the 2004 enforcement campaign, administrative fines remain far too low to deter pirate activity and criminal cases have been extremely rare despite Chinese promises to use the TRIPS-required remedy.

According to one newspaper report, the legitimate home video market in China represents about 5% of the estimated total market of $1.3 billion (which is itself a very conservative estimate). Of the 83 optical disk factories licensed by the government (and an unknown number of "underground" unlicensed plants), many continue to churn out pirate DVDs. The export of pirated home video products, which had slowed to a trickle after the US Section 301 action (and threatened retaliation), has resumed and is growing. The total optical disk plant production capacity, a significant amount of which is devoted to producing pirated products, is now close to 2.7 billion units annually. Optical disks sourced in China and containing pirated films have been seized in more than 25 countries around the world. The massive quantity of pirated movie products available in China is evidenced by the fact that pirate prices start around $0.60 per unit, the lowest price in Asia.

As with the other copyright industries, any enforcement that occurs is conducted by administrative agencies, with overlapping jurisdiction and often little coordination, and fines imposed are a mere "cost of doing business." A recent anecdotal study, conducted by the Motion Picture Association (MPA), revealed that the average fine imposed per pirate home video product (DVD and VCD) seized in raids resulting from MPA complaints is only slightly higher than the cost of purchasing a blank disk—clearly of no deterrent value. The lack of deterrent administrative penalties is a key reason, in addition to the almost complete lack of criminal enforcement, that piracy rates persist at 90% of the market and above.

Accompanying and reinforcing this piracy situation are onerous market access restrictions, including a government-owned monopoly importer, very limited competition in distribution, and a quota of 20 theatrical films allowed into China annually on commercial terms. The pirates capture 100% of the market for films not permitted legally in China. Even those films permitted theatrical release suffer piracy rates of 70%–75%, because of the long delays before most American films are given screen time. Another consequence of the lack of competition in importation and distribution is the non-competitive pricing in the Chinese market. Cumbersome licensing requirements burden the retail sale of legal home entertainment products, holding down revenue potential and helping keep the market in the hands of the pirates.

The Entertainment Software Industry

The entertainment software industry, one of the fastest growing copyright-based industries, faces similar high piracy rates and estimates the value of pirated video games in the market at $510 million in 2004, but today's market is unknown and could be estimated at very close to or over a billion dollars. Demand for entertainment software products is growing rapidly but is being soaked up primarily by the pirates. This demand is exemplified by the exploding popularity of "massively multiplayer online role-playing games" (MMORPGs) where literally thousands of players can compete against one another simultaneously. Demand for MMORPGs in China has grown to at least 40%–45% over expectations in 2004 when the last serious research was performed and made available. This increasing demand has fueled, in part, the growth of Internet cafés in China. (It is estimated that there are close to 200,000 Internet cafés in the country, with a seating capacity of between 100 and 300 seats, of which 60% are involved in game play.) While US game publishers, represented by the Entertainment Software Association, have engaged in some licensing of the cafés, the vast majority of the product used is pirated, either available at the café or downloadable from the Internet. This dire situation has been all the more exasperating since the Chinese government extensively regulates the activities of these Internet cafés and often and vigorously revokes licenses for actions the government deems inappropriate. However, as far as the US knows, the Chinese government has never truly sought to include in this extensive regulatory scheme prohibitions against the widespread and blatant piracy at these cafés in its business licenses (which are otherwise very thorough). Moreover, no copyright enforcement of any kind has occurred. The legal infrastructure governing the Internet still is not helpful to copyright enforcement. Takedown of pirate sites is negligible, and penalties are nonexistent.

Cartridge-based handheld games are also hard hit by the pirates with manufacturing and assembly operations throughout China and with exports throughout Asia, Latin America, the Middle East, and Europe. Enforcement attempts have been relatively successful in terms of raids and seizures but, like with other industries, administrative fines are non-deterrent and criminal enforcement action is very rarely undertaken, even against factories generating millions of dollars in illicit profits. Entertainment software products are also subject to a protracted content review process, by two separate agencies contributing to market entry delays. Given the immediate nature of the demand for and life cycle of best-selling games, pirates virtually become uncontested in the market prior to the official release of a new title. There are also Internet and investment restrictions that must be significantly eased or abolished.

The Book Publishing Industry

The US book publishing industry, represented by the Association of American Publishers, faces both significant offset printing of pirated books, primarily in translated editions, and massive commercial photocopying of textbooks and reference books on and near university campuses.

There are at least 600 or more licensed state-owned publishers in China, at least 50 of which are considered major. There are only a few privately owned publishers, but they must buy publishing rights from the state-owned publishers. US publishers issued 4500 translation licenses in 2004, a significant number but far below China's potential. All the best-selling books are then virtually immediately pirated by outlaw "printers" and made available through independent bookstores, stalls, and street vendors.

To give an example, the famous self-help bestseller *Who Moved My Cheese* sold over 3 million copies in China. It is estimated, however, that the pirates sold another *6 million* copies.

The Harry Potter books and other best sellers like Hilary and Bill Clinton's books *Living History* and *My Life*, John Grisham's books, and others all face a similar fate from the pirates. Former General Electric President Jack Welch's biography, *Winning*, has sold more than 800,000 copies but with an equal number of pirate copies available in the market.

English language textbooks are also heavily photocopied in their entirety and there are six known web sites that make available entire copies of textbooks that are downloaded and then photocopied. Enforcement against this vast piracy is spotty and all done administratively through the local and national copyright bureaus. Any resulting administrative fines are non-deterrent. The book publishing industry also faces market access barriers—US publishers are not permitted to publish, sign authors, or print their books in China.

The Recording Industry

The recording industry, represented by the Recording Industry Association of America, did experience a minor reduction in the piracy rate for sound recordings, from 90% in 2003 to 85% in 2004 in "hard goods" piracy, but with significant increases in Internet piracy. Losses remain in excess of $200 million per year from continued optical disk manufacture and distribution within the Chinese market and significant levels of audiocassette piracy (still an important format in China). The recording industry faces many of the same problems with optical disk piracy confronting the motion picture industry. Millions of pirated music CDs are readily available throughout China. Some of these pirated products have found their way into the export market. China continues to rely on its failed administrative enforcement system, which relies on numerous inspections, product seizures, and, when the pirate doesn't flee, the imposition of small, non-deterrent fines.

Internet piracy in China, as in other countries in the world, has become a huge problem for the recording industry. Thousands of active web sites such as www.9sky.com and www.chinaMP3.com are giving away, or offering links to, thousands of pirated songs. (These not-for-profit acts of piracy are not penalized in China, as they are, for example, in the United States.) International criminal syndicates are apparently using Chinese servers to hide their illicit activity (www.boxup.com) and many Asian pirate sites' businesses are thriving in China, such as www.kuro.com from Taiwan.

Market access restrictions are severe, contributing to piracy and market losses. US record companies cannot "publish" or release a recording without permission of a state-owned company and cannot manufacture, distribute, or engage in retailing of its products, which artificially segments the market and makes it extraordinarily difficult for this world-class industry to participate in the Chinese market. Its products are subject to censorship while domestic (as well as pirated) recordings are not—a national treatment violation.

Congressional Hearings on Chinese Piracy

So many Congressional hearings take place over various legislative sessions that it is sometimes hard to find out what they are really covering outside of the hearing title. One needs to delve into it as many subareas, some closely and others not so closely related, are discussed with experts. Over time, specific information can be obtained on a given subject matter area. During one hearing, the area of Chinese piracy was discussed. A section of that particular hearing is provided below.

Piracy has become one of the most lucrative businesses in Asia and, indeed, throughout the world. By our best information, organized criminal syndicates, organized principally out of Taiwan, Hong Kong, and into the mainland, and in other countries in East Asia, have a solid lock on this business. And their lock is so solid that it is very difficult for governments to unlock it. Governments need to assert their political will to break these syndicates.

Realize that copyright piracy and counterfeiting are serious problems that do not merely affect private companies' bottom lines in the short term. They also discourage investment and innovation in the long term, which will eventually lead to fewer consumer choices—a repercussion that affects entire societies and economies. Governments must work together to reward creators and punish thieves.

IP is at the heart of the American success story. Over the last 200 years, the United States has emerged as the leader in innovation and development of new technologies, and these innovations and developments are in turn the heart of the American economy. IP systems that encourage innovation made this possible.

Unfortunately, bad actors scorn the protection of innovation and development and favor systems that foster free riding on the backs of others. US trade partners must respect IP. They not only must have laws on the books proscribing infringement but also must have enforcement mechanisms in place to make them stick. I am particularly concerned about recent revelations that pirating operations may be operating on land owned by the Russian government.

California industries have seen billions of dollars of losses. These losses do not only involve losses to the recording and movie industries, though I am very sympathetic to the particularly large losses in those sectors. American products from shaving razors to automobile parts to pharmaceuticals are also being copied and sold in violation of international law. Former attorney Ashcroft reported in late 2004 that IP crimes cost the US economy $250 billion and 300,000 jobs. DVD piracy alone reportedly accounts for $3 billion a year in losses to the US economy.

The same holds true whether the piracy is sponsored by the government itself or funded by individual citizens. While the concept of private ownership of property is relatively new in many of the formerly communist countries, the value has not been lost on them. Any government that wants the benefits of trade with America, and who is currently benefiting from trade preferences, has a responsibility to respect American innovation.

Breadth of the Counterfeiting Problem

Counterfeiting and piracy are costing the US consumers and American companies billions of dollars every year. But the problem is more insidious than that. It damages investment and innovation, has potentially devastating economic consequences for small businesses, puts a severe strain on law enforcement agencies, nearly always escapes taxation, threatens public and health safety, diverts government resources from other priorities, and has links to terrorism and organized crime.

Counterfeiting and piracy, once viewed as "victimless" crimes mainly consisting of selling cheap products such as sunglasses and watches, have mushroomed in recent years to endanger every product. From dangerous substandard replacement parts for airplane engines, to ineffective pharmaceuticals, to illegally copied compact discs manufactured in clandestine factories around the world, sales of counterfeit and pirated products are skyrocketing. Profits from these illicit sales are being funneled worldwide into the pockets of everyone, from groups associated with known terrorists to organized crime elements.

The problem of counterfeiting and piracy goes beyond the manufacture, distribution, and sale of cheap, unauthorized goods. It threatens our national security, lessens the value of legitimate brand names, and erodes the profits of nearly every business in America.

In sum, for all the above, some statistics might be helpful to illustrate the magnitude of the problem we face today. Approximately 5% to 7% of world trade is in counterfeit goods, according to the Federal Bureau of Investigation, Interpol, and the World Customs Organization. That's the equivalent of as much as $512 billion in global sales. Of that amount, US companies lose between $200 billion and $250 billion in global sales. US Customs and Border Protection estimates that counterfeit merchandise is responsible for the loss of more than 750,000 American jobs. Finally, note that the World Health Organization (WHO) has estimated that counterfeit drugs account for 10% of all pharmaceuticals. Incredibly, in some developing countries, WHO suggests that this number is as high as 60%. These statistics exemplify US concerns about the growing epidemic of IP.

In total, then, China is ripping off America big time, and we only encourage it by purchasing the products that have been made with our stolen patents, designs, software, engineering and machine designs, ideas, and concepts (Figure 5.1).

FIGURE 5.1 Products made with stolen US patents, designs, software, engineering, and ideas only funnel more US dollars into China's pocket and encourage further IP theft and espionage.

6 Who, What, and How China Targets*

Any nation conducting clandestine intelligence-gathering activities desires to keep it secret so you won't learn about it and take appropriate countermeasures to thwart their intentions and activities. On the other hand, though—and all businesses and governments know this—much information can be gathered from open-source data that are publicly available to anyone.

Open-source intelligence gathering can be performed over the Internet. Using a vacuum cleaner approach, an opponent can scarf up just about anything of value—or possible value—in the here and now, or possibly useful in the far-term future. They don't have the need-to-know in the legitimate sense, as people within a given business would, to have access to the information in the performance of their duties.

But the phrase "need to know" means different things to different people, and different things to different countries, businesses, and organizations. China's need-to-know is not a legitimate one, but it means anything they deem of interest or of possible interest for the development or expansion of their economic base, creating or expanding business ventures, increasing military strength, or just increasing their political might and potential for world leadership in one manner or another. In essence, if it might at some time become useful, they will try and obtain it, knowing that, in the long run, just about everything can be put to some use.

China looks to all world nations for information to exploit, but when it comes to America, China wants, desires, demands, and insists upon getting anything that could be perceived to be of value. Think of the United States as the greatest shopping center in the world, and China has a very big shopping list, so they demand an even bigger shopping cart. Next, think of all those other people without a list. To get items on their shopping list means being creative and looking at potential opportunities to learn, glean, access, acquire, or otherwise obtain something of value. We have lots of "stuff" and they are interested in just about all of it.

At the top of the list will be virtually any technology available or known about. Published studies, reports, interviews, company brochures and press releases, and even job opening announcements and advertisements for newly created products and related product manufacturing facilities can lead a shopper to look at our emerging or new technologies and also to consider one that is just an idea or in the incubation state. Newly found start-up companies look for investors and really talk up their product (and potential company future) to anyone who will listen, and the Chinese are more than willing to listen and even toss in some dollars if they can benefit from it in the short-term or long-term future.

Now, specifically, what is China looking for? In this, we go to the best lists possible, for general and specific technologies. These lists include the National Critical Technology List, the Military Critical Technology List, and the Developing Science and Technology List. Each of these lists is like a book. No, they just don't list the technology topics, which are essentially some 20 to 30 items, but proceed to break down each of these as general headers and underneath delineate every possible thing of value that can be considered as a national, economic, or defense critical technology or an

* The contents of this chapter, including extensive verbatim passages, come from official government documents—including the Annual Report to Congress on Economic Collection and Industrial Espionage, for the years 1995 to 2011, but especially the 1995 and 2007 editions—and were prepared by the Office of the National Counterintelligence Executive.

emerging technology within a given subject field. These lists, with all the varying details, can easily extend to several hundred pages with untold amounts of detailed data being listed.

From such data, a potential collector can start determining the types of specific businesses and industries that might be targeted to obtain any data that could relate to a specific technology item.

Simply put, China will target any nation, any organization, any business, or any web site anywhere in the world that will allow it to obtain information. The United States is not alone, but since the United States has the greatest technological advances across the board in just about every technology, it is reasonable that China will target the nation for the best, up-to-date information they can possibly obtain.

As an example, in March 2012, in Taiwan, security personnel were able to detain and arrest a Chinese spy at a northern air force base. This was not the only person charged with spying for China in 14 months. This particular base houses the very sensitive and highly classified US Patriot surface-to-air missiles. A couple of other people recently arrested included a high-ranking officer and a civilian: the first had access to a command and control system that had been designed by the United States, and the other wanted to obtain Patriot missile secrets. All three of these definitely show that China was and still is interested in information about the missile and support systems. The major concern here is that the systems were designed and built with US technology.

In looking at Taiwan, China, the author believes, is probably focused on these two systems—the Patriot missile system and a command and control system—not only because of what they can do in terms of performance but also because their technology is far beyond what China now has or is capable of producing in the near future. Lockheed Martin built the latter, and Raytheon developed and built the Patriot missile defense system. These systems, then, combine and demonstrate the highest technology within the missile field. No wonder China will do anything to get them.

Without the command and control system and the Patriot missile setup, Chinese military forces would not be able to pass critical battlefield information instantly. Without the Patriot radar system, which is exceptionally sophisticated and can track incoming aerial threats and then destroy them, China would also be at a major loss. With the radar system and its subsequent data, China would be in an excellent position to develop appropriate countermeasures, which means China would then have the ability to jam the missile system or else redirect the missile, possibly back to its point of origin.[1]

Besides Taiwan, other countries will also be targeted by China for US technology, mainly because they do not necessarily maintain high standards of protection. Unfortunately, the United States, though having high standards, must recognize that individual breakdowns in the system will always allow for the theft of trade secrets and other items of value to China.

TARGETED INFORMATION AND TECHNOLOGIES

Targeted information and technologies include biotechnology; aerospace; telecommunications, including the technology to build and maintain the "information superhighway"; computer software/hardware; advanced transportation and engine technology; advanced materials and coatings, including "stealth" technologies; energy research; defense and armaments technology; manufacturing processes; and semiconductors. Proprietary business information—that is, bid, contract, customer, and even sales strategy processes in each of these sectors—is always aggressively targeted. China also shows an interest in government and corporate financial and trade data.

All of these areas provide a strategic interest to the United States as they produce very classified and sensitive unclassified products for the government, can produce dual-use technology that is used in a variety of sophisticated and technology-enhanced areas within both the government and private sectors, and are also responsible for leading-edge technologies critical to maintaining US economic security. There are many other US high-tech industrial sectors that have been targeted. Any company that competes for the sale or a piece of a market share, regardless of the specific market, could resort to intelligence activities as a "force multiplier" to improve its chances of economic success.

The United States currently has no formal mechanism for determining the full qualitative and quantitative scope and impact of the loss of this targeted information. Over time, various industry companies that have fallen victim to stolen information have reported that the losses are in the range of hundreds of millions of dollars, thousands of lost jobs, and a discernible drop in their market share. However, these reports tend to be ad hoc and often are only acknowledged after public exposure of the loss. It is understandable that the US industry is reluctant to publicize occurrences of foreign economic and industrial espionage. Such publicity typically adversely affects a company's stock values, customers' confidence, and, ultimately, its overall competitiveness and market share.[2]

METHODS USED TO CONDUCT SUCH ESPIONAGE

Chinese practitioners of the espionage arts seldom use just one method in isolation but combine them into concerted collection programs to maximize their collection abilities. Although countries or corporations have been known to turn legitimate transactions or business relationships into clandestine collection opportunities, some of the methods below are most often used for legitimate purposes. While their inclusion here is not intended to imply illegal activity, they are listed as potential elements of a much broader, coordinated intelligence effort.[2]

Traditional methods are those primarily reserved for collecting national defense information and they are now being applied to collect economic and proprietary information. Traditional awareness training is most suitable for fulfilling these collection methods.

a. *Classic Agent Recruitment.* An intelligence collector's best source for information will be a trusted person inside a company or organization to whom the collector can easily task to provide proprietary or classified information. The collector's interest in employees is not necessarily commensurate with their rank in the company. Researchers, key business managers, and corporate executives can all be targets, but so can support employees such as secretaries, computer operators, financial data personnel, engineers and other technicians, and maintenance people. The latter frequently have a good, if not the best, level of access to competitive information mainly because they move through a large section of a building or other complex and can observe (even after hours) what may be happening or what changes are being made because of a new or improved product, or observe various papers that have been left unattended (or, also, suddenly hard locked away). Additionally, the lower pay and rank of these people can usually provide fertile ground for manipulation.[2]
b. *Volunteers.* Volunteers are those individuals that are most likely to improperly acquire a company's information, and they are in a position to do so because they are the company's own employees. Such individuals resort to stealing information for several reasons, such as the exhibition of the same motivations and human frailties as the average thief or spy: illegal or excessive use of drugs or alcohol, money problems, personal stress, and just plain greed. In past cases, the volunteer (when an American) was in it for the thrill, challenge, and a desire to accumulate a lot of money in a short period. When the volunteer is an intern, student, or otherwise associated with China, such as a second-generation family, it is because of loyalty to the family, loyalty to China as an ancestral home, or, again, just plain greed, as the information he or she intends to steal can be sold to a commercial company in China, and then the person can quit the company, move back to China, and assume a much more important position with a greater income value accumulation because of his or her knowledge of the product and its associated information.[2]

c. *Surveillance and Surreptitious Entry.* Economic and industrial espionage may involve simply breaking into an office containing desired information. In the past, companies have reported break-ins in which laptop computers or disks were stolen even when there were more valuable items in the same vicinity. Also to be considered is when a break-in occurs and nothing is stolen, or the office is tossed (items thrown about and some destroyed, perhaps only a few miscellaneous items stolen), and the computers are left untouched or just damaged. These instances are not always reported, or reported as merely break-ins, without considering the possibility that the target was information rather than equipment. As a side note, in such instances, the information technology (IT) manager should check the system to see when it was last accessed and what files were accessed. When the times coincide with the break-in, then consider the information that was accessed and its value to a competitor, in this case, China.[2]

   Some countries convince hotel operators to provide intelligence collectors with access to visitors' luggage or rooms. During these surreptitious break-ins, known colloquially as "black bag operations," unattended luggage is searched for sensitive information, and any useful documents are copied or simply stolen.[2]

d. *Specialized Technical Operations.* This includes computer intrusions, telecommunications targeting and intercept, and private-sector encryption weaknesses. These activities account for the largest portion of economic and industrial information lost by US corporations. Because they are so easily accessed and intercepted, corporate telecommunications, and in particular, international telecommunications, can provide a highly vulnerable and lucrative source for anyone interested in obtaining trade secrets or competitive information. Because of the increased usage of the Internet links for bulk computer data transmission and electronic mail, collectors find telecommunications intercepts cost-effective. For example, there is the interception of facsimile transmissions through government-owned telephone companies. You may not think that a fax would be targeted, but approximately half of all overseas telecommunications are facsimile transmissions. In this category, there are also the innovative "hackers" who connect to a company's computers, using a variety of hacking tools to evade controls and firewalls in order to obtain company information. In addition, many American companies have begun using electronic data interchange, a system of transferring corporate bidding, invoice, and pricing data electronically overseas. The more newer and sophisticated is the system that is being used, the more likely that it can be hacked in the short term. Only after a period of time will many of the more subtle bugs be located and removed. But, always, the hackers are very inventive and will continue to target, either subtly or by using brute force tactics to get into the computer, take over the role of administrator, insert backdoors for future access, add hidden access permissions and passwords, and also download immediately interesting and possibly very valuable company information.[2]

e. *Economic Disinformation.* There is the use of disinformation campaigns to scare companies or any potential clients away from dealing with certain US companies. The press and government agencies frequently discuss foreign economic and industrial intelligence activities, but often in vague, nonspecific terms. The disinformation issue has been used to paint foreign competitors or countries as aggressive and untrustworthy, even if the company has no tangible evidence of any collection activity. Some countries have widely publicized their efforts to set up information security mechanisms to protect against their competitors' penetration attempts, and frequently the United States is mentioned as the primary threat. The author believes, in very few cases, that it is true, but overall, it is the United States that should be building greater IT barriers against the threat. Check your newspapers and web sites weekly. You will find the threats are out there and IT is a major way of protecting against these threats. But the concern over disinformation will continue, as individuals and countries make it look like they are protecting their secrets from everyone else, hoping that, somehow, the disinformation campaign will work against you, allowing them some sort of access to your information.[2]

OTHER ECONOMIC COLLECTION METHODS

In addition to the previous collection methods utilized, the Chinese also have used—and are believed to continue the use of—the following techniques to access and acquire U.S. technological information.

a. Tasking Foreign Students Studying in the United States. The Chinese government, through various organizations and companies, will task their students in the United States to acquire information on a variety of economic and technical subjects. In some instances, the students have been recruited and tasked before they ever entered the United States to study, having them send any technological information they acquire back to China. Other students will be approached after arriving and are ensconced on a given college or university campus. They are then recruited or pressured based upon a sense of loyalty or fear to obtain information and pass it back to China.[2]

   In some instances, at a collector's behest, graduate students would be directed to serve as assistants at no cost to professors doing research in a targeted field. The student then has access to the professor's research and can learn various applications of the technology.
b. Tasking Foreign Employees within US Firms and Agencies. Chinese companies and Chinese government representatives at various levels sometimes recruit or task compatriot employees within a firm to steal proprietary information. Although this is similar to clandestine recruitment that would be used traditionally by the intelligence service, often there is not an intelligence service involved, but only a company or non-intelligence Chinese government agency. The collector then passes the information directly to the private company or the government agency.[2]
c. Debriefing of Chinese Citizens to the United States. China will actively debrief their citizens after foreign travel, asking for any information acquired during the trip abroad. Sometimes, these debriefing sessions are usually accepted as part of the deal for going abroad. If the citizen has a military background, is a scientist or an engineer, or has particular knowledge gained could be useful to China. Thus, information that was acquired by observation, listening or when discussing topics of mutual interest, are passed on to Chinese officials conducting the debriefing.[2]
d. Recruitment of Émigrés and Other Ethnic Targeting. Collectors find it particularly effective to target persons of their own ethnic group. The Chinese watch for and target those Chinese ethnics or émigrés that work in US military and research and development (R&D) facilities or have access to proprietary and classified US technology. The repatriation of foreign ethnic scientists is very beneficial to China because of the knowledge the individuals have gained over time. The greatest desire often comes from those who have worked in the areas that allow the person to carry out "in their heads" detailed information that essentially avoids the problem of any bans on technology transfer. Past cases that have been reported in the news include the "repatriation" of ethnic scientists back to their home country from the United States. Ethnic targeting for collection purposes will include attempts to recruit and task naturalized US citizens and permanent resident aliens to assist in acquiring science and technology information. Frequently, the appeal to a person's patriotism and ethnic loyalty is strong within the Asian community. Some countries' collectors resort to threatening family members that continue to reside in their home country.
e. Conferences, Meetings, Symposia, and Trade Shows. Any meeting at which Chinese are present is a sure indication of the importance of the subject matter being presented. Also,

it is a prime location for "like-minded" people to get together, socialize, and also discuss items of mutual interest, specifically topics of the conference, any work-related information that may pertain, and, also, the old "what are you working on now" line of questioning. Just friendly banter, of course.

Events, such as international conferences on high-tech topics, trade fairs, and air shows, attract many scientists and engineers, providing foreign intelligence collectors with a concentrated group of specialists on a certain topic. Collectors target these individuals while they are abroad to gather any information the scientists or engineers may possess. Sometimes, depending on the foreign country and the specific circumstances, these elicitation efforts are heavy handed and threatening, while other times they are subtle.[2]

Whether local, regional, national, or international, seminar audiences may include leading scientists and technical experts from China or surrogate representatives, who pose more of a threat than any intelligence officers because of their level of technical understanding and ability to exploit immediately the information they may collect. During seminars, the individual will attempt subtle approaches such as sitting next to a potential target and initiating casual conversation. This activity often serves as a starting point for later exploitation. Membership lists of international business and technical societies are increasingly used to identify potential US targets. One of the most common targeting techniques is to use collectors who have common cultural or ethnic backgrounds with the target such as origin of birth, religion, or language.

These public venues are laden with opportunities for collectors to interact with US experts and glean information regarding dual-use and sensitive technologies. Collection in these open forums accounted for about an average of 5% of all reported suspicious incidents.

Other large-scale international events, particularly athletic events, have also emerged as venues for increased economic espionage against the United States. US corporations often sponsor such events and send thousands of employees to the festivities. The Summer Olympic Games in China, the 2010 World Expo in Shanghai, and the forthcoming 2014 Winter Olympics in Sochi, Russia, all take place in high-threat environments.[3] Such events offer host-country and other intelligence agencies the opportunity to spot, assess, and develop or even recruit new sources within the US private sector and to gain electronic access to companies' virtual networks and databases through technology brought to the events by corporate personnel. The 2012 Olympics in London provided China an excellent venue. Chinese companies donated massive amounts of telecommunications in support of the Olympics. Imagine all the communications equipment having the electronics configured so that Chinese companies can monitor every communication made or received. More importantly, the equipment will stay in Great Britain as a "gift" from China. The equipment will certainly not just sit on the shelf after the Olympics are over, but will be put to use. Who will use the equipment and, incidentally, the information that will be passed over it during the next few years? China! Who is in a position to collect the information because of possible alterations to the equipment? Again, the answer is China!

f. All-Expenses-Paid Trips. Collectors sometimes attempt to recruit scientists by inviting them on expense-paid trips abroad for conferences or sabbaticals. The individuals are treated royally, and their advice is sought on areas of interest. When they return to the United States, collectors re-contact them and ask them to provide information on their areas of research.

There are also the politicians at various levels that are heavily courted with free trips. China is increasingly aggressive in trying to recruit local "agents of influence" to advance their own economic and political objectives. These can range from discrete political support of local events, funneled through sympathetic associations or business leaders, to glamorous hospitality junkets.

The most obvious is the all-expenses-paid "fact-finding" trip in which the people being courted are "treated like an emperor."

The greatest concern is not the trip itself, but the level being offered. Whether a subject matter expert or a politician, not one of the trips are offered by the Chinese without the hope of being able to influence the individuals. Such trips, which might not be to mainland China, but even to speaking at a Chinese-sponsored (directly or indirectly) event, especially one being held in the Southeast Asia region, are very carefully planned. The host organization committee goes to great extremes to provide anything and everything to make the visitor feel welcome, but in the end, the host is always seeking some form of a long-term relationship and "understanding." China does not plan to spend thousands of dollars to court someone of influence without an expectation of getting something back. The bottom line is that the sponsors want, above all, influence on our politics, trade relations and international positions, and specific points of contact with businessmen and their businesses.[2,4]

g. Commercial Data Bases, Trade and Scientific Journals, Computer Bulletin Boards, Openly Available US Government Data, and Corporate Publications. Collectors will always take advantage of the vast amounts of free competitive information that is legally and openly available in the United States. Open-source information can provide personality profile data, data on new R&D and planned products, new manufacturing techniques, and competitors' strengths and weaknesses. A legitimate collector, such as a regional competitor, would use this information for its own worth in their normal day-to-day business competition. But China would use the openly available information as leads to refine and focus their clandestine collection and to identify individuals and organizations that possess desired information.[2]
h. Clandestine Collection of Open-Source Materials. Because China believes (and rightly so) that they are closely monitored by US counterintelligence, their traditional intelligence services will resort to clandestine methods to collect even open-source materials. They will use false names to access open-source data bases. At times, they may also ask that a legal and open relationship be kept confidential.[2]
i. The Use of Private-Sector Organizations, Front Companies, and Joint Ventures. China uses a "must/need" approach to exploit existing non-government-affiliated organizations or create new ones. They may include friendship societies, international exchange organizations, import–export companies, or any other entity that could provide a gateway to frequent contacts with American companies. All this in order to develop contacts, develop close business ties, gather intelligence, and station their own collectors in positions that will help them extract privileged company information. The Chinese government will conceal their involvement in these organizations and present them as purely private entities in order to cover the collection operation. The organizations can then spot and assess potential victims to recruit with whom they have contact. Such organizations also then also openly lobby US government officials to change policies they consider unfavorable.[2]
j. Corporate Mergers and Acquisitions. The use of mergers and acquisitions to acquire technology is not unknown and has been going on for quite a few years. The vast majority of these transactions are made for completely legitimate purposes. However, a close examination of some mergers can determine they were made specifically to allow an independent (i.e., not government owned, operated, or controlled) company to acquire US-originated technologies without spending their own resources on R&D.[2]
k. Headhunting and the Hiring of a Competitors' Employees. Whenever possible and feasible, a Chinese company will advertise for or typically hire knowledgeable employees of competing firms to do the same corresponding work. The company may be wholly owned, a front company, or a research/R&D firm desiring to go into a specific business. The hiring is done to specifically gain inside technical information from the employee.[2]

l. Corporate Technology Agreements. Chinese companies also use potential technology sharing agreements as a primary conduit in order to receive proprietary information. In such instances, the Chinese company would demand that, in order to complete the negotiations for a final agreement, the US company would have to divulge large amounts of information about its processes and products, sometimes much more than is justified by the project being negotiated. Often, the information requested is highly sensitive and treated as such by the US company. In such cases, the Chinese company will either terminate the deal after receipt of the information or refuse to negotiate further if denied the information.[2]

m. Sponsorship of Research Activities in the United States. The desire by US technical personnel to expand their research capabilities can include their exploitation by China or its surrogates. The United States has always been a nation with a favorable research climate for the sponsoring of research activities at numerous US universities and research centers. Generally, both countries would likely benefit from the finished research. In China's case, however, you must assume that the "sponsor" is somehow being directed by the government or one of its many seemingly non-government-affiliated organizations, and they will use the opportunity as a one-sided attempt to collect research results and proprietary information. They will also use these efforts as platforms to insert specific individuals who will act solely as information collectors for the initial information being sought, as well as for other information that could be of value down the road.[2]

n. Hiring Information Brokers and Consultants. Information brokers and consultants scour the world for valuable proprietary data that can be used by someone else. What they cannot obtain legally or by guile, some information brokers will end up purchasing. The broker then verifies the data, puts it into a usable and easily accessible format, and delivers it to interested clients in China. Consultants, for the most part, are highly respected in their field, and are well known. With such credentials, they sometimes have an easier time contacting the appropriate people to gain information or insight. Unfortunately, China would use such subject matter experts to gain insights under differing guises, such as getting a better awareness on the technology, developing a technical book or article, and requiring background. Such individuals tend to start out looking for specific data (for which there is no need to really protect) and then slowly expand their questions and areas of interest to the real subject data being desired.[2]

   The following advertisement published in the *Asian Wall Street Journal* in 1991 illustrates this activity:

   > Do you have advanced/privileged information of any type of project/contract that is going to be carried out in your country? We hold commission/agency agreements with many large European companies and could introduce them to your project/contract. Any commission received would be shared with yourselves.

   The ad was followed by a phone number in Western Europe.[2]

o. Fulfillment of Classified US Government Contracts and Exploitation of Department of Defense–Sponsored Technology Sharing Agreements. At times, classified US government contracts are awarded to companies that are partially or substantially controlled by a foreign government. Although US government security agencies closely monitor these contracts, the contract or technology-sharing agreement can still provide a foreign government with unauthorized access to information. The foreign country may not have the same security protection standards, and may also have Chinese or their surrogate personnel working on the contract. Thus, the information can be obtained and China benefits from it. Typically, non-allies seldom are included in such contracts, but depending upon the contract, such non-allies like China could work their way into the organization as a subcontractor or as a regular employee.[2]

p. Tasking Liaison Officers at Government-to Government Projects. During joint R&D activities, foreign governments routinely request to have an onsite liaison officer to monitor progress and provide guidance. American allied countries have taken advantage of these positions as cover for liaison (intelligence) officers assigned with collecting as much information about the facility as possible. As above, the Chinese may also attempt to influence the intelligence officer or other individuals associated with the project, which are located in the liaison officer's home country in order to obtain the information.[2]

 Using their close access to their US counterparts when conducting joint R&D, particularly in the defense arena, these liaison officers have been caught removing classified or restricted documents that have been clearly marked as such.

q. Known or Unknown Source that Concerns Classified, Sensitive, or Export-Controlled Information. The fact that the individual or company soliciting the information has little or no reason to know about the technology, by itself, should be sufficient enough for US government contractors or companies to be suspicious of the inquiry. Such requests typically are often more of a probing exercise than an actual attempt to acquire the information. Those making the inquiries often provide few specific details on product requirements and even less end-user information.[2]

r. Attempted Acquisitions. Acquisitions are a great method of obtaining information. The acquisition need not be completed, for during the somewhat drawn-out negotiation process, the targeted company will be providing technical details about the sensitive products being sought. Further, relevant requesting material, supply, and pricing information will be revealed. On occasion, these acquisition attempts gain access to sensitive technologies that have been made by purchasing a US company outright. Attempted acquisitions usually bypass the usual marketing offices and go, instead, to a senior-level individual inside the company. When sensitive information of a defense or economic value is at stake, such attempted acquisitions should immediately heighten the concerns of the company in terms of what is really happening. When appropriate, government contractors should contact their contract security officer for guidance. Such inquiries, in and of themselves, are not illegal, but US firms should initially respond by requiring end-user information or by pointing out that export licenses are required before the technology can be delivered. From the requester's view, these details are simply ignored. Overall, the vast majority of these direct requests yield no positive results, but it alerts the requester that security is important to the company to protect its information. Considering the almost cost-free nature of this technique, however, the search simply continues until a supplier is located that, for the right price, will dispense with or circumvent legal prohibitions and export the restricted technology. The short-term profits go, unfortunately, to the US firms most willing to bend or break the rules. Often those making the requests are operating on behalf of unidentified end users.[2]

 Sometimes, the requesters will operate out of front companies, making it even more difficult to determine the true end users. Several different collectors may initiate nearly identical inquiries over a period of a few months. This indicates that a single end user hopes to increase the chance of success by going through multiple channels without revealing the actual individuals or motives behind the acquisition. Often such firms generate most of their revenue doing legitimate business. China is reported to have over 3000 front companies located in the United States, and depending upon the company name and what they actually do or make, it might be difficult to determine whether or not a requester represents one of these front companies or not.[2]

 These firms play an important role in the illegal transfer of sensitive technologies abroad. Each collector, then, may approach several potential suppliers. Sometimes, requests to potential suppliers fail to identify a final destination for the product. Other times, a collector will falsely identify an end user. When the true end user is a less developed country that lacks the means to make large purchases, a collector may deliberately supply misleading information and identify the end user as a large country in an effort to dangle high-volume, high-profit prospects in front of the seller. This sometimes results in less than perfect attention by the selling company to such details as verifying the bona fide credentials of the recipient and adhering strictly to US export-control laws. By establishing offices in the United States, foreign collectors sometimes take possession of sensitive goods ostensibly for domestic use. Later, the technology is smuggled out of the country.[2]

s. Marketing of Foreign Services and Products to US High-Tech Firms. This collection technique is one of those that is favored for accessing sensitive US technologies. Individuals with technical backgrounds will offer their services to US research facilities, academic institutions, and even cleared defense contractors. They hold the appropriate credentials and knowledge base, so using this tool is a favorite. Selling the hardware and software provides an immediate "in" with the purchasing company, and the seller has people standing by to install and provide service and maintenance under a low-cost service contract for their products. Maintenance and servicing is a method to acquire access to the facilities and technologies that might not otherwise be available.[2]

  Temporary access to IT networks has the potential to turn into long-term access if there is the ability to install a Trojan horse or backdoor into sensitive computer networks. The beauty of this approach is that the servicing personnel are invited in and actually paid for providing a service while, at the same time, gaining direct access to technologies that would not otherwise be available to them.[2]

t. Technical Areas That Have Direct Application to Their Work. Unsuspecting scientists can be easy targets of opportunity because they underestimate the importance of the information they share. They essentially let their guard down when talking to peers on arcane technical subjects and, in doing so, inadvertently provide proprietary, sensitive, or classified information. Also, when the scientists are attending a conference or symposium, the exhibits and technical materials available will offer a unique opportunity to study, compare, and photograph actual products in one location. Of even more importance, events that are held on the collector's home territory are vulnerable to exploitation by traditional technical means (e.g., electronic surveillance) and by the use of entrapment ploys, such as inducing targets into compromising situations.[2]

u. US Travelers Abroad. They have traditionally been another important source of information on sensitive US technologies, and the last two years were no different. The free flow of information in the United States and the willingness of US scientists and scholars to engage in academic exchange make US travelers particularly vulnerable not only to standard electronic monitoring devices—installed in hotel rooms or conference centers—but also to simple approaches by foreigners trained to ask the right questions. Targeting occurs at airports and includes luggage searches, unnecessary inspection and downloading of information from laptop computers, and extensive questioning beyond normal security measures. Other travelers have received excessively "helpful" service by host government representatives and hotel staffs.[2]

v. Requests for Information. Direct and indirect requests for information continue to top the list of methods most often reported by the CI community. These types of approaches often include requests for classified, sensitive, or export-controlled information that are not sought or encouraged by the target. The Defense Security Service (DSS), Air Force Office of Special Investigations, and Army Counterintelligence Center (ACIC) all report that this technique is the method of choice for both government and non-government collectors. ACIC numbers indicate that over 85% of targeting incidents involved direct requests in person or via e-mail, telephone, or fax, while DSS reporting shows that 26% of its targeting incidents fall under this category.[3]

w. Solicitation and Marketing of Services. China also seeks entry to US firms by pursuing business relationships that enable them to gain access to sensitive or classified information, technologies, or projects. For example, a businessman would submit an unsolicited business proposal offering a variety of services such as product design, software, or engineering to US military facilities conducting work involving sensitive technologies.[3]

x. Solicitation and Marketing of Foreign Services. One of the most popular tactics used to gain access to US R&D facilities is to have foreign scientists submit unsolicited employment applications. Facilities that are the targets of this kind of solicitation work on such technologies as electro-optics, ballistics, and astrophysics. Other approaches included offers of software support, internships, and proposals to act as sales or purchasing agents. In addition, of growing importance is the greater use of foreign research facilities and software development companies located outside the United States to work on commercial projects related to protected programs. Any time direct control of a process or a product is relinquished, the technology associated with it is susceptible to possible exploitation.[3]

y. Acquisition of Technology. The direct and indirect acquisition of technology and information via third countries, the use of front companies, and the direct purchase of US firms or technologies are proven methods of acquisition that collectors continue to exploit. They can disguise their activity by passing US technologies through fictitious companies, multiple layers of freight forwarders, multiple countries, or Free Trade Zones. They also commingle illicit and legal trade to obscure their activity.[3]

z. Official Foreign Visitors. Chinese government organizations, including intelligence and security services, also frequently target and collect information through official contacts and visits to the United States. These include visits to US military posts, armament-producing centers, and national laboratories. Some visitors may be trained to verbally elicit information, some may brazenly ignore the security parameters of a tour, and others will use concealed recording devices to collect information. Some information may seem innocuous, such as the facility layout, but that seemingly innocuous request could be very valuable to them and provide one or more clues about your products or how to run their own facility better. In one instance noted in the past, a visitor played with his wristwatch in a manner that made the host suspicious that a micro camera might be in the watch. Other visitors had double-sided tape on the soles of their shoes in order to collect slivers of metal alloys from the floor of a production plant for US military planes. They later analyzed the slivers to determine the exact metallic components used in the planes.

  There are a number of commercially available audio and video recording devices disguised as pens, sunglasses, buttons, key fobs, cigarette packs, and so on. It may be nearly impossible to keep such devices from entering your facility. When you have concerns, check out the data provided by the Federal Bureau of Investigation (FBI), which is located at: fbi.gov/about-us/investigate/counterintelligence/risks-mitigations-of-visitors.[3,5]

aa. Exploitation of Joint Research. Increasingly, groundbreaking R&D is the product of cooperative efforts between US and Chinese experts. As noted in a recently released Department of Commerce–sponsored study, individual US firms, along with their international competitors, were building global research enterprises. American universities who establish campuses abroad are also creating joint educational programs with foreign institutions and then partnering with faculty members in the conduct of cutting-edge research. China is in this area in a big way and will continue to expand its efforts. If an American university has a campus in a foreign nation and research in any area may result, a reasonable check will show that the Chinese have students on the campus, have provided subject matter experts to teach on the campus at a reduced salary, have observers located on or nearby the campus, or will have provided funds for some campus departments to set up and run R&D or other laboratories in order to gain insight into the result of any academic research that is conducted.[3]

Overall, though, scientific exchange is integral to research across the complex of component laboratories throughout the world. Although most government organizations, educational facilities, and private-sector firms employ varying levels of risk mitigation strategies to protect against illegal technology transfers and loss of trade secrets, the volume of joint research underway is such that is presents very temping targeting opportunity, either through human-to-human contact or via technical means. These laboratories get a lot of visitors. During one year alone, there were over 10,000 foreign visitors to Department of Energy facilities, of which over 4500 were Chinese.[2]

bb. Cyber Attack and Exploitation. Over the past two decades, cyber threats have grown to tremendous levels. US government, government contractor, and private-sector networks have all experienced intrusions that appeared designed for intelligence collection purposes. In the past decade, the United States has identified China-connected computer network intrusions that have compromised thousands of hosts and hundreds of thousands of user accounts and exfiltrated numerous terabytes of data from US and private-sector computer networks. Other computer attacks have been people pretending to be someone else; these can be labeled as a subset of all intrusion activity. Most if not all of this massive cyber attack on US IT systems are affiliated with China. They have used socially engineered e-mails to compromise the computers of cleared defense contractors. Continually, also, the US government networks are being probed and targeted by both state and non-state people for numerous reasons, which include legitimate cooperative scientific research. China has thousands of networks that are the source of a significant amount of malicious activity targeting computers in the United States, but it is often difficult to attribute the origin or specific intent of any given activity.[3]

"Spear phishing" is a more recent intrusion method and is becoming a burgeoning social engineering–based method used by hackers to gain access to sensitive information. In contrast to the broader phishing schemes—known as "spamming"—spear phishers involved in espionage usually target their attacks on just a few individuals of higher value by using open-source information to develop e-mail messages that can, on their face, appear to originate from a trusted source and that contains just enough valid information to entice the person being contacted to open a malicious attachment or access a malicious web site. This is according to a Microsoft alert.

In February 2007, several high-ranking business executives received a spear phishing e-mail. For all intents and purposes, it was allegedly from the US Better Business Bureau. The e-mail claimed that some complaints had been filed against the executives' companies. The e-mail then directed them to download complaints by accessing the listed web site. The fraudulent download was designed to install a key logger on the victims' systems in order to capture all key strokes related to financial and government web sites visited by the victims.[3,6]

cc. Targeting of US Travelers Overseas. Collectors also target US travelers, such as businessmen, government employees, and contractors, when they are in an overseas environment. Collection methods will include everything from eliciting information during seemingly innocuous conversations to eavesdropping on "private" telephone conversations to downloading information from laptops or other digital storage devices after surreptitiously entering hotel rooms.[3]

dd. Exploiting Internet Discussion Groups. The anonymity of the Internet makes it a more than perfect medium for collection attempts using e-mail, search engines, and discussion groups. You can expect the Chinese to expand their collection using such exploitation as listserv. This is an e-mail-based discussion group that is organized along topics of interest and open to anyone. If there isn't a specific group topic, they will probably create such a topic area and then have other personnel send various e-mails in an attempt to draw other users into discussions. If the new subject area is crafted right, the possibility exists that people from other groups can be more easily drawn in and then exploited. Subscribers who join a list can send e-mail messaged to the list. The messages are then sent to all members of a given group by the listserv, which provides subscribers with e-mail addresses of all other members. This procedure provides an easy method to facilitate discussions involving research advice on specific technical challenges. All of it is permanently archived and searchable. Such exchanges will pose various serious threats to economic and technological security for two reasons. The first is that it is not uncommon for concepts, research, development, testing, and evaluation of a technology to take place in an open environment because, after all, the information isn't all that sensitive, but just information that may help someone else advance a theory or idea, and also the sender might receive additional information that would help him. This is particularly significant when the information relates to dual-use technologies, proprietary information, or possible new groundbreaking concepts that can be put to use. Second, the listserv site provides a Chinese (or other foreign) national who is involved in collecting information on future programs or in acquiring research being conducted in another country, with the mail addresses of everyone involved in the discussion area. From that, further research can reveal the person, where they work, and provide a link for learning more about the person for use in the future.[7]

OTHER ECONOMIC COLLECTION EFFORTS

Foreign governments and industry also collect economic information from US firms through standard business practices, such as mergers and acquisitions, strategic alliances, and licensing agreements, as well as gathering publicly available information. Although these activities are an accepted element of the business world, various reports received by US government intelligence agencies that track espionage activities have indicated that these activities have generated a considerable portion of the technology and economic information obtained; they clearly do not constitute any illegal behavior. However, the open-source collection activities have included the review of trade journals or corporate annual reports, market surveys, and attending conferences and symposia. There are instances, however, that indicate that these types of collection efforts could well be the precursors for illicit collection activities, or they can indicate a specific intelligence collection interest. For example, an attempt to persuade a US employee of a firm to gather information from the firm's library could well be the first step in setting up a source that would eventually collect proprietary documentation. Similarly, a joint venture or licensing agreement can provide the ideal opportunity to obtain non-public information from a company.[2]

a. Acquisition of Technology and Companies. Acquisitions are on the rise. This is the latest manifestation of an increased trend to acquire sensitive technologies through purchase. According to DSS reporting, 88% of all reported suspicious acquisition activities involved third parties. Third parties are not the actual entities acquiring the technology but are the ultimate end users. Third-party acquisitions are often an indicator of a possible technology transfer or diversion because when the ultimate recipients are determined, they are often countries that are on embargoed lists for the acquired items. One method that is commonly used involves setting up a freight forwarder, that is, a cooperating US-based company that will provide the ultimate foreign recipient with a US address to subvert US export-control laws. The reader must remember, though, that not all freight forwarding companies engage in such activities. Many are wholly legitimate. Those few that are willing to subvert US laws and export controls are willing to provide false paperwork and false end-user licenses (and the associated legitimate third countries) and look only to the cash in hand for such transactions.[8]
b. Exploitation by Trade Delegations and Technical Groups during Visits to US Companies. During the past couple of years, efforts have continued to exploit visits to US facilities. Some examples of exploitation techniques include the following: wandering around facilities unescorted, bringing unauthorized cameras or recording devices into cleared facilities,

or pressing their hosts for additional accesses or information; adding last minute or unannounced persons as part of the visit, arriving unannounced, and seeking access by asking to see an employee belonging to the same organization as the visitor; hiding true agendas, for example, by trying to shift conversations to topics not agreed upon in advance; and misrepresenting a visitor's importance or technical competency to secure visit approval.[8]

c. Internet Activity (Cyber Attack and Exploitation). This category addresses cyber attack and exploitation via Internet-based requests for information. The majority of Internet endeavors are foreign probes searching for potential weaknesses in systems for exploitation. One example was a network attack that, over the period of a day, involved several hundred attempts to use multiple passwords to illegally obtain access to a cleared defense facility's network. Fortunately, the facility had an appropriate level of protection in place to repel this attack. This example reflects the extent to which intelligence collectors are attempting to use the Internet to gain access to sensitive or proprietary information. Given the considerable effort that is under way in the cyber attack and exploitation arenas, substantial resources will need to be allocated in the future to ensure adequate security countermeasures.[8]
d. Exploitation of Joint Ventures/Research. Joint ventures place foreign personnel in proximity to US personnel and technology and can thereby facilitate access to protected programs. This is of special concern when foreign employees are in place for long periods. In this scenario, there is always a danger that foreign employees will be more readily accepted as full partners, and the security vigilance of US colleagues may wane. Some examples of suspicious activity in joint ventures/research include the following: foreign workers seeking access to areas or information outside the purview of their work agreement, enticing US companies to provide large quantities of technical data as part of the bidding process, and foreign organizations sending more representatives than reasonably necessary for particular projects.[8]
e. Illegal Collection Activities. The unlawful acquisition of export-controlled technologies by foreign collectors remains a considerable concern. Methods of operation employed to circumvent the export-control process include the following: using front companies within the United States and overseas, illegally transporting products to an undisclosed end user by utilizing false end-user certificates, and purchasing products that have been modified during the manufacturing process to meet export-controlled specifications.[9]
f. Theft of Trade Secrets and Critical Technologies in Overseas Environments. US businessmen traveling overseas are increasingly becoming targets of foreign collection activities. There are numerous examples of briefcases or laptop computers showing evidence of unauthorized access after being left unattended in hotel rooms. In addition, there is evidence of travelers being photographed during business meetings in foreign countries for future targeting.[7]
g. Use of the Freedom of Information Act (FOIA). The FOIA provides another important method for collecting open-source material. US adversaries have used FOIA requests to obtain information from government agencies that have provided valuable intelligence on economic policy, insights into proprietary technologies, and information concerning intelligence and military operations. This information has also been used to identify classified activities.[10]

   As an example, Mitsubishi filed around 1500 FOIA requests in one year alone, all in an effort to enter the space industry using the information and resulting technology developed in the United States.
h. Data Contained in the US Patent Office (USPO). The USPO is another great source of freely available proprietary information. When a patent application is filed, detailed data and drawings are required. Unless the Defense Department or another agency can determine with some exactitude that revealing the actual patent application would endanger national security, when the patent is approved and a number assigned, the patent will forever remain protected from public release and viewing. If the patent does not fall into the national security arena, any individual can walk into the patent office, see the patent, and make a copy. To make it easier, the USPO lists recent patent filing and those that have been approved. How

much easier could it be for the Chinese to look at and copy the latest patents. As a side note, if a patent application includes information that would be considered proprietary information to the company, such as a trade secret, then when the application is approved, that information is, suddenly, no longer proprietary, and freely available to anyone to use as they desire.

CASE STUDY OF A CHINESE COLLECTOR[3]

The 2007 conviction of a Chinese-American agent who operated in the United States for more than 20 years illustrates the elusive collection threat. The agent, a Chinese engineer, entered the United States via Hong Kong in 1978. With his background and knowledge base, he was soon hired in his chosen field and began a steady rise to positions with increasing access to sensitive information, including a position with a major US intelligence and defense contractor. In interviews with the FBI after his arrest, the agent admitted that he had passed information on sensitive projects to China beginning in 1983. By 1985, he and his wife became naturalized US citizens, and in 1996, he was granted a secret security clearance. He continued espionage activities on behalf of China, traveling there with his wife approximately once every two years to deliver information to his handler in the People's Liberation Army (PLA) and receive additional tasking. In May 2001, the Chinese agent's younger brother, a former PLA propaganda officer, his wife, and their son immigrated to the United States. They became permanent resident aliens, while working as couriers for the PLA. The agent uploaded sensitive US defense information to removable media and passed it to his brother. The brother and his wife traveled to China, often flying from Vancouver to Hong Kong in an effort to obscure their final destination. Their adult son also traveled to China, where he met with the PLA officer and received various tasks that, upon his return to the United States, he passed to the agent. The case offers insights into clandestine operational methods employed by the Chinese Intelligence Services to obscure their activities. For example, for communications security, the agent and family members avoided phone calls from the United States to China. They also avoided direct flights. Additionally, they encrypted information on laptops and disks and employed code words. Most importantly, the case demonstrated the People's Republic of China's (PRC's) patient and purposeful approach to espionage. The agent was allowed time to slowly infiltrate a company until he was in a position to provide sensitive information, showing the range of information and technologies that China may task a single, well-connected asset to collect against. Tasking documents recovered by the FBI included instructions to "join more (professional) organizations and participate in more seminars with special subject matters and then compile the special conference material on a disk." Also included was a list of military technologies that the agent should target, including space application, propulsion technology, nuclear attack technology, and a host of other sensitive technologies.

OTHER INTERESTING CASES OF CHINESE ESPIONAGE

Below are some quick summaries of five espionage cases conducted by China as reported in the National Counterintelligence Center's Annual Report to Congress on Foreign Economic Collection and Industrial Espionage. More information on them can be located in the press through Internet searches.

CASE 1

Two businessmen, one a Chinese national, who is the president of a Beijing-based firm, and the other a naturalized Canadian citizen, pleaded guilty to charges of illegally exporting fiber-optic gyroscopes to the PRC without the required State Department permits. Export of these gyroscopes to the PRC is prohibited. The two men bought the gyroscopes from a Massachusetts company and planned to export them to the PRC via a Canadian subsidiary of the Beijing-based firm. The gyroscopes can be used in missile and aircraft guidance systems, as well as smart bombs.

Case 2

Two naturalized US citizens were convicted of conspiring to illegally export weapons parts to their native China. They used their exporting company to purchase surplus US missile, aircraft, radar, and tank parts from the Defense Reutilization and Marketing Service and then ship them to the PRC. The exported items were on the US Munitions List that prohibited them from being shipped without a license from the State Department.

Case 3

Two Chinese scientists and a naturalized US citizen who was born in China were arrested for stealing product designs from a major US telecommunications firm and passing them to a Chinese government–owned company in Beijing. Both Chinese scientists had received technical degrees from US universities before being employed by the US firm.

Case 4

A Chinese company based in Orlando, Florida, was charged with illegally exporting radiation-hardened integrated circuits to Chinese missile and satellite manufacturers in the PRC without the required Department of Commerce licenses. The affidavit prepared by the Department of Commerce described three illegal diversions of the missile microchips. According to weapons proliferation specialists, the microchips have military applications and could be used by the Chinese military to improve their long-range missile-targeting capabilities.

Case 5

A naturalized Chinese national was arrested for attempting to smuggle a defense-grade Radiance high-speed (HS) infrared camera to the PRC. Since the Radiance HS camera is on the US Munitions List, companies must file with the Department of State to legally export such items. The camera was destined for the Chinese State Ship Building Corporation, a state-owned conglomerate of 58 companies that is based in Beijing and Shanghai.

REFERENCES

1. Enav, Peter, Chinese spies target Taiwan's U.S.-made defenses, *The Washington Times*, March 12, 2012.
2. National Counterintelligence Center (NACIC), Annual Report to Congress on Foreign Economic Collection and Industrial Espionage, Washington, D.C., July 1995 [The information, in various forms, is also included in numerous other NACIC and ONCIX annual reports].
3. Annual Report to Congress on Foreign Economic Collection and Industrial Espionage, Office of the Counterintelligence Executive (ONCIX), Washington, D.C., 2007.
4. Stewart, Brian, Why other countries pay for our politicians to visit, July 7, 2010, found at: http://bc.ca/news/Canada.
5. Visitors: Risks and Mitigations, found at: http://fbi.gov.
6. Microsoft Safety and Security Center website, found at: http://microsoft.com/security/online-privacy/phishing-faq.aspx.
7. Annual Report to Congress on Foreign Economic Collection and Industrial Espionage, Office of the Counterintelligence Executive (ONCIX), Washington, D.C., 2000.
8. National Counterintelligence Center (NACIC), Annual Report to Congress on Foreign Economic Collection and Industrial Espionage 2001, Washington, D.C.
9. Annual Report to Congress on Foreign Economic Collection and Industrial Espionage, Office of the Counterintelligence Executive (ONCIX), Washington, D.C., for the years 2000 and 2001.
10. Intelligence Threat Handbook, IOSS, Washington, D.C., The Interagency OPSEC Support Staff, April 1996, revised May 1996.

7 The China Spy Guide and Open-Source Information

"Those inscrutable Chinese" is a phrase that has been echoed numerous times over the years. Inscrutable, perhaps, but in commerce as in politics, they are very deliberate and methodical. As a nation, and as a people, China exemplifies the value of taking small, calculated, methodical steps, and couples it with a carefully crafted educational system that demands that everything to be done would be developed like a college term paper to assure oneself that everything has been carefully researched, thought through, and that only great success would be assured.

In this term paper instance, a paper is based on innumerable research sources, each carefully vetted, and each proposed idea in the paper must have a proven worth to be included.

China has taken this approach in its intelligence-gathering research field in order to develop an espionage technique base, a base created upon desired results to benefit the political, military, and economic sectors of the government.

It started in the 1990s when two PhDs, Huo Zhongwen and Wang Zongxiao, veteran spies, who now teach intelligence in Beijing, created a master's degree–level course. As with any course, such as a college course you might take, it requires that a formal textbook be available. Like any academic exercise in developing a course model from scratch, they had an appropriate background in intelligence gathering, but wished to formalize the process. They used hundreds of hours of reading and research, viewed other academic reports, looked to the great Chinese libraries for information, went on the Internet and delved into everything that could possibly be related, and pulled data from a myriad of sources. Once collected, they (along with many others, it is presumed) refined the data, pared it down, developed a specific outline for such a course in intelligence gathering, and, requiring a specific target, used the United States as the base from whence to obtain the desired materials. Using open-source information easily available in the United States, these two men carefully crafted a textbook that could be used by any nation that would be interested in obtaining defense, weaponry, and scientific and technical information; innovation; and other related data that could be used to increase the viability and economy status of China. The textbook developed by these two men is known by its formal English title as *Sources and Techniques of Obtaining National Defense Science and Technology Intelligence*. Later on, after a copy was obtained and translated in the United States, it came to be known as the "China Spy Manual." The entire document can be found on http://www.fas.org/irp/world/china/docs/sources.html.

Once created, reviewed, and finalized, the manual was used to teach a generation of spies what information to look for, where it is most likely to be found, and then how to go about acquiring the information. One can presume that since 9/11 and the government's review of thousands upon thousands of untold documents, as well as the reduction of information found on the Internet from various government and government contractor web sites, in addition to other information once easily available to the general public, the China Spy Manual has undergone a somewhat extensive revision to keep up with the changes in US policy and protective features for a wide variety of information.

Published in Beijing in 1999, the 200+ page manual was immediately put into use. The following provides an outline of the major segments within the manual.

Chapter 1—A Summary of Collection Work
- Section One—Establishing New Concepts of Collection Work
- Section Two—Information, Intelligence and the Target of Collection
- Section Three—Sources of Intelligence and Sources of Information
- Section Four—The Substance of Information Collection Work
- Section Five—Theoretical Approaches to Guiding Collection Work

Chapter 2—A Brief History of the Development of Collection Work
- Section One—The Period of Collection Acts
- Section Two—The Period of "Collection Work"
- Section Three—The Period of Collection Work as a Science and a Technology
- Section Four—Regarding the Reform of Information Collection Work
- Section Five—The Rational Overall Arrangement of S&T Information

Chapter 3—Overview of Information
- Section One—Explanation of Symbols
- Section Two—What Information Is
- Section Three—Categories of Information
- Section Four—The Essential Elements, Attributes and Functions of Information
- Section Five—Data Banks and Databases
- Section Six—Evaluation of Information
- Section Seven—The Present State of Technological Information and Trends for Development

Chapter 4—National Defense S&T Intelligence Sources Discussed
- Section One—Examples of the Concept of Information Sources Most Commonly Seen in China and Elsewhere
- Section Two—Categories and Characteristics of Intelligence Sources and Information Sources
- Section Three—Output Characteristics of Information Sources
- Section Four—Parameters for Evaluating the Status of Information Sources
- Section Five—Characteristics of National Defense Intelligence Sources and Information Sources
- Section Six—Results of Intelligence Source and Information Source Research
- Section Seven—Introduction to Typical National Defense Intelligence Sources and Materials

Chapter 5—Consumer Intelligence Needs Studies
- Section One—Basic Concepts
- Section Two—Significance of Consumer Intelligence Needs Studies
- Section Three—Essential Attributes of Consumer Intelligence Needs
- Section Four—Consumer Intelligence Needs Studies: What It Consists of and the Forms Its Achievements Take
- Section Five—Assessment Standards for Consumer Intelligence Needs
- Section Six—Types of Consumer Intelligence Needs and Their Relations with Collection Work
- Section Seven—The History and Current State of Consumer Intelligence Needs Studies
- Section Eight—Research Methods for Consumer Intelligence Needs
- Section Nine—The Laws of Consumer Intelligence Needs and Intelligence Behavior
- Section Ten—Basic Characteristics of Consumers of National Defense S&T Intelligence
- Section Eleven—National Defense S&T Intelligence: Case Studies in Consumer Intelligence Needs Research

Chapter 6—Information Transmission Channels
- Section One—The Concept of Channels
- Section Two—Categories of Channels
- Section Three—The Properties of Channels
- Section Four—Channel Interference and Anti-Interference Measures
- Section Five—Channel Confidentiality

Chapter 7—Methods and Techniques of Obtaining Information
Section One—Information Collection Systems
Section Two—The Basic Process of Obtaining Information
Section Three—Basic Methods of Information Collection
Section Four—Information Collection Methods
Section Five—Selection Techniques
Section Six—Modernized Collection Operations and Computer Applications
Chapter 8—A First Approach to the Study of Intelligence, Information, and Collection
Section One—Brief Review of the Development of Information Science
Section Two—Current Thinking on Intelligence, Information, and Collection
Section Three—Comparison of Study Subjects in Intelligence, Information, and Collection
Section Four—Disciplinary Characteristics of Intelligence, Information and Collection
Section Five—General Methods to Study Intelligence, Information, and Collection
Section Six—Significance of Intelligence, Information, and Collection Research

What makes the manual exceptionally interesting is that any country could use it to target the United States for the purposes of attempting to gain the desired information, that is, not just China, but virtually every country that wishes to target the United States, if desired. Also, any country could use the manual as a blueprint for revisiting it and creating a specific manual against any other country.

Well, that is except for one little, itsy-bitsy detail: openness. The United States is the most open nation in the world. The manual was developed based upon that simple fact. No other nation allows such openness in terms of access to government, private industry, think tanks, developing technologies, and the like. The following sections include extensive excerpts and passages taken from the Interagency OPSEC Support Staff IOSS publication *Intelligence Threat Handbook*.

CHINESE INTELLIGENCE OPERATIONS

The People's Republic of China (PRC) has a significant intelligence collection capability, much of which is focused on regional adversaries, in particular, Russia. That said, the United States has become the primary target of China because of its role as a global superpower; its substantial military, political, and economic presence in the Pacific Rim and Asia; and its role as a developer of advanced technology. China wants, needs, and requires the technology to ensure its own economic growth. All the intelligence functions within China are controlled and directed through the Central Committee of the Communist Party and then further through the General Staff Department of the Central Military Commission. All ongoing intelligence operations are coordinated through the General Office of the Central Committee, and all intelligence reports must be reviewed by this office prior to presentation to the Chinese leadership. China's structure is such that it maintains four intelligence organizations from which to conduct collection activities that are directed at the United States: the Ministry of State Security, the Military Intelligence Department, the Third or Technical Department of the Central Military Commission, and the New China News Agency.[1]

CHINESE INTELLIGENCE COLLECTION ORGANIZATIONS

Although China uses numerous "non-government/non-official" organizations to collect intelligence, there are several specific government organizations that have a vested, full-time, interest in collection and are highlighted below.

a. *The Ministry of State Security (MSS).* The MSS was created in 1983 by the Communist Party Central Committee to provide for the centralization of foreign intelligence and counterintelligence functions. The MSS is headed by the Minister of State Security, who reports to the Central Committee. It conducts counterespionage operations within China, and HUMINT and limited SIGINT operations both inside and outside of the PRC. The MSS centers its collection operations on regional adversaries with which China has shared borders, including Russia, India, and Vietnam, and on nations that are militarily, politically, or economically important to China. The latter category includes the United States, Taiwan, South Korea, and Japan.[1]

Key intelligence collection objectives for the MSS include the following:

- Acquiring foreign military and civilian high technology
- Collecting information on adversary military planning, foreign policy, and foreign trade positions concerning China
- Monitoring Chinese dissident groups overseas[1]

HUMINT is the primary discipline used by the MSS for intelligence collection within the United States and other targeted nations. The MSS also has a limited covert SIGINT capability. The Chinese will use both overt and clandestine HUMINT collection to gather information required by their leaders. Additionally, the MSS attempts to gain information on foreign targets through surveillance of foreigners visiting China.

b. *The Chinese Army's Military Intelligence Department (MID).* The MID is responsible for basic order-of-battle intelligence, studies of foreign weapons systems, and analyses of the capabilities of foreign military organizations. The collection of relevant information comes from military attaches, a constant review of open-source literature, various clandestine HUMINT operations, and joint business ventures with foreign commercial entities. The MID is believed to play an integral role in obtaining advanced military technologies to bolster China's military capabilities and improve those weapons systems vital to China's export arms business. In the past, the MID has played a most significant role in the development of clandestine relationships with Israel and other nations to gain expertise in the development of advanced weapons systems. Together with the Commission on Science, Technology and Industry for National Defense (COSTIND), the MID continually works to obtain vital military technologies that can have current and future application to the Chinese military. Much of this technology is obtained through technological diversion and reverse engineering of products purchased from the West. The MID is also responsible, in concert with the COSTIND, for the development of China's space reconnaissance program.[1]

c. *Technical Department.* The Technical Department, or Third Department of the General Staff Department of the Central Military Commission, is a national agency responsible for managing China's strategic SIGINT program. The Department was established over a half-century ago with Soviet assistance to provide the Chinese General Staff with a limited SIGINT capability and strategic communications support.[1] Over the past decades, China has built up its SIGINT program to become a major player, relying on their own creativity and an ever-increasing ability to build on newer technology from other sources.

d. *The New China News Agency (NCNA).* The NCNA is the primary official domestic and international news agency for the PRC. The NCNA has a staff of over 5000 employees operating out of over 90 bureaus and 300 offices in China and abroad. The NCNA serves as a legitimate news organization in the collection of information and also as a cover for clandestine Chinese intelligence operations. As a new agency, the NCNA constantly monitors newspapers, magazines, and broadcasts from around the world, and conducts open-source analysis for the Chinese leadership.[1]

Chinese Collection Operations

a. HUMINT. The MSS is the primary Chinese HUMINT collection organization, although the MID is also involved in HUMINT collection. The MID is primarily involved in the overt collection of technical information through visits to trade shows, through military exchange programs, and through the military attaché program. The MSS's responsibilities include both overt and clandestine collection. It will use students, diplomats, businessmen, and scientists in its attempts to gain information. China promotes an extremely aggressive program of HUMINT collection activities in the United States. As such, China has more than 2600 diplomatic and commercial officials in various parts of the United States. A substantial percentage of these personnel are actively involved in collecting intelligence. At the college and university level, there are over 40,000 students from the PRC in attendance in the United States, and many of these students have been tasked to collect information by the Chinese government. In addition to all of these personnel, some 25,000–30,000 or more Chinese visit the United States annually as members of official delegations. On top of all these people, there is also the additional 20,000+ Chinese immigrating to the United States annually.

The MSS, through all of these individuals and their activities, has been able to obtain high- and mid-level technologies not cleared for export to the PRC. The MSS has developed a three-pronged means to obtain such technology: first, recruiting agents in China and sending them abroad to acquire technology; second, acquiring American firms that produce a desired technology; and lastly, the use of MSS-operated front companies. The Chinese use a number of different methods to gather HUMINT. In the past, they have used various pressure tactics to gain information from the Chinese immigrant community, especially targeting those Chinese that have access to high technology or military data. They also "encourage" Chinese students to remain in the United States as long-term penetration agents. MSS personnel have acted as intelligence collectors using cover as NCNA reporters, trade office representatives, and accredited diplomats.[1]

The MSS has determined that scientific exchange programs have proven to be an extremely useful means to gather information. The Federal Bureau of Investigation has stated that virtually all Chinese citizens allowed to leave the PRC for the United States are given some type of collection requirement to fulfill. While the bulk of Chinese operations are not sophisticated operations in any sense of the word, the continually large number of ongoing Chinese operations makes it more difficult for American counterintelligence to identify and subsequently counter their espionage activities. In the past decade or so, the Chinese have been the subject of approximately half of all cases initiated by US law enforcement agencies concerning the illegal diversion of technology from the United States.[1]

b. SIGINT. The Technical Department has provided the PRC with a wide range of SIGINT collection and monitoring capabilities. The Chinese maintain, by far, the most extensive SIGINT capability of any nation in the Asia-Pacific region. They operate several dozen SIGINT ground stations deployed throughout China, which allows for continual monitoring of signals from Russia, Taiwan, Japan, South Korea, India, and other parts of Southeast Asia. Signals from US military units located in the region are of significant interest to these monitoring stations. A large SIGINT facility at Hainan Island is principally concerned with monitoring US naval activities in the South China Sea. The Chinese appear to be developing a spaceborne ELINT system that is mounted on their photoreconnaissance and communications satellites. In this regard, though, there have been no open-source information confirmations that this capability presents a significant threat to US forces in the region. Even so, they have the capability, equipment, and manpower to take advantage of any situation that could arise. The Chinese also actively monitor international communications satellites from SATCOM intercept facilities on Hainan Island and outside Beijing. Additionally, the Chinese have developed a series of SIGINT collection vessels that monitor US military operations and exercises in the Asia-Pacific region.[1]
c. IMINT. The Chinese have a spaceborne photoreconnaissance capability that focuses on collecting imagery over the Russian border. In studying China over the past decade, the author believes the Chinese IMINT capability has been greatly expanded to cover the entire Southeast Asia, particularly those where US forces, or forces supported by the United States, are evident and have advanced technologies supporting the military. The Chinese also use a

variety of fixed-wing aircraft to collect photographic imagery. These systems could present a substantial intelligence collection threat to US forces in the region. US intelligence agencies believe that China will likely develop a mid- to high-resolution electro-optic imaging system that can then provide the Chinese with vastly improved capabilities.[1]

Chinese Intelligence Collection Trends

Currently, and into the foreseeable future, the PRC will continue to use its intelligence services to gather information about the United States and to obtain access to advanced technologies. It can be expected as the Chinese technological base continues to grow and expand, there will be a greater ramping up of their collection efforts. An integral part of this effort will be the greater use of open-source information gathered by students, scientific researchers, and the NCNA. This must be considered as a firm reality since the question of limiting open-source information is such that it will not be abated. Everyone wants to contribute, through blogs and business and subject area web sites, so the information will be out there, and China will grasp it firmly and never let go. As the sources expand, China will take their ability to expand and improve both its SIGINT and IMINT capabilities, increasing the collection threat to the United States. Through this, the Chinese will continue to use intelligence collection to improve their economic position in the global economy.[1]

The various Chinese intelligence agencies targeting economic information generally combine a number of collection techniques into a concerted collection effort that ensures a maximum level of collected information on any given subject area. Many of the collection techniques used to gather economic intelligence are legitimate practices that do not involve illegal activity. However, they are important elements of a broader, directed intelligence collection effort. The National Counterintelligence Center examined the threat posed by foreign intelligence in their collection of economic information and determined the most used collection tactics.[1]

The following identifies the classic and traditional collection methods being employed:

- Classic agent recruitment
- Volunteers
- Surveillance and surreptitious entry
- Specialized technical operations
- Tasking of foreign employees of US firms
- Elicitation during international conferences and trade fairs
- Foreign government use of private-sector organizations, front companies, and joint ventures
- Tasking of liaison officers at government-to-government projects

Since the China Spy Manual emphasizes the advantages of open-source collection and the myriad information that can be obtained through this method, let's move on and study this valuable resource area.

OPEN-SOURCE COLLECTION

It is estimated that some 80% to 90% of all intelligence gathering comes from open sources, that is, publicly available information. We learned during the Cold War that Russia almost always had one or more individuals sitting in on Congressional hearings that might provide information of value. They also haunted the US Patent and Copyright Offices, collecting vast amounts of the latest patents and copyright information so that, where possible, they could obtain the specifics on the open market. And then, the collected data, Congressional reports, notes taken, USPTO papers, and any contacts made were forwarded to Moscow where it was carefully sifted, translated, filed, studied, and passed on to academia and others for their use. Information that was not immediately put to use was filed away for future consumption.

China, basically, does the same. Their vacuum-cleaner approach scoops up everything of value, and then it is carefully sifted through and the debris is filed away somewhere else; just in case, and the real nuggets of the most current data are then passed to people in business, academia, research and development, think tanks, the military, and the political organs of government.

If you go on the Internet and check out the China Spy Manual, you would see the value of OSINT as a valuable source of information, all of which, at the time of its writing, were somewhat easily obtainable.

The Chinese, *more than any other nation*, collects information via open source. They have the people, those direct and indirectly working for the nation as a whole, to scoop up data. This section will examine the threat posed by the growing availability of information through open sources. As noted earlier, open-source information is publicly available information appearing in print or electronic form. It may be transmitted by radio, television, and newspapers, or it may be distributed through commercial databases, images, and drawings. It is the openness of the US society and the wealth of technical, scientific, political, and economic information available through the media that provide China with its greatest windfall of intelligence. Information has traditionally been extracted from technical journals, trade magazines, Congressional documents, government reports, periodicals, newspapers, and legal documents. These traditional sources of information remain available to adversaries and cannot be ignored. However, in the past decade, the amount of detailed, accurate, and timely information available to the public and US adversaries has expanded dramatically.[1]

Benefits of Open-Source Information Collection

The use of open-source information as an intelligence source has a number of benefits for China. First, the information is relatively cheap to obtain and makes up the greatest volume of information accessible to an intelligence collector. Next, the collecting of open-source materials is legal in the majority of instances, and the collector is not subject to the danger of prosecution for espionage. Frequently, it is possible to derive sensitive information by aggregating and comparing data concerning a particular activity or facility. Various reports and data on the same subject from a number of sources will provide the same information as well as slightly different specific bits of data because each report was written for a different audience. As such, the information has a slightly different approach. By looking at the variations in the topic materials, a subject matter expert or analyst can discern patterns and, by aggregating the information into one "article" as it were, come up with data that were not available in any of the initial articles that were written. All this was possible because the author(s) used slightly different approaches, data, initial sources, and different interpretations of the same date, based on the writer's background, experience, and knowledge of the subject area. The types of information that are useful in such instances include technical journals, newspaper articles, maps, photographs, budgetary documents, environmental declarations, lawsuits, and advertisements requesting services or offering employment. Another distinct advantage of open-source information is that it may be the most timely and accurate information available.

Finally, the combination of open-source data and classified material often provides a more complete picture of a targeted activity than classified information would alone. However, open-source materials also have some disadvantages. For example, information may have been planted in an article as part of a greater deception program. The point here is that the information in the aggregate would become extremely sensitive or fall within the classified arena. But when the information is planted, it can give the analyst pause, and he might go chasing off in a different direction, or presuppose the information to be truly accurate and move on, passing the information to someone who then uses countless man-hours, resources, and funds to accomplish something that has no value. Further, such a deception might lead a person or team to attempt to develop and produce an item and give fanfare to it before the item is found to be worthless. In such cases, the individual/country that put out the initial disinformation data can determine that the collector/country is seriously interested in a particular area and thus confirm previously held suspicions. Also, the area of censorship for the information needs to be considered, ensuring it is not released through an open-source method. In this case, the information is protected early on, and this is a disadvantage to China. But if there is no censorship (or self-censorship) of the material, the resulting open source is extremely valuable to US adversaries.[1]

The Changing Nature of Open-Source Information

The advent of Cable News Network (CNN) and other near real-time information services has increased the quantity, quality, and timeliness of information available from open sources. Detailed information on the activities of the US government, the military services, and the private sector can be obtained from news services, television, online databases, electronic bulletin board systems (BBS), and a wide range of specialized publications available in full text from online services. The effort and the value that adversaries place on this type of information can be illustrated by the Persian Gulf War of the early 1990s. Television crews covered every aspect of the ground and air war in the Persian Gulf region. After the war, it was revealed that the Iraqis viewed the CNN coverage constantly, using it as a near real-time intelligence system, from which they used to obtain political and military information. China, we can suppose, also does this, and probably has in place a continuing program to train intelligence officers and others to gather information using these methods.[1–3]

Not only is a great deal of desired information readily available, it is relatively inexpensive to access and, in many cases, has already had some level of analysis performed by a news agency, bulletin board operator, government body, or university. Issue-oriented groups on the Internet, hackers, students, and hobbyists have taken an increased interest in many classified or sensitive programs. In some cases, these groups have performed fairly sophisticated analysis of these activities. Intelligence can also be derived from the commercial imagery products. Currently, the Russian government is selling imagery with a ground resolution of 2 meters. Until China comes up with the appropriate satellite imaging system that can meet or exceed Russia's effort, China will assuredly use the Russian satellite imagery in their collection effort. With the advent of a new generation of commercial imaging satellites that are becoming operational, imagery products with 1 meter in resolution will become available. Foreign intelligence services and even terrorist groups, news services, and economic competitors will all be able to gain access to this information.[1]

The threat posed by the growing availability of information to China is increased only by the availability of improved analytical workstations and software tools on the commercial market. Expert systems that can quickly examine raw computerized data and extract information pertinent to established search parameters are available. Online search engines and other Internet tools currently allow intelligence collectors and analysts to rapidly sort through massive quantities of information, extracting that information pertinent to their area of interest, while leaving the initial data pristine for another search later on or by someone else. In the area of imagery analysis, there are a number of commercially available programs that can provide China with the means to conduct detailed analysis of digitized imagery. These capabilities will grow as better technologies become available to the public.[1,2]

Traditional Open-Source Assets

As discussed earlier, open-source information has always been exploited by China in their targeting of the United States. The former Soviet Union found open-source intelligence to be so lucrative that it established organizations within its intelligence services and academic institutes dedicated to analyzing open-source data. China is no different, except they have many more resources to devote to it. For example, they would use the initial data derived from analysis to further target clandestine HUMINT and technical intelligence collectors against these organizations, businesses, and activities. They see open sources as valuable for gathering information on political, military, scientific and technical, and economic matters. Their collectors can attend Congressional hearings, examine major newspapers on a daily basis, extract data from the publications of academic and research organizations, and obtain information from technical journals. Right now, depending upon the Congressional hearing, you can expect to find representative of the Chinese government attending, or at least their new media, front company business representatives, or just plain "interested individuals" who happen to be of Chinese heritage.[1]

The Chinese have a large, dedicated open-source collection and analysis capability that operates under the auspices of the NCNA. The NCNA monitors over 40 foreign news agencies and at least 30 foreign broadcast facilities. Data derived from this monitoring are provided to China's leaders, giving them the latest information on world political, economic, and military trends. The Chinese government has available for its use at least six research institutes to gather and analyze open-source information and provide Chinese leaders with detailed assessments of areas of interest.[1]

The Freedom of Information Act (FOIA) provides another important method for collecting open-source material. US adversaries have used FOIA requests to obtain information from government agencies, and the information provided has given the collectors valuable intelligence on economic policy, insights into proprietary technologies, and information concerning intelligence and military operations. This information has also been used to identify classified activities.

Electronic Databases

The number of electronic databases available to the public has grown dramatically in the past few years and will continue to expand. The information available through them has also expanded and includes a vast quantity of data on political, technical, economic, and military topics that would be valuable to China. Chinese intelligence, businesses, hackers, students, and the average person in small businesses have all realized the value of the databases and are exploiting them for intelligence collection. There are substantial incentives to do so. For example, the Department of Energy's (DOE's) national laboratories are targeted because of their emphasis on the development of advanced technologies, many of which have military applications. Virtually all of the DOE laboratories have Internet access, and many provide for public access to a variety of research data. It is possible for an intelligence collector to derive information from these laboratories and associated private and academic facilities that would permit significant insight into US technological efforts. It is interesting to note that the largest users of the DOE databases have come from foreign corporations and governments.[1,3]

A number of nations have engaged in gathering open-source information through electronic databases. The Russian Institute of Automated Systems at Moscow State University hosts the National Center for Automated Date Exchanges with Foreign Computer Networks and Data Banks (NCADE). NCADE was subordinate to the KGB and is now believed to play a central role in SVR computer intelligence collection activities. NCADE has direct access to data networks in the United States, Canada, Germany, the United Kingdom, and France, and is a client of several online databases. These databases include the US Library of Congress, the LEXIS/NEXIS data service, the US National Technical Information Service, the British Library, and the International Atomic Energy Agency. The Russians have also established direct connection with Internet service providers such as COMPUSERVE, TYMNET, and the European Union's EUNET. During the Cold War, the Bulgarian Security Service (DS) was a major client of Lockheed's Dialog online database service. Dialog information was available to all hosts connected to the Bulgarian packet switch network, BULPAC. These connected hosts included DS computers, the computers of the Bulgarian military intelligence organization, and the Bulgarian research and development institutions. It's no wonder that the Chinese, Japanese, and South Koreans have been particularly active in collecting open-source economic and technical data by exploiting electronic databases. By time this book comes out, there will be more databases of value; the Chinese know it, and they will be standing in line to access the databases to determine what information is available for the taking, what contacts can be made, and what new technology might be available that was unknown only a couple of years ago. They will go with a vengeance to obtain the information for their own purposes, all because it is open source and the United States, individuals, industries, and businesses do nothing to stop their shopping for the information.[1,3,4]

Another threat that has grown in importance is electronic BBSs. BBSs, some of which track sensitive US government activities, or can provide information on proprietary activities performed by government contractors, have grown rapidly on the Internet. These systems consist of a host computer with one or more modem lines for remote access. Most BBSs have two main areas: the remote file transfer section and the message base. By tradition, these systems have been used by hobbyists and hackers as a means of distributing information on topics of interest to a particular group. Many of the hobbyist BBSs have engaged in a sophisticated analysis of classified US government programs. Bulletin boards track space launches and speculate on the capability of US reconnaissance satellites. Other bulletin boards track classified programs through the Congressional budget process and attempt to publicize programs that are being managed under special access provisions. Hacker BBSs even provide detailed information on the vulnerability of telecommunications and computer systems. They are also able to display data that have been stolen from computer systems that have been compromised by the hacker group. It is believed that many of these bulletin boards are actively monitored by others who are using these systems to gather sensitive information concerning US capabilities.[1,5,6]

Commercial Imagery

Another area of growing importance related to open-source collection is the increasing availability of imagery products to anyone who has the money to pay for them. Available imagery products include synthetic aperture radar images, electro-optical (EO) images, and multi-spectral imagery (MSI) products. Each of these imagery product types provides information that can be used for intelligence exploitation. Radar imagery applications provide a day/night, all-weather imagery capability, and they can potentially be used for detection of submerged vessels or underground facilities. Electro-optic imagery provides a digitized panchromatic product that offers visible information at high spatial resolutions. Essentially, EO imagery provides a black-and-white picture of the targeted facility or area. Finally, MSI provides spectral range coverage, recording energy visible, near-infrared, short-wave infrared, and medium infrared wavelengths of the spectrum of light.[1,7]

These systems provide for a medium resolution with wide-area coverage capabilities. Their utility for targeting, mapping, and monitoring was demonstrated during the Persian Gulf War. As commercial EO systems become better and are made available to all, they will have a ground resolution of approximately 1 meter. This is sufficient in most cases for the precise identification of most types of facilities and will provide a significant level of detail for any required technical analysis. Currently, there are about a dozen or so commercial imaging satellites under development or just recently put into use, of which at least five will be able to provide a 1-meter-resolution imagery. The use of multiple sensor systems, such as with the use of EO, SM, and MSI imagery to cross-reference a particular feature or facility, will allow change detection analysis, layover analysis, and other sophisticated imagery assessments to be performed. These analyses will present a significant threat to sensitive activities that can be observed by Chinese orbiting satellites.[1,8,9]

CLOSING COMMENTS

In March 2004, American university researcher and Chinese national Zhan Gao pled guilty to illegally exporting technology that can be used in missile guidance and airborne battle management systems for a $590,000 payment from China. Chinese nationals Jian Guo-qu and Ruo Ling Wang were arrested in Milwaukee for conspiring to illegally export more than $500,000 in restricted electronic military radar components to China. Kwonhwan Park, a Korean national, pled guilty to illegally exporting Black Hawk helicopter engines to China through a Malaysian front company.[10–12]

There is no nation that engages in surreptitious illegal technology acquisition for purposes of both commercial piracy and military advancement on a scale that approaches that of the PRC. China is, literally, number one on the list of the United States for its engagement in espionage for the wholesale theft of American technological secrets. As was aptly stated by Ms. Sheila Jackson Lee in the hearing before the Subcommittee on Immigration, Border Security, and Claims, Committee on the Judiciary back in 2005:

> Foreign access to sensitive information with both military and conventional applications has eroded the United States military advantage and the greater US intelligence community's ability to provide information to policymakers and undercut US industry … New electronic devices have vastly simplified the illegal retrieval of storage information, of massive amounts of information, including trade secrets and proprietary data. Globalization has mixed foreign and American companies in ways that have made it difficult to protect the technologies that these firms develop or acquire, particularly when that technology is required for overseas operation. Lastly, sophisticated information systems that store and transmit data have become increasingly vulnerable to cyber attacks.[13]

The larger and more complex the systems are, the greater is the need for numerous complex firewall systems to be installed, maintained, and constantly monitored. Also, the more complex, the greater the possibility is that a way will be found to get in and steal data from the system.

REFERENCES

1. The Interagency OPSEC Support Staff, *Intelligence Threat Handbook*, IOSS, Washington, D.C., *April 1996* (revised May 1996).
2. U.S. Army Training and Doctrine Command, Concept for information operations (Final Draft), TRADOC Pamphlet 525-XX May 5, 1994.
3. Madsen, Wayne, Intelligence agency threats to computer security, *International Journal of Intelligence and Counterintelligence*, 6:4, Winter 1993.
4. DeGenaro, William, How foreign spies are destroying U.S. jobs, *Presentation to the Fifth National OPSEC Conference*, McLean, VA, May 1995.
5. Office of the Manager, National Communications System, The electronic intrusion threat to National Security/Emergency Preparedness (NS/EP) telecommunications, Arlington, VA: OMNCS, December 1994, E-1.
6. Christy, Jim, Special Agent, Air Force Office of Special Investigations, Briefing on countering the computer intrusion threat, September 26, 1994.
7. Barrett, Randy, Spy-grade satellite pix, anyone? *Washington Technology*, March 24, 1994, p. 4.
8. Armani, Robin, Testimony on commercial remote sensing before the Senate Select Committee on Intelligence November 17, 1993.
9. Gupta, Vipin, New satellite images for sale: the opportunities and risks ahead, *International Security*, 20:1, Spring 1995, pp. 102–109.
10. Fact Sheet, *ICE Arms and Strategic Technology Investigations*, U.S. Customs and Immigration Enforcement (ICE), Washington, D.C., October 1, 2005.
11. U.S. Department of Justice, United States Attorney, Eastern District of Wisconsin, News Release, Manitowoc Resident Sentenced to Prison for Exporting Restricted Electronic Components to China, January 19, 2006.
12. U.S. Department of Justice, United States Attorney, Eastern District of Wisconsin, News Release, Manitowoc Resident Sentenced to Prison for Exporting Restricted Electronic Components to China, December 22, 2005.
13. Hearing before the Subcommittee on Immigration, Border Security, and Claims, Committee on the Judiciary, Sources and methods of foreign nationals engaged in economic and military espionage, House of Representatives, 109th Congress, First Session, document serial no. 109-58, Washington, D.C., September 15, 2005.

8 The Intelligence Cycle and Collection Effort

Whether it is your competition, your opposition, or just a "gut feeling" that someone is targeting you and your organization for information, it is not a haphazard approach if they intend to really glean your information. It might be called opposition research (politicians do it all the time when running for office), economic espionage, industrial espionage, or another name, but the goal is the same: getting information. In terms of this book, consider that China is your only opposition, and that they are willing to do everything possible to obtain your information. As such, they will use the basic intelligence cycle and its resulting collection effort in targeting your company, those companies that are subcontractors, those suppliers, those equipment manufacturers you deal with, and also your customers, all in order to learn your secrets.

So, be forewarned and consider carefully the thought process that goes into planning for the collection of information. China is most adept at detailing what they are looking for in terms of a baseline intelligence cycle process.

The actual collection of information could be by highly trained individuals, a lowly tourist, a student or a businessman, a trade mission representation, an exchange official, a trainee with the company, or a subject matter expert working at a medium- to high-level job within the organization. For China, though, it is mostly volunteers, those Chinese or others of Chinese descent, who are collecting your information. Certainly, there are those professionals who enter the scene, but they are in a minority.

No matter who has the knowledge or access to the information, and no matter what level of protection has been afforded that information, if the information was—at one time or another—identified as being of interest or of a specific value, it was then put onto a collection list and became part of the intelligence cycle in terms of desired information. Where the information was positioned on the list was determined by a number of factors including how critical it is to current short-range planning, its sensitivity, how difficult it is to obtain, where it is currently (or believed to be) located, how and where does it fit in with current political and economic thinking and planning, its short- and long-term value, and who or what types of individuals can be assigned to collect it.

In this regard, experts in the field who work full-time in the subject areas provided assistance. Intellectuals, manufacturers, designers, scientists, engineers, agro-chemical specialists, and a myriad of others have contributed to the first part of the cycle. But, more than most, there is at some point, a national-level decision made to target the information. It might be a very generic statement, like "we need to move to the forefront in communications development and technology."

From this statement, a general set of requirements would be made: (a) What do we currently know in relation to the technological advanced nations? (b) What are they doing that we could be doing? (c) Who is doing it and where are they located? (d) How much do we know about the company's research and development (R&D) efforts, on the basis of studies, reports, and so on? Is there any corporate information publicly available? (e) What types of job openings do they have and what specialties are they looking for? This list would continue to expand with various levels of finite questions until a complete package of questions is enumerated and prioritized, and then the work will begin in terms of answering the initial generic statement.

When all is said and done, the information is fitted into the intelligence collection cycle from whence it will be determined which collectors will be assigned to that specific project. Realize, up front, that such collectors can be at any level and may well have a number of projects they are working on. In some cases, such projects are very specific and the new collection requirement(s) can be neatly folded into their current assignments. In other cases, a shotgun approach could be used because the information may well reside in a number of places and, sooner or later, any one of a number of collectors may come across it, directly or inadvertently.

In the final collection effort, the information may not have been targeted by a specific collector, but just found buried among other items the collector is looking for. Such a collector would not dismiss it because the information was not on his "list," but it would be gathered and forwarded with other information up the line.

To understand this in the overall process, the following highlights the intelligence collection activities and the disciplines.

DEFINING INTELLIGENCE*

Intelligence is the product that results from the collection, collation, evaluation, analysis, integration, and interpretation of information. It is a specialized process that provides information necessary for China to further its national and economic interests. One of the most important functions of intelligence is the reduction of the ambiguity that is inherent in the observation of external activities. In the most obvious case, China seeks information concerning political, economic, and military capabilities; proprietary data; or other matters that can directly affect or threaten its own national security, military strength, and economic stability and growth. Simply defined, then, intelligence is information that has been analyzed and refined so that it is useful to policymakers in making specific decisions.

The Federal Bureau of Investigation and the other organizations that make up the US Intelligence Community use the term *intelligence* in three different ways:

1. Intelligence is a *product* that consists of information that has been refined to meet the needs of policymakers.
2. Intelligence is also a *process* through which that information is identified, collected, and analyzed.
3. Intelligence refers to both the individual *organizations* that shape raw data into a finished intelligence product for the benefit of decision makers and the larger *community* of these organizations.

China has the same concept in use. In each of these cases, the information sought may provide an edge and might allow China to implement a well-developed strategy to reach its goals. In most cases, the development of an intelligence product involves collecting information from a number of different sources. In some cases, information may be disseminated immediately upon collection on the basis of operational necessity and potential impact on current events within the military, political, or economic areas.

The raw intelligence is usually based on fragmentary information about current events and may contain substantial inaccuracies or uncertainties that must be resolved through subsequent report and analysis. Finished intelligence products contain information that is compared, analyzed, and weighted to allow the development of conclusions. Finished intelligence refers to data produced through the analytical review of the collected information maintained in the intelligence process.

* Much of the information, in whole or part, in the remaining sections of this chapter is derived from the *Operations Security: Intelligence Threat Handbook* (The Interagency OPSEC Support Staff, *Operations Security Intelligence Threat Handbook*, 1055, Washington, DC, April 1996, Revised May 1996). As appropriate, data have been customized to meet the needs of this book, mainly the Chinese effort to acquire U.S. economic secrets.

The intelligence process confirms a fact or set of facts through a multiplicity of sources to reduce the chance of erroneous conclusions and susceptibility to deception.

Intelligence can be divided into strategic and operational intelligence. Strategic intelligence provides policymakers with the information needed to make national policies or decisions of long-lasting importance. This type of collection often requires integrating other information concerning politics, military affairs, economics, societal interactions, and technological developments. It typically evolves over a longer period and results in the development of studies and estimates. Operational intelligence is concerned with current or near-term events and can be used to determine the current and projected capability of a program or operation on an ongoing basis. It does not result in long-term projections.

The intelligence cycle is the process through which intelligence is obtained, produced, and made available to users. In depicting this cycle, let's look at the US Intelligence Community's use of a five-step process. China and other nations may describe this cycle differently; however, the process is largely the same. The steps in the intelligence cycle are depicted in Figure 8.1.

The intelligence cycle steps include planning, requirements, and direction; collection; processing and analysis; production; and dissemination.

a. *Planning, Requirements, and Direction.* This initial step involves the overall development and management of the entire intelligence effort, from the identification of a need for data to the final delivery of the intelligence product to the consumer. The process consists of identifying, prioritizing, and validating intelligence collection requirements; translating those requirements into observables; preparing collection plans; issuing requests for information collection, production, and dissemination; and continuously monitoring the availability of collected data. In this step, specific collection capabilities are tasked, based on the type of information required, the susceptibility of the targeted activity to various types of collection activity, and the availability of collection assets.
b. *Collection.* Step 2 of the process includes both the acquisition of information and then transmitting such collected information to those people who will process it and produce a final product or products. The collection process encompasses the management of various activities, including developing collection guidelines that ensure optimal use of available resources. These requirements are developed based upon the needs and requirements of the potential consumers, which could be a Chinese manufacturer, academic institution, R&D facility, the military, or one of the political organs of the government. On the basis of identified intelligence, the requirements collection activities are given tasks on what information to collect. These tasks are generally redundant and may use a number of different intelligence disciplines for collection activities. Tasking redundancy compensates for and ensures against the potential loss or failure of a given collection asset. It ensures that the

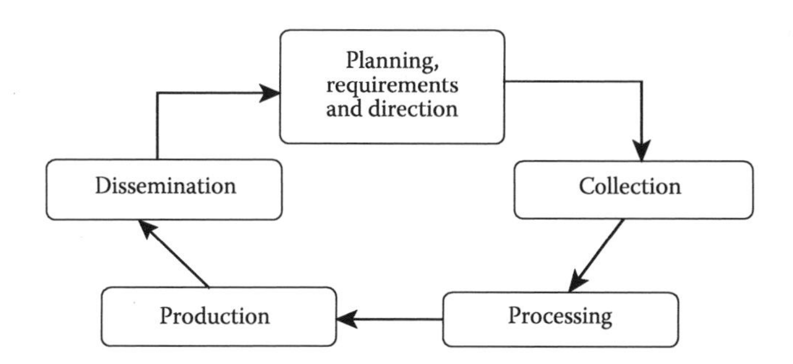

FIGURE 8.1 The intelligence collection process.

failure of a collection asset is compensated for by duplicate or different assets capable of answering the collection need. The use of different types of collection systems contributes to redundancy. It also allows the collection of different types of information that can be used to confirm or disprove potential assessments. Collection operations would typically be a "bottom–up" process, which means that the information is sent vertically instead of laterally to the recipient processing and analysis center. It is not passed back and forth for review by others. Unlike intelligence collection during wartime, it is not critical that it be rapid, but only that it be redundant to maximize success and should have a reliable system of communication to allow for the information to be forwarded for processing.

c. *Processing and Analysis.* Here is where collected information is converted into a form suitable for analysis. Incoming information is converted into formats that can be readily used by various analysts to produce usable data. The more specialized the data, the more likely that subject matter specialists, engineers, chemists, academia, and the like will study it in order to produce viable detailed analysis and comparison with other information to ensure its accuracy and potential use. Other types of processing include video production, photographic processing, and correlation of information collected by technical intelligence platforms.
d. *Production.* This step processes the information with further analysis, evaluation, interpretation, and then integration of the raw data and information into finished intelligence products for known or anticipated purposes and applications. The product may be developed from a single source or from multiple collection activities and databases. To be effective, it becomes necessary that the intelligence production *must* focus on the consumer's needs. It should be objective, timely, and, most importantly, accurate. As part of the process, the elimination of information that is redundant, erroneous, or inapplicable to the requirements of its intended recipient will be undertaken by subject matter specialists. As a result, it may be determined that additional collection efforts are necessary to fill in any gaps left by previous collection or existing intelligence databases. The final product must provide the consumer or end user with an understanding of the subject area and draw analytical conclusions supported by available data.
e. *Dissemination.* This final step is getting the finished product to the consumer in a usable form. Depending upon the consumer needs and requirements, the final product will be provided in a wide range of formats including verbal reports, written reports, imagery products, and databases. Dissemination is accomplished through physical exchanges of data and through interconnected data and communications networks.

COLLECTION DISCIPLINES

There are five basic intelligence information sources, or collection disciplines. Below is a quick summary of each, followed by an in-depth discussion of them.

1. Signals intelligence (SIGINT) includes information derived from intercepted communications, radar, and telemetry.
2. Imagery intelligence (IMINT) includes both overhead and ground imagery.
3. Measurement and signature intelligence (MASINT) refers to intelligence data technically derived using means other than imagery and SIGINT. It employs a broad group of disciplines including nuclear, optical, radiofrequency, acoustics, seismic, and materials sciences. Examples of MASINT include the distinctive radar signatures of specific types of aircraft or new missile system.
4. Human-source intelligence (HUMINT) involves clandestine and overt collection techniques to obtain information. Some of the principal types of collection associated with HUMINT include the following:

   a. Clandestine sources collecting information (including photography, documents, and other material) of value.
   b. Overt data collection by individuals assigned to or working for the US government, its varied contractor companies, and those in the private sector wherein the company has information or a product or does R&D in areas of interest to China.
   c. The debriefing of people who have traveled abroad or have access to foreign information.
5. Open-source information is publicly available information appearing in print or electronic form. It may be transmitted by radio, television, and newspapers, or it may be distributed through commercial databases, graphics, drawings, magazines, or books.

It is important to understand that information from collection sources is information, not intelligence. Raw information is often incomplete or—when taken out of context or without understanding its origin and purpose—possibly misleading. It can be subject to misinterpretation, or just plain wrong. Information becomes intelligence only through its processing, exploitation, and analysis.

All these intelligence disciplines are used by the Chinese and their agents, front companies, allies, or co-opted individuals, to acquire information. The known disciplines the People's Republic of China (PRC) will use include human intelligence (HUMINT), signals intelligence (SIGINT), imagery intelligence (IMINT), measurement and signatures intelligence (MASINT), and open-source intelligence (OSINT).

Open-source intelligence is the surest source of general and sometimes specific information in China's success in targeting the United States because of the openness of the American society. Technical and professional journals are often lucrative sources for information concerning government and commercial activities in the United States. In recent years, the growing number of online databases has increased the capacity for China to develop and create tailored data products on US government and industry activities. Through the use of such databases, China can review large quantities of information in very short periods. Search parameters used for these databases can be structured to extract only pertinent information for analysis.

The open-source collection effort by China becomes more of a threat as a greater amount of information becomes electronically accessible. Every information technology manager needs to become aware of China's potential for open-source collection against their activities and must ensure that protective countermeasures are developed to prevent inadvertent compromise of program activities through publication of data in publicly available media. So the company puts up the latest firewall. That's great, but as soon as the new firewall is known, hundreds of Chinese hackers (if not more) will begin their attempts to break through it using brute force attacks or subtle probing for possible problem areas within the program itself, or they may look for ways to circumvent the firewall altogether.

Even though over 80% of all data collection is from open-source literature and the news media, the Chinese collection effort will also utilize and make maximum use of its IMINT, SIGINT, and MASINT capabilities to obtain the more difficult data that could not be easily acquired otherwise. These collection capabilities, however, are only limited by the technological capabilities that China possesses. China's advances in these three areas have changed dramatically in the last few decades; hence, there is tremendous potential in the area of collection. Not realized by the average person is that various SIGINT technologies are proliferating throughout the world and are being sold by a wide variety of suppliers to numerous nations, and China will be at the top of the list to obtain the latest and put it into immediate use.

Imagery products are becoming more readily available as such commercial products that can approach the quality of Western nation collection systems become available for sale. MASINT, however, up until the last decade, was still a relatively arcane collection discipline and only a limited number of nations had access to such collection capabilities, China being one of them. The following discusses each collection discipline and the type of information collected.

HUMINT

Human intelligence is derived from human sources, that is, people, either acting on their own, or being directed by someone else. To the public, HUMINT remains synonymous with espionage and clandestine activities, yet, in reality, most HUMINT collection is performed by overt collectors such as diplomats and military attaches around the world. China may be the exception to this, as they employ, in one fashion or another, a vast amount of HUMINT individuals, of which a very small portion (probably anywhere from 5% to 15%) are professionals. The rest come from business travelers, students studying abroad, "overseas" Chinese, and visitors making trips to the United States. For China, it remains the mainstay of their collection activities. HUMINT includes overt, sensitive, and clandestine activities and the individuals who exploit, control, supervise, or support these sources.

Overt activities are performed openly. These collectors of your sensitive corporate information can include military attaches, diplomatic personnel, and members of official delegations, among others. Their activities will include exploiting unclassified publications, conference materials, and Congressional hearings, and debriefing travelers who have traveled to the United States or to another country where the information has been transferred, or wherever there is similar technology available. As long as valued information can be obtained for China, someone representing the PRC will soon be there in an attempt to collect it for China's use. Sensitive HUMINT activities may depend upon the same methods as overt activities; however, the sponsor (which in China's case will be the military or some other government organization directly coordinating the collection effort) of the activity must be protected from disclosure. In this regard, China goes to great lengths to distance itself from the admission or even implication they are conducting espionage. Thus, in many cases, direction of the collection activity is performed by an individual that cannot be directly tied to the Chinese government, such as a private business, an individual "acting on his own," a student, or a visitor. None seem to have direct ties to the PRC and its intelligence gathering process, but if the person could be backtracked, the source of any tasking would certainly have the imprint of senior PRC officials or some agency.

Clandestine HUMINT sources will include those agents who have been recruited or have volunteered to provide information to China. They also include those foreign nationals who successfully infiltrate an organization with a cover story. The latter cases are not rare for China since they use literally thousands of "stand-alone" individuals who have come to the United States under various guises such as students, business individuals, trade representatives, accredited press, or other guises. Once in the United States, over time they will work themselves into positions that allow them to gather political, technical, or economic information.

The operation of more sensitive collection systems will require a number of support personnel, and some of these personnel are likely to be intelligence collectors. Collectors in these situations are those who have been specially trained to collect specific types of data. Many may well enjoy the advantages of diplomatic immunity, working out of an embassy or consulate. It is also likely that such personnel will attempt to obtain intelligence through observation of facilities, through meetings with numerous ethnic Chinese (to include the "overseas" Chinese), students, and the like, plus the elicitation of information from facility personnel when they have an opportunity to take a factory tour, and from the collection of generally available documentation.

Over the past few decades, there has been an explosion of more technical intelligence capabilities; nevertheless, HUMINT still provides information that even the most proficient technical collector vehicles cannot, such as access to internal memoranda and to that information held within close-hold, limited access facilities where human contact is necessary to see it. Most importantly, though, is the fact that human collectors have the ability to provide key insights into the thoughts and intentions of the individuals working on a project, whereas technical collection systems can be limited in their determination of capabilities. HUMINT can be used to reveal plans and intentions, or uncover scientific and weapons developments before they are used or are even detected by technical collection systems. HUMINT also can provide documentary evidence such as blueprints of facilities, copies of adversary plans, or copies of diplomatic or policy documents. These are not readily accessible by other means. Finally, HUMINT is extremely cost-effective when compared with technical collection systems and does not require a significant technological production base for support.

SIGINT

Signals intelligence is derived from signal intercepts comprising, either individually or in combination, all communications intelligence (COMINT), electronic intelligence (ELINT), and foreign instrumentation signals intelligence (FISINT), however transmitted. COMINT, one of the primary SIGINT disciplines, includes information derived from intercepted communications transmissions.

COMINT targets voice and teleprinter traffic, video, Morse code traffic, or even facsimile messages. Because of the numerous advances that have been made in telecommunications technology, the commonplace cell phone is ripe for hacking and listening. Look at your cell phone and its packaging and find the "made in…" blurb; it probably was not made in the United States. Almost all cell phones come from overseas, the Far East, and any that may come from other places around the world probably have a number of electronic parts including the memory and transmission capabilities; those critical parts of the cell phone were developed and manufactured in the Far East. It is not too far to assume that hackers and others are using some form of SIGINT capabilities to listen in on your cell phone calls and gleaning data. Always assume that access is possible. COMINT can be collected from the airwaves, cable, fiber optics, or any other transmission medium.

ELINT includes the interception and analysis of non-communications transmissions, such as radar. Such collection is used to identify the location of an emitter (transmitter), determine its characteristics, and, from that, infer the characteristics of supported systems.

FISINT consists of intercepts of telemetry from an opponent's weapons systems as they are being tested. Telemetry units provide information on a prototype's guidance system operation, fuel usage, staging, and other parameters vital for understanding operational characteristics. These data enable the designer to evaluate the performance of the prototype. When intercepted, they also provide an adversary with the ability to estimate the capability of the prototype. If China cannot get its hands on the actual equipment used, then the technical specifications, computer operating code, and various working manuals are the next best target, and can provide enough information to allow the starting development of countermeasures.

Signals intelligence collection can be performed from a variety of platforms. Examples include overt ground collection sites, ships and aircraft, and covert locations inside the United States. Check out the number of satellites circling the earth at any given time. Month by month, more satellites are sent aloft. Many are of a commercial nature, but a lot are from government facilities that can monitor transmissions from communications satellites, as well as terrestrial facilities. This is particularly important because many international transmissions originating in the United States are dependent on communications satellites for passage overseas. Communications satellites supporting the transmission of US government, private sector, and public communications include the International Maritime Satellite system (NMARSAT), the International Telecommunications Satellite system (INTELSAT), and the European Satellite system (EUROSAT). International communications satellites are routinely monitored by the Chinese intelligence services. The majority of collection capabilities targeting the United States are either ground or sea based, and target line-of-site or satellite communication systems. Space-based collection systems can also collect COMINT, FISINT, and ELINT.

MASINT

MASINT includes all the scientific and technical intelligence information obtained by quantitative and qualitative analysis of data derived from specific technical sensors for the purpose of identifying any distinctive features associated with the source emitter or sender. This information is then used to facilitate the subsequent identification or measurement of the same type of equipment. The term *measurement* refers primarily to the data collected for the purpose of obtaining metric parameters. The term *signature* refers primarily to those data that indicate the distinctive features of phenomena, equipment, or objects as they are sensed by the collection instrument. The signature is used to recognize the phenomenon, equipment, or object when its distinctive features are detected.

Examples of MASINT disciplines include radar intelligence (RADINT), infrared intelligence (IRINT), and nuclear intelligence (NUCINT). Because it works in different parts of the electromagnetic spectrum, MASINT detects information patterns not previously exploited by sensors. MASINT sensors collect information generally considered by the targeted nation to be peripheral in nature. As a result, these signatures are often not protected by any countermeasures.

IMINT

IMINT is a product of imagery analysis. Imagery includes representations of objects reproduced electronically or by optical means on film, electronic display devices, or other media. Imagery can be derived from visual photography, radar sensors, infrared sensors, lasers, and electro-optics. IMINT includes the exploitation of data to detect, classify, and identify objects or organizations. It can be produced from either hard- or soft-copy (digital) imagery. Hard-copy imagery is synonymous with film, while soft-copy imagery is displayed on electronic terminals. Both types of imagery sources can be analyzed and interpreted for various purposes by different users.

At one time, the imagery intelligence threat was largely restricted to the former Soviet Union and later to the Russian Federation. This is no longer true. The proliferation of space-based imagery systems permits a much greater use of imagery products by nations that previously did not have access to them. Currently, imagery can be purchased from a variety of sensors. These systems include the Landsat multi-spectral imagery (MSI) system operated by the United States, the French SPOT MSI and pan-chromatic imaging system, the European Space Agency's ERS-1 synthetic aperture radar imaging system, and the Japanese JERS-1 multi-sensor imager. Additionally, the Russians are selling 2-meter or better imagery from their space-based reconnaissance systems. China can be considered a prime purchaser of products from all these systems. They would use all because various technically created items, such as military rocketry and the like, are scattered around the globe. Likewise, US companies have far-flung interests throughout the world, with facilities and test sites being in areas that lend themselves to being observed by satellites. The commercial imagery market is very likely to continue to grow at an exponential rate, and additional collection systems are currently being developed. These will include imaging systems produced by US companies that will be capable of producing 1-meter-resolution electro-optical digitized imagery. One-meter imagery is sufficient to conduct technical analysis of terrain, determine key facilities in an urban area, and conduct detailed analyses of industrial facilities. Other nations such as France, Germany, Japan, and Canada produce advanced imagery platforms that could be used to target sensitive facilities. Existing imagery systems and developmental commercial systems will be discussed in greater detail further in this chapter. An additional factor that must be considered is the growing availability of sophisticated imagery work stations and analytical tools. These capabilities will allow China to conduct in-depth analysis for targeting and technical intelligence gathering.

The 1992 Open Skies Treaty also poses an imagery collection threat. This treaty established a regime of unarmed aerial observation flights over the entire territory of its signatories. The treaty was negotiated between the members of the North Atlantic Treaty Organization and the former Warsaw Pact as a means to promote openness and transparency of military forces and activities. The observation flights could be performed from aircraft provided by the observing nation, the observed nation, or a third participating party. All aircraft had the ability to be equipped with panoramic and framing cameras. The camera would have the capability of taking pictures with a ground resolution of no better than 30 centimeters; video cameras would have a ground resolution of no better than 30 centimeters; infrared line scanning devices would have a ground resolution of no better than 50 centimeters; and synthetic aperture radar systems would have an impulse response rate resolution no better than 3 meters. Ground resolutions of 50 centimeters or less provided significant detailed information for an imagery analyst. Using the imagery derived from Open Skies flights, analysts could identify particular types of equipment by type and capability and also perform detailed analyses of rail, port, industrial, and military facilities. Although the agreement did not include China, any aircraft flying over the United States could be equipped with the appropriate imaging devices to collect information. What the Open Skies Treaty probably did not envision at the time was that the imagery cameras could also look down on new construction. Major factories in some instances required certain configurations for the construction and assembly of their projects. Knowing the factory layout, its size, observation of certain equipment and machinery that would have to be positioned before some walls could be constructed would allow a nation such as China to make many discrete observations about the manufacturing plant. Also, test ranges and movement of transportation vehicles accessing a site could be viewed in terms of who would be supporting the product in terms of subcontractors and their supplies. This was not necessarily anticipated at the time the Treaty was made, but China (or any nation for that matter who flew over the site) could take advantage and collect valuable imagery to support their expanding industrial base with information not otherwise available.

Imagery provides significant benefits for China as it collects intelligence data against the United States in several ways. First, properly mensurated imagery can provide geolocation accuracies for weapons systems targeting or other intelligence collection platforms. Second, the imagery allows any ground activity to be detected, their target characteristics to be studied in detail, and equipment and facilities to be enumerated and delineated. Third, large areas can be covered by imagery sensors for the mapping of large areas or swaths of land that are of key importance.

With everything that is collectible, imagery also has limitations. Except for synthetic aperture radar, imagery quality is normally degraded by darkness and adverse weather. This allows a targeted organization or area to use these periods of darkness for a time to conduct activities that should go unobserved. Knowing that an organization or its activities are being targeted by imagery systems, the organization can use camouflage, concealment, and deception (CC&D) techniques to obscure ongoing activities or to provide a misleading image to the imaging camera devices. The effective use of CC&D can also result in erroneous conclusions being made based on the observed organization's capabilities and activities. Finally, imagery collection usually requires a technologically oriented infrastructure. While this requirement may seem to be lessened, the ongoing technical capabilities of enhanced technology make it seem somewhat nil. Even so, to maintain the effectiveness of collected imagery, there will always be the requirement for well-educated, trained, and technically competent analysts, of which China has many.

OSINT

Although discussed in other places in this book, open-source intelligence involves the use of materials available to the public by Chinese intelligence agents or their surrogates. Estimates range as high as up to 90% of intelligence collection is derived through open-source information. The level of intelligence obtained by China is not known with complete assurance, but the author believes that it is in the range of 70%–80%. With the proliferation of electronic databases, it has become easier to collate large quantities of data and structure information to meet the needs of the adversary collector. Open-source information can often provide extremely valuable information concerning an organization's activities and capabilities. Frequently, open-source material can provide information on organizational dynamics, technical processes, and research activities not available in any other form. When open-source data are compiled, it is often possible to derive classified data or trade secrets. This is particularly significant in the case of studies published in technical journals. An understanding of R&D efforts of an organization or company can often be derived by analyzing journal articles published by different members of a research organization. Finally, open-source information is generally more timely and may be the only information available outside the place or origin or use.

Open-source intelligence collection does have its limitations. Often articles that appear in military or scientific journals represent a theoretical or desired capability rather than an actual capability. Censorship—self or imposed by some directive or regulation—may also limit the publication of key data needed to arrive at a full understanding of the information being acquired. In some cases, the press may be used as part of a conscious deception effort, giving out data that can be expected to become public in the near future while holding back other data, and providing another range of information that when acquired would lead China in a different direction or to draw conclusions that would not be warranted, thus making the information collection effort somewhat unusable.

COMPUTER INTRUSION FOR COLLECTION OPERATIONS

It is unclear to what extent China uses computer hackers to obtain proprietary data or sensitive government information, or whether it has developed the capability of using computer intrusion techniques to disrupt telecommunications activities. But it is known that such intrusions are on a very large scale. Whether they work directly for the Chinese government or the military, come from academia, or are "solo" artists cannot be confirmed, but there are many thousands of them at work daily. There have been way too many instances of computer intrusion over the past decade, and their efforts have picked up in the last couple years. Various reports and articles have come out, laying the perpetrator as China, but China will never admit to hacking.

What is known about China's hacking capabilities can be noted in the press on a weekly basis. Literally thousands of attempts are made every day, attacking US government and private-sector computer systems. Of these attempts, at any given time, the press can report with confidence from people who monitor and analyze such attacks that while a portion will come from Europe and some smaller world areas, the heaviest attacks emanate from China.

9 Corporate Rivals

People tend to think about espionage as country rivals stealing secrets for military or political purposes. It was certainly that way in the past. By the 11th century, economic espionage had reared its ugly head, and economic espionage was used for military and political purposes. And it still continues today.

This chapter is more of a discussion. It will look at corporate espionage because businesses want to know what their competitors are doing, what new or improved products may be emerging, where a competitor stands in relationship to their own similar products, and what new ideas, concepts, or products are being developed that an unethical company might desire so as to make and sell the product themselves. To really get ahead of a competitor, you must outthink, outproduce, and outsell the competition. Thus, competitive intelligence has become the norm. Competitive intelligence, when done openly, is not a problem in terms of illegality. It is when manufacturers and developers of products step over the line from simple research on the competition into what the competition is actually doing in terms of their intellectual property, corporate secrets, and whatnot that it becomes a form of economic espionage. In considering competitors, remember that China will use the same strategies and more to uncover your valued secrets.

Obtaining a competitor's secrets is derived from a strategy of learning what they are doing; knowing their suppliers and what is being purchased in the way of tools, equipment, and materials; looking openly on the company web site to develop insights; listening to employee talk at after-hours bars or during luncheons; delving into their trash (legally and illegally); and taking a company tour when possible, but the best method would be to get a person on the inside as an employee.

Some of these tactics are legal while others are illegal. Crossing the line is easy, and some companies do it. Others stick to a strict code when conducting competitive intelligence. There is a code of ethics for competitive intelligence professionals, but here we are concerned with those who step over the line. And China certainly does that. By far and above, almost all their espionage ventures constitute the illegal side. And, evidently, China has no qualms about it. From the news and a bit of Internet research, you can learn how far China, in one form or another, is willing to go in order to learn the secrets of others. Yes, the government may shout or scream a bit about someone being caught, and China will be blamed, but they will deny that the government had anything to do with it. Simple research will show who does what and who directs and controls; the links seem tenuous, almost non-existent, but they are there.

That said, it is not only China or other nations that will seek out company secrets. Competitors in your business or an allied business and even just a start-up company that wants to get into the same business as you are doing it also. You may know them, or at least know of them. They are found in local telephone books, business directories, and at industry trade shows. Yes, your competitors are looking for an edge up to grow their business also.

The question arises: Have you ever made the wrong decision, or no decision, because you had no information, or inadequate information?

Numerous businesses will argue, many with conviction, that they have plenty of information, and the information came from reading and talking to competitors, interviewing customers, and studying and analyzing the marketplace. Every business can and probably does do that, but it is when the information is properly assimilated and managed to become "expert" knowledge that the correct decisions can be made to allow the company to develop and sell new products, expand the customer base, and make more money.

How often have you thought, "If I knew then what I know now, things would have been a whole lot different?" In business, the thought probably comes up every couple of weeks. The use of competitive intelligence strategies reduces the risk of you making a wrong decision and, at the same time, making the right decision for you and the company. You don't walk into a dark cave without a flashlight to seek out the unknown, so why would you make a decision without the best information about a competitor when deciding to go forward with a new product or when developing a new technology in your research and development (R&D) lab?

Of course, some businesses might do it and succeed, but those are so few and far between to make it almost statistically nil. When you have all the data collected from competitive intelligence, you are more likely to succeed, mainly because your decisions are grounded on better facts and knowledge.

The best results will only come from making the best decisions. The quality of any decision will be the result of the amount and quality of information collected and analyzed objectively. To ensure that the information is the best, it must come from asking the right questions, looking ahead to consider and ponder any potential roadblocks that might be in the way of success.

Businesses must understand the current marketplace and be constantly looking to a better future and how any changes might affect the business model for success. One, several, or many competitors can change the long-term outlook of a business, mainly because the impact of what they do from day to day affects your business success. Who will seize the market first and to what extent will that company move to the forefront is based upon leadership and knowledge of the ever-changing marketplace. Competitive intelligence helps the company advance in the marketplace, develop better success strategies, and succeed.

A company relies on the employee's years of experience in the business and knowledge of the overall industry, where it stands now, how it has advanced from the past, and what is ahead for the future. But none of it makes sense if success is not taken into account when considering the competition. The old "gut" feeling doesn't cut it anymore. The market is moving too fast to just guess the future. Certainly, experience is important, but change is continually taking place and knowledge is the key to advancement and success, and the latest knowledge comes from a continual study of the competition through competitor intelligence.

The company will look at public information, but public information comes in many forms, and not all of it is truly public as most people think of the term. True public information can be obtained from daily newspapers, radio, television, and magazines. Even the Internet provides a tremendous amount of data. But there are other data sources to be studied. The sources and information are public, but not in plain sight and used by everybody. Look at the Uniform Commercial Code. This is a collection of business filings, required filings that cover business assets, capital investment, equipment that is being purchased, and collateral for loans. Knowing what equipment is being ordered and used can allow a person to determine what it is used for and what product(s) could be made using the equipment. The investment cost for one or more pieces of the same equipment determines the amount of use and number of products that might be made. One item might mean just one production line, but several of the same indicates a ramped-up series of product lines.

Consider court records, various filings required by each state, and government hearings where various business representatives testify about the state of the market or even their own company. Various records dealing with land purchases, building permits, and design plans have to be filed in various local offices. Environment impact statements are available as well. All these contain important information about a competitor's future plans and finances, as well as various groups that oppose the business. A pending venture may likewise provide interesting data about the competitor.

Exactly what are competitors looking for? Just about anything. But in reality, they usually target just one or two sectors of a company. That being said, some of the more seemingly generic items of interest and value might also include the following:

- Business models
- Client lists
- Company brochures, flyers, job announcements
- Copyrighted materials

- Customer billing data
- Expansion plans (including designs, possible builders, permit applications, etc.)
- Financial data (product specific, general, confidential)
- Inventions (in development or not yet patented)
- Marketing plans
- Personnel records
- Pricing strategies for a specific product
- Product designs
- Production processes
- R&D blueprints, research data, conceptual designs, and thoughts or ideas for new products or technologies
- Recent patents
- Trade secrets

The ever-increasing stakes of espionage are carried out by individuals, companies, and countries on a continuous basis. They want the data that provide a competitive or financial edge over other competitors.

According to the Society of Competitive Intelligence Professionals, the market for business intelligence can be at least $2 billion or more. All this to seek out each other's secrets.[1]

A decade ago, companies lost more than $45 billion in corporate data, and today who knows what that figure might be.[2] With the advent of the computer and the Internet, ferreting out secrets has been made a whole lot easier, and it can be done from anywhere in the world. Almost all companies keep just about everything on their computers, and those computers are attached to a system and, in some form or fashion, to the Internet. There may be firewalls, but hackers and corporate spies versed in computer technology can slowly break down all except for the most powerful firewalls in order to obtain secrets.

Let's look at an example of economic espionage between two companies.

Each company has a large computer network, staffed by information technology (IT) professionals with a background in computer security. These companies are also connected to the Internet, and when so, they usually (but not always) restrict who can download certain information, who can copy onto disks certain materials, or who can even print out data. The limitations can be put into motion, but then, there is a problem. It takes "time" to get the materials and jump through all the hoops, so, just perhaps, people take shortcuts.

Joe, over development, needs something that is used by engineers, but he will have to get permission or a special password and have his access approved for a short period. So he walks over to Rick and asks a favor of him. Rick complies, because he had the same type of problem just a month or so ago, and someone did him a favor. They saved time and effort, and he told nobody what happened. The problem here is what else was obtained at the same time. Joe saw Rick type in his password for some project data. Joe remembered it long enough to write it down. Now he has access to a whole bunch of data from Rick, and Rick doesn't know about it. Joe could jump onto his own computer and get more information, but then the IT security people would notice that his computer was accessing information not authorized. So Joe goes to Rick's computer at lunch time or after work, or whenever Rick is not around, and browses the site and finds what he wants and also some other interesting data, and then Joe downloads it all because he knows Rick is authorized to do so. Further, he copies it onto a disk.

And Joe doesn't worry because Rick is the person that people are going to talk to, not him. For now, and perhaps forever, Joe feels safe, so he slips the disk into his coat pocket, closes out the file, and leaves as if nothing had happened.

In two months, Joe is going to quit the firm and move to another company where he will be getting a promotion. To ensure that promotion, he is going to collect as much data on disks as possible to take with him. He will pull it off of Rick's computer. Maybe he can get a few passwords of other people and expand his data collection. The more sensitive and confidential data he has from the company, the more valuable he will be at his next job, and he will surely be in for bonuses and ever higher salaries because of his part-time efforts on Rick's computer.

Rick, on the other hand, has some financial worries. But he is about to eliminate them.

The company has a new product under development. Rick should know because he performed a lot of work on the engineering specifications and, in doing that, learned how long it would take for the product to move from concept to final design and to the actual product ready to sell to the public.

In various meetings, he learned about the costs involved, various contracts and subcontractors required for parts and materials, and what new tools and equipment would be required, and perhaps, he helped design some of them. He filed away this information, picking up a couple of sheets of paper here and there with specific data on them. All this went into a new file he created and took home with him each week. He also started downloading the product data design, specifications, and anything else onto disks and took these items home.

Over time, Rick has built up a fair amount of information on the product. He even got the opportunity to talk with advertising and sales because they had to know about the product and some of its technical and engineering features in order to start a very big public relations campaign to roll out the product when it was ready. Rick, fortunately, was able to get more information, such as rough drafts of the product flyers and press kits for a future product trade show. After all, he had to vet the materials to ensure their accuracy. Joe reported back any problems or concerns, provided new ideas, but told them he went ahead and destroyed the paper materials since he was "security conscious" and didn't want it to end up where it shouldn't belong. Advertising was proud of Joe for his concern over the new product.

They should have been more concerned. Rick was a real busy beaver. He went on the web, checked out the competition, found several companies of interest, and also looked at start-up companies and smaller ones that had a lot of money and minimum cash flow problems, but needed to jump into the big arena. To do so, they would have to spend several years of R&D, a few more in actual engineering and design development, and then purchase certain items of manufacturing equipment and specific tools related to the machinery equipment (which they could afford, but needed to design a number of technical specifications for the new product, and that would take more time).

After a while, he found a small, emerging company with a lot of capital behind it. The company was hungry for business. Joe made one call, then a few more. He didn't give his name at the time, but just dropped a few tidbits of information. Yes! They were interested. Real interested. A meeting was set. The company, a state away, would require a few days out of the office. Rick decided to take a long mini-vacation, being on leave on Friday and Monday. A whole four days.

He was packed and ready Thursday morning. Immediately after work, he headed out and started driving. Six hours later, he was in the city of the company's main offices. He got a motel for the weekend and made a late night phone call; the Friday morning meeting was confirmed.

By Monday evening, he was back home, ready to go back to work. His meeting had gone better than expected. He left a large file of information with his newfound friends, picked up a chunk of cash, and even learned that there would be more when he provided more specific product data. He had it already at his home, but held it back at the meeting. Now, he would make more money. And he did.

Everything went well for several months, and he worked longer and harder than others. He went in the office every day, even evenings and weekends. He was provided an e-mail address to send information to the potentially new employer as soon as he obtained it. He sent some, but not all. He was starting to like the idea of money coming in, all that non-taxable cash. He liked the idea of a new life. He bought a new car, then a fancy van. He picked up new clothes and started hitting some of the higher-end restaurants and other places he had never gone before.

Unfortunately for Rick, he created a beautiful hole for himself. It might have been lined with cash, but it was still a deep hole. At one restaurant, a senior manager across the room noticed him.

He later commented about seeing Rick to another manager, who knew Rick and never expected him to eat at such an expensive place. He had also noticed Rick's new car one day, and later his new van. The manager knew Rick made good money, but this was just a tad overboard. He talked to his boss, who then checked with personnel, and found that Rick wasn't getting any bonuses to account for his newfound wealth. Next, security was called in. Rick's computer was closely monitored. All the extra time on evenings and weekends wasn't purely work. He was downloading a lot of data that really didn't fit in his job description, information peripheral to his job, but that he had access to but didn't need to download. IT security found he was copying material almost every night and weekend. Printouts of various information and items of interest were also made.

Before that week was over, two miniature CCTV cameras and a microphone were set up to monitor his activities. All the video and audio were put onto disks and secured each day. Legal was called in to review the tapes and take down details of what was happening, and experts from security and IT were consulted. Within two weeks, it was determined that Rick was a danger to the company. Security monitored his off-hours activities and recorded various activities.

Now it was serious. To stay above board, the regional office of the Federal Bureau of Investigation (FBI) was contacted, and a meeting was set up outside the company at another location. Information was provided, and the FBI had their IT people confirm several details. A case file was open, and a search warrant for Rick's home was obtained and, after he left for work, the FBI went in and checked out his house. On his computer, they found e-mails going to an unknown site, in which a lot of company data had been sent. Going through his house, they found copies of disks with company data on it, a lot of Rick's notes, and a new bank account with a lot of money being deposited over a very short period. The FBI determined that Rick was probably selling information, just as the company had suspected.

Very shortly thereafter, Rick was arrested for theft of trade secrets and the violation of several other laws, both state and federal. Employees of the recipient company were also targeted for arrest. It was over. Rick was just too greedy.

As for Joe, he hasn't been caught yet. As soon as he learned about Rick's arrest, he destroyed everything he had accumulated and cleaned up his act. He's been on the straight and narrow ever since. But he will always be looking over his shoulder, just in case.

One person got caught, and the other is just left hanging, never knowing. Either way, both of them committed a crime against their own company, whether they went through with the actual crime or not.

Had Rick's venture been totally successful, his information would have been used by the competitor, and then they would be developing the same or a similar product, saving time and money, and as it sells to the public, they would cut into their rival's profits.

While this is just an example, it could very easily happen. And if China is interested enough, it probably will happen.

All companies collect and make use of information about their competitors. They take a close interest in the products, policies, and even various processes of rival companies. The collection of information is just a part of doing business, a part of the standard and very conventional market research that is carried on daily. If one company doesn't have a benchmark relating to another company's products, where they stand, and possibly where they might be expanding, then their research department is not doing a very good job.

Look at the airline industry, specifically Virgin Atlantic and British Airways. In the early 1990s, British Airways targeted Virgin with the aim of putting them out of business. Allegedly, they assessed confidential passenger information, stole documents, started a smear campaign, impersonated Virgin staff, and even tried to poach customers as they stood in line for tickets. Ultimately, Lord King, British Airways chairman ended up issuing a public apology in court to Virgin Atlantic.[3–5]

This happened over 15 years ago, but don't think corporate spying and dirty tricks have ended in terms of companies spying on each other.

The two big companies Proctor & Gamble (P&G) and Unilever have also gone at it in a big way using corporate espionage. They are fierce rivals in competition for a larger market share and also for greater profits. Their blatant espionage scandal really exploded in 2001. P&G private investigators (PIs) needed to know more about Unilever's business, specifically their hair products.[6–8]

At this time, both companies were in the process of vying for the Clairol hair care brand (P&G eventually got it). Dumpster diving, the art of sifting through garbage in search of some nuggets of information, really paid off. The PIs were able to collect reams of unshredded documents relating to the shampoo market. Be aware that depending which state a company is in, dumpster diving may be illegal or not. If the dumpster is on public property, such as a street, it is usually fair game. If it is on private property, that is another matter.[6,7]

P&G had internal security guidelines on intelligence gathering. Even so, the PIs broke them with abandon. As for Unilever, all those documents were not just tossed in one day; it went on over an extended period. Knowing that P&G was probably monitoring them continually, Unilever determined that their own security procedures were probably at fault concerning the shredding of corporate-sensitive data. They were changed.[6,7]

In the end, P&G came clean to Unilever. This author suspects that P&G tied everything to various rogue PIs acting far and above their own authority and any guidelines they were supposed to follow, but this is actually unknown.

P&G didn't get off easy; an out-of-court settlement cost P&G an estimated $10 million to resolve their actions against Unilever.

NATURE OF THE INFORMATION

The difference between ethical competitive intelligence and corporate espionage stems from several criteria.

First, would the nature of the information being sought, or actually obtained, be considered confidential by the company? Is it closely held, limited to a small circle of individuals? Does the company have specific written guidelines in place, and has security been consulted in terms of any physical protection requirements?

Second, how was the information obtained? Were the tactics and techniques used to get the information determined to be way beyond what any reasonable person would deem to be ethical or as part of a legitimate acceptable business practice or procedure, or would the legality of it being obtained be in question?

Finally, for what purpose would the obtained information be and how will it actually be used? Would it be for pure information, would it be used in some way against the public interest at large, would it be tied to further questionable information collection tactics that would embarrass (financially, commercially, or politically) the company obtaining it, or to deliberately damage the offended company?

These are questions that cannot always be easily answered.

The nature of the information being sought or actually obtained can say a great deal about the level of ethics involved. When the information is definitely the property of a company, appropriately marked and protected far beyond that of other company data, and is the type of information the company would want to keep away from the general company, that is, not freely available to the general public as in a company advertisement or brochure, implying that the information is such that a moral or legal protection might actually exist, then that information would be off-limits to an ethical researcher.

A company brochure that is taken to a trade show with the intention of being given to whomever is clearly within the bounds of ethics and can be used for competitive intelligence research. When the brochure is just in the initial stages of development with information that has not been reviewed by the security office, the legal office, or the actual developers of the product, and the draft has indications (perhaps by question marks, a concern stated or otherwise indicated) that the information is too pointed or covers something that should be held away from public viewing and discussion, then the line of ethics can easily be crossed at that point. This is a minefield for ethics. The boundary between what must stay within the company and be protected versus what is allowed out in the open for the public is difficult.

Is the company information closely held being limited to just a few people? Does such information come with certain protective markings on it? Does the information have certain company policies that must be followed in order to protect it? Finally, are those policies actually being followed? If any of the answers are "no," then it can raise the red flag of ethical violations. When the information is clearly marked as such, policies are in place, employees know about them, the limits of distribution of specific knowledge of the information are kept to a bare minimum, and the information is protected when not actually in use, then clearly the restraints against public disclosure are in place and the ethical level has been determined, and that is one that should not be breached.

Suppose the draft brochure is tossed into the trash. Two questions arise. First, should it have been destroyed in a more secure manner, such as by shredding or burning to protect all the information on the draft? Second, if not, was the trash on company property where only a private trash contractor has access? If the second applies, then consider that the contractor might be actually destroying the information versus tossing it into some trash dump. But if the dumpster or trash barrel is, for one reason or another, set outside the legal boundaries of the company, such as in a public alleyway or on the street, the ethics question might be wholly moot.

During the time Henry Kissinger was Secretary of State, newspaper reporters trolled through the personal trash at his residence. The individuals were taken to court. The result? Henry had put the trash out for disposal, but further, he set it out into the street, off his property, and thus, it was fair game for anyone to go through. So what did the trash contain? Travel plans (think personal security here) for an upcoming trip to Europe. Nobody else outside of a few people in the State Department had such detailed information.

Suppose the people developing a new product brochure had taken a break, perhaps a long working business lunch outside the company boundaries, and they obtained a large corner table with few people seated near them or perhaps a private room. Their voices were loud, and they make notes to themselves and worked on the brochure, the specifics of information that should and should not be included. Perhaps the waiter overheard them talking specifics and was allowed to carry away any of the notes that had been discarded, or the waiter passed on what he has heard to someone outside the room without their knowledge; the ethical question of obtaining the information is thus not in doubt. The rules for protecting it were broken; the information is available for anyone who obtains it to use it in any manner they desire.

There are various ethical boundaries that may be crossed when performing corporate intelligence collection.[9]

The right of privacy is difficult at best to determine within a public company, but closed and locked doors, restriction signs, and specific rules for protection of information do certainly lend credence to a level of protection and privacy being sought and ethically maintained for certain items of company information. It is now easier to say that such information is company protected and limited in its access when it is indicated in one manner or another to be a patent or copyright, as such have certain legal implications for their protection and ownership. The trade secrets and other company confidential protected data fall closely within this area and have certain legally enforceable protections. Just because they may be intangible, such as a new idea, an untested formula, a software algorithm, or a chemical formula or recipe, these too are afforded a given level of protection, and obtaining them outside in the trash area or from overhearing at an off-site meeting not only would put such company rights in jeopardy concerning their ownership rights but also would allow another individual to obtain and use them with a certain level of legitimacy.

Hence, in looking at the nature of the information, we have already crossed over into the tactics employed to obtain such information. The ethical or the moral issues of using such information are closely intertwined. A bevy of lawyers could go on for weeks defending either side, and various court decisions would support either side. The bottom line to all this would be a given individual's ethical and moral value in terms of how the information was obtained, and then the ethical and moral values of the company or its representatives in using such information.

If the information wasn't from the trash or from an off-site meeting, was it gleaned through the use of long-range microphones set up outside the boundaries of the company property? Or via the use of concealed microphones or via hidden and monitored cameras? Or perhaps from a factory tour, an interview, a news or magazine article, learned about on the trade room floor, or obtained from other customers of the company? Perhaps by putting together numerous pieces of information already publicly available, the answer was then determined through analysis of the information. All these tactics to obtain information have been and will continue to be used by people seeking company secrets.

Depending upon their use, the actual tactic used may be legal, but the moral and ethical issues will still continue to be a point of contention. If you use it against them and obtain something the company values as protected, would you allow them to do the same to you? If not, then the ethical and moral judgments are in place and you know it shouldn't be done!

Finally, why was the information obtained in terms of how it is going to be used? It might fall under anti-competition behavior. It could be used to destroy a company, drastically lowering its stock and actual revenues until bankruptcy is declared.

Suppose the information has a national security interest? Many years ago, a book was published, titled *Mushroom: The True Story of The A-Bomb Kid*,[10] and was the true story about Princeton University student John Aristotle Phillips who wrote his senior thesis on how easily one could design an atomic bomb. Using publicly available information, he got so far because much of the physics about such design were already public knowledge. He needed specifics. So he went to the initial information sources, several certain companies, and he explained that he was writing a paper and asked specific questions. They gave him specific answers. In the end, he didn't get his paper back, but he did get an "A" for it. The paper, via his student advisor, was determined to contain information of sensitive national security value. Here, the information obtained was mainly publicly available, but when put into the aggregate, it raised an issue of public trust, national security, and ethical and moral value as to whether such information should be given to the public at large.

Companies that are involved with military defense products have the same concerns. Most, if not all, have government contracts that spell out what they can and cannot release, and what information, design, engineering specifications, and so on are classified or otherwise protected under US government security programs. This protection is for the common good—the greater good—and is protected as such. When a foreign government obtains such sensitive information, it could imperil a nation's national defense posture or, worse, could threaten the world if used indiscriminately. So now, the consequences of protecting the information come into play because society, at one level or another, or one region of the world or another, can have great harm inflicted because certain defense or weapons type of information was not properly protected and held away from public knowledge.

Since companies are becoming multinational in their scope of manufacturing and selling of products, this globalization raises the level of competition to newer and greater levels. Foreign competition, as best seen as that coming from the Far East, has opened doors unheard of 50 years ago. The emerging international markets directly affect the value of a given country's economic power base. Companies, then, have to remain innovative and creative and to maintain a lower cost base to ensure continued profits and growth. Economic espionage by competitors attacks these very issues and permits one company to take on and perhaps drive another out of business or at least lower its customer base.

In order to protect corporate secrets from rivals, companies are required to institute a variety of security policies, procedures, and practices. They all cost money; sometimes, a lot of money. Unfortunately, much of that money can be wasted because some companies attempt to apply the security standards across the entire spectrum of the company. Security planning should, at the start, be developed as a general plan for the company. Then, it must be increased as various aspects of the security plan are determined by the value and sensitivity of the information or specific items within the company that must be protected at a higher level. Not everything needs to be protected at the same level, and not everything can actually be protected at a higher level of security.

Company security planners first determine what needs real protection in terms of sensitivity and value. Each is looked at for the short term and also for the long term. Short term because some aspects of a given item or secret may well become public, while other parts of the same item may well continue to be protected into the distant future.

This chapter has provided you with some food for thought, food that you must digest in order for you to see how it could concern your company or organization. Protecting your corporate secrets from a competitor is in your best interests, and also that of your employer. It is also necessary to look beyond your local, regional, and national competitors, and observe, more importantly, your international competitors as well. China is definitely a competitor, no matter what you create, produce, and sell. If there is a profit in it, especially a large profit, if it can be presented in such a way that more people will want to buy it, and if it has a potential military value, then China will most certainly be interested. So, sit back and think about what you do, and look at your company and its products from a competitor's point of view. Then, you can begin to understand the real value of your company, its products, and its trade secrets.

REFERENCES

1. Strategic and competitive intelligence professionals, Falls Church, VA, as seen on the SCIP web site scip.org.
2. Robinson, Shane, Corporate espionage 201, SANS INFOSEC Reading Room, SANS Institute, 2007, found at: sans.org/reading_room.
3. Gregory, Martyn, How the dirty tricks campaign was run, abstract from the *Independent*, located at http://faqs.org/abstracts/Retail-industry.
4. Airliners.net (blog discussions that include the British Airways and Virgin Atlantic incident).
5. Battle of the airlines: how the dirty tricks campaign was run: Martyn Gregory, reporting on BA's 'dirty tricks' campaign, during the period where he was a producer/director of Thames Television's *This Week* program, January 12, 1993.
6. Jordan, Jennifer and Prof. Finkelstein, Sydney, *The Ethics of Competitive Intelligence*, Tuck School of Business, Hanover, NH. [Case Study #1-0095, reprinted in Competitive Intelligence: An Introduction, Ghose A. ed.], 2007, Hyderabad, India; Icfai University Press.
7. Andrew Crane, *In the Company of Spies: The Ethics of Industrial Espionage*, International Centre for Corporate Social Responsibility, Nov. 15, 2003, Dirk Matten, ed., ICCRE Research Paper Series ISSN 1479-5124, Nottingham University Business School, United Kingdom, 2003.
8. Procter & Gamble vs Unilever: a case of corporate espionage, located at http://cmrindia.org/casestudies.
9. Myers, Robert H., Jr., Legal and ethical issues in obtaining and sharing information, Morris, Manning & Martin, LLP, 2012, located at http://mmmlaw.com/media-room/publications.
10. Phillips, John A. and Michaelis, David, *Mushroom: The True Story of the A-Bomb Kid.* HarperCollins, 1978.

10 Sources of Information*

Information comes in many forms, from many places, some of which are wholly unexpected. It could be a press release; a speech at a trade show; a business magazine; a flyer; the company newsletter or annual report; a Department of Commerce document about business trends; from television, newspapers, or radio; from employees within a company; from various web sites (both government and business); or from a blog on the web. Information is everywhere.

As you read this, be very aware that what is covered in this chapter is most assuredly happening today in the United States. And such information collection will continue in the years to come. China uses any method possible to collect information, including the old tried-and-true methods that have been identified in the past, as well as creative measures[1–3] that may take years to come to fruition.

The Chinese have a long history of collecting information, both governmental in nature and also for private ventures. Counterfeit items have been created in China for hundreds of years, and even with today's high-tech environment, it continues.

For China, collecting information is part of business and a part of government. It is about trends, new products on the market, and what is coming down the pipeline from various competitors. Collection is also about seeing the future and what can be accomplished—not necessarily with what is at hand, but being able to take several seemingly unrelated items and putting them together to develop, make, and then sell a new item that suddenly becomes a "necessity" to have.

Collected information may sit on the shelf for a week, a month, a year, or much longer, before someone sees value in it; takes that bit of collected information; puts it with an idea, a concept, another product, or a product under development; and, from that, moves to the next level or leap several levels to come up with a wholly and seemingly new product. But without that initial bit of collected information, the item would not exist. Unfortunately, for the United States or another nation, the essential bit of information was probably acquired illegally in some fashion by China.

People talk. Do you have a cordless telephone? In-house cordless phones or the ubiquitous cell phone and other such handheld device actually broadcast information for a distance that can be picked up blocks away by cell phone frequency scanners. With cell phones, there are several ways to pick up your conversations. High-frequency scanners can hear every word on your phone. Also, hacking the phone is quite common in today's environment. The 2011 scandal in London wherein the press used private investigators to listen in and tap the phones of celebrities is one example.

* Many sources were reviewed for pertinent background in the identification and development of the various methods and techniques used by the Chinese in order to collect America's technological secrets, whether those methods are legal or not. The various techniques and methods identified in this chapter come from official government documents. The *Annual Report to Congress on Foreign Economic Collection and Industrial Espionage*, for the years 1995 to 2011, were prepared by the Office of the National Counterintelligence Executive (ONCIX) and its forerunner, the National Counterintelligence Center (NACIC); other background information was derived from the Defense Security Service/Counterintelligence, Quantico, Virginia, and Linthicum, Maryland; DSS press releases #981210-02, #981210-01, #981210-05, #981228, #981211-0, #990106, and #981210-06; DSS brochures: Elicitation and Recruitment: can you recognize it, Insider threats, Foreign Travel Vulnerability, Preparing for Foreign Visitors, and the DSS Job Aid: Procedural Guide for Conducting Classified Conferences. Other reports include Targeting U.S. Technologies: a Trend Analysis of Reporting from Defense Industry, 2011, 2010, 2009, 2008; and Office of the Assistant Secretary of Defense, Public Affairs, release 97-S-1431 (prepared by the DSS for the OASD/PA). Other data included within the various methods come from the author's background, personal notes, and papers. Although these sources might be considered "dated" by some readers, be very aware the methods and techniques are still in use today, being further refined and updated to meet current espionage collection expectations. Further, as this is being written, be assured that newer and more creative methods are being developed and used.

Another example is the wireless headsets that office workers use. Talking back and forth, they can easily broadcast confidential information around the office and even outside for a distance. Wireless computers broadcast their signals into the ether, and with the right electronics equipment, these, too, can have their signals intercepted.

China, over the decades, has learned quite well the various techniques of modern espionage in order to collect information. From the Russians, a vast amount of intelligence collection techniques were learned, as well as other techniques from the French, English, Germans, and Americans. Too much information about the "how to" is published in books and on the Internet and is provided in terms of techniques to gain information. And China is currently exploiting these methods for its own use.

The information China is looking for can be open, hidden, or classified by government regulations. At some point, information in any of these categories can be targeted when necessary. Getting the information may be another matter though.

OPEN SOURCES OF INFORMATION

What is desired is, in essence, in plain sight. It is available for a little work, a little travel, or a little time.

Initial places to search out data include the following:

- US Patent and Trademark office
- Government Printing Office (GPO)
- Congressional hearings and their associated reports
- Federal budget and related documentation (from Congressional hearings)
- Trade shows
- Specialty organizations and clubs
- Local and national newspapers (especially the *Wall Street Journal* and the *New York Times*)
- Commerce Business Daily
- Military newspapers (*Army Times*, *Navy Times*, *Air Force Times*, and individual military base papers)
- Foreign Military Sales (FMS) documents
- Conferences, meetings, and symposia
- Technical publications
- Air shows
- Diplomatic affairs
- Military bases: displays, publicity, contracts, personnel, contractors
- Web chat rooms and blogs (search by product name, subject, manufacturers, suppliers, contracts on specific subjects, etc.)
- Factory tours
- Contracts: request for proposal, request for bids, and so on
- Organizations (some have specialty groups within them)
- Research organizations and foundations related to subject or topics of interest
- Building permits
- Industry-related magazines
- Professional contacts
- College courses at advanced levels
- Internships
- Freedom of Information Act (FOIA)
- Visual media (photographs, videos, etc.)

The amount of information to be gained from the above areas can keep a medium-sized business occupied forever. Some data are easily available; the sifting and analysis of data would be continual, requiring hundreds of people. Think of how much data China desires. They are keeping thousands of people fully occupied analyzing information obtained.

Below is what China can obtain from various sources of information.

- *US Patent and Trademark Office.* The latest patents and copyrights on newly developed technology, information technology, engineering, aeronautics and space programs, agriculture, medical, and many other areas are available to China. Patents detail out who invented or developed it, and provide specifics about why the patent is different from anything else and what it can be used for in creating a new business module, product, or whatever. Patent drawings are detailed enough to provide very valuable data about a product's construction. There are enough specifics that a Chinese agent can quickly be directed to a given person or company where the required data reside and, more importantly, to the specific company that will be developing and building the next generation of a product.
- *Government Printing Office.* The US GPO is a trove of treasures just waiting to be picked up. The GPO prints thousands of documents, some as few as two or three pages, to those weighty tomes of several volumes covering thousands of pages from the Agriculture Department, and various committee reports from the House and Senate sections of Congress, as well as Department of Defense technical data. China takes advantage of our openness in government and picks up data for a song.
- *Congressional Hearing and Reports.* While most Committee reports are published, the Chinese can also sit in on all publicly open hearings. Sometimes, data that do not necessarily make it into the final report are discussed. Also, it is easy to note that when a session is cut short for a "closed" session, something of extreme value and interest is being covered, something the public is not entitled to hear. These closures provide areas for attempts to determine what was said. Once a session is completed, it can be a while before a report comes out, but by having individuals sitting in on each open session, information is picked up immediately. Speakers on a given topic provide insights into their thinking and rationale, but it also identifies them as points of interest or for possible contact in terms of a business or government organization for where to go in order to obtain more information. Essentially, numerous links in a chain of collection can be obtained from these sessions.
- *Federal Budget and Related Documentation.* The Federal budget is covered in detail during hearings from both the House and Senate sides of Congress. Each department essentially defends its budget. In doing so, the hearings highlight what each believes is most critical in terms of funding. Supporting documentation, costs figures, and, once published, the detailed figures of personnel involved in various efforts also provide telling information. Some say that the Budget document is one of the most important since it really lays out where the money is being spent, how much is being spent, what is the level of importance of each allocation in the budget, and what guidelines and time frames may be necessary to accomplish something.
- *Trade Shows.* A trade show is a collection of like-minded, associated, and direct and indirectly related businesses that come together to provide a showcase of the latest products or services they provide, give examples of their latest ventures, exhibit the latest technological feats of wonder, and also provide lectures and discussions about the industry. Some of the lectures are general, some specific, and others VERY specific, going into great detail. Exceptionally valuable information is gleaned from these trade shows. Additionally, the amount of brochures, specific product data sheets, speaker handouts, product illustrations and pictures, designs, contacts, and other information is tremendous. I attended a trade show where I ended up sending two full boxes of information home, carrying more in my suitcase and briefcase, and then having more mailed to my office. I had documents covering technical specifications, engineering data detailing several products, copies of production designs, and a couple product samples—all for asking politely, inferring a special relationship between us.

- *Specialty Organizations and Clubs.* Every profession has some sort of organization, whether it is local, national, or international. The larger ones have local and regional chapters so that members can attend meetings, meet with their colleagues, learn what is happening locally and regionally, provide contacts with other like-minded interested individuals, and also provide for a cross-fertilization of information exchange.

Larger national and international organizations hold symposia and conferences where there is a constant flow of information from lectures, training sessions, specialty subgroups, and the ubiquitous related product trade show.

Major manufacturers may also use private rooms ("for selected and interested individuals") to provide further information in the hopes of a major sale. In all these instances, a lot of detailed data are provided, making such venues worth more than its basic costs to the information collector.

I, for example, have obtained factory manuals and technical design data not normally available to the public. A simple request followed by a supposedly convincing interest in the technical details so that I could better "develop a proposal" that could include the products because of their value was all it took. Salespeople are always ready to provide if there is any possibility of a future sale of value.

An invitation to a factory tour and sample products may not be too far behind if the company representatives are approached in the right manner. In most cases, visitors are encouraged. Simply showing interest, having a part of the subject area as a hobby, and especially just opening a business that uses certain products, or if a student, a desire to learn more to become a better professional after the end of one's educational years, will always get an invitation to attend. Outsiders are usually warmly welcomed as the group attempts to increase its membership.

Foreigners (with some exceptions because of subject matter) are very welcome because they can provide insights as to what is happening elsewhere. Again, an exchange of information. When properly done, the Chinese will agree to give a presentation in the near future. As such, he provides some insights, provides information the group isn't aware of, and dangles a few tantalizing pieces of information in front of them.

During Q&A sessions, he can easily determine their knowledge levels, what they are really interested in, and, thus, conclude where they have information that he desires.

Informal discussions after the meeting lead to contacts and invitations to their company, and thus, he slowly and effectively can worm his way into areas that will provide the information he is seeking or may have a future interest of obtaining.

If your interest is unique or comes close to something the Chinese are designing or creating, they will just about fall over backward to assist you so they can get into the inner circle and pick up tidbits of information not otherwise obtainable. In some cases, also, they put out feelers that might well provide employment right where the desired information is located, making it much easier to steal it.

- *Local and National Newspapers.* Nationally, the *Wall Street Journal* and the *New York Times* tend to lead the way. The business sections of the *New York Times* and the entire *Wall Street Journal* are a boon of information: what's happening across the entire spectrum of business, what's new, what's being developed, and, more importantly, who's who in the industry. Interviews and articles by experts in various fields are found weekly. In local and regional newspapers, a Chinese operative can target job listings, newsworthy articles about start-up plants and companies, new product ventures, capitalization ventures, development, new ideas, and a who's who of local employees, including their union and union representative who can also provide information about the company. Business licenses, public hearings, expansion of the company, and contractors and subcontractors are usually mentioned. Many of them advertise and give points of contact for further information along with their web site. The local papers provide a personal slant in the information that is available, but the company web sites and job listings are usually the most informative in the long run because they are up to date, while the data in various articles about a company can contain both old and new information.

- *Military Newspapers.* The *Army Times, Navy Times, Air Force Times*, and other military-related papers and magazines cover the entire spectrum of interest. Interest comes from knowing specific personnel and their jobs, to new contracts, to base contacts, and to the status of ongoing projects at various bases. Also, each military base has its own paper, covering what it is doing. Just as with local and national papers, these papers provide contacts, contracts, people of interest, job openings, interesting advertisements by contracting companies, and web sites. A lot of information in the base papers will never be seen in the national-level military newspapers.
- *Foreign Military Sales.* The FMS program is a government-to-government method for selling US defense equipment, services, and training. Responsible arms sales further national security and foreign policy objectives by strengthening bilateral defense relations, supporting coalition building, and enhancing interoperability between US forces and militaries of friends and allies. From a Chinese perspective, the great thing about the FMS program is that when items are shipped to foreign countries, they may not have the same level of security protection as is afforded in the United States. Thus, the possibility of theft with the specific item, or contact with personnel who will be working with the item, is typically far easier than in the United States. Also, with differing levels of security, access to the item might be easier, or the item itself might become available through a corrupt individual or via direct purpose when, in some instances, various officials are either negligent or unaware of any security conditions or resale conditions for the item in question.
- *Commerce Business Daily.* Effective January 1, 2002, Federal Business Opportunities (FedBizOpps) replaced the Commerce Business Daily (CBD). Many people still refer to it as the CBD. It provides data on federal procurement bidding opportunities, contracts awarded, special notices, and surplus government sales. Searches using keywords or phrases relevant to your business or selection from over 100 business categories mean that contracts being let can be identified by organization, and those just completed are identified along with who has the contract. In accordance with the recent changes in the Federal Acquisition Regulation, FedBizOpps has been designated as the single point of universal electronic public access on the Internet for government-wide Federal procurement opportunities that exceed $25,000. There are more than 20,000 business opportunities for small to large contractors. Thus, these opportunities are also available to China to peruse and take advantage of, whether it be shopping just for the information or using the opportunity to get in on the ground floor and provide a product under the program. Remember, in the latter case, that getting a low-level contract provides an opportunity to delve further into a given organization and obtain information that can be used to further China's own needs and desires.[1–3]
- *Specialty Conferences, Meetings, and Symposia.* Like trade shows, these events are a tremendous source of information and contacts. A conference is usually very specific about a single or series of topics to be presented or will cover an entire field of endeavor. All have handouts, transcripts may be available, and the opportunity for the Chinese businessman to meet subject matter experts in the field is a tremendous incentive for attendance.

When possible, joining the organization provides long-term benefits, the best being one-on-one contacts and an organizational directory of exactly what they do, their goals and objectives, and everybody and anybody at all levels of government and business that are of interest in the organization's subject area and its various subsets. Very few are government exclusive, but for those that are non-government, ease of access can be acquired by being part of a small business that has some relationship to the subject matter involved, professing academic or research credentials (not usually very well checked), just being interested in the subject matter, or just being a student. Cost is usually a major factor, with conference fees, hotel fees, and the ability to look professional. All have display tables from various subject-related vendors, others have full-blown exhibition halls for hundreds or thousands many items, and still others might provide product demonstrations at a local or regional factory that deals with the subject matter. All in all, for the Chinese, these are well worth attending as the ability to obtain lots of excellent information is usually guaranteed.

Whenever possible, a contact employee may help arrange for visits to some scientific, engineering, or other conferences that are unique and the Chinese might not know about or normally attend. The Chinese go to those conferences and, in return, or sometimes, after a short interlude, an individual is invited to present at a Chinese conference of "like-minded" individuals for the exchange of views and a determination of where the subject area is in terms of the advancing of scientific knowledge. While the invited individual receives a certain amount of status, will see a paper published in an international journal, and the like, the Chinese will take advantage of the conference. Since it is on China's home ground, the invitee can be more easily used to obtain information he or she would not normally give away.

The Chinese attend meetings to develop specific further contacts for the future. In these types of conferences and meetings, the Chinese attendees will be exceptionally knowledgeable about the subject area and, after a period of time, start asking more pointed questions, drawing out the invitee into more sensitive areas. Using the ploy of international friendship and the bit about "we're all just scientists here exchanging information for the betterment of all," the invitee is slowly drawn into a deceitful web of passing on knowledge that is sensitive, protected, or even classified. The Chinese would have no qualms about bringing up sensitive topics and then showing their abilities and passing on information they have previously obtained to further ingratiate themselves with the invitee. With the appropriate question, perhaps led by an example that includes already learned information that the invitee would realize is sensitive or a protected company secret, they attempt (and are usually successful) in breaking down barriers and slowly drawing the invitee out into revealing more information.

At this point, the Chinese would probably slow the discussions, move on to other benign topics as if the previous answers were no big deal, and maybe not touch on it again for a day or so.

The promise and perhaps assistance of working with a Chinese colleague in writing an article for a journal gives an openness of information sharing that is usually unprecedented for the invitee. While discussing a paper to be developed, specific areas that will be "off-topic" for the paper are touched upon and the Chinese co-author might suggest, since it is not for normal publication, to just drop the off-topic subject and then move onto something safer that can be put into the paper. Unfortunately, just a minor reference is enough for the Chinese to start further research, develop other contacts, and know exactly what else they should be searching for in order to complete a specific puzzle.

Whether or not the paper is published is of no real concern to the Chinese, since they have obtained other tidbits of information. If the invitee is in a very enviable position or will be working his or her way up the corporate ladder into greater positions of authority and responsibility, the paper will surely be published. What the Chinese are now doing is targeting the invitee's ego and status. Publish the paper in scientific journals, making sure it gets into the Internet and is translated into a number of languages. Those who read it will offer comments, perhaps expand on some point, and, voila, the Chinese have just obtained another open-source contact to further their economic espionage effort.

It is even possible, with some credence given to history concerning the Soviets, that perhaps nearly all scientists, engineers, and the like traveling to the United States are associated to some degree with the collection effort. For security purposes, higher-level specialists traveling abroad should be automatically assumed to be working on projects in which further collection of information is necessary. They will be directly or indirectly working for and with the military, intelligence, and government services. They are not formally affiliated with the state organs but have willingly accepted certain collection requirements. Their motivation in cooperating may vary, such as certain financial rewards, personal recognition, job promotions, and the like. They may say it is for the obtainment of knowledge, but more likely it is because of patriotism.

- *Technical Publications.* Every professional has his or her own publication. Some are national, with international ones also being available, providing worldwide data and advertisements about the subject matter. Advertisements, classified sections, articles, and information request cards are usually contained therein, and any individual worth his salt looking for specific or general information in a given field will have a plethora of information to be found.
- *Air Shows.* Air shows, general service airplanes, transports, jets, helicopters, and other specialized planes are of great interest to the Chinese as they build and expand their civilian and military air fleets. Besides the standard display of planes and displays, test flights of various planes are usually available where government interest is shown. All the supporting crafts, especially electronics, mechanical, design and development, air frame manufacturers, and other specialized plane features, are also represented at these events. The annual Paris Air Show is the biggest. As visitors walk through the displays, talk with the technical specialists, much information is gleaned. Since the United States produces a wide variety of planes, company representatives will be sought out and drawn out in terms of information to be obtained about the latest developments. Whenever possible, a factory tour might be arranged where other data may possibly be obtained. Some of the best kept secrets of airplane design and manufacturing can be learned or hinted at on the factory floor through judicious questioning of the technical experts.
- *Diplomatic Affairs.* The average Chinese citizen won't get into diplomatic affairs, but those from the embassies, legations, and consulates will be invited. Meeting with their American counterparts, the Chinese can at least find points of interest and potential directions in which to point their lower-level collectors of information. It is mainly the contacts made that are important. Depending upon the event, a variety of specialists in one field or another from business, government, or academia are sure to be at the diplomatic event. They may not be top tier in a company, but they are usually more valuable as a source of information because they work more with a product than senior management who, for one reason or another, will only have a passing knowledge of the product and not the specific data that are really desired.
- *Military Bases.* The military community provides a tremendous amount of information and the opportunity for China to expand its collection efforts to improve its military technology. From bases, directly and indirectly come public displays, publicity, contracts, personnel, contractors, and a lot of trash that is collected by off-base companies. Some military bases are closed to the general public, while most others require at least a military or other government identification card for entry. Most bases, at one time or another, hold some form of open house or have other events to which the general public is invited to attend. All bases have numerous supporting vendors, contractors, and subcontractors that work on or near the base, with more and more of these contractors having offices for their personnel that are integrated with the military offices, or they will have entire buildings devoted to their support of military activities. This is where simple open-source information is obtained by the Chinese. Simply monitoring commercial vehicles entering the base and noting the company represented is important. The more vehicles, the more military work they support. A base directory, a base map, the local base paper, and other information will lead a Chinese agent to determine what is actually going on and where it is located.

The supporting contractors and their personnel are sources of further information. The base web site usually indicates, via some sort of listing, what organizations are on the base, which leads to further research into what each one does. Knowing what commercial companies work on the base can provide areas on their web site to scour. Names, possible contacts, and contracted military organizations lead to further research of value.

Job announcements for the base can indicate sensitive projects or new ones. By noting the number of openings, whether or not a security clearance is necessary (and at what level), an agent can get a very good feel of the potential information that should be targeted.

Creating a list of contractors and other vendors can lead to an excellent list of potential personnel to target.

Not everyone eats lunch on the base. Where these personnel go at lunch time or after work, those restaurants and bars within a couple miles of a base entrance are places to pick up tidbits of information about ongoing or future projects. The huge problem in protecting information is that Americans like to talk, to brag, and to show they are superior. Lunch gossip is no different. Give them a heavy workload and the employees will talk, many times around a project, during lunch. A single word or a series of words uttered before realizing a sensitive subject is being broached is enough for an agent to pick up on. Adding those words to an ever-growing compilation gives insight and possible inroads for further collection efforts. Like a private investigator or other espionage agent, China would not be adverse to planting simple bugs at tables frequented by base and contractor personnel. Short-distance listening devices (bugs) concealed under a table are not far-fetched. Further, should the restaurant be owned or controlled by Chinese, the likelihood of more sophisticated, permanent bugs and even video cannot be discounted.

Military bases let contracts for trash pickup by outside firms. Unless such trash is properly destroyed on site by shredding, expect it to be picked over after being collected. Sure, it is all unclassified, but like a puzzle, putting the pieces together will allow a view of the entire picture. You may have a shredder, but if it is a strip shredder, you might as well not shred at all. If it is a high-security shredder, and the shred is 1/32" × 1/2", you are okay. A high-security shredder easily shreds a given piece of paper into some 25,000 pieces or more. But, more likely, the trash is just unshredded paper, making it so much easier to use... thanks to your minimal security concerns for unclassified data.

Recall that after the Iranians invaded the US Embassy in the early 1980s, there were no high-security shredders, but strip shredders. Iranian women spent countless hours carefully going through the trash and putting the information back together again. And you don't think the Chinese wouldn't do that also?

With some judicious planning and, perhaps, some luck, a Chinese agent could get a job on the base. Not necessarily as a contractor, but as a vendor, refilling soda and snack machines. Every base, every building, every person will, at one time or another, get a soda or a snack. Even contracting to work in or provide the services of a contract fast-food eatery on the base should not be dismissed. The more control one has over a given enterprise, the greater the opportunity to install listening devices at, in, near, or around tables or at vending machines, and this should not be dismissed as well.

- *The Web, Chat Rooms, and Blogs.* Base personnel have computers. They also have their own laptops, cell phones, and other electronic devices. They talk to each other during the day and after hours. The possibility they will include something that discusses their work can be expected. Also, cell phones and laptops with WiFi cannot be discounted because, after all, who makes these products? China! The possibility they have installed backdoors into the system to allow information to be periodically downloaded or, in the case of cell phones, methods to covertly listen in on conversations, must be a given.

Personnel also use chat rooms and blogs to talk about work, to complain, and to pass in current project data with questions, comments, and concerns. Many of these can be found by computer hackers and others with some command of the computer system and judicious use of a keyboard. Searching for products by name, subject, manufacturer, locations, and so on, can allow someone to listen in, or even participate. In the latter case, getting into a chat room or blog is not difficult. In fact, since everyone used some catchy name, nobody really knows who is getting the information. When questions come up, people tend to respond. Just a word or two, and the conversation can take a different approach. Being an anonymous blogger means nothing when sensitive data are being disclosed. This is especially true when people are complaining about work, supervisors, project deadlines, overtime, and anything else that doesn't keep them happy. An agent would take great care to help you with your problem and perhaps, lend some advice. But to get to the core of your problem, you would have to provide just a "bit more background" so they could better help with your problem or concern. You give a bit more information, and "bingo," they know where to further lead you to get further information. Now, you've made a new friend over the Internet, and he's helped you with a problem. But, in return, you gave out some information that really helped him in terms of getting closer to collecting the desired information he wanted.

- *Factory Tours*. Many US factories have stopped giving tours. From a public tour, engineers and specialists in a given subject area can learn a lot. Certain types of equipment do certain things. Knowing what equipment is on the product line and what machinery is used to mix certain types of chemicals or powders in a formula for something help immensely in determining exactly what you are producing. Product X, for example, requires a mixing of seven different powders and three liquids. Certain machinery is necessary. The powders might have to be mixed in certain proportions in a given order. If a person watches a full cycle, timing the flow of the various powders gives relative percentage amounts of each. The same is true for liquids when the approximate flow can be determined. Through observation of the boxes or bags of the powders and liquids, the observer may exactly know what product items are being mixed. It won't take a couple of scientists and chemists long to determine the exact formulation.

When new metal or plastics are created, a factory tour might include taking visitors across a small section of the factory floor. Minor metallic or plastic particles will fall onto the floor. A pair of shoes with a slight adhesive on the sole allows particles to be picked up and later retrieved for analysis. This becomes an easy way to determine the composition of the metal or plastic.

Depending upon the type of factory or manufacturing facility, other opportunities are also available. Suppose a Chinese company wants to compete with your newfangled soda product. A factory tour to see the types of equipment, steps in the process, and a sampling of the product at the very end is useful. Perhaps the plant has a new soda line to be released in the next few months. And they have decided to test it with visitors. This becomes an excellent opportunity to pick up a sample for analysis. From the analysis, the formula can be fairly well deduced. Not as specific as they might like, but close enough so that some quick variations of the various formula components and, voila, they now have an almost perfect replica of your new soda, and they just might beat you to the market with it, because they will work 24/7 to get it out ahead of you.

A lot of information may be deduced from factory tours. A tour guide will discuss the various "steps" in a process for a product, point out machinery, encourage you to ask questions, perhaps take photos—especially if they are in the photo—and encourage you to sample the product if it is food or a soda. Literature, a history of the industry or the particular factory or manufacturer, is always available. You can ask to be put on their web site, and they will cheerfully tell you where to go and how to do it. The helpful tour guide usually has not been thoroughly indoctrinated by security in terms of what they can discuss and what they should hold back. More importantly, a tour guide that has been employed for a number of years has also interacted with other employees. From this interaction, they have picked up items of information that will make the tour talks more informative. And they want to pass on this information; it makes them feel good to be so knowledgeable, and it makes the collector happier because he is collecting a better level of information that expected.

- *Contracts*. Both government and private industry cannot do everything themselves. They must contract out for a product, a piece of equipment, a design development, or a service. So they put out a request for proposal (RFP), a request for bids (RFB), or something similar.

The government uses the FedBizOpps web site to list proposals. Chinese agents will know of this, but they will also look under "contracts" + "xxx business," or something similar to see what contracts are available.

An RFB or RFP provides interesting reading in itself. Either may tell who is letting the contract; when must data be submitted; who is the point of contact; what is his or her contact number; what on-site tour will be available to prospective bidders, if any; and what services are being requested. A site tour is excellent since it allows prospective bidders—as a group—to get a mini tour of a portion of the facility. While miniature cameras might not be authorized, many bidders bring an audio recorder because they can't write fast enough. Also, the recorder picks up all the questions that are asked as well as the answers, and gives the collector an opportunity to include his or her own insights at the same time. With all this, a camera phone might be used (if possible) and can go unnoticed in place of a miniature covert camera that could be concealed on the person. The point here is just about everyone carries a cell phone and all a person would have to do is lift the phone like they are taking a call and quickly take a picture while pretending to talk with someone.

A second advantage to a group tour is finding out who else is there. An exchange of cards means that other companies are interested in the bid and might well become future sources of information because they will have other contracts to bid and work on, thus giving insight into other products or projects of current or future interest to a collector.

- *Organizations for Students.* Thousands of organizations exist, some purely social, but the vast majority (and some have specialty groups within them) are specific to a given professional, such as chemistry, space science, engineering, computer programming, and computer design. Some have unique subgroups, like research for a discerning subject area, while others, like mathematics, could well include physics, discrete math, sophisticated algorism design, and so on, within them. Most organizations have student chapters; hence, China would look to its overseas students to join the groups. Short- and long-term relationships typically evolve from such organizations, whether the inductee is a student, professional, or just someone interested in the subject or wanting to learn more about it. Some do have specific entrance requirements, such as having many years of experience in a particular area, knowledge base factors, professional credentials within the field, to name a few. No two groups have the same requirements, but most all have a student category, and this is the one best exploited in terms of gaining insight and information and making the right contacts. For students, this is excellent.

Knowledgeable Chinese students know that manufacturers and scientific and technical organizations are always looking for part-time people, especially for intern programs. Companies want students that are at the graduate level, and Chinese students attending US colleges and universities typically go for advanced degrees. These companies would want students who are truly interested in the subject area and who are willing to do untold hours of research at a minimum salary compared to full-time employees. The students, though, benefit more than the company because while they are learning and researching, the ability to collect specific and also related materials is gained. Many times, long-term interns will seem like regular employees and get the opportunity to mingle freely and learn about other aspects of the company. Further, the give-and-take conversation during and after working hours leads to a closer relationship with company professionals. This makes the next step much easier, that of obtaining full-time employment with the company.

Full-time employment means getting further on a specific project and then moving on to other related projects. In some cases, interns and other employees attend either in-house or other meetings or training sessions. Those with proven abilities and are very closely aligned with a project may well be one of several individuals attending a conference or trade show to tout the new product. In such cases, they will then meet with other like-minded professionals, thus expanding their knowledge base and collection of contacts that can be used down the road, perhaps moving to another company where the intellectual pickings might be better. All the knowledge, training, and techniques that are acquired can then be transmitted back to China, or when they leave the company, they carry it back with them to China. No matter which way is employed, the knowledge is lost and the United States is the poorer for it.

- *Building Permits.* This is one area that not a lot of people think about, but a good information collector will certainly look at building permits and building designs in their quest for information. A building permit and associated designs are normally available to the public for perusal. Certain types of production facilities, research and development (R&D) facilities, assembly lines, and others require certain amount of space, electrical power, specialized equipment, storage space, and so on. Architectural designs for buildings are submitted along with requests for a permit. A lot can be learned. Assume an automobile manufacturer is starting a new production line for a new vehicle in another state instead of expanding a current plant. The manufacturing layout, the amount of storage space, electrical requirements, and so on, can be discerned from the drawings. From this, also, is exactly where the plant is to be built and when construction will start. Observation at the construction site will provide information as to the level of manufacturing equipment required, specific machinery to be used, its general or specific placement (based on when it arrives and how it is transported into the various building structures), and, from that, the amount of personnel required. Further, the loading dock for materials and parts is normally in an open area, which means the subcontractors for various parts can be identified from labels on the items being off-loaded or from the names on the delivery trucks coming from the subcontractors. Long-range handheld cameras, small remote control airplanes, and helicopters with cameras are also used. For large areas, even satellite pictures can be obtained and used to determine many details of a manufacturing facility, especially those under construction.
- *Industry-Related Magazines.* Every industry has several magazines that address topics necessary to that particular industry. These may well be different from the technical publications that are also available for the industry as a whole. Such magazines provide data about new contracts, building expansion, what they are doing, long-term corporate goals and objectives, where they will be exhibiting new or improved products, job announcements, and advertisements that provide clues to what is going on within the company, as well as interviews with industry leaders, insights in corporate thinking, photo displays from within the company, and other items the company wants others within the industry to know. While some of it is plainly public relations, getting their name out, touting the greatness of the company, showing how they intend to lead the industry or jump ahead of others, a gold mine of information is available.
- *Professional Contacts.* The majority of the above topic areas provide leads to professional contacts. Even checking the Internet by subject area will provide names of people who are subject matter experts in the field. Many have their own web sites or even businesses (part-time consulting work off the company books) and provide articles and a lot of specific information that can be used. Such individuals also love to receive questions. From questions come answers, and from answers come more questions. The give and take of Internet web sites provides a continually expanding collection of information not normally available. This is because all these "experts" love to talk about themselves and show just how great they are. Unfortunately, in doing so, they give away information that should be held back. It's not classified, but it may be a company secret, something that should be held back from the competition or other individuals looking for specific information.
- *College Courses at Advanced Levels and Specialty Training.* Thousands of Chinese students attend American colleges and universities. Many are true students interested in furthering their own education to better themselves, but there are others who, while interested in learning, have a secondary role of collecting general or specific information in a given field.

In looking at those students in particular, the undergrads are looking to learn more about a specific subject area, hence their major. Most of the time, the major is in the applied sciences, engineering, math, and science fields. Technology is a worthy field, and that is where the greatest technological strides are being made and where you will normally find the largest concentration of students.

Graduate students have been more specialized and take a somewhat narrower course of study. The majority of their courses, naturally, reflect their major interest. Here, more than the undergraduate student, they will work in science and technical laboratories, review more specialized papers, and meet with other professionals and scientists in a related field where they can also apply what they are working on.

In many instances, they will have the opportunity to work with various R&D facilities, manufacturers, think tanks, and so on, to gain further insight, "share" knowledge, and develop a greater appreciation for their subject area. At the same time, both the graduate and undergraduate students are in an excellent position to develop contacts, make close friends, go to conferences and meetings, and get closely involved with the R&D of a product, chemical, new medical device, or whatever. Concurrently, they can collect this information, download it off the computers they are able to access, and have that information ready to provide back to China, either via the mail system, over the Internet using their e-mail, or by delivering it in person.

With so many Chinese students, it is virtually impossible to pick out the one that is targeting your information. Thus, the question arises as to why we use them. Often they are willing to work long hours, in some cases for less money, and they are very bright, energetic, and eager to help. Hence, you should ask yourself, at what price? What is the risk and what is the potential data or information that could be compromised?

- *Freedom of Information Act.* The FOIA is great when dealing with government. When documents are released by the government under a FOIA request, materials within may be redacted (blacked out), limiting what is really being said. But anyone with enough knowledge can make some fairly accurate guesses about what such information might contain. When it is just a few words, the work is probably easy, but when redacted information covers a paragraph or several pages, then the chances of determining that information are usually nil. But the rest of the document is available, and from that, a great amount of information can be learned, again depending upon the subject area.

All government web sites normally have a FOIA identification indicated on their web site. By clicking on that, an information collector can view information that has been recently released by the government because of an FOIA request. A lot will not be useful, but might point the way to something more interesting. What most people don't realize is that through the FOIA, all sorts of information can be made available. If it hasn't been requested before, or if it has, and the information was not provided, this can be learned. While the FOIA portion of the site is interesting, sometimes such items as government regulations, requirements, training manuals, and so on, can be obtained. Do not think that the Chinese would never use the FOIA in order to obtain information. Researchers do it every day in order to further a paper, develop a book, or whatever. Of course, any information collector worth his salt would also do it.

- *Visual Media.* This will include video, photographs, and the like. Information gleaned from this typically has a short life span, especially in the R&D, design, and manufacturing industries.

A case in point: a company was building a new manufacturing plant. A specialized piece of equipment, extremely large, had to be put into the building before one wall could go up. During the time the particularly unique piece of equipment was being installed, an airplane flew over and took pictures. From an off-site location, using a long-range camera with a powerful lens unit, other pictures were taken. The company eventually went to court, claiming the equipment was proprietary. They lost. Since they took no precautions to cover up the equipment during its installation, which would have included large draping material over the open roof and also protection to the sides, the expectation of privacy from public eyes was lost.

Satellites are not only government but also commercial in nature. From commercial satellites—for a price—a person can obtain pictures of a given site. The resolution may not be the greatest, but it may be the only way to obtain an overhead view and learn something of interest.

Cameras are becoming small, very small. And just about everyone has a camera phone. What is easier than using a camera phone to take a picture when the opportunity occurs. Many companies, especially those in sensitive designs, manufacturing, and R&D may have controlled areas, or at least some have put up a sign telling people to leave their camera phones in their cars or leave them with some administrative person. But on no account should they take pictures. Just knowing such a sign exists is a temptation even for company employees. Who checks to make sure a visitor or someone at the factory on some level of business actually turns in their cell phone. On the other hand, a miniature camera built into a tie clip, a button, a pocket pen, or other clip-on device provides the opportunity to take pictures unknowingly.

- *Hidden Information.* Hidden information is that type of data that may or may not be known, but is not available openly. It could fall into the area of information that may be classified and protected through government regulations, policies, and procedures. It may also include closely held information within a corporation or small start-up business venture. Such information in this case is that which are considered the "crown jewels" of the organization. Without it, the company will flounder and die. For the purposes here, consider it as non-classified, not normally available to the public, and harder to obtain.

Hidden information easily falls within the emerging technologies fields, especially scientific and technical, and to the R&D arena. Any information that can give a major jump-start to something, create or expand something, or is wholly new and will be desired by many is hidden until it becomes absolutely necessary to acknowledge its existence. As such, the smaller the number of people that even know of its existence—those who work in developing and testing it—the more protected and hidden the information will be.

Probably one of the best examples of hidden information that later became publicly known was the *New York Times* preparation for and publication of "The Pentagon Papers." The *Times*, upon receiving the information, worked closely with legal; moved to another site to review, edit, and prepare the special edition of the paper; had well-trusted employees work on all phases of the project; and then carefully kept the secret until the paper was actually published. Everyone involved realized the critical nature of the information that was to be published and they kept the secret well.

Another example of hidden information was the U-2 airplane. Some information was available in a hobby magazine, but nobody took notice of it. Not until a U-2 was shot down over the USSR did the general public learn of its existence, saw pictures, found out who developed and built the plane, who controlled it, and what was its mission.

The Stealth airplane, while acknowledged to the general public, still has many pieces of hidden information, some classified, others not. It may be decades or more before much of the unclassified hidden information becomes known and only because another nation may have determined how to create its own Stealth plane or such a plane crashes and sensitive parts are obtained and the information is shared or sold.

If only one bit of hidden information becomes known, by accident or design, then a target can be designated, and anything about it can be researched. Again, like with general research on a new product at a manufacturing facility, knowledge of supplies, contactors, subcontractors, job openings, and skill qualifications required provide indirect information that can be used to learn about the hidden information.

Realizing, of course, that many employees may have signed non-disclosure agreements, secrecy agreements, and whatnot, the information remains hidden, but sooner or later, an off-remark out of the office or a phrase overheard in a bar can provide better direction into what is going on and another source for access to the hidden information may be developed.

CLASSIFIED GOVERNMENT INFORMATION

Classified information is always the hardest to obtain. It has been developed and is continually controlled by the government or by a government contractor. There are rules, regulations, and implementing procedures that are necessary to protect the information. Only those individuals, having the appropriate security clearance and need-to-know (NTK), are authorized access and use of the information. Legally binding non-disclosure agreements (NDAs) have been signed, and they stipulate that unauthorized disclosure could result in the arrest, trial, and, eventually, jail time for the concerned individual. When the information is provided a contractor, the NTK and NDAs are again used to protect the information. Contractors also put their own spin on protection, many times more stringent than government. To lose information might well cost the company the contract and excessively large fines. Additionally, they could be barred from working on other government contracts. Hence, it is in their best interest to protect the information beyond that of what a government contract requires.

Each government department or agency, each government contactor or subcontractor, and each military service also have further instructions, procedures, and levels of security, with the levels becoming more stringent as the information becomes more sensitive. Whether it be Confidential, Secret, or Top; Secret, or falls within a code word area, each succeeding security level has more stringent protective requirements than the previous. Unfortunately, though, what can be made by man can be defeated by man. People talk ("loose lips sink ships"), people love to brag, to show off, and in doing so can inadvertently leak some of the information. Once something becomes known, such people may assume that what they were doing is no longer so stringently protected, and they will talk more.

There is so much information created every day and every year that much of it must be physically destroyed. Much of it is properly destroyed, but so much is also retained, in hard copy form, be it for historical purposes, by law, or just because someone wants to keep a copy of it around because they worked on it in the past. Such information, over time, gets shuffled to the back, misplaced, stored, and forgotten and then might be assumed to be unclassified by an unfamiliar person and tossed into the trash, or improperly declassified, and, suddenly, the information suddenly becomes available.

In the past, scientists and researchers on various government projects kept their own notebooks aside from official records. When they moved on to another job or retired, the notebooks went with them. The information was never marked as classified. The person dies, or the material is lost, and then whoever looks at it sees nothing of value and it goes to the scrap pile, becomes available at a yard sale, is given over to a university for their use, and so on. Somehow, somewhere, the information becomes public.

In these instances, it may be decades after the event, so nobody really studies it for current purposes and applications. But some do, especially if they are researchers at the university on a particular topic. Suddenly, the old information is of value to them, and depending upon where they are from (can you say "China"?), the information may become of great value and such information is copied and transmitted back to China. From there, it will be put to some use by someone.

Hidden government unclassified (but still sensitive) information is hard to come by, but not necessarily that hard. It is not like a government classified document, but it is surely protected. For the commercial intelligence collector, this is the area of importance. Corporate secrets, sensitive financial materials, roll-out data on a new product, or the advertising plans and dates are sensitive and protected, as are many customer lists and details about customers that would be of value to a competitor, or to a Chinese company considering a similar product. A lot of this can be related to government contracts; hence, companies will protect the information in order to maintain a contract. After the contract ends, the classified information goes back to the government, but not some of the unclassified but still sensitive information. It is maintained at the contractor facilities because they may still be entitled to use it, but sooner or later, it will be tossed into the trash or destroyed. Unfortunately, it is usually just tossed. The garbage collection companies that service such companies are then in a unique position to collect the older data, which are mixed in with the daily trash that also has potential practical value.

Finding hidden information takes a lot of time, needs a considerable amount of money, and necessitates contacts. Contacts are developed over time and could include a student, an employee who is hard up and needs some extra cash, or a person in a position to supply such information. Getting any such individual takes creativity and the ability to motivate the person, through trust, to obtain and provide the information to the collector. Sometimes, bribery, sex, or blackmail may be employed, but these are areas best left to the true professional espionage agent who is targeting a company for its secrets. The old tried-and-true methods of friendship, employee bonding, and close affiliation to a project or subject matter usually works the best. And it is the safest and the cheapest route to go for the information.

Since we live in a technological society, everyone has cell phones, and some from an older generation may actually hang on to their cordless phones, and everyone who is anyone sends text messages all the time. People know they shouldn't talk about classified information over an unsecured device, so they "talk around it"; that is, they hint at it without actually saying it. The person on the other end knows exactly what is really being talked about and figures nobody else will know, so it must be safe. It isn't!

Most cordless phones broadcast conversations for blocks. People with scanners can hear every word on the phone from your home. Wireless baby monitors do the same thing.

Think about a receptionist, a secretary, or any other office worker who uses a wireless headset. A call comes in for Mr. Smith. The receptionist picks up the phone and asks "what's it about?" and the caller refers to a new product being developed. The receptionist then passes the call to Mr. Smith's secretary, who talks to the caller and (since she works closely with Mr. Smith) says, "Oh, you mean the new Widget being developed with Zelo Company." Bingo! The caller has just picked up a piece of valuable information. He now knows it is a new widget, and Zelo Company is working with them. He can now target Zelo, or perhaps, if Mr. Smith is in, the secretary patches him through. Talking to Mr. Smith, who doesn't really know the caller, more information can be learned and if the caller is really persuasive, he can get an invite to meet with Mr. Smith or use Mr. Smith as a way to get into the Zelo Company plant floor and learn more about the new widget. On the other hand, wireless headsets also often broadcast confidential information and, depending upon the range of the headset, the information can also be heard and even recorded some distance away.

PAPER SHREDDING

Shredding of classified or sensitive document is a common practice. You can purchase a shredder at your local office supply store. But, a 1/4" strip shredder does nothing to protect the information on that sheet of paper. It can so easily be put back together. Further, the paper goes into the trash and, if it is not burned on-site, or transported by a company specializing in destroying sensitive office paper, it very likely could be separated from other trash and quickly put back together. So, who takes care of the trash? Normally, an outside contractor, who gave the lowest bid to collect your company's trash. If you have a trash or disposal company that specializes in destroying sensitive company paper, is that trash company bonded? Did you check to see if the company is what it represents itself to be? And do you really trust them to destroy everything? Your janitors also, if not in-house employees, are capable of collecting minute bits of information, along with the trash, and passing it on to someone else.

Sending paper out without shredding is an invitation to dumpster divers. A cross-cut shredder is necessary for real protection of sensitive material that is thrown into the trash. When planning for executive copy rooms, be certain to include a cross-cut shredder that can take handfuls of paper.

Creativity is required to obtain the information. Unless an individual mistakenly tosses the document into the trash, or it is improperly destroyed, or makes an unauthorized copy ("because the rules are too stringent and I need to work on the project at home") and then does not properly destroy it, the document is bound to become lost somewhere along the way.

People also duplicate the document or portions thereof, without ensuring that the controls placed on the initial document are carried over to the duplicated copy. The document may be copied without the knowledge of the legal document owner, and no controls are in place for the document except what the person who copied it determines is necessary. In this instance, it will be probably be removed from the work site and taken home to work on, then, hopefully destroyed. If their home was broken into and the document stolen, are they going to report it stolen? Probably not, because then they would have to admit to creating an illegal copy of the document, its removal from an authorized location to an unauthorized location, and also the fact that it was not being properly protected. The result? Loss of document and its information, job loss, and perhaps some jail time. Given all these, people will still do it.

A better method is *long-term employment* with a company. In the past, Chinese information collectors have worked long and hard for a company. Some obtained US citizenship, received a security clearance, and spent decades working for a company. During that time, they are able to collect and transmit volumes of data back to China. Other individuals, but for much shorter periods, collect the information and then either directly transmit it to China over the Internet or accumulate it and carry it back to China themselves, usually just after quitting the company after only a few years of employment. They provide it to others, or use it themselves or with others to create a start-up company that will be a direct competitor of the company from which the information was stolen. This has happened in the recent past, and will continue into the future.

Because the Chinese act as "individuals" and not as a direct agent of the government, China can truthfully say that the individual, if caught, was not working for the government, although in one fashion or another, the idea or "assignment" to collect the information came from someone within the government or working on their behalf.

Since China uses some professional spies, business people, and students to collect information, the latter two are becoming more and more the choice for collectors.

While much can be collected openly, and a lot over the Internet, in the long run, people will be essential. Knowledgeable individuals within a given subject area, such as the scientific community, engineers, chemists, agriculturists, and the like, are all useful in collecting information. Open-source venues allow them to interact more closely, develop friendships (both professional and personal), and gain trust and worm their way into obtaining the desired information.

Learning from the Soviets, China effectively collects scientific and technical information through these professional contacts. As the world grows smaller, the influx of Chinese to the scientific and technical communities has grown tremendously.

These types of individuals have been tasked as collectors of our know-how for a number of decades, not necessarily by the government itself, but through its various business-related organs that direct the flow and expansion of commerce, as well as the military and political direction of the country. These collectors of information are long-term, not ad hoc, assets. The high-level ministries, committees, and business heads control the collection effort and respond to other tasks.

All the activities in which such personnel might come into contact are filtered to evaluate and recruit assets (knowingly and unknowingly) into the collection process and give guidance and further leads for collection, which might include the names of companies, other counterparts, and laboratories wherein further or other information of value can be obtained. In order to assess the individual collection efforts, those individuals to which the Chinese interact are reported on and, if of value, a certain level of contact is maintained for future reference.

Chinese collectors should be considered adept at exploiting personal relationships between their scientific counterparts.

Since almost all thefts of economic information cannot be directly tied to the Chinese, their collection efforts are seen as legitimate activities that would not in some way identify or stigmatize the individual as a specific intelligence collector.

Bilateral agreements of one type or another, especially with businesses, help the Chinese acquire seriously needed information.

The US scientific community is viewed by the Chinese as a bonanza for scientific and technical information. The Chinese have programs to identify, exploit, and recruit those individuals whose expertise could advance the military, scientific, and economic sectors of government and industry.

Items of particular interest would include physics—plasma, nuclear, light and sound; missile, space, and aircraft technology; all phases of the computer industry, especially semiconductors and algorithms; chemistry; new metals and materials; medicine; biology; and agriculture.

The United States is perceived as the ideal place for collection because of two essentials: data are widely available, and scientists working on sensitive or classified projects are accessible. Frequently, US research facilities are involved in both classified and unclassified activities. In conjunction with unclassified work, many foreign nationals visit a variety of US facilities.

American scientists are considered relatively easy targets because of the following: sociability, liberal politics, egoism, materialism, and careerism.

- *Social Contacts and Personal Interaction.* Americans are a social creature. Even with casual contacts, Americans want to be liked and work at being friendly. They will talk just to keep a conversation going.

In terms of liberal politics, one may think the government may differ, but people are people. Scientists are often antiestablishment to some degree and see it as fashionable to rebel. The Chinese will promote the idea that science and the passing of knowledge have no national boundaries.

Think materialism, because money and belongings are viewed as a measure of success and status.

Coupled along with materialism is egoism. They want to feel smarter than most people; thus, they become susceptible to flattery, especially from fellow scientists.

Finally, careerism. This compromises integrity for professional recognition, honors, and power.

China has long recognized the potential value of scientists as long-term collectors of information. Scientific and technical collection efforts against the United States range from harmless visits to scientific conferences, to exchanges of personnel in order to gain access to potentially valuable information. Apparently, Chinese scientists are willing to collect scientific data, publications, and materials as well as information about other scientists that can then be evaluated for their potential. The reasons are materialistic, professional, and patriotic in nature. Compensation sometimes may come in the form of extra benefits, better and longer travel stays overseas, increased prestige at home, better job advancement via promotions, and, for a few, just the knowledge that they have obtained information of value to China.

Professional recognition among their other Chinese peers is invaluable. It is career enhancing to attend professional meetings outside China, publish in both domestic and foreign journals, or attract well-known American scientists. Coupled with this recognition is the opportunity to collect data that could advance or enhance the ongoing research effort.

THE DIRECTION OF THE COLLECTION EFFORT

All collection activities, whether specifically stated from above, have in one way or another been filtered through specialized elements of various government ministries, business groups, or scientific coordinating cells that are either directly or indirectly attached to government.

Major collection targets include academic institutions. Applied military-related technology and scientific data are often both found at the same place. The collection of information from scientific conferences, academic centers of R&D, and defense contractors will always be productive.

Information collected from professional and academic conferences on the applied science and technological areas will always help both the military and industrial bases in China. Conferences with such subject areas as composite materials, missiles, engineers, lasers, computers, marine technology, space, microelectronics, chemical engineering, radars, armaments, and optical communications are just some of the more interesting ones that the Chinese will try to attend. Data from these types of conferences will be among the most significant contributions to their projects.

As examples, let's consider the following types of conferences that might be held during a year and what could be gained from it by the Chinese.

- A conference on integrated optics might produce information on a new category of integrated optical devices that could be used in fiber-optics communications.
- A radar conference might help with the improvement of circuit designs for satellite radars and aircraft over-the-horizon radars.
- An aerospace and electronics system conference could well expand the known knowledge about low-altitude target detection radars.
- A symposium on solar energy conversion could increase efficiency and decrease costs of space vehicle solar components.

The appropriate information gleaned from any of these above conferences could produce millions of dollars in savings in addition to time and personnel research efforts that could be cut dramatically.

Sources of information also involve US scientists and other personnel who have direct knowledge of, or access to, specific types of information. In order to get information from them, knowledge about the scientists must be obtained. This would entail the collection of biographical and assessment data on the targeted individual or company. Chinese scientists might visit or at least correspond on a professional level and develop what is hoped as a long-term relationship that can be exploited in the future. The individual's professional capabilities are evaluated, along with any potential personal vulnerabilities and also their receptivity to any form of possible recruitment.

When possible, China (as indicated above) might invite them to visit, allowing the scientist to be observed under certain controlled conditions.

By using scientists, dealing with other scientists on a one-to-one personal basis, the Chinese increase their chances of fulfilling various collection needs. Chinese scientists have the advantage over any average person in collecting specific information because they have a unique access to both published and unpublished material through their US counterpart and they are discriminating in knowing what information is of value and what is not.

Additionally, one-on-one personal visits also provide ways to access scientific laboratories and other scientific and technical facilities. The collection of biographic data on other specific scientists, their families, friends, and colleagues, as well as data on the status of their programs, is more easily to come by. At times, even samples of sensitive materials or formulas are possible. Two examples come to mind. The first involves a delegation taking a factory tour where a new metal used in aircraft was being developed and put to use. Naturally, the visitors couldn't get the materials themselves, but while walking the factory floors, with their shoes coated with a light adhesive, they were able to pick up metal files that could then be analyzed later on; thus, just a walk-through of the factory produced the information they would need. The second case is set at a trade show, where a new product formula was being exhibited. Unfortunately, the booth personnel had some of the liquid on display, in an open-topped container. A moment's distraction and a necktie was dipped into the liquid. Analysis of the liquid that was then embedded in the tie would determine exactly its chemical makeup. Thus, the collection system seems relatively inexpensive and risk free when such little effort is required to obtain necessary data.

The Chinese scientist program functions well on two levels. It fulfills scientific and technical requirements in terms of gaining desired information and, equally important, it often directly helps the Chinese scientists' own works. This effect can be immediate and dramatic, saving time and money while advancing a career. This added incentive ensures highly motivated and very helpful scientists and information collectors.

The net impact of using only scientists to collect information is not totally clear, but with China's growing military and economic desires and goals, their commitment to technology modernization makes such collection a very high priority. Such evidence would seem to indicate that Chinese activity in just this one area alone will continue unabated into the distant future. It also seems likely that over time, and with a desire to improve their economic base, the Chinese will become more cautious and inclined to avoid any high-risk practices that would tarnish their image. This would place increasing importance on the use of scientists as collectors because of the low-risk aspects of this collection program.

Twenty-five years ago, China had more than 1500 diplomats and commercial representatives at some 70 establishments and offices in the United States. China also has some access to students studying in the United States, around 15,000, and also to more than 10,000 individuals arriving in about 2700 delegations each year.[4] All these were used to target our military and industrial bases for economic reasons. Additionally, these visitors were in an excellent position to seek to exploit the large ethnic Chinese communities scattered across the United States. Since that time, the numbers of diplomats, businessmen in delegations, individuals, and just plain visitors have grown tremendously. The numbers are constantly changing, but what they desire isn't.

As far back as 1988, it was determined that intelligence collectors were very interested in dual-use equipment and technology. Just knowing what was of interest and then going to the Internet and typing in the subject areas would provide a variety of manufacturers and R&D companies for such items. The following is a list of such dual-use items from the Department of Defense publication *Hostile Intelligence Threats to U.S. Technology*. Even in today's highly driven desire for technology, the items on the list are of continuing interest because these have continually expanded and become more sophisticated.

Microelectronics
- Advanced Integrated Circuits
  - GaAs devices
  - Memories
  - Micoprocessors and peripherals
  - Very-High Speed Integrated Circuit (VHSIC) devices
- Automatic integrated circuit and printed circuit board besters
- Chemical Vapor Deposition (CVD) equipment, especially Metal–Organic CVD Systems
- Computer-Aided Design (CAD) systems
- Integrated optics

Computers
- Array-transform processors
- Artificial intelligence systems
- Data display equipment
- High-density disk storage systems
- Internal memories
- Software development systems
- Stand-alone mainframe computers
- Supercomputers
- Super-minicomputers

Material Fabrication
- Metals and alloys
- Composites
  - High-strength fibers and filaments
  - Carbon–carbon manufacturing

- Ceramics
- Materials processing
  - High-temperature-resistant coatings
  - Isostatic presses
  - Lasers for surface conditioning and material processing
  - Material joining and bonding equipment
  - Nondestructive test and evaluation equipment
  - Precision shapers and formers
  - Vacuum furnaces, including those for single crystal growth
- Fracture mechanics

Command, Control, Communications, and Intelligence (C3I)

- C3I software
- Computer networking systems
- Telecommunications
  - Fiber-optics transmission systems
  - Digital switching systems
  - High-speed modems
  - Satellite communications systems
  - Terminal displays
- Ion-beam and plasma etchers
- Ion-implantation equipment
- Lithography equipment, especially electron beam, ion-beam, and x-ray systems
- Molecular Beam Epitaxy (MBE) systems
- Semiconductors
  - III–V and II–VI compounds
  - Heteroepitaxial materials
  - Specialized crystal pullers
  - Quality silicon for Very-Large Scale Integrated (VLSI) circuits

Computer Integrated Design and Manufacturing

- Computer-Aided Design (CAD) software, methods, and equipment
- Computer-Aided Manufacturing (CAM) software
- Computer numerical controls
- Metalworking machines
- Coordinate measuring machines
- Flexible Manufacturing Systems (FMS)
- Finite Element Analysis
- Plant control software
- Robotics

Miscellaneous

- Gas turbine engines
- Large floating drydocks and equipment
- Space launch vehicles and space craft
- Navigation, guidance, and control technologies
- Nuclear energy
- Directed energy
- Microwave
- Superplasticity
- Underseas systems
- Sensors
- Developments in genetic engineering[4]

Have you ever heard of many of the above items? Probably not. This is the science and technology of the future. Some have come to fore and have been repurposed with newer advances, while others are still unheard of by the multitudes. It is no wonder, then, if you haven't heard about them; they probably are still in the research state, development and experimental stage, or testing stage, or, just perhaps, great strides have been made, but such strides are being kept undercover because China is also very interested in the subject matter. Just be aware that the above areas are in the private sector, that information (some or a lot) may be on the Internet, and that China is looking very carefully and following the strides that are being made. And they can do it because the information would be considered "open source" and not being shielded behind government security measures as long as it is in the formative or R&D stages. Now, think for a moment. If you were an intelligence collector and saw this list today, would you be interested in the status of all these items? Well, China has seen the list. In fact, be assured that they have had the list since 1988 and are still working on it… and you just found out about the list!

The implications, then, for many of these items of dual-use and advanced technology is that the PRC is in direct competition with American businesses and government for the prestige, the dollars earned, and the possession of advanced technology and, from that, the influence they can have around the world.

In examining the open sources discussed above, you should have noted many that correlated to the direction in the China Spy Guide in terms of seeking out information. Do not think of these as the only areas that Chinese information collectors use. Any and all methods, not just the tried and true, are considered. Great plans are made, but chance and opportunity are never ruled out when information may become available. As a last thought here, if you can think of a way to collect information on a given subject, be assured that they have probably had the same thought, but they probably did something about it. That you haven't heard about it means one of two things: they haven't obtained it or they have been caught attempting to obtain it, or second, they obtained it, but in such a way that you will never know for sure.

REFERENCES

1. Commerce Business Daily Network, FedGovcontracts.com, Washington, D.C., December 28, 2001.
2. Department of Commerce, CBDNet, *The Commerce Business Daily*, Washington, D.C.
3. About Commerce/Business Daily, found at: http://gpo.gov.
4. Office of the Assistant Secretary of Defense (Counterintelligence and Security). *Hostile Intelligence Threat to U.S. Technology*, DoD pamphlet 5200.1-PH-2, November 1988.

11 The Economic Espionage Act

Economic Espionage is the greatest threat to our national security since the Cold War.

Louis Freeh
former FBI Director[1]

The Economic Espionage Act (EEA) of 1996 did not just come about overnight. The United States realized over a long period of years that the theft of secrets, whether political, military, or economic, was hurting our nation's best interests. Americans had relied on the Uniform Trade Secrets Act; the Arms Control Act; the State Department Privacy Act; the Food and Drug Administration; the Department of Commerce; the Department of Defense; International Trafficking in Arms Regulation; the Food, Drug and Cosmetic Act; the Digital Millennium Copyright Act; and other laws and regulations to protect information. In the early 1990s, it was determined that current laws and regulations were not enough. It was hoped that any given law could only deter US citizens who were more likely to want to avoid a lengthy prison sentence and large fines if caught. For foreigners, the laws meant nothing, really, except, perhaps that they should be a bit more careful to avoid being caught. After all, the best thefts of secrets were those that were never found out and where the perpetrators were never caught.

The EEA of 1996 actually became a law because of one major economic theft that was a few years in the making: that of the Avery & Four Pillars Enterprises. This case is summarized in Appendix B, and we include an excerpt of the US code to provide the gist of the act:

(a) Whoever, with intent to convert a trade secret, that is related to or included in a product that is produced for or placed in interstate or foreign commerce, to the economic benefit of anyone other than the owner thereof, and intending or knowing that the offense will, injure any owner of that trade secret, knowingly—
  (1) steals, or without authorization appropriates, takes, carries away, or conceals, or by fraud, artifice, or deception obtains such information;
  (2) without authorization copies, duplicates, sketches, draws, photographs, downloads, uploads, alters, destroys, photocopies, replicates, transmits, delivers, sends, mails, communicates, or conveys such information;
  (3) receives, buys, or possesses such information, knowing the same to have been stolen or appropriated, obtained, or converted without authorization;
  (4) attempts to commit any offense described in paragraphs (1) through (3); or
  (5) conspires with one or more other persons to commit any offense described in paragraphs (1) through (3), and one or more of such persons do any act to effect the object of the conspiracy, shall, except as provided in subsection (b), be fined under this title or imprisoned not more than 10 years, or both.

(b) Any organization that commits any offense described in subsection (a) shall be fined not more than $5,000,000.[2]

The EEA of 1996 (18 U.S.C. § 1831–1839) was signed into law on October 11, 1996, creating a new federal crime—the theft of trade secrets.

The Federal Bureau of Investigation (FBI) investigates such crimes under the EEA while the Department of Justice has sweeping authority to prosecute the theft of trade secrets in the United States.

OVERVIEW OF THE EEA OF 1996

The EEA of 1996 criminalizes two types of trade secret misappropriation in Title 18. Section 1831 punishes the theft of a trade secret to benefit a foreign government, instrumentality, or agent. Section 1831 punishes the commercial theft of trade secrets carried out for economic advantage, whether or not it benefits a foreign government, instrumentality, or agent.

Although § 1831 (foreign economic espionage) and § 1832 (commercial economic espionage) define separate offenses, they are nevertheless related. Both sections require that the government be able to prove beyond a reasonable doubt that: (1) the defendant misappropriated information (or conspired or attempted to do so); (2) the defendant knew or believed that this information was a trade secret; and (3) the information was in fact a trade secret (unless the crime charged is a conspiracy or an attempt). Both § 1831 and § 1832 criminalize the following: the knowing purchase, receipt, or possession of a stolen trade secret as well as the destruction or misappropriation of a trade secret.[3,4]

Regarding prosecuting such cases, Assistant US Attorney Sean Condron, in a 2006 presentation on the topic *Economic Espionage & Trade Secret Theft*, explains:

> To establish that foreign economic espionage did actually occur under 18 U.S.C. § 1831, the government must also prove that the defendant knew that the offense would benefit, or was intended to benefit, a foreign government or a foreign government instrumentality or agent. If a foreign connection does not exist or cannot be proved, the government may still establish a violation of 18 U.S.C. § 1832 by proving, in addition to other elements, that: (4) the defendant intended to convert the trade secret to the economic benefit of anyone other than the owner; (5) the defendant knew or intended that the owner of the trade secret would be injured; and (6) the trade secret was related to or was included in a product that was produced or placed in interstate or foreign commerce.[3]

As such, the EEA can be applied to a wide variety of criminal conduct. It criminalizes attempts and conspiracies to violate the EEA and certain extraterritorial conduct. The EEA also provides for several remedies that are unusual in a criminal statute: civil injunctive relief against violations, to be obtained by the Attorney General, and confidentiality orders to maintain the trade secret's secrecy throughout the prosecution.

As Matthew J. Bassiur, a federal prosecutor in the Computer Crime & Intellectual Property Section of the United States Department of Justice, stated in his 2007 paper, *Intellectual Property—An Introduction*:

> A trade secret is really just a piece of information (such as a customer list, or a method of production, or a secret formula for a soft drink) that the holder tries to keep secret by executing confidentiality agreements with employees and others and by hiding the information from outsiders by means of fences, safes, encryption, and other means of concealment, so that the only way the secret can be unmasked is by a breach of contract or a tort." *ConFold Pac. v. Polaris Indus.*, 433 F.3d 952, 959 (7th Cir. 2006) (Posner, J.). Or, as Judge Posner could have pointed out, it can be unmasked by a criminal act.
>
> Until 1996, no federal statute explicitly criminalized the theft of commercial trade secrets. Some statutes could punish trade secret theft in limited situations: 18 U.S.C. § 1905 for the unauthorized disclosure of government information, including trade secrets, by a government employee; 18 U.S.C. § 2314 for the interstate transportation of stolen property, including trade secrets; and 18 U.S.C. §§ 1341, 1343, and 1346 for the use of mail or wire communications in a scheme to use information in violation of a confidential or fiduciary relationship.[5]

The EEA's definition of a trade secret is based on the trade secret definition in the Uniform Trade Secrets Act. Cases that address trade secrets outside the EEA should, in most cases, be relevant in EEA prosecutions. This chapter will consider several areas, and include extensive text excerpts, from this excellent publication by Bassiur.

ELEMENTS COMMON TO 18 U.S.C. §§ 1831, 1832

a. The Information Was a Trade Secret. As mentioned above, a trade secret is really just a piece of information (such as a customer list, or a method of production, or a secret formula for a soft drink) that the holder tries to keep secret, so that the only way the secret can be unmasked is by unlawful activity. Whether particular information is a trade secret is a question of fact. The EEA's definition of a trade secret is very broad. Examples of trade secrets include the following:[5]
    - A computer software system used in the lumber industry
    - Measurements, metallurgical specifications, and engineering drawings to produce an aircraft brake assembly
    - Information involving zinc recovery furnaces and the tungsten reclamation process
    - Information concerning pollution control chemicals and related materials
    - Information regarding contact lens production
    - Pizza recipes

    In cases alleging attempt and conspiracy, the government need not prove that the information actually was a trade secret.
b. Employee's General Knowledge, Skill, or Abilities Not Covered. The EEA does not apply to individuals who seek to capitalize on their personal knowledge, skill, or abilities to which they may have developed in moving from one job to another. The statute is not intended to be used to prosecute employees who change employers or start their own companies using general knowledge and skills developed while employed. It is not and was not designed to punish competition, even when such competition relied on the know-how of former employees of a direct competitor. It was, however, designed to prevent those employees (and their future employers) from taking advantage of confidential information gained, discovered, copied, or taken while employed elsewhere.[5]

    It is not enough to say that a person has accumulated experience and knowledge during the course of his or her employ. Nor can such a person be prosecuted on the basis of an assertion that he or she was merely exposed to a trade secret while employed. A prosecution that attempts to tie skill and experience to a particular trade secret should not succeed unless it can show that the particular material was stolen or misappropriated.

    These principles are often cited when a purported trade secret is one in which the defendant remembered only casually. As an example, one court held that a terminated person could not be prohibited from using skills that he acquired, or casually remembered information that he acquired, while employed by the principal. In another case, a court ruled that "remembered information as to specific needs and business habits of particular customers is not confidential."[5]

    The court cited two reasons for finding that remembered information concerning customer preferences was not a trade secret. First, no evidence was offered that the defendants intentionally memorized information, or that they stole it in any other way. Second, the information in question could easily be recalled or obtained subsequently by the defendants.[5]

    Moreover, any employee who changes employers or starts his own company cannot be prosecuted under the EEA merely on the grounds that he was exposed to a trade secret while employed. Rather, the government must clearly establish that he actually stole or misappropriated a particular trade secret, or at least that he conspired or attempted to do so.

SPECIFICATION OF TRADE SECRETS

The government must ascertain (beyond a reasonable doubt) which specific information the victim claims as a trade secret early on. Here, the prosecution must clearly establish a specific and particular piece of information that a person has stolen or misappropriated. This helps avoid the defendant's defense that he was merely relying on his general knowledge, skills, and abilities along, perhaps, with legitimate reverse engineering. The defense in such instances, however, does not have the right to take pre-trial depositions of the government's expert witnesses to determine what the government will claim is a trade secret and why.[5]

a. *Novelty.* Unlike patents or copyrights, which require higher degrees of novelty, trade secrets must possess only "minimal novelty." In other words, the trade secret must contain some element that is not known and that sets it apart from what is generally known. The Justice Department does not strictly impose a novelty or inventiveness requirement in order for material to be considered a trade secret; looking at the novelty or uniqueness of a piece of information or knowledge should inform courts in determining whether something is a matter of general knowledge, skill, or experience.[5]
b. *Secrecy.* The key attribute of a trade secret is that the underlying information "not be generally known to … the public" and that it "not be readily ascertainable through proper means by the public." The "public" may not necessarily mean the general public. The phrases "readily ascertainable" and "the public" must be understood to concentrate attention on either potential users of the information, or proxies for them (which is to say, persons who have the same ability to "ascertain" the information). In other words, information will not necessarily be a trade secret just because it is not readily ascertainable by the general public.[5]

In the view of the Seventh Circuit Court, the information would not be a trade secret if it is readily ascertainable by those within the information's field of specialty. If a scientist could ascertain a purported trade secret formula only by gleaning information from publications and then engaging in many hours of laboratory testing and analysis, the existence of such publications would not necessarily disqualify the formula as a trade secret under the EEA, since the scientist's work would probably not qualify as "readily ascertainable by the public."[5]

The formula would not be a trade secret if it could be ascertained or reverse engineered within a relatively short time. Such measurements could not be called trade secrets if the assemblies in question were easy to take apart and measured. A Mississippi court found and held that a company's bid estimating system was readily ascertainable by using simple math applied to data on past bids, and thus was not a trade secret.[5]

A trade secret can also include elements that are in the public domain if the trade secret itself constitutes a unique, "effective, successful and valuable integration of the public domain elements." In fact, a trade secret can exist in a combination of characteristics and components, each of which, by itself, is in the public domain, but the unified process, design, and operation of which, in unique combination, affords a competitive advantage and is a protectable secret.[5]

For example, in the case of *Metallurgical Industries, Inc. v. Fourtek, Inc.* [790 f.2d 1195, 1202 (5th Cir. 1986)], when the company modified a generally known zinc recovery process, the modified process could be considered a trade secret even though the original process and the technologies involved were publicly known, because the details of the modifications were not available or known to the general public.[5]

DISCLOSURE EFFECTS OF A TRADE SECRET

A trade secret can lose its protected status through disclosure. To prove secrecy, the government often has the difficult burden of proving a negative, that is, that the information was not generally available to the public. For this reason, any prosecution must determine early on whether the purported trade secret was ever disclosed and to what extent those disclosures affect the information's status as a trade secret.[5]

a. *Disclosure through the Patent and Copyright Processes.* Information that has been disclosed in a patent application can nevertheless qualify as a trade secret *between the times* of the application's submission and the patent's issuance, as long as the patent application itself is not published by the patent office. The patented process or device is no longer a trade secret once the application is published or the patent is issued, because publication of the application or patent makes the process publicly available for all to see. In return for the disclosure, however, the owner enjoys patent protection against other companies' use of the technology.[5]

A subsequent refinement or enhancement to the patented technology may be a trade secret if it is not reasonably ascertainable from the published patent itself. Substantially, the same analysis applies to information that has been submitted to the United States Copyright Office for registration. Submitting material to the Copyright Office can render it open to public examination and viewing, thus destroying the information's value as a trade secret, unless the material is submitted under special procedures to limit trade secret disclosure.[5]

b. *Disclosure through Industry Publications or Conferences.* Information can lose trade secret protection through accidental or intentional disclosure by an employee at a conference or trade show, or in technical journals or other publications.[5]

c. *Disclosure to Licensees, Vendors, and Third Parties.* Information that has been disclosed to licensees, vendors, or third parties for limited purposes can remain a trade secret under certain circumstances. The trade secret owner must take some security measures to maintain secrecy during any disclosure.[5]

d. *Disclosure through Internet Postings.* A trade secret can lose protected status when posted anonymously on the Internet, even if the trade secret was originally gathered through improper means. If the Internet posting causes the information to fall into the public domain, a person who republishes the information is not guilty of misappropriating a trade secret, even if he knew that the information was originally acquired by improper means.[5]

Disclosure over the Internet does not, however, strip away a trade secret's protection automatically. For example, in *United States v. Genovese*, the court held that a trade secret could retain its secrecy despite a brief disclosure over the Internet: "(A) trade secret does not lose its protection under the EEA if it is temporarily, accidentally or illicitly released to the public, provided it does not become 'generally known' or 'readily ascertainable through proper means.'" Publication on the Internet does not destroy the trade secret's status "if the publication is sufficiently obscure or transient or otherwise limited so that it does not become generally known to the relevant people, i.e., potential competitors or other persons to whom the information would have some economic value."[5]

e. *Disclosure during Law Enforcement Investigations.* Disclosures to the government to assist an investigation or prosecution of an EEA case should not waive trade secret protections. In one case, it was held that a victim's disclosure of trade secret to government for use in a sting operation under oral assurances that the information would not be used or disclosed for any purpose unrelated to the case did not violate trade secret status. Disclosure to the government is essential for the investigation and prosecution of illegal activity and is expressly contemplated by the EEA.[5]

The EEA specifically encourages disclosures to the government, stating that the EEA "does not prohibit... the reporting of a suspected violation of law to any governmental entity of the United States... if such entity has lawful authority with respect to that violation." Second, 18 U.S.C. § 1835 authorizes the court to "enter such orders and take such other action as may be necessary and appropriate to preserve the confidentiality of trade secrets, consistent with the requirements of the Federal Rules of Criminal and Civil Procedure... and all other applicable laws." Section 1835 gives "a clear indication from Congress that trade secrets are to be protected to the fullest extent during EEA litigation." Together, these sections demonstrate Congress's intent to encourage the reporting of an EEA violation.[5]

Laws other than the EEA similarly limit the Department of Justice's disclosure of trade secrets without the consent of the trade secret owner or the express written authorization of senior officials at the Department. Information does not lose its status as a trade secret if the government discloses it to the defendant as "bait" during a sting operation. To hold that dangling such bait waives trade secret protection would effectively undermine the EEA at least to the extent that the government tries... to prevent an irrevocable loss of American technology before it happens.[5]

f. *Disclosure by the Original Misappropriator or His Co-Conspirators.* The person who originally misappropriates a trade secret cannot immunize himself from prosecution by disclosing it into the public domain. Although disclosure of a trade secret may cause it to lose trade secret status *after* the disclosure, disclosure does not destroy trade secret status retroactively. Consequently, the person who first disclosed the information may be prosecuted, whereas one who distributes the information post-disclosure may not, unless he was working in concert with the original misappropriator.[5]

Let's focus mainly on the provision in EEA that criminalizes trade secret theft intended to benefit a foreign power, given that it was designed specifically to tackle the problem of Chinese espionage. According to X: The EEA provides two distinct but related offenses. 18 U.S.C. §§ 1831–1832 (1996). The first offense, § 1831, applies to economic espionage, which involves the misappropriation of a trade secret with the intent to benefit a foreign government, foreign instrumentality, or foreign agent. The second offense, § 1832, involves the misappropriation of a trade secret with the intent to convert the trade secret to the economic benefit of anyone other than the owner and to injure the owner of the trade secret. Since the Act's passage, a number of articles reviewing the law have focused on the domestic provisions. It is no coincidence that a large majority of cases under this provision involve the Chinese government: it is an essential tool for them to boost its long-term military, technological, and economic aspirations.[5–7]

COMMON ISSUES AND CHALLENGES IN TRADE SECRET AND EEA CASES

Let's look at the most impending and recurring challenges in trade secrets relating to the EEA. The remainder of this chapter will use portions, including extensive excerpts, from the Department of Justice article *Common Issues and Challenges in Prosecuting Trade Secrets and Economic Act Cases*, prepared by Mark Krotoski, US Department of Justice, Executive Offices for United States Attorneys.

Trade secrets represent one form of intellectual property and are a key part of the innovation process; it is important to protect the development of new ideas as well as established information that derives value from not being publicly known. A substantial portion of the US economy continues to be based on innovation and the development of new technologies and knowledge-based ideas. A trade secret may take a wide variety of forms.[6]

One classic trade secret example is the Coca-Cola soft drink formula. If the formula is revealed, the company could lose its competitive advantage in marketing, producing, and selling the drink product. For software companies, trade secrets may include source codes for the software. If a source code becomes available to others, then third parties can produce the software, or other versions of it, either in the same domestic market or around the world.[6]

The misappropriation of trade secrets can impose severe economic and other harm not only to the owner of the trade secret but also on many others. The adverse consequences may affect company employees whose livelihood is based on the continued success of the company, a community dependent on the company contributions to the local economy, or even the health of a particular industry or the national economy. In other cases, disclosure of a trade secret can harm national security. Misappropriated technology such as US munitions list materials, which also qualify as trade secrets, in the hands of adversaries may provide a previously unattainable advantage against the United States.[6]

In cases involving aggravated conduct, criminal prosecution is necessary to deter and punish the misappropriation of a trade secret. The following case scenarios highlight different trade secret misappropriation scenarios that a prosecutor could be called upon to consider:[6]

- State-sponsored targeting of trade secrets and technology misappropriated with the intent to benefit a foreign government or an instrumentality of a foreign government.
- A trusted employee with access to valuable company information who, after becoming disgruntled, downloads and transmits the information to others outside the company who offer it to the "highest bidder."
- An employee, who after learning how a new prototype is made, decides to form his own company and use the trade secret and other proprietary information to launch his own competing product.
- A competitor who devises a scheme to gain access to company information for use in fulfilling an international contract.
- Employees who execute a plan to steal proprietary information and take it to another country and are stopped at the airport.
- After being offered a senior position with a direct competitor, and before tendering his resignation, an employee uses his supervisory position to request and obtain proprietary information he would not normally be entitled to access. After taking as much proprietary information as he can, he submits his resignation and takes the materials of his former employer to his new position and employer.

The above scenarios also have some of the common issues and challenges for prosecutors involved in trade secret and economic espionage cases. As such, the prosecutor must consider the very primary objectives as to why protection is necessary.[6]

Primary Objectives

In his Senate testimony, then-FBI Director Louis J. Freeh, an early key proponent and architect of the statute, described the significance of promoting and protecting the innovation process to the economic growth of the United States:

> The development and production of intellectual property and advanced technologies is an integral part of virtually every aspect of United States trade, commerce, and business.
>
> Intellectual property, that is, government and corporate proprietary economic information, sustains the health, integrity, and competitiveness of the American economy, and has been responsible for earning our nation's place in the world as an economic superpower. The theft, misappropriation, and wrongful receipt of intellectual property and technology, particularly by foreign governments and their agents, directly threatens the development and making of the products that flow from that information. Such conduct deprives its owners—individuals, corporations, and our nation—of the corresponding economic and social benefits.[6]

Three Parts to Trade Secrets

Both § 1831 and § 1832 cases require *proof of a trade secret.* Consequently, it is important to understand how a trade secret is established under the EEA. A trade secret, as defined under 18 U.S.C. § 1839(3) (A), (B) (1996), has three parts: (1) information, (2) reasonable measures taken to protect the information, and (3) which derives independent economic value from not being publicly known.

a. Information. Information expansively includes: "all forms and types of financial, business, scientific, technical, economic, or engineering information... whether tangible or intangible, and whether or how stored, compiled, or memorialized physically, electronically, graphically, photographically, or in writing...." These are merely illustrative as Congress intended that the "definition be read broadly." Trade secrets are not restricted to formulas, patterns, and compilations, but now include programs and codes, "whether tangible or intangible, and whether or how stored."[6]
b. Reasonable measures. The trade secret owner must have taken reasonable measures to keep such information secret. The federal statute confers special intellectual protection where the trade secret owner takes certain steps to safeguard the trade secret.[6]

   The owner of the information must have taken objectively reasonable and active measures to protect the information from becoming known to unauthorized persons. If the owner fails to attempt to safeguard his or her proprietary information, no one can be rightfully accused of misappropriating it. It is important to note that an owner take reasonable measures to protect this information. It will be up to the court in each case to determine whether the owner's efforts to protect the information in question were reasonable under the circumstances, but not necessarily that the owner be required to have taken every conceivable step to protect the property from misappropriation.[6]

   Reasonable measures may include a layered or tiered approach. One layer may involve physical security, such as isolating the trade secret to a particular area and limiting access on a "need to know" basis, using security cards to monitor and restrict access, or requiring sign-in sheets to record visitors.[6]

   Another layer may involve computer or electronic limitations, such as multiple passwords, secure laptops, data encryption, and no remote or Internet access in the area where the trade secret is used. As another layer, most companies protect trade secrets through employment policies and practices including employee non-disclosure agreements, marking trade secret and proprietary information as "confidential," training and reminders about the importance of protecting the company trade secrets, employment manuals, and exit interviews upon an employee's departure to ensure proprietary materials have been returned and to underscore confidentiality obligations.[6]
c. Independent economic value. The third part of the trade secret definition requires that "the information derives independent economic value, actual or potential, from not being generally known to, and not being readily ascertainable through proper means by, the public." Illustratively, some means to establish this element may include showing (a) competitive advantages for the owner in using the trade secret, (b) the costs for an outsider to duplicate the trade secret, (c) lost advantages to the trade secret owner resulting from disclosure to competitors, or (d) statements by the defendant about the value of the trade secret.[6]

   The study of numerous court cases can provide a much greater insight into the methodologies, targeting, and what was identified in terms of the court case. Further, it is the author's contention that by having a legal view of what has happened in the past, a person with a trade secret or other intellectual property can be forewarned about what to do and not to do in order to ensure maximum protection under the EEA. The following are just a few case references that you may wish to read for further edification.[6]

Intellectual Property Cases

Many cases have been prosecuted under the intellectual property statutes, such as 18 U.S.C. §§ 2318, 2319, and 2320. The following lists various cases that might be of interest to the reader as further background reading relative to the judiciary and courts. The first three items are specific government intellectual property operations undertaken. All can be located on the Internet.

Operation Site Down
Operation Buccaneer
Operation Fastlink

Copyright Cases. Charged under: 18 U.S.C. § 2318 (counterfeit or illicit labels); 18 U.S.C. § 2319 (criminal copyright infringement); 17 U.S.C. § 506 (criminal copyright infringement).
U.S. v. Shao (Fu, Fu, Chen, Li) (S.D. Fla.)
U.S. v. Yuan (Chen Rodriguez, Waziry, Karwan, Zhuang, Ma)
U.S. v. Zheng (Jin) (Operation Cyberstorm)
Digital Millennium Copyright Act Cases (DMCA). Charged under 17 U.S.C. § 1201 et seq.
U.S. v. McWaine
U.S. v. Buchholz (N.D. Cal.)
Trademark Cases. Charged under 18 U.S.C. § 2320
U.S. v. Nguyen
Trade Secret/Economic Espionage Cases
U.S. v. Dimson, et al.
U.S. v. Zhang
U.S. v. Tsai
U.S. v. Zhu
U.S. v. Okamoto

REFERENCES

1. Wilke, John R. Two silicon valley cases raise fears of Chinese espionage, *Wall Street Journal* online, January 15, 2003.
2. 18 USC Chapter 90 – Protection of Trade Secrets, found at: uscode.house.gov and 18 U.S.C. §1831 and §1832 Code, Department of Justice, Washington, D.C.
3. Department of Justice, Computer Crime and Intellectual Property Section (CCIPS), Washington, D.C., found at: http://USDOJ-crm.gov.
4. Executive Office for United States Attorneys, a manual for Computer Crime and intellectual Property Section, *Prosecuting Intellectual Property Crimes*, 3rd ed., U.S. Department of Justice, Washington, D.C., September 2006.
5. Bassiur, Matthew J., Intellectual property – an introduction, American Intellectual Property Law Association (2007) found at: http://www.aipla.org/learningcenter/library/papers/SM/SM07Materials/Documents/Bassiur_M-Paper.pdf.
6. United States Attorney's Bulletin, Common issues and challenges in prosecuting trade secrets and economic act cases, article prepared by Mark Krotoski, U.S. Department of Justice, Executive Offices for United States Attorneys, Washington, D.C., vol. 57, no. 5, November 2009.
7. Lewis, Jonathan Eric, The economic espionage act and the threat of Chinese espionage in the United States, *Chicago-Kent Journal of Intellectual Property* (Spring 2009).

12 The U.S. Response to Economic Espionage

You might as well sell this to us. We are going to get it anyway.

FBI records quoting the US representative of a firm brokering technology transfer to a major foreign power[1]

The Economic Espionage Act (EEA) is but one part of the various federal laws that can be applied to various types of theft. Besides the EEA, there are the laws governing copyright and patent protection and theft, the Digital Millennium Copyright Act, Trade Secrets Act, and a few others, some of which seem minor, but could be put into play when absolutely necessary. Congress is concerned about espionage, but its response through the crafting of relevant laws, is slow. Various Congressional Committees and Subcommittees will hold many hearings on the subject, trot out innumerable experts, spend an inordinate amount of time deliberating the 'tragedy' that has befallen America, and finally issue a report on what should be done. Any laws, or change to laws, will then be considered. Unfortunately, what could've, should've, or would've happened are many times disparate.

US GOVERNMENT AWARENESS

Over the past dozen or so years, senior US policymakers have become increasingly aware of the inseparable link between economic security and national security. Even the annual issues of the White House's *National Security Strategy*[2] have emphasized the fact that economic security has become a very integral part of US national interest and of national security. The intertwining of these was not recognized so much two decades ago. But in the February 1995 edition,[2] included in President Clinton's list of America's three central strategy goals is bolstering economic revitalization. He underscored the concept that "the strength of our diplomacy, our ability to maintain an unrivaled military, (and) the attractiveness of our values abroad" were all dependent (at least in part) on our economic strength. These ideas reaffirmed in the following year's edition of *National Security Strategy of Enlargement and Engagement.*[3]

Even earlier, on November 4, 1993, speaking before the Senate Foreign Relations Committee, Secretary of State Warren Christopher stated that: "In the post-Cold War world, our national security is inseparable from our economic security." He went on to emphasize that there must be a "new centrality of economic policy in our foreign policy."[4] This economic policy means that America's genius is what is marketed around the world through the products created. Vibrant market forces worldwide are affected by this genius of innovation but, further, if it does not encourage inventive viability, then the economy can and will be hobbled by outside forces who would strive to strip it, reducing the US economy and its resultant financial gains. Hence, the use of intellectual property (IP) rights must be controlled and maintained for the economy to prosper.

Consistent with such policy, in 1992, the Federal Bureau of Investigation (FBI) began to refocus its counterintelligence (CI) resources to provide greater protection to US economic security.

By 1994, the FBI had initiated an Economic Counterintelligence program. Its mission was to collect information and engage in activities that allowed the Agency to detect and counteract foreign power–sponsored **or** coordinated threats and activities that were being directed against US economic interests, especially when those acts involved economic espionage. The program began as being defensive in nature with the ultimate goal of protecting US national security. To accomplish this goal, the FBI applied a full range of investigative tools, techniques, and remedies available through the authorities and jurisdictions assigned to both their Foreign Counterintelligence and Criminal Investigative Programs.[4]

Through this economic CI program, the FBI developed significant information on foreign economic threats, including the identification of those acting nations that posed the threats, their targets, and the methods they utilized.

On January 5, 2001, a mere two weeks before leaving office, President Clinton issued Presidential Decision Directive (PDD) 75, "U.S. Counterintelligence Effectiveness—Counterintelligence for the Twenty-first Century." The PDD outlined specific steps enabling the US CI community to better fulfill its mission of identifying, understanding, prioritizing, and counteracting the intelligence threats faced by the United States. The system was designed to be predictive and proactive in providing integrated oversight of CI issues across the spectrum of US national security agencies.

PDD 75 also presented specific measures enhancing the ability of the numerous member agencies and organizations of the US CI community to identify and counteract threats.

Among the provisions of PDD 75 was the establishment of the Counterintelligence Board of Directors, chaired by the director of the FBI, and composed of the Deputy Secretary of Defense, the Deputy Director of Central Intelligence, and a senior representative of the Department of Justice (DOJ). PDD 75 also created the position of a CI executive (NCIX).[5]

The National Counterintelligence Executive (NCIX) was to serve as the leader of national-level CI and coordinates and supports critical CI missions for the US government.[6]

The NCIX directs all CI activities at the national level, reports to the FBI director as board chairman, but is accountable to all board members, having the responsibility of advising them on CI programs, policies, and challenges.[5]

The PDD stipulated that the NCIX would chair the National Counterintelligence Policy Board (NACIPB), whose members would include (at a minimum) senior CI officials from the Departments of State, Defense, Justice, and Energy, as well as from the Joint Chiefs of Staff, Central Intelligence Agency (CIA), FBI, and National Security Council (NSC). The NCIX would also oversee the Office of the National Counterintelligence Executive (ONCIX), which would replace the old National Counterintelligence Center (NACIC).[5]

NACIC BACKGROUND AND THE CHANGE TO THE OFFICE OF THE NCIX

The NACIC was initially established under the authority of the NACIPB, in accordance with Presidential Decision Directive/NSC-24 "US Counterintelligence Effectiveness," in May 1994. During 1994, President Clinton ordered a review of the overall effectiveness of US CI, which resulted in the establishment of a new CI policy and coordination apparatus for the US CI community. It eliminated the policy structure that was then held under the Director of Central Intelligence and established the NACIPB as the primary functioning body for addressing CI policy issues. The NACIC was designed to be an autonomous entity reporting to the NACIPB and the NSC. Its employees were drawn from CI and security professionals from the FBI, the CIA, the National Security Agency (NSA), the Department of Defense (DOD), and the Department of State.

As a result of its policy role, the NACIC's main concern was with coordination of national-level CI activities. Within the NACIC, a community training branch responsible for the development of organizing and implementing training throughout the CI community and private industry was established. In some cases, there were joint efforts with federal agencies or with private organizations. A quarterly newsletter, *Counterintelligence News and Developments*, was published by the NACIC along with various brochures and reports. Various public educational materials were continued when the NACIC was transformed into the NCIX. While the new office of the NCIX was ultimately under the leadership of the FBI, the NACIC had been attached to the NSC. In this capacity, the NACIC had operated a threat assessment office that compiled information—both from the US Intelligence Community and from open sources in the media and elsewhere—on activities by foreign entities and their intelligence agencies that posed potential threats to US companies. It also analyzed possible espionage concerning emerging technologies from the United States, as well as threats to US executives or business personnel, additionally keeping a close watch on the effects of foreign ownership, technology transfers, and joint ownership that could impinge upon US economic concerns.[5,7]

AN EXPANDED OUTREACH TO THE PRIVATE SECTOR

The new office of the NCIX broadened its appeal to the private sector by expanding its outreach through seminars to the somewhat few private-sector security organizations (such as the American Society for Industrial Security, the National Classification Management Society, and various Industrial Security Advisory councils that were smaller organizations tied to government contractors). Continuing these efforts into the present, the NCIX makes available to the private sector a vast array of CI awareness products. The office publishes its *Annual Report to Congress on Foreign Economic Collection and Industrial Espionage* online. It also publishes booklets and brochures designed to inform and advise Americans to the ways that they might become targets of foreign intelligence collection activities. At its web site (ncix.gov), the office of the NCIX has available various publications and links of value. It also has security awareness posters created to heighten awareness of CI.

NO ELECTRONIC THEFT ACT

On December 16, 1997, President Clinton signed into law H.R. 2265, the No Electronic Theft (NET) Act. The NET Act provided for the enhanced protection of copyrights and trademarks by amending provisions in Titles 17 and 18 of the US Code. The NET Act permitted for the federal prosecution of large-scale, willful copyright infringement even where the infringer does not act for a commercial purpose or for private financial gain. This amendment closed a gap in statutory protection that was discussed in *United States v. LaMacchia*, 871 F. Supp. 535 (D. Mass. 1994).[8–10]

Within this and other acts, the Congress has provided a clear way for a greater variety of prosecutions that could take place for the theft of economic data. The listing below highlights the variety of prosecution subject areas for cases involving economic espionage and the theft of America's IP secrets. The subjects cover a great swath through American companies and industries.

- Bootlegged video tapes
- CD manufacturing piracy
- Computer damage and access device fraud
- Computer fraud
- Conspiracy to steal/sell (as in Coca-Cola trade secrets)
- Copyright infringement
- Copyright protected software and video games
- Counterfeit baby formula
- Counterfeit clothing and accessories
- Counterfeit Compaq computers
- Counterfeit computer chips
- Counterfeit drugs
- Counterfeit DVDs

- Counterfeit goods (general)
- Counterfeit labels
- Counterfeit luxury goods (such as Louis Vuitton handbags)
- Counterfeit Rolex watches
- Counterfeit software
- Counterfeit trademarks
- Counterfeit Viagra
- Counterfeit, adulterated, and mislabeled pesticides
- DNA cell lines
- Drug delivery system formulas
- Engineered drug theft
- Genetic screening discoveries
- Illegal copying, reproduction, and distribution of movies
- Intellectual property (general)
- Microprocessor research
- Money laundering
- Music piracy
- Network switch plans
- Piracy/modifying X-Box game consoles
- Pirated copies of business software
- Pirated satellite TV access cards
- Pirated satellite TV interception devices
- Proprietary pricing information
- Securities broker customer and account data
- Smart card technology
- Software piracy
- Test materials
- Theft of computer source codes
- Theft/sale of software, music, movies, and games
- Theft/sale of trade secrets and proprietary databases
- Trademark violations
- Ultrasound machine plans

The list emphasizes the ingenuity and creativity of American scientists, engineers, doctors, bio-engineers, and others in the creation of various items in technology, engineering, medicine, and other fields. At the same time, it highlights various areas in which counterfeit items have been created to attack the economic ends of these items by foreign entities. In the 2010 *Joint Strategic Plan on Intellectual Property Enforcement*, released in June 2010 by the White House, Victoria Espinel, US Intellectual Property Enforcement Coordinator (IPEC), stated that:

> Our (the United States) entrepreneurial spirit, creativity and ingenuity are clear comparative advantages for America in the global economy. As such, Americans are global leaders in the production of creative and innovative service and products, including digital content, many of which are dependent on the protection of intellectual property rights. In order to continue to lead, succeed and prosper in the global economy, we must ensure the strong enforcement of American intellectual property rights.[11]

The Prioritizing Resources and Organization for Intellectual Property Act directed the IPEC to coordinate the development of a Joint Strategic Plan against counterfeiting and infringement. President Obama, on March 11, 2010, said "We're going to aggressively protect our intellectual property. Our single greatest asset is the innovation and the ingenuity and creativity of the American people. It is essential to our prosperity and it will only become more so in this century."[12]

The *Joint Security Plan on Intellectual Property Enforcement* goes on to state that:

> Americans work daily to create a better world. We create products and services that improve the world's ability to communicate, to learn, to understand diverse cultures and beliefs, to be mobile, to live better and longer lives, to produce and consume energy efficiently and to secure food, nourishment and safety. Most of the value of this work is intangible—it lies in America's entrepreneurial spirit, our creativity, ingenuity and insistence on progress and in creating a better life for our communities and for communities around the world. These intangible assets, often captured as copyrights, patents, trademarks, trade secrets and other forms of "intellectual property," reflect America's advantage in the global economy.[11]

The federal government has continually supported the strong enforcement of IP rights for a number of reasons: (1) the growth of the US economy and the creation of jobs for American workers and that supports US exports, (2) the promotion of innovation and security of America's comparative advantage in the global economy, (3) the protection of consumer trust and safety, (4) the national and economic security, and (5) the validation of those rights as enumerated and protected under our Constitution.[11]

The Joint Security Plan also stated that American industries "depend on intellectual property employ engineers and chemists, artists and authors, and manufacturers and laborers. From the Silicon Valley to the Raleigh/Durham research triangle area and up the Northeast corridor, Americans bring new, life-changing pharmaceuticals and medical devices, creating from an idea the development of environmentally-conscious technologies, envisioning and creating innovative software products, building new communication networks."[11] Essentially, it means that anyone vested in any enterprise must also be dependent upon IP protection. With the United States as a global leader in developing new technologies through innovation or emanating from pure research, everyone has to remain strong and vigilant to ensure the protection of their IP. However, without the appropriate protection in place, it also means that America is the world's target for theft of all these types of items.

Congress, in this regard, must continually make and update those appropriate laws, providing generous resources for law enforcement to use to combat theft. To that end, government as a whole and not in a fragmented sense must pull together to:

1. Combat foreign-based and foreign-controlled websites that infringe on our IP rights.
2. Enhance foreign law enforcement cooperation.
3. Promote an effective enforcement of US IP rights through our various trade policy tools
4. Use the US Trade Representative's special 301 "action plans" identifying various foreign countries and alert US organizations and companies as to which nations are on the priority watch lists.[13]

One item Congress had not truly addressed, identified, or really concerned itself about is, probably through the Department of Commerce, to assess the economic impact of intellectual property-intensive industries. No attempt has been made (to the author's knowledge) that actually attempts to measure and quantify the economic contributions of our numerous property-intensive industries within all the US business secrets. Such improved measures, if linked with measures of economic performance, would help the government understand the actual role and breadth of the IP and could, thus, be used as a formal basis for developing and implementing a national policy and various associate resource decisions for future enforcement.

Take note that any such actions would, invariably, assist others in targeting specifics, much less identify for targeting any recent state-of-the-art items, technology, and so on, that would become available with the latest IP information made public. As such, any report that Congress might issue would have to be generic enough so that potential thieves could not then identify and target specific companies. While the Congress has not acted in this area, enough open-source information is currently available to allow a great deal of targeting to be done today. Thus, Congressional inaction would be necessary in this regard, but if action were to be taken, regretfully, Congressional hearings for such would be open to the general public for the most part, and some if not a lot of the areas that should be protected in terms of company or manufacturing identification would still become public knowledge.

As stated in the 2010 Report, a variety of actions must be taken. While no given individual action or combination of them can completely stop IP and other thefts, it is a start. I believe that the major problem is the time taken to complete any given data action. Such things as "tracking and reporting," "coordination with…," "improving…," establishing committees, enhancing, and so on, are all just buzzwords that mean time, more time, and lots of generated paperwork without any true, final decisions made that can be effective.[11]

All in all, the report may read well, but will also require a lot of time, effort, and dollars expended to put the various recommended actions in place. Other countries, in the meantime, can and will move faster to acquire what IP we are developing or currently have, much faster than we can create specific plans and procedures to protect such from theft by these countries or their agents and supporters.

Remember that Congress must take the lead, and then the various departments and agencies of the government will start to act. Let's take a look at a few of them more closely here. The following summaries of departments, agencies, and offices are abridged versions derived from the 2010 *Joint Strategic Plan on Intellectual Property Enforcement*:

a. *Department of Commerce, International Trade Administration (ITA).* The ITA is set up to strengthen the competitiveness of US industry, promote trade, and ensure fair trade through a rigorous enforcement of trade laws and agreements. The Office of Intellectual Property Rights develops (and coordinates with ITA on) trade-related IP rights policies, programs, and practices, and assists companies to overcome challenges to protect and enforce their IP rights overseas. As part of an overall strategy to educate the US business community, small- and medium-size businesses, IP agreements, and the US Patent and Trademark Office (USPTO), they have set up a web site that provides the businessman with market-specific toolkits with detailed information on protecting IP in specific key markets that include the ever-bulging China.[11]
b. *US Patent and Trademark Office.* The USPTO has a long history of supporting trade partners and has created a flexible team enterprise that meets the challenges of IP enforcement within today's global economy. They meet the challenges by (1) carrying out statutory and internal treaty obligations with developing nations in implementing accessible and effective IP enforcement systems; (2) responding rapidly to changing global and international conditions; (3) establishing alliance with other national and international IP organizations to strengthen, protect, and enforce American IP rights globally; and (4) working with other government agencies, national IP enforcement authorities, and international organizations to increase the accessibility, efficiency, and administration and criminal enforcement mechanisms.[11]
c. *Department of Health and Human Services (Food and Drug Administration, FDA).* As part of the FDA mission, it takes reports of counterfeits very seriously and rapidly responds to emerging threats by strengthening the ability to prevent the introduction of falsified medical products and foods into the US distribution chain, identifying falsified medical products and foods, and minimizing the risk and exposure of patients and consumers to falsified products. As part of these efforts, they also investigate reports of suspected falsified products and coordinate counterfeit investigations with other international, federal, state, and local law enforcement. The issue of falsified medical products and food is truly a global issue, one that requires a global solution, thus compelling the FDA to work with

international regulatory partners to address the public health aspects of counterfeit medical products and foods.[11]

d. *Department of Homeland Security (DHS).* DHS plays a key role in protecting IP rights, in the pursuit of an effective IP enforcement strategy. Its aim is to ensure the facilitation of legitimate trade, while enforcing US trade and IP rights laws and investigating IP violations, specifically trademark, counterfeit, and copyright piracy.[11]
e. *Customs and Border Protection (CBP).* The CBP is in a position to inspect, seize, and require forfeiture of goods that infringe on trademarks, trade names, and copyrights. The CBP has a partnership program to facilitate legitimate trade, enhanced targeting, and training to intensify the drive against IP-infringing goods that enter the United States.[11]
f. *Immigration and Customs Enforcement (ICE).* ICE is the lead agency that investigates criminal IP violations involving the illegal production, smuggling, and distribution of counterfeit and pirated products, in addition to associated money laundering violations. ICE established an IPR Center to more effectively counter the flood of infringing producers. This center addresses and combats predatory and unfair trade practices that threaten our economic stability and national security, or restrict the competitiveness of US industry in world markets.[11]
g. *US Secret Service (USSS).* They investigate violations relating to counterfeiting of monetary obligations and securities. Also of great interest to the USSS are financial crimes that include access device fraud, financial institution fraud, identify theft, computer fraud, and computer-based attacks on our financial, banking, and telecommunications and critical infrastructure.[11]
h. *Department of Justice.* Here, we have the most aggressive enforcement of IP laws that consistently have high priority within the DOJ. Using the full resources of the Criminal Division, US Attorneys' Offices and Civil Division, as well as investigatory and law enforcement from the FBI, their IP priorities include the investigation and prosecution of IP crimes involving health and safety, trade secrets and economic espionage, and commercial online piracy and counterfeiting.[11]
i. *Federal Bureau of Investigation.* The FBI is extremely aggressive in pursuing trade secret theft and IP enforcement. The FBI's Intellectual Property Rights Unit (IPRU) became fully operational in April 2010, has dedicated FBI agents, and employs over 50 Special Agents exclusively devoted to pursuing IP investigations. Additionally, the IPRU works with the Criminal Investigative Division and Organized Crime and Health Care Fraud Units, as well as the Counterintelligence Division Economic Espionage Unit, for the coordination and tracking of the theft of trade secret investigations that have a state sponsorship nexus, in attempting to prevent the loss of trade secrets to foreign agents, governments, and instrumentalities.[11]

These are the major players, but not necessarily all of them. While the knowledge of these agencies and organizations described previously is important, remember that without the Congress passing specific laws and developing appropriate information in order to strengthen current laws, nothing will happen.

Three lists of importance that are critical to America's economic welfare and to the overall defense of the nation are the National Critical Technologies List, followed by the Militarily Critical Technologies List (MCTL), and the Developing Science and Technologies List. The first covered the nation and its industrial base as a whole, the second concerns itself with those technologies that are specifically relative to the defense of the nation, while the last is that which concerns itself with emerging technology and innovation within the scientific fields. We will focus on the MCTL in the following section with excerpts utilized from the document *The Militarily Critical Technologies List (MCTL)*, issued by the DOD Security Institute.

MILITARILY CRITICAL TECHNOLOGIES LIST

The MCTL is a detailed compendium of information on technologies that the DOD assesses as critical to maintaining superior US military capabilities. The MCTL contains definitions of specifications and thresholds that make each technology critical to the military. The majority of the MCTL technologies are dual-use technologies, which means they can be used for both military and civilian applications. For example, new, rugged, high-power lasers have a specialized civilian application, but they are also adaptable to sensitive military applications.[14]

An intelligence collector may attempt to use the alleged civilian use as a plausible cover for seeking information or materials that have military applications. Dual-use items would make a significant contribution to their military and are on the Department of Commerce's Commodity Control List; a license is required for their export. The acquisition of any of these technologies by a potential adversary would lead to the significant enhancement of the military–industrial capabilities of that country to the detriment of US security interests. A check of prosecutions over even a short period would reveal that dual-use technologies are being targeted.

The MCTL provides everyone concerned with a singular volume of knowledge about the greater degree of sophistication and sensitivity for those technologies that must be protected and what may be freely exchanged with our foreign counterparts. It is the technical foundation for decisions on:[11]

- Proposals for export control and for implementation of licensing and export control policies
- Pre-publication review of scientific papers prepared by government, industry, and academia
- Tasking for intelligence collection
- Research and development planning
- International technology cooperation and transfer

The overall MCTL document is quite lengthy. Currently, the MTCL site has been removed from the web, although a diligent search might provide some data on web sites other than the Defense Technical Information Center (DTIC). The Department of Commerce should be consulted for up-to-date information relating to specific cases.

The major technology categories in the MCTL include the following:[14]

- Aeronautics Systems Technology
- Armaments and Energetic Materials
- Biological Technology
- Biomedical Technology
- Chemical Technology
- Directed and Kinetic Energy Systems
- Energy Systems Technology
- Electronics Technology
- Ground Systems Technology
- Information Systems Technology
- Lasers, Optics, and Imaging Technology
- Processing and Manufacturing Technology
- Marine Systems Technology
- Materials and Processes Technology
- Nuclear Systems Technology
- Positioning, Navigation, and Time Technology
- Information Security Technology
- Signature Control Technology
- Space Systems Technology
- Weapons Effects Technology

For each of these major technology categories, there is a general discussion on how this technology is used by the military and detailed information on each technology that is subject to export control and other regulations.

There are several DOD agencies that maintain records of suspicious foreign attempts to obtain MCTL technologies. The MCTL technologies most sought after by foreign intelligence collectors tend to remain unchanged for years. They are as follows: information systems (software and hardware), sensors (the eyes and ears of many military systems, including high-speed cameras, night vision equipment, and sensor platforms placed on unmanned aerial vehicles), aeronautics (unmanned aerial vehicles, composite materials, onboard computer management systems, experimental aerospace platforms), and electronics (used in virtually every weapons system to enhance performance and reliability while reducing size and increasing power).[14]

Often though, the need for secrecy directly conflicts with the normal MCT research environment. The success of the United States in maintaining MCTL secrets can be described as marginal at best. Just knowing that the United States has identified a specific military critical technology and what it can be possibly used for gives the intelligence collector a baseline from which to act in searching out where to obtain the technology. Table 12.1 identifies sample technologies, possible uses, and their value. As such, it would demonstrate the lure of potential money, patriotism for another nation, and why it would be valuable to another nation. Perhaps the most famous case of MCT espionage would be that of Julius and Ethel Rosenberg who were executed in 1953 for giving away atomic bomb technology. Other spies such as Aldrich Ames, Jonathan Pollard, Earl Pitts, Harold Nicholson, and Robert Hanssen all serve as reminders that the threat is active, real, and ongoing even as some American's greed for money or other status overrode their patriotism. Somewhat recently, Brian Regan, a former Air Force intelligence analyst, was convicted of giving technical information on spy satellites to China and Iran. Such cases serve as reminders and underscore the very fact that we must safeguard our MCT from those intelligence collectors that are highly skilled in espionage activities.[14]

TABLE 12.1
Selected Examples of Military Critical Technologies

Military Critical Technology	Overview	Example Capability
Aeronautics systems	Aircraft, gas turbine engine	Combustion >2800°F
Armaments, energetic materials	Ammo, bombs, mines	Kinetic penetration >400 mm
Chemical and biological system	Chem bio detection, decon	Protection for 24 hours against all known liquid chemical agents
Directed energy systems	High-energy laser, particle beams	>20 kW laser
Electronics	New-generation microchips	Signal processor >1 GHz
Ground systems	Sensors, advanced diesel engines	Power output >750 kW
Guidance, navigation, and control	GPS	<1 M 3D accuracy
Information systems	Data proc, info storage	4 hours for 72-hour weather forecast
Information warfare	EW and hacking	Memory speed >200 MHz
Processing and manufacturing	Production of equipment	
Materials	Armor, anti-armor	Body armor, stop AK47 at 100 m
Nuclear systems	Fission	U235 enrichment to 90%
Sensors and lasers	Acoustic, optical sensor	Locate a direct fire weapon with 10 m accuracy out to 500 m

Source: Office of the National Counterintelligence, Executive (ONCIX), Annual Report to Congress on Foreign Economic Collection and Industrial Espionage, FY 2008, NCIX-007-09 July 23, 2009, Retrieved April 3, 2013 found at: http://www.ncix.gov/publications/reports/fecie_all/fecie_2008/2008_FECIE_Blue.pdf.

Over the years, various government studies have described the "defensive" measures that the US government applies to counter foreign collection of US economic-related intelligence and information. These studies would list and discuss to some extent the US targets and the methods used to obtain US economic and technological information, including, at times, US government information that directly affects US industry.[14]

To provide a full scope of foreign economic collection efforts targeted at US firms, such reports tend to examine "foreign industrial espionage" as well as other types of collection efforts that potentially could be damaging to US national and corporate interests. Any report will include in general the collection efforts by foreign intelligence services, but would not specify the country involved unless it was the subject of a prosecution. Open-source searches on the Internet can sometimes identify specific countries involved, as well as when a government agency or company makes known that espionage has occurred. Also, there are private-sector reports, especially from within the computer security industries, that track electronic IP theft (successful attempts or otherwise) back to their originating source and report such.[14]

ESPIONAGE AND ILLICIT ACQUISITION OF PROPRIETARY INFORMATION

The *Annual Report to Congress on Foreign Economic Collection and Industrial Espionage*, prepared by the NACIC several years ago, highlights some of the issues of espionage and theft of proprietary information and trade secrets, focusing on some of the roles of domestic agencies in thwarting such activity. The next several sections are adapted from and use several excerpts from the recommendations of the report.

The government of the People's Republic of China (PRC) and its thousands of varying businesses and industries, either state controlled or closely related through business ventures, collect economic information from US firms through standard business practices, such as mergers and acquisitions, strategic alliances, and licensing agreements, as well as gathering publicly available information. These activities are an accepted element of the business world and are largely peripheral to the scope of this report, and these activities can generate a considerable portion of the technology and economic information they obtain. These open-source collection activities include, but are not limited to, review of trade journals or corporate annual reports, market surveys, and attending conferences and symposia. In some instances, however, these types of collection efforts could become the precursors to the collection of information that was earlier determined to be of an intelligence interest.

For example, an attempt to persuade an employee of a US firm to gather information from the firm's library could be the first step in setting up a source that would eventually collect proprietary documents. Similarly, the use of legal joint ventures and licensing agreements provide the ideal opportunities to gather non-public information from US firms. After all, what better way to collect such information than having your own Chinese citizens working within the company, having access to the information on a daily basis, or being in a position to motivate others to provide it so the individual "can do a better job."[15]

POLICY FUNCTIONS AND OPERATIONAL ROLES

Any Congressional mandate tends to direct the method and types of information required in any report of the size necessitated by the subject matter, especially in the case of foreign espionage. The report will spend a great deal discussing the respective policy functions and operational roles of all the varying agencies of the Executive Branch that are in the position to identify and counter the threats to US industry posed by one or more foreign entities, and then giving a general summary of the manner in which such functions and roles are coordinated.

The US government's primary methods for identifying and countering foreign economic espionage and illicit acquisition of proprietary information are through those various national-level CI operations and law enforcement investigations. CI and law enforcement agencies monitor intelligence collection, ascertain how and against whom it is directed, and determine the optimum remedy to counter the threat.[15]

CI efforts are directed at monitoring, penetrating, and neutralizing foreign intelligence activities targeted against US national interests, including economic and industrial interests. Law enforcement agencies take advantage of CI information as well as develop their own information through investigations. At times, these two communities have proceeded separately without effectively coordinating their efforts. This is the big problem as each organization wants to "protect its own turf" and each also wants to get all the credit when the espionage is uncovered and the individuals involved are caught.[15]

The FBI is the government agency responsible for collecting, analyzing, and investigating foreign threats to US industry. Because of its role as both the US government's primary CI agency with regard to foreign intelligence activities within the United States and the lead criminal investigative agency, the FBI is able to use both types of remedies against economic and industrial espionage.[15]

The US ICE (formerly just the US Customs Service) is the primary border enforcement agency. For example, ICE would be responsible for enforcing the Arms Export Control Act and the Export of War Materials Act, which involve munitions control and trafficking activities. It is also responsible for the enforcement of export controls of high-technology material and information under the Export Administrations Act. Economic and industrial espionage have been found to be quite often connected to trade sanctions and embargoes against designated countries, strategic trade issues, and protection of IP rights.[15]

The DOD and each military service have CI and criminal investigative components that conduct CI operations and investigate foreign economic and industrial intelligence activities as they relate to DOD programs and systems. Hence, when a potential espionage concern is raised by a DOD contractor facility, it will be the Defense Investigative Service (DIS) or the individual military intelligence organization that performs the initial investigation. Dependent upon the level, sensitivity, who might be involved, and so on, it is quite possible that the FBI will be brought in to provide other professional support and assistance. The military services work closely with the FBI when the activity involves violations of federal laws or intelligence activity targeted against US persons. The information developed through this support is disseminated and coordinated throughout the CI and security programs communities.[15]

CI and law enforcement investigative agencies rely on several sources within the US government for CI information and criminal leads that they can further develop through investigations and operations, and they will include the following.

The FBI, in the 1970s, instituted a program called the "Development of Espionage, Counterintelligence, and Counterterrorism Awareness," but by the mid-90s, the program morphed into the Awareness of National Security Issues and Response (ANSIR). ANSIR provides an interface with the US corporate community through which the FBI not only conveys information but also obtains investigative leads from corporations concerning foreign government and corporate attempts to illicitly collect US economic and technological information. Michael J. Waguespack, Deputy Assistant Director, National Security Division, FBI, speaking before the House Committee on Government Reform, Subcommittee on National Security, Veterans Affairs, and International Relations, in Washington, D.C., on April 3, 2001, stated:

> The FBI's ANSIR Program's awareness message is principally aimed at U.S. corporations, although other government agencies and law enforcement also benefit from it. The principal method of disseminating FBI awareness information is through ANSIR e-mail described in the following section. The ease of replicating email communication accounts for the global nature of the dissemination. American interests abroad receive ANSIR awareness communications primarily from their headquarters in the United States which relays ANSIR e-mail to them.

The CIA informs the FBI and other appropriate US government agencies when it learns, in the course of its broader foreign CI and economic intelligence gathering activities, about a foreign government or company targeting US industry.

For example, the CIA would relay to the FBI or the DOJ economic espionage information acquired from foreign government sources, in addition to the State Department and other appropriate government agencies of instances of economic espionage or state-supported unfair trading practices, such as bribery of contracting officials. In this regard also, the CIA prepares analyses on any country engaging in economic espionage and questionable trading practices.

The Counterintelligence Division of the Department of Energy (DOE) manages a defensive CI program to identify and counter any identifiable threats or potential threats of foreign economic and industrial intelligence collection activities against DOE personnel and facilities. They collect information through reports of foreigners visiting DOE facilities and through the debriefing of DOE employees and contractors who may have been targeted by foreign governments or corporations. It then furnishes this information as CI leads to the FBI when there is evidence of foreign intelligence targeting.[15]

The Defense Security Service (DSS), formerly the DIS, systematically collects CI information developed through personnel security interviews and industrial security inspections. The Designated Approving Authority (DAA) is the approval point of contact for certification, accreditation, oversight, and management of government cleared contractor computer facilities. The DAA headquarters' Counterintelligence Office analyzes this collected information and, when appropriate, provides it as CI and criminal investigative leads to agencies such as the FBI, US Customs Service, and the military services.[15]

US GOVERNMENT SUPPORT TO PRIVATE INDUSTRY

Any report to federal officials or the Congress relative to economic/industrial espionage will also indicate the means by which the federal government communicates information on industrial espionage threats and on methods to protect against such threats to US industry in general and to US companies that are known to be targets of foreign espionage. Government agencies identify and counter foreign economic espionage and illicit efforts to acquire proprietary information from two distinct but integrated approaches: CI and law enforcement. As a subset of those approaches, and taking advantage of the information that the respective communities develop, the US government also counters those activities through security education, awareness, and training.[15]

Such security education and awareness programs are designed to provide government and private audiences with information relative to the foreign threat information, which is necessary in order to better protect classified and proprietary economic information. Government contractors receive the vast majority of threat information through formal training, brochures, and briefings.[15]

The primary US government programs that pass threat information to non-government-affiliated corporations are the FBI's ANSIR Program, the State Department's Overseas Security Advisory Council (OSAC), and, on occasion, certain programs of training and education from the CIA. The ONCIX has various implemented initiatives to work with these various programs to provide more timely or relevant threat information to the private sector.[15]

After obtaining information indicating that a specific US company is being targeted, this information is provided to the FBI, which may inform the company about the threat.

The FBI can then brief appropriate personnel in the company about the threat and work with them to counteract that threat. Information of a more general nature is also shared with the State Department's OSAC representatives for passage to the private sector.

The OCNIX can also join forces with OSAC to share threat information, particularly on the US technology–targeted and collection techniques used by foreign governments. The following highlights awareness and briefing programs within each US government agency that provides threat information to private-sector companies:[15]

a. *Federal Bureau of Investigation.* The ANSIR Program is the FBI's public voice and educational medium for communicating threat information, especially within the economic espionage arena, to the private sector. The program has been an integral part of the FBI's foreign CI program. ANSIR coordinators in each of the FBI's field offices have regular liaison with companies located in the field offices' territories. The coordinators furnish briefings, videotapes, pamphlets, and other materials to help the private sector understand and recognize foreign economic espionage threats directed at them. The content of briefings and material provided is always tailored to the specific needs and concerns of each company. The coordinators also discuss the various methods employed by a foreign entity to accomplish their collection goals. The FBI will also provide briefings at academic institutions, laboratories, and state and local governments.

The ANSIR Program is a national effort with management, direction, and analytical support from FBI headquarters. As needed, the FBI provides field offices with information, materials, and speaker support to facilitate a specific request or need. It relies on dynamic and direct communication between the ANSIR coordinator and executives, security directors, and personnel within US corporations.[15]

b. *Department of State.* The State Department's OSAC is a joint venture by the Department and US businesses to resolve overseas security problems of mutual concern, including foreign economic threats. OSAC is administered under the State Department's Bureau of Diplomatic Security. Over 1400 private-sector organizations participate in its activities and receive information and guidance.[15]

   OSAC also oversees "Country Councils" in selected foreign cities that consist of US embassy security officers and other post officials working with security managers of US private-sector enterprises to exchange unclassified security information in a timely fashion. There are Country Councils in more than 25 foreign cities. Country Councils enable OSAC to pass threat information to the industry and to gather information from US corporations concerning threats to US economic security.[15]

   Government and business representatives have joined with OSAC to produce a series of publications providing guidance, suggestions, and planning techniques on a variety of security-related issues, including a booklet titled *Guidelines for Protecting US Business Information Overseas.*

   To exchange threat information as expeditiously as possible, the State Department created the OSAC Electronic Bulletin Board (EBB). The EBB is an unclassified online system available to OSAC member companies that serves as the focal point for the exchange of information between the Department of State and the US private sector. More specifically, the Office of Intelligence and Threat Analysis (ITA) uses the EBB to provide corporations doing business abroad with timely, unclassified security-related information. US firms can supplement ITA's information by voluntarily submitting accounts of security or crime incidents affecting their own or other US overseas operations. The EBB maintains reports of various types of overseas threats.[15]

c. *Central Intelligence Agency.* The CIA provides information to the FBI for use, as appropriate, in accordance with memoranda of understanding and executive orders. On occasion, the CIA briefs US corporate officials directly concerning the foreign intelligence threats. The CIA presents these briefings, which describe the ways used to conduct economic intelligence collection to individual corporations and at industry-wide conferences, often with FBI participation. The briefings can cover foreign economic activities worldwide, focusing on intelligence-gathering techniques used by specific countries.[15]

d. *Department of Defense/Defense Intelligence Agency.* The Defense Intelligence Agency (DIA) conducts briefings at conferences attended by government-affiliated contractors and provides current threat information for training courses for DOD contractor personnel. Briefing subjects include economic intelligence collection activities and threats of illicit technology transfer. The DIA also prepares CI risk assessments on foreign ownership of DOD-affiliated US corporations and studies on the foreign intelligence threat to DOD programs and operations, including contractor programs.[15]

The DIS shares information with the industry about the targeting of specific technologies or specific contractors based on its analysis of information from databases such as the Foreign Ownership, Control, or Influence database and various elements of the Foreign Disclosure and Technical Information System. The focus of the DIS program is to safeguard classified information, but its efforts also help protect proprietary information. As DIS becomes aware of the targeting of specific technologies or specific contractors, that information is shared with the industry and other US government agencies as appropriate.

Foreign threat information can also be developed by DIS Special Agents during personal security interviews by industrial security representatives under the auspices of the National Industrial Security Program and through liaison with other US agencies. Appropriate reports are disseminated throughout DOD, throughout the intelligence community, and to cleared defense contractors during industrial security actions.[15]

DIS has a program in place to identify those cleared contractor facilities that are involved in critical technologies and may have currently or in the near future interface with foreign interests. DIS will then spearhead a briefing/debriefing program for contractor personnel who host foreign national visitors, conduct foreign travel/visits, interface with on-site foreign national visitor groups, and are assigned overseas. The focus of this program is to identify attempts by foreign nationals to circumvent or undermine disclosure decisions.[15]

DOD service CI components each have comprehensive programs to brief the defense industry and the acquisition community on the political, military, and economic threat to sensitive technologies and programs and the multidisciplinary threat posed by foreign countries, visitors, and economic entities. Military CI components can provide a full range of CI support to the military research, development, test, and evaluations community; acquisition program offices; and contractors they serve. Their overall goal is to detect, deter, neutralize, and exploit attempts by foreign entities to acquire restricted DOD systems and technologies.[15]

The DOD Acquisition Systems Protection Program (ASPP) works to unify the acquisition, CI, and security communities to prevent losses of information. Under the ASPP, the acquisition community identifies the most essential elements of DOD acquisition programs, known as EPITS (essential program information, technology, and systems), as well as other pertinent information about DOD technologies. The CI community identifies threats to the technologies in general and to specific EPITS by location as far as possible. The security community then tailors countermeasures to offset the threat and vulnerabilities of the program.[15]

e. *National Reconnaissance Office (NRO).* NRO's counterintelligence staff runs a CI threat and awareness program to brief its contractor-based personnel on the intelligence threat targeting their systems and programs.
f. *National Security Agency.* The NSA conducts briefings and develops and organizes courses, seminars, and conferences to sensitize its contractors cleared for special compartmented information to the foreign intelligence threat domestically and overseas. NSA provides general and country-specific threat information in all indoctrination and orientation briefings, debriefings, and special briefings (e.g., defensive travel briefings, courier briefings, special access briefings, etc.).[15]
g. *Office of the National Counterintelligence Executive (formerly the NACIC).* The ONCIX under its predecessor NACIC was established in 1994 in accordance with Presidential Decision Directive/NSC-24, titled "U.S. Counterintelligence Effectiveness." It is the NACIPB's primary mechanism to guide all national-level CI activities, including countering foreign economic and industrial intelligence collection activities.[15]

The Threat Assessment Office compiles intelligence and open-source reporting on the clandestine targeting of US industry and technologies by foreign powers or their intelligence services. It fulfills this in cooperation with other US government agencies in three ways:[15]

1. By providing analyses on threats to emerging or existing technologies and on threats to critical facilities in the United States or overseas.

2. By identifying and broadly disseminating information on human and technical collection methods used by foreign powers against the United States, including threats encountered by US businessmen at home or overseas.
3. By assessing the CI aspects of foreign disclosures, foreign ownership, technology transfers, and joint ventures.

In cooperation with other US government agencies, the ONCIX can provide reports, as appropriate, to US private firms with and without classified government contracts. The ONCIX has responded to limited tasking from US corporations for threat information and seeks to make this service more available to private-sector customers.

h. The *ONCIX* maintains an awareness section, which also serves as a body for CI training and awareness programs. As such, it can facilitate both the development and monitoring of the effectiveness of US government awareness programs to both the public and private sectors. CI information describing the threat to US industry is incorporated into these awareness presentations.[15]

i. *Department of Energy.* DOE's CI Program mission is to deter and neutralize foreign intelligence activities in the United States directed at or involving DOE programs, facilities, technology, personnel, and sensitive unclassified and classified information. The DOE Counterintelligence Division communicates the foreign threat through its awareness training program, analysis program, foreign travel briefing and debriefing programs, and the dissemination of intelligence threat information to employees, scientists, managers, and security personnel. The Counterintelligence Division regularly publishes classified and unclassified analytical studies. Bulletins, newsletters, and other information about foreign intelligence threats to DOE facilities and personnel are also made available. This threat information is also shared with other US government agencies and US corporations who have entered into Cooperative Research and Development Agreements with the DOE.[15]

j. *Department of Commerce.* Although the Department of Commerce does not have a formal program to provide CI support to US business, it provides informal assistance through security awareness briefings to contractors and consultants with access to classified information. Its Office of Export Enforcement conducts an industry outreach program that provides information to numerous industry officials each year on CI as it relates to illegal technology transfer. Various Department of Commerce components also publish newsletters and magazines that contain highlights of security incidents and illicit export practices.[15]

k. *US Customs.* In support of its multifaceted mission, Customs has for years operated several education and outreach programs designed to familiarize the private industry with the export laws and regulations and with the Customs Service roles in enforcing them. These programs have included threat information when it applies to export issues.[15]

l. *National Aeronautics and Space Administration (NASA).* NASA provides specific threat information to NASA employees and contractors involved in Special Access Programs through approximately 1500 security awareness briefings annually. Although there are no NASA resources solely dedicated to conducting awareness briefings, security specialists are usually assigned the tasks.[15]

OPTIONS FOR CONSIDERATION

Report the specific measures that are being or could be undertaken in order to improve the activities referred to in the above paragraphs, including proposals or any modifications of law necessary to facilitate the undertaking of such activities.

CI efforts are governed by presidential directives, executive orders, and statutes, many of which were established during the Cold War and were designed to counter a corresponding threat: that is, foreign intelligence activities directed against US military and political information. Over the past decade, some of these guidelines have been adapted to better confront the post-Cold War reality that economic and technological information are as much a target of foreign intelligence collection as military and political information.[15]

Law enforcement efforts are similarly limited because economic and technological information are often not specifically protected by federal laws, making it difficult to prosecute thefts of proprietary technology or IP. Law enforcement efforts instead must rely on less specific criminal laws, such as espionage, fraud and stolen property, and export statutes, to build prosecutable cases against foreign economic and industrial intelligence collectors and to deter such activity. Previous administrations have considered (and now the current administration is considering) legislative options to strengthen current federal statutes, as well as new laws that would specifically forbid theft of IP and proprietary information.[15]

While other options are under various stages of consideration, the following are included as examples.

Executive Branch Policy Options. Increase resources available to US CI and law enforcement organizations to investigate and, where appropriate, prosecute entities involved in industrial and economic intelligence collection activities targeting US information.

As attested by the Aldrich Ames espionage case, or the more recent and specific cases involving Chinese espionage over the past decade, the end of the Cold War has not stopped the collecting of information through espionage. CI agencies continue to allocate resources against traditional intelligence threats. However, while such threats have continued, an increasing portion of CI and law enforcement resources are also being drawn to thwart economic and industrial intelligence collection activities.[15]

Institutionalize the concept that economic security is an integral part of national security.

The goal of CI must be and is to identify, penetrate, and neutralize foreign intelligence activities threatening America's national security. CI has traditionally been directed at military, ideological, or subversive threats to national security.

In today's world in which a country's power and stature are often measured by its economic and industrial capability, foreign government ministries—such as those dealing with finance and trade—and major industrial sectors are increasingly looked upon to play a more prominent role in their collection efforts. While a military rival steals documents for a state-of-the-art weapon or defense system, an economic competitor sets out to steal a US company's proprietary business information or government trade strategies. Just as a foreign country's defense establishment is the main recipient of US defense–related information, and when foreign companies and commercially oriented government ministries are the main beneficiaries of US economic information, then China can consider such targets as a possibly easier way to obtain economic and technical secrets since many countries do not have higher levels of security protection and their personnel are not as well trained and educated against the PRC threat. The aggregate losses that can mount as a result of such efforts can reach billions of dollars per year, constituting a serious national security concern.[15]

The March 1990 and February 1995 national security strategies published by the White House focus on economic security as an integral part not only of US national interest but also of national security. If nothing else, the reader should look to these past strategy reports and see how they impact the current world. A few names and methods may have changed, but the bottom line is still the same: get America's secrets.

In February 1995, President Clinton published *A National Security Strategy of Engagement and Enlargement*[3] in accordance with the Goldwater–Nichols Defense Department Reorganization Act of 1986. It identified the US central goals as:

- To sustain our security with military forces that are ready to fight
- To bolster America's economic revitalization
- To promote democracy abroad

The report identified US intelligence capabilities as critical instruments of national power and noted that:

> The collection and analysis of intelligence related to economic development will play an increasingly important role in helping policy matters understand economic trends. That collection and analysis can help level the economic playing field by identifying threats to US companies from foreign intelligence services and unfair trading practices.

The report also describes the US government partnership with business and labor, noting:

> Our economic strategy views the private sector as the engine of economic growth. It sees government's role as a partner to the private sector—acting as an advocate of U.S. business interests; leveling the playing field in international markets; helping to boost American exports; and finding ways to remove domestic and foreign barriers to the creativity, initiative and productivity of American business.

Guidance issued from 1990 to the present has continually directed the intelligence and CI communities, specifically the latter, to detect and deter foreign intelligence targeting of US economic and technological interests, including efforts to obtain US proprietary information from companies and research institutions that form our strategic industrial base.[15]

Consistent with US national security policy since 1990, then, the CI community has emphasized economic security in operations, reports, and briefings designed to fulfill the guidance indicated above, designing and implementing a coordinated CI and law enforcement approach and appropriate collection and analytic requirements to address foreign economic and industrial intelligence collection activities.

Previous reports that have been sponsored by the executive and legislative branches have found that efforts across the spectrum of government to investigate and counter economic and industrial intelligence collection activities were often fragmented and uncoordinated. The CI and law enforcement communities have usually not truly been effective in harmonizing their efforts. With any government bureaucracy, there have been numerous interagency working groups and committees formed to discuss the problem while, at the same time, a number of individual agencies were exerting efforts on their own. This lack of coordination resulted in many partially informed decisions and diverging collection and analytical efforts. A coordinated CI and law enforcement approach and appropriate collection and analytic requirements needed to be developed.[15]

There have been numerous efforts to determine the CI needs of various traditional and nontraditional intelligence consumers, and in the process of surveying agency customers, it was learned that many needs have not fully been met in the past, either because no mechanism was in place to fulfill the needs or because the existing mechanism was malfunctioning. As part of a program of determining CI needs, there needed to be a better approach in forming the appropriate and manageable requirements to ensure that (1) necessary information was being collected, and (2) once the information is collected, it reaches those that need it in a timely manner.[15]

Collectors are continuing to seek out that broad range of civilian technologies, such as pharmaceuticals, biometrics, nanotech/miniaturization, manufacturing processes, and public safety systems. These areas, 20 years ago and even today, further exemplify the range of restricted or proprietary civilian technologies that needed to be protected.

CI COMMUNITY EFFORTS TO PROTECT TECHNOLOGY

Proactive would be the greatest approach, but over the years, it seems that reactive approaches are being used. This is mainly because the specific threat is not identified to a given topic area, at a given location, and the collector(s) are not identified; the greater action is thus not taken until it is too late. In May 2012, the FBI started putting up billboards across the nation, using public awareness, newspapers, and television to get the word out to the American populace, that America's economic secrets are being stolen. The FBI web site provides information that should be reviewed by all citizens, especially those involved in new or continuing businesses, wherein economic secrets are possessed and might be vulnerable. As stated in *Report to Congress on Foreign Economic Collection and Industrial Espionage, FY 2008* released by the ONCIX, the CI community "encompasses a broad set of Federal agencies and departments, each of which works to protect sensitive information and technologies from unlawful foreign acquisition. It includes intelligence collectors, analysts, and law enforcers, who meet regularly in a variety of forums to ensure the timely sharing of information and rapid prosecution of key cases."[16] This effort by the FBI will greatly assist them in determining if there are potential threats to any given company and its trade secrets. The FBI will be the central point in collecting and then disseminating information received by the various intelligence community members. A sample of the support provided by community members, excerpted from the Repot, includes the following:

- The ONCIX spearheads a number of efforts that provide impetus to, and an organizational hub for, the intelligence community to combine resources to track CI threats to the nation. The CI Community also supports the ONCIX Community Acquisition Risk Section (CARS), which evaluates the risk to the IC posed by US commercial entities that conduct business with foreign firms. CARS, with CI Community support, also provides threat assessments to the Committee on Foreign Investment in the United States (CFIUS) to help ensure that foreign investment does not endanger US strategic interests.
- The Air Force Office of Special Investigations (AFOSI) identifies critical Air Force technologies, analyzes threats against those technologies, directs measures to mitigate those threats, and investigates suspicious activities by foreign nationals when warranted. AFOSI also shares related intelligence with other US government agencies and cooperatively tracks and analyzes the changing nature of the threat to American technologies.
- The Army Counterintelligence Center (ACIC) supports the DOD in characterizing and assessing the efforts of foreign entities—government and private—to unlawfully target or acquire critical US technologies, trade secrets, and proprietary technology information. ACIC produces assessments for technology programs based on data resident in the SENTINEL CI database and assesses a foreign country's ability and willingness to protect US technology from unauthorized transfer or disclosure.
- The DIA assesses foreign intelligence efforts to obtain classified and critical US technologies. The DIA examines the means used to collect against US targets, including those by foreign intelligence and security services, and the impact of theft. In addition, the DIA supports DOD acquisitions by working with CARS to protect against foreign intelligence collection. The DIA also helps protect critical DOD technologies through its participation in the intelligence community process to examine foreign ownership, control, and influence of US assets and provide input to CFIUS.
- The DOE has a number of facilities and national laboratories that employ a variety of CI countermeasures to protect against the loss of critical nuclear technologies. The DOE Office of Intelligence and Counterintelligence oversees a number of programs aimed at countering the threat from foreign acquisition. The programs include policy development, field oversight, professional training, awareness training, analysis of CI threats, and investigations and operations support. DOE CI personnel have limited investigative authority to support the FBI in the conduct of CI investigations and offensive CI operations.
- The DSS implements the National Industrial Security Program for over 12,000 cleared defense contractor facilities across the United States. DSS CI specialists provide threat awareness briefings, give referrals of suspicious incidents to investigative agencies, and produces intelligence information reports for dissemination throughout the CI Community. On the basis of suspicious incidents reported by contractors, DSS CI personnel trace and analyze the changing nature of the threat to US technologies. CI specialists team with DSS

Industrial Security Specialists for security reviews of contractor facilities, using current threat information to assist contractors in developing tailored security countermeasures. The DSS maintains a training facility outside Baltimore, Maryland, providing formalized security training for government contractors. Security awareness information and various brochures and pamphlets are available from their web site.

- The FBI's Counterintelligence Division is responsible for most of the Bureau's efforts to prosecute and prevent economic espionage in the United States. The division relays the seriousness of foreign threats to US companies, laboratories, and other US entities by providing presentations, publishing tactical and strategic intelligence products, and hosting meetings and working group sessions. Within the Counterintelligence Division, the Counterespionage Section handles investigations that fall under the purview of the EEA. This section administratively supports and gives operational assistance to FBI field divisions that undertake these investigations. The Counterintelligence Division's Domain Section, which began operations in August 2005, oversees efforts to identify and address CI vulnerabilities and threats to critical technologies. The section maintains national security–related liaison initiatives through business and academic alliance programs and provides strategic CI operational leadership and focus through national and regional working groups.
- The Office of Counterintelligence of the National Geospatial-Intelligence Agency (NGA) works to protect the Agency's capabilities, personnel, and facilities. NGA maintains a Threat Mitigation Center, designed to further integrate and enhance NGA collaborative efforts in areas such as operational security, industrial security, and information assurance. To achieve synergy between the CI and law enforcement communities, NGA has a full-time presence within the ONCIX. The NGA has also created a Research Technology Protection Oversight Council to design, develop, implement, and evaluate tactics, techniques, and procedures required to protect new technologies through all stages of the acquisition, research, development, test, and evaluation process.
- The NRO has worked to improve the identification of espionage threats to its operations, programs, and personnel as well as increase the awareness of targeting efforts by nontraditional threat countries and groups. In support of its contractor community, there are tailored briefings of current threats to technology and targeting methods. In addition, the CINet system is a secure, automated, web-based intranet system that uses electronic forms to streamline the reporting of foreign contact and foreign travel, allowing for the dissemination of threat information and briefings to security officers and authorized users within, and outside of, government facilities. The CINet further provides users with a means of submitting requests for specific CI services. They also work closely with the FBI and other mission partners to protect NRO resources.
- The Director of National Intelligences' Open Source Center (OSC), which opened on 2005, advances the intelligence community's exploitation of openly available information to include the Internet, databases, press, radio, television, video, geospatial data, photos, and commercial imagery. The Center's functions will include collection, analysis and research, training, and information technology management to facilitate government-wide access and use. The Center will build on the established expertise of the CIA's Foreign Broadcast Information Service, which has provided the US government a broad range of highly valued products and services since 1941. In this regard, it contributes to the CI community's effort against China by monitoring foreign-language publications and Internet web sites for indications of threats and sharing this information with appropriate agencies, including law enforcement. OSC translates significant open-source materials on CI issues. It monitors European media reporting on economic intelligence and industrial espionage. OSC has taken the initiative in organizing community conferences and working groups aimed at countering specific CI challenges and has supported a wide variety of ad hoc requests from offices throughout the intelligence community.

The Center's establishment is a step toward the National Intelligence Strategy of the United States of America's goal to build an integrated intelligence capability and tap expertise where it resides.[16]

REFERENCES

1. Office of the National Counterintelligence Executive (ONCIX), February 2004.
2. *National Security Strategy*, The White House, Washington, D.C., February 1995.
3. *A National Security Strategy of Engagement and Enlargement*, White House, Washington, D.C., February 1995.
4. Hearing on Economic Espionage, Senate Select Committee on Intelligence and Senate Committee on the Judiciary, Subcommittee on Terrorism, Technology and Government Information, Washington, D.C., Feb 28, 1996.
5. Office of the Press Secretary, Fact Sheet, The Presidential Decision Directive on CI-21: counterintelligence for the 21st century, The White House, Washington, D.C., January 5, 2001, found at: http://fas.org/irp/offdocs/pdd/pdd-ci-21.htm.
6. Support to countering foreign intelligence, found at: http://cia.gov/library/reports.
7. Federal Register, National Counterintelligence Center, Privacy Act of 1974: Establishment of a New System of Records, February 27, 1997 (Volume 62, Number 39) [Notices, Pages 8995–8998], [DOCID: fr27feb97-115], from the Federal Register Online via GPO Access, found at: http://wais.access.gpo.gov, located at cryptome.org.
8. Department of Justice, The No Electronic Theft ("NET") Act, Computer Crime and Intellectual Property Section, Washington, D.C., undated.
9. Statement of Marybeth Peters, The Register of Copyrights before the Subcommittee on Courts and Intellectual Property Committee on the Judiciary, United States House of Representatives, 105th Congress, 1st Session, September 11, 1997, No Electronic Theft (NET) Act of 1997 (H.R. 2265).
10. Bill Text Versions, 105th Congress (1997–1998), H.R.2265, No Electronic Theft (NET) Act, found at: http://thomas.loc.gov.
11. 2010 Joint Security Plan on Intellectual Property Enforcement, White House, Washington, D.C., June 2010.
12. The White House, Office of Management and Budget (OMB), Office of the U.S. Intellectual Property Enforcement Coordinator, Remarks by the President at the Export-Import Bank's Annual Conference, March 11, 2010.
13. 2011 U.S. Intellectual Property Enforcement Coordinator Annual Report on Intellectual Property Enforcement, the White House, March 2012.
14. *The Militarily Critical Technologies List (MCTL), Security Awareness Bulletin*, Number 2-95. Richmond, VA: Department of Defense Security Institute.
15. Annual Report to Congress on Foreign Economic Collection and Industrial Espionage, July 1995, National Counterintelligence Center (NACIC), Washington, D.C.
16. Office of the National Counterintelligence, Executive (ONCIX), Annual Report to Congress on Foreign Economic Collection and Industrial Espionage, FY 2008, NCIX-007-09 July 23, 2009, Retrieved April 3, 2013 found at: http://www.ncix.gov/publications/reports/fecie_all/fecie_2008/2008_FECIE_Blue.pdf.

13 The DOD View of IP Theft
*A Trend Analysis of Reporting on Foreign Targeting of US Technologies**

Eternal vigilance is the price of liberty.

Attributed to John Philpot Curran[1†]
Dublin, Ireland, 1790

The above quote is equally applicable to the United States in the present era. Each and every day, various foreign entities attempt to break through our collective defense systems to illegally acquire US technological secrets. Some succeed; some don't, and they try again and again. As such, US national security rests deeply upon the collective success of all government agencies and organizations, government contractors, researchers, manufacturers, research and development (R&D) units, information technology (IT) security professionals, and just plain interested and involved individuals who want to thwart these persistent attacks.

As a nation, the United States has the most open society and government of the world. Because of this simple fact alone, sensitive, classified, and developmental items of information about the government, in addition to the private sector from whence comes the majority of the development of new ideas and products, are extremely ripe for those individuals, foreign corporations, and nations who target these areas for economic information via espionage. Much to the chagrin of many people, a lot of valuable information is available in various government reports and Congressional hearings. While much of the reports seem to be dry reading, the value comes from the knowledge that certain programs are now available, various items are being researched, new military weapons and aircraft are being built, the names of various government contractors and researchers are known since they may well be testifying in Committee hearings, and, oh yes, new methods of doing something are identified or at least pointed in a general direction of where further information might be obtained.

Any decent collector gleans these items of information and puts them on their "to do" or "to find out more about" lists. How much is known about foreign espionage attempts are laid out in striking detail, identifying who, when, where, and how such espionage is being conducted. Were it not for this fact, this book might never have been written. In any other country of the world, such information, to include the open press, would not have the ability to provide such information to the general public should they desire to read and learn about it. The author has taken the liberty of obtaining a

* Much of the information for this chapter, in some cases extensive verbatim excerpts, originates from the Department of Defense Publication *Targeting U.S. Technologies: A Trend Analysis of Reporting from Defense Industry* from the years 2009 to 2012. Note: For the serious reader, the author recommends going onto the Internet and reading the various DSS' Trend Analysis for the past half-dozen years to obtain a complete and more detailed understanding of what is happening in terms of technology thefts.

† An early use of the words "eternal vigilance." *Bartlett's Familiar Quotations*, at least, lists this as the source of "eternal vigilance is the price of liberty" (15th ed., p. 397, footnote 8, 1980).

great deal of fascinating data through various government reports and Congressional hearings and also that which comes out of the Department of Defense (DOD).

The stakes are high in the battle against foreign collection and espionage targeting US technology, trade secrets, and proprietary information. Not only is national security at risk but also any technological edge, which is closely tied to the health of the US economy and the economic success of the cleared contractor community. Most importantly, every time an adversary gains access to restricted information, it jeopardizes the lives of the military warfighters, since an adversary can use the information to develop more lethal weapons or countermeasures.

Preventing such loss is a team effort. The Defense Security Service (DSS), a part of the DOD in this effort, supports national security by overseeing the protection of a portion of the nation's technological base as it covers both US and foreign classified information in the hands of government and cleared industry. The DSS Counterintelligence Directorate seeks to identify and stop those who would attempt to or actually succeed in penetrating US defenses. In this mission, DSS relies on the support of cleared contractor employees and the US intelligence and law enforcement communities.

To do this, it is necessary for the DSS to collect an extremely wide variety of data from many sources, and then the DSS draws it together, using a variety of analysis techniques to verify the information, puts it in order of importance, determines what percentages of the threats are from given areas of the world and any country in particular going after one or more specific types of information, looks at the past threats from a given area or country, compiles the data, and then clearly articulates the various identified threats to US information and technology resident in defense contractor–cleared industries. Once completed, the DSS publishes annually a valuable publication entitled *Targeting U.S. Technologies: A Trend Analysis of Reporting from Defense Industry.*[2–5] It provides an overview of what is happening since the last report and includes a statistical analysis of those suspicious contact reports (SCRs). The information contained in this annual publication helps employees, companies, intelligence, and law enforcement professionals to better understand the continuing yet changing nature of the threats. For the reader, whether within or outside government, or is one who is just plain interested, the report gives rise to numerous insights about the actual espionage concerns that are not normally known by the average individual.

In the latest fiscal year report reviewed, federal investigative or intelligence agencies opened more than 200 operations or investigations based on information that industry provided to the DSS.

BACKGROUND

The DOD requires the DSS to publish each year a classified report detailing any suspicious contacts occurring within the cleared contractor community. Suspicious contacts in this case refer to or mean any contact that is not legitimate in terms of the contractor's business with the government. Sometimes such contacts are wholly innocent such as a misdialed telephone number and the follow-on conversation that piques the interest of the contractor, or it might be a written or e-mail request for information (RFI) from a legitimate researcher, but in these cases, the material or information sought is just a bit too close to a government project, thus the individual needs to be checked out. All these requests, even if they are unintentional, require that an SCR is made to the DSS.

The DSS will go through the reports and then focus on various threat indicators that show a potential threat for the compromise or exploitation of cleared contractor personnel, or on methods that might be used to illegally obtain, or to gain unauthorized access to, sensitive or classified information or technologies resident in the US-cleared industrial base. For the average person interested in the subject of foreign espionage, and Chinese espionage in this particular case, much less other countries around the world, the DSS also releases an unclassified version of the report that is also available to the general public. Unfortunately, this report is seldom seen by the majority of potentially interested people as they just don't know about it or have never taken the time to seek it out.

THREAT ENTITIES

The DSS groups the various threat entities into the following sectors:

Commercial—Those entities whose span of business endeavors includes the defense sector.

Government Affiliated—All research institutes, laboratories, universities, or contractors that are being funded by, representing, or otherwise operating in cooperation *with a foreign government* or government agency, whose shared purposes may include acquiring access to US sensitive, classified, or export-controlled information.

Individuals—Any person who, for financial gain, or ostensibly for academic or research purposes, will seek to acquire some form of access (legitimate or otherwise) to US sensitive, classified, or export controlled information or technology, for the purposes of transferring it out of the country.

Government—Ministries of Defense (by any name) and branches of the military, as well as foreign military attachés, foreign liaison officers, and the like. The author believes this could also include, but is not necessarily limited to, diplomatic personnel attached to embassies, consulates, and legations, or other foreign government entities that are legitimately in the United States. While the DSS does not specifically ascribe to this, it is probably true in some instances, but not necessarily proven.

Unknown/Other—Those instances wherein no attribution of a contact that could be identified as being tied to a specific end user could be directly made.

As of the latest data available, the DSS noted that the RFI is the most common method of operation (MO), followed by suspicious network activity (SNA). The RFI has always been a major route in seeking information or at least a simple way that would allow a collector to "gain a foot in the door." Despite a dramatic lead in the past, the percentage of SCRs reporting RFIs have decreased somewhat across the board since FY09. In East Asia and the Pacific, that area of the world we are truly interested in, SNAs have continued to increase significantly both in numbers of reports and in the percentage of the overall total contacts being made against US government–affiliated contractor companies. This, the author surmises, is because the use of the computer and Internet makes it much safer and less time consuming, and is at a minimal cost for the potential return.

The use of RFIs makes it very likely that the collectors expect to obtain the required information (or at least some portion or another source that could possibly be used) without using the time-consuming and expensive resources employed by a traditional intelligence officer. Thus, RFIs can and will always offer an approach that is characterized by low cost yet offers the potential for a high reward return. The DSS has assessed that East Asian and Pacific collectors will almost certainly continue a substantial use of this MO.

The author must note that the electronic type of RFI requests will continue and always be with us, and that their expansion will increase more and more not only because it is easier and quicker but also because just about everybody is more readily adaptable to an almost entire electronic communications contact with other people. On the street; in the car, plane, train, or bus; or even with a given organization, the use of the cell phone or other devices is just so much easier than having to meet face to face. And the greater concern here is nobody thinks that anyone would be listening in, that the data will disappear when the discussion is completed, or that the security office will never know they may have disregarded security policy and procedures when discussing information in an unsecured and unprotected manner.

The reader must understand that the DSS does not identify specific countries in their unclassified report, but rather only regions of the world, grouping countries in that area into a block for reporting purposes. You only need to determine the level of technology available to a given country, their priorities, and their ability to acquire specific information to determine which country is in the best position to obtain and exploit the information. In the case of the East Asian and Pacific collector category, China, Japan, and Korea would lead the way in a descending order. It is also important to note that Japan and Korea do not even come close to what China is looking for in terms of sensitive data and trade secrets. Also, China has the money and people to really go after such items of value.

The DSS has, in their annual reports over the years, identified the various methods that are currently in use and those that are expected to be used in the foreseeable future, and they include the following:

- *Requests for Information*: Via phone, email, or webcard approaches, these are attempts to collect protected information under the guise of price quote or purchase requests, marketing surveys, or other direct and indirect efforts.
- *Suspicious Network Activity*: Via cyber intrusion, viruses, malware, backdoor attacks, acquisition of user names and passwords, and similar targeting, these are attempts to carry out intrusions into cleared contractor networks and exfiltrate protected information.
- *Solicitation or Marketing*: Via sales, representation, or agency offers, or response to tenders for technical or business services, these are attempts by foreign entities to establish a connection with a cleared contractor vulnerable to the extraction of protected information.
- *Academic Solicitation*: Via requests for or arrangement of peer or scientific board reviews of academic papers or presentations, or requests to study or consult with faculty members, or applications for admission into academic institutions, departments, majors, or programs, as faculty members, students, fellows, or employees.
- *Exploitation of Relationships*: Via establishing connections such as joint ventures, official agreements, foreign military sales, business arrangements, or cultural commonality, these are attempts to play upon existing legitimate or ostensibly innocuous relationships (Figure 13.1).
- *Conferences, Conventions, and Trade Shows*: This refers to suspicious activity at such events—especially those involving dual-use or sensitive technologies that involve protected information—such as taking of photographs, making sketches, or asking of detailed technical questions.
- *Official Foreign Visits and Targeting*: Via visits to cleared contractor facilities that are either pre-arranged by foreign contingents or unannounced, these are attempts to gain access to and collect protected information that goes beyond that permitted and intended for sharing to gain unauthorized access.

FIGURE 13.1 Seeming legitimate joint ventures, or overtures to partner and share technologies, are often one-way streets to turning valuable assets and information over to China.

- *Seeking Employment*: Via resumé submissions, applications, and references, these are attempts to introduce persons who, wittingly or unwittingly, will thereby gain access to protected information which could prove useful to agencies of a foreign government.
- *Targeting US Travelers Overseas*: Via airport searches, hotel room incursions, computer/device accessing, telephone monitoring, personal interchange, and the like, these are attempts to gain access to protected information through the presence of cleared contractor employees traveling abroad as a result of invitations and/or payment to attend seminars, provide training, deliver speeches, and the like.
- *Criminal Activities*: Via theft, these are attempts to acquire protected information with no pretense or plausibility of legitimate acquisition.
- *Attempted Acquisition of Technology*: Via direct purchase of firms or the agency of front companies or third countries, these are attempts to acquire protected information in the form of controlled technologies, whether the equipment itself or diagrams, schematics, plans, spec sheets, or the like.

DSS KEY FINDINGS

In their key findings, the DSS reported that collectors of information will continue to remain active in all the various collection areas. Such foreign collectors are making the most attempts to collect US information and technology using an ever-increasingly wide range of methods. You need only to peruse various newspaper reports on spying and espionage activities by China on a weekly or monthly basis to notice that a *bold and aggressive agenda* is being undertaken in China's multifaceted, pervasive, and innovative collection effort.

The collection entities and methodologies that China would consider as the most likely to yield the greatest *and most desired results* will come from their heavy reliance on commercial agents. This is important to understand because as much as the Internet is used in attempts to obtain information, the Internet is rather more of another tool to get specific direction or to target individuals, and that is what makes the Internet exceptionally valuable. At that point, the use of individuals now becomes more important since China doesn't want just the small nuggets of information that might be obtained from general open sources. They will try whatever means and methods possible to go to the actual source of information in order to obtain as much information at one time as possible. If they can succeed just once, then targeting and control of a targeted individual can result in a wider and greater amount of other useful information obtained over a shorter amount of time. Some individuals have worked for a number of years passing on information to the Chinese. As such, the US-cleared industrial base will continually find itself confronted by government, government-affiliated, individual, and unidentified collectors, each of which provide advantages in particular contexts.

The collection MOs will always span the range between the direct, immediate, and seemingly legitimate approaches to potential targets. These will include the usual and varying RFIs from "college students," researchers, and so on, who will use the Internet or mail system to seek information, to the indirect, long-term, and more opaque approaches, such as academic solicitation, individuals seeking employment, and the solicitation or marketing of services (support, R&D, design, construction, etc.), to the often obscure suspicious network activities that seek to penetrate US industry networks through computer trojans, viruses, brute force attacks, the insertions of bugs, weevils, backdoors, and so on.

Often, if one does any research at all, it will be found that many collectors do not truly discriminate between the desired technological information and other available information; rather, they will collect anything that might be of possible value. But with the many continued technological advances in the United States, whether they be measured by development level or interest across the board by industry, the open-source information that becomes publicly available will always continue to attract attention and, in doing so, identify new information sources and targets for collectors.

In some cases for the targeting of information, there is a more subtle approach, such as an RFI going from commercial-grade to military-grade specifications and systems. This approach is typical and more likely when they are with a cleared government contractor. In an attempt such as this, the "purchaser" has already developed a friendship or at least a business-like relationship with the contractor company. At some point in the negotiations, the purchaser may quickly or slowly upgrade the RFI or a product's specifications. The subtle undertone of such attempts would indicate to the contractor that the purchaser has a lot more money to throw into the pot, or that the deal might not be consummated if the upgraded specifications are not made available "for review." Either way, any reasonable person should realize that something wrong is happening. Attempting to upgrade specifications or system demands midway through the purchasing process likely constitutes a gross attempt to circumvent the US export control process for the protection of such sensitive information via misdirection or to use the cleared contractor's desire to complete a sale already in process, which would allow the supposed purchaser to gain access to otherwise restricted technology information.

While many of the attempts to obtain information are unsophisticated, in the past couple of years, there has been an increase in the number of relatively advanced "spear phishing" attempts over the Internet, pretty much in e-mails sent to specific individuals. These attempts also have a dangerous side to them.

In order to convince employees to download malicious applications, the prober would craft the e-mail in such a way that it appears as if it was being sent from within the company, and the recipient would see on their screen (such as when a person highlights the incoming e-mail then right-clicks on "properties") the appropriate contact information and uniform resource locators (URLs) designed to match or resemble those affiliated with the cleared facility. The URL might look legitimate, but upon close examination, it might have a misspelling in it, or the location of the site is not exactly the same as the company site, and is usually in a foreign country. Beyond lending an assumed credibility to the e-mail, the use of cleared contractor naming conventions in the URLs is also likely to facilitate the storage and organization of collected information, implying collaboration between multiple requesting entities. If the recipient does not really know the full company URL, the scheme may well happen because of the "trust factor" that the information request is from a legitimate user with appropriate access. When the attachment is opened, it becomes too late, as the prober now has some form of internal access, because a piece of concealed software within the attachment has just entered the computer system without anyone's knowledge.

The author is wary of attachments to e-mails as such phishing attempts almost always have one. This is one reason the author never opens such attachments unless the sender can be verified (usually with a quick phone call), so don't take such e-mails too lightly.

The proper phisher, if he (or she) is really good, will have studied the URL site information and crafted his (or her) e-mail to be business-like, or perhaps slightly "chatty" using buzzwords and terms that would be acceptable and reasonable for the intended recipient to feel at home and assume that the e-mail actually came from someone he had met at work, or a project, or in a professional capacity. These, when they work, are usually tried at larger companies where not everyone will know everyone else because of the sheer size of the organization. Adding an attachment to the e-mail for downloading helps when dealing with a request for specific information. The recipient of the e-mail downloads the attachment and then it is too late. A trojan, backdoor, or several lines of code in the attachment may well allow access to information or another way into the system, or automatically send information to an off-site computer controlled by the initial sender. In any of these cases, security is breached, a firewall is made ineffective, and information can be lost.

TARGETED TECHNOLOGY CONCERNS

If China acquires US information or technologies, or gets its hands on the specific product, they will go to great means in order to reverse engineer the acquired technology/product. In some cases, this will likely be to advance their R&D capabilities so as to meet national mandates, including the development of countermeasures, while in other instances, it will likely result from a desire to re-export the technology for profit.

With the above information now at hand, the reader can understand and reliably conclude that the technology base of the United States is under constant attack. This most pervasive and enduring threat is like the weather: ever present yet ever changing. Any perceived lull in attacks against a given technology base is like the eye of a storm: if you wait five minutes, the aggressiveness and nature of the attack will change. However, unlike the weather, the Chinese are calculating, cunning, and manipulative. Their motivations may vary from striving for the advantage on some future battlefield to simply stealing information and technology for economic gain now or in the long-term future. No matter the motivation, any loss of technology to an adversary or competitor degrades a nation's strength, both militarily and economically.

During the last fiscal year, US defense contractors have witnessed a stunning increase close to 150% in the number of SCRs that were determined to be of intelligence value. By the time this book is released to the public, the percentage may well have risen to above 160% or maybe up to about 175%. Identified percentage increases likely result not only from aggressive foreign collection targeting cleared industry but also from the diligence of cleared industry in identifying and reporting suspicious activity. Although not all suspicious activity is actually that of a collector, some could probably be identified as that of just plain aggressive people seeking information in order to make a business proposal or for their own personal research into a subject area of interest to them or perhaps even professional interest. When suspicious activity reports involve actual targeting, then the DSS is very interested. For example, improved general awareness about computer network operations could easily account for a major increase in the number of reports on suspicious activity at cleared contractor facility networks. This is only because people became aware and wanted to know more about network operations for their own edification. Ask any newspaper reporter in the IT or business sector. If it piques their interest and a possible article can result, they will doggedly and diligently dig to find a few scraps of information. And when somebody else, like a collector, reads the article, their interest is also piqued and they start digging. And the collector probably has a lot more resources to target this item of interest.

Realizing that technology collection spans the entire spectrum of categories on the Military Critical Technologies List, continual industry reporting would show that information systems are currently receiving the most attention.

The low-cost advantage of targeting US technologies by using RFIs is extremely common and accounts for nearly half of all the reported suspicious incidents. Computer network operations, as they are categorized under the term *suspicious network activity*, have had the greatest increase in reporting by industry. This very likely reflects a persistent constant cyber collection attack that has been specifically directed toward industry and also shows the greater use of improved network monitoring to see these sometimes subtle attacks on the network system.

During the past several years, academic solicitations have also enjoyed a significant increase in targeting and collection. These academic solicitations—where students, professors, scientists, and researchers are used as collectors—were recently identified more specifically and then became a new category for the DSS. Previously, the DSS had classified academic solicitations as belonging to the old categories of seeking employment, direct requests, and foreign travel, depending on the specific situation as determined by the SCR. Recently, though, the use of academic solicitations has been noted to account for a higher percentage of all suspicious contacts than in the past. Because the increase continues, it is reasoned that this MO is a very viable information collecting method and will very probably continue to gain in popularity in those regions of the world lacking the capacity for more sophisticated computer network operations or experiencing difficulty in acquiring technology due to export controls or economic sanctions. That being said, China would not be averse to using other locations from around the world where they have a foothold to use academic solicitations. A solicitation from a country that is trying to develop a sense of increased economic development might not be viewed as suspicious as one that could be traced back to China.

The author notes that in addition to China being more sophisticated than other countries in the Far East and Mid-East regions, it has supplemented regional populations with its own citizens. From various other countries then, these Chinese can seem like legitimate "academics" in their RFIs, assistance, looking for jobs in their regions, and so on. Employers then will not see them as "specific Chinese" but rather people from another country and might be caught unaware or at least let their guard down somewhat when a solicitation arrives in their inbox.

OVERALL DOD CONCERNS: A SUMMARY

Because maintaining US high-technology protection and, thus, maintaining US world competitiveness require access to and application of the latest technologies, the DOD contract facilities and their employees must always be aware of the potential for direct, indirect, and subtle attempts to obtain information. Not just in the United States, but anywhere else in the world where the DOD has contacts and contracts and where it provides high-technology products and services, can you find contractor facilities working alongside other local government organizations. Developing innovative technology requires time and resources; some countries save both time and money by pilfering technology developed by others. Others save money by outsourcing the work, or by having it performed by a company spin-off or an overseas division of the same company. Security procedures may well become more lax, and local personnel may turn a blind eye to minor infractions, not ever realizing what is really happening right under their noses. In such areas or situations, foreign collectors, whether government, commercial, or individuals, will attempt to steal technology to gain a military or economic advantage. Their need for technology and their willingness to acquire it through questionable and highly illegal means will continue and probably grow in the near future. As such, government contractors will continue to be the prime target for anyone seeking to obtain the latest technologies. Further, it can be expected that collectors can and will target the entire spectrum of technology to improve their military capabilities, develop countermeasures to US and other Western systems, or introduce rival systems into the commercial market for sale to other countries.

The author has spent the last few pages on RFIs because, except for having a person on-site to collect information, it is, as some have found to their regret, the easiest way to get information. While RFIs will very likely remain the most common MO for collection attempts, any organization with an adequate security education program that covers the topic with their employees will see that the foreign collectors will increase their use of SNA and academic solicitation to the maximum. They may not succeed because of good security practices, but any item of information obtained will provide them a further target or means to attempt to collect the rest of the desired information. The dependence on information systems for project development, for the storage of information, and for the continual use of communication will always be there to create vulnerabilities for any system that is connected to the Internet. The most important thing is that the more complex the system, the greater the possibility that a flaw or method will be found to exploit the system, no matter how great the firewalls. With the convenience of the Internet comes the greater possibility of computer network vulnerability and its exploitation by sophisticated adversaries.

Due to the availability of vast amounts of data stored on systems and networks connected to the Internet, there will always be collectors continuing to attack such systems, and they will be more likely to increase their attempts to exploit the Internet to obtain information from the DOD's cleared industries.

Additionally, just because a company is not directly affiliated to the DOD, such commercial businesses could be targeted because of their business affiliation with identified government contractors. The anonymity of the Internet and its applications, such as e-mail and web cards, allows collectors to hide their identities, so a company might believe a request is coming from a government contractor for information on possible products or items the contractor is interested in, or the reverse, the contractor receives a missive from a known company and acts upon it in ignorance of where the request is really coming from, and, again, information of value is lost to the collector.

Combine all this with the difficulty of tracing sophisticated cyber attacks simply points toward the likelihood of an increase in the number of attempted collections.

Next, because of their unique position and business with the US government, specifically the DOD, cleared contractor companies typically have the advanced expertise for the creation and development of newer and higher technologies that may not be found anywhere else in the world for even a decade or two to come. These then become advanced and highly sought-after technologies. This makes the companies the primary targets by collectors. Because of this, the threat to technology will always continue as the United States maintains its position as a leader in technological advancement. This will continue for the foreseeable future and collectors will take advantage of any avenue that will provide them access to the cutting-edge technology that will give them the ability to reverse engineer, restructure, or further develop their competitive edge both economically and militarily.

The ever-increasing trend toward using non-government-affiliated commercial surrogates as collectors to diffuse suspicions will certainly continue and increase more in the future. Since China has funds and the ability to send people worldwide for indefinite periods in attempts of further obtaining technology, it can be expected that they will utilize both authentic commercial businesses and illicit front companies in their attempt to acquire controlled technologies. Nevertheless, those non-traditional methods, especially from the college, university, and graduate student sector with the hope of gaining even a somewhat limited access to restricted US technology, will continue mostly unabated. China is more than willing to use this multidimensional approach, thus becoming a greater threat to US resources since it takes time and resources for counterintelligence and security personnel to determine exactly what is happening and then develop innovative and proactive countermeasures on the part of security personnel, the government contractors, and the public sector business enterprises.

This should be a much greater concern to Americans, but at times, it doesn't seem so. The rapid globalization of world economies means that traditional borders are quickly dissolved as commerce tends to rule more than politics. This includes defense-related industrial sectors and will drive an unprecedented degree of interface between US industry and foreign governments eager for information and technologies resident in the defense industry. Concern must be given to foreign entities because if such advanced technologies are provided, especially to emerging Third World countries so that they can possess viable military and technical competencies, understand that it will be much easier for China to obtain the information, data, or product there since security protection is not as high, and for a developing country, more money than they could ever dream will always sway a potential seller of sensitive information and technology.

Like the cutting-edge technical advancements they represent, the United States' dual-use technologies will always generate a sustained interest, irrespective of whether the collector has any actual interest in the specific commercial or military applications. Foreign commercial entities and joint enterprises will continue to complicate the defense industry's ability to distinguish between legitimate global business practices and illicit attempts to acquire US technologies. As always, this multidimensional threat environment will continue to require a concerted team effort between cleared contractors and security professionals to develop innovative and proactive countermeasures to secure the integrity of information and technology in the defense industrial base.

Another cause of concern for the DSS is the somewhat small percentage of traditional collection attempts that came from an unknown origin. In essence, it is not really known where the attempt actually comes from. To understand this, realize that some collection activity may not always be the ultimate end user of the targeted technology. Collectors can use various anonymous proxies or base their collection activity in another region of the world to conceal their intentions or the identity of the ultimate end user, or they use various third party people who don't really know what is actually being planned to attempt to gain the desired information. Such proxies might be a "for hire" type, someone masquerading as someone else (an individual, company, think tank, etc.), or it could just be a middleman in a much more complex venture to obtain information.

No matter where a suspicious request comes from, one can never be sure of the actual sender or of the actual recipient. This is somewhat disturbing since it muddies the water in terms of which nation, company, or individual is seeking the data and to what purpose it might be ultimately used.

REFERENCES

1. Curran, John Philpot, *Election of Lord Mayor of Dublin*, speech before the Privy Council, July 10, 1790. The Speeches of the Right Honorable John Philpot Curran, Davis, Thomas, ed., 1847, pp. 94–95.
2. Targeting U.S. Technologies: A Trend Analysis of Reporting from Defense Industry, 2009, unclassified, Defense Security Service, Washington, D.C.
3. Targeting U.S. Technologies: A Trend Analysis of Reporting from Defense Industry, 2010, unclassified, Defense Security Service, Washington, D.C.
4. Targeting U.S. Technologies: A Trend Analysis of Reporting from Defense Industry, 2011, unclassified, Defense Security Service, Washington, D.C.
5. Targeting U.S. Technologies: A Trend Analysis of Reporting from Defense Industry, 2012, unclassified, Defense Security Service, Washington, D.C.

14 Intellectual Property Rights *Patents, Copyrights, and Trade Secrets*

An individual has certain intellectual property rights (IPR) that derive from a patent, copyright, or trade secret. Such individual may wholly own them and do with such rights as they please, and many do, via licensing them to various manufacturers and companies to produce and sell the products, allowing a royalty type of revenue to accrue to the initial owner. Inventions and their impending patents, copyrights on books, records and CDs, and trade secrets of a company are items in need of protection. Protection through the law can be misunderstood, but is necessary to establish an owner's legal rights to the product, no matter what that product may be. This chapter is concerned with the various laws and what they say. Where appropriate, the reader will be directed to further information that cannot be included here due to its data size and level of detail.

In the publication *International Crime Threat Assessment*, the White House outlined succinctly, the threat and impact of patent information, breach of copyright and IPRs:

> Most intellectual property rights (IPR) affecting US businesses involve the theft of trade secrets and copyright, trademark, and patent violations. Criminal violations of intellectual property rights—particularly the sale of counterfeit or illegally manufactured products—distort international trade, undermine the legitimate marketplace, and cause extensive revenue losses to legitimate U.S. industries. The explosion of digitization and the Internet have further enabled IPR violators to easily copy and illegally distribute trade secrets, trademarks, and logos.
>
> U.S. businesses are particularly vulnerable and especially hard hit by counterfeiting and other forms of copyright, trademark, and patent infringement because the United States leads the world in the creation and export of intellectual property—primarily in motion pictures, computer software, sound recording, and book publishing. These industries contributed more than $270 billion to the US economy in 1996, or approximately 3.65 percent of GDP, according to International Intellectual Property Association estimates. Copyright industry products have surpassed agricultural products as the single-largest export sector in the US economy, and America's three largest software companies are now worth more than the steel, automotive, aerospace, chemical, and plastics industries combined.[1]

The value of many companies *lies in its intangible property*: those varied patents and trademarks, copyrights, inventions, as well as those specific and sometimes unique trade secrets, which also include the licensing of these properties to others to use and sell. Because of the value of such intellectual property (IP), America has a variety of laws to protect (to the extent possible) these properties from blatant theft.

Trade secrets are just one part of a family of laws known as IP, which also includes patents, copyrights, and trademarks, and although the laws provide a certain level of protection, these are, at times, seemingly confusing because they can overlap. There may be a wonderful invention developed, but the care in protecting a specific process is not always the best, such as in a patent application where too many details are given. Once the patent is issued, the details are now public but still protected by the patent. Such details are also now available to the People's Republic of China (PRC), which can then take them and develop its own product ... all because too much specific data were provided in the patent application, allowing the sensitive IP to become known to the general public.

US patent and copyright laws are among the most stringent in the world. Filing in the United States allows you only to sue a Chinese company in US courts, providing that company has offices or a subsidiary in the United States. Because the United States is such a great market for goods, every Chinese firm that wants to make a really big profit desires to sell its products in the United States. Having a strong, substantive patent is no assurance the item won't be stolen, but for the Chinese, it will at least slow down their attempts because of the possibility of being sued, and their products, confiscated. When the Chinese use blatant espionage to obtain data not within the patent and then recreate the product—with another name and possibly a few slightly different features—they are taking a chance the counterfeit items won't be stopped and confiscated by US customs. Since inspection of products from China are so numerous, the possibility of only a few being confiscated still allows many more to enter the United States and be sold.

The protection of IP is somewhat complex and can fall into various realms, including legal, information technology, and even human resources. The categories of IP for concern, consideration, and protection are patents, trademarks, copyrights, and trade secrets.

PATENTS

Patents protect the world of inventions.

To qualify for a utility patent, an invention must be

- Useful, that is, it is capable of performing its intended purpose.
- Novel, that is, it must differ in some way from the publicly known or existing knowledge in the field of the invention.
- Non-obvious, that is, persons working in the field of the invention would consider the invention unexpected and surprising.[2]

Patents are the grant of a property right to the inventor(s), being issued by the US Patent and Trademark Office (USPTO). Patents provide the inventor(s) the right to exclude others from making, using, offering for sale, or selling the invention within the United States or importing the invention into the United States and such products made by that process, referring to the specification for the particulars thereof. Applications for patents must be filed in the USPTO. Any person who "invents or discovers any new and useful process, machine, manufacture, or composition of matter, or any new and useful improvement thereof, may obtain a patent," including practically everything that is made by humans and the processes for making the products. "If the invention is a process, of the right to exclude others from using, offering for sale or selling throughout the United States, or importing into the United States, products made by that process, referring to the specification for the particulars thereof," that can also be patented. There are also "business process" patents that protect certain "ways of doing" that produce material or services.[2,3]

Patent law is specific to the subject matter of the application (the invention) in that it must be "useful"; that is, the subject matter has a useful purpose. The application must also include operativeness (it "works" as described). The subject matter sought to be patented must be sufficiently different from what has been used or described before (think "another patent") that it may be said to be non-obvious to a person having ordinary skill in the area of technology related to the invention. For example, the substitution of one color for another, or changes in size, are ordinarily not patentable.[2]

Types of Patents

There are three types of patents: utility, design, and plant, with utility patents being the most common form. Utility patents are available for inventions that are novel, non-obvious, and useful as detailed in 35 U.S.C. § 101.[4,5]

According on the US Patent Office, here is a list of what can be patented—utility patents are provided for a new, non-obvious, and useful:

- Process
- Machine
- Article of manufacture
- Composition of matter
- Improvement of any of the above

Note that in addition to utility patents, encompassing one of the categories above, patent protection is available for (1) ornamental design of an article of manufacture or (2) asexually reproduced plant varieties by design and plant patents.[6]

On some of the specific patents available, the US Patent Office outlines the following:

Utility Patent. This form of patent is issued for the invention of a new and useful process, machine, manufacture, or composition of matter, or a new and useful improvement thereof, and it generally permits its owner to exclude others from making, using, or selling the invention for a period of up to 20 years from the date of patent application filing, subject to the payment of maintenance fees. Approximately 90% of the patent documents issued by the USPTO in recent years have been utility patents, also referred to as "patents for invention."

Design Patent. These are issued for a new, original, and ornamental design for an article of manufacture. It permits the patent owner to exclude others from making, using, or selling the design for a period of 14 years from the date of patent grant. Design patents are not subject to the payment of maintenance fees.

Plant Patent. Issued for a new and distinct, invented or discovered asexually reproduced plant including cultivated sports, mutants, hybrids, and newly found seedlings, or other than a tuber propagated plant or a plant found in an uncultivated state. A plant patent permits the owner to exclude others from making, using, or selling the plant for a period of up to 20 years from the date of patent application filing. Plant patents are not subject to the payment of maintenance fees.[7]

Design patents do not apply to plants since it wouldn't make much sense to allow a plant application patent (often referred to as a PAP) on design patents because design patents only cover the near or exact ornamental appearance as shown in all the views; thus, your design really would have to be 100% done to count as supporting any subsequent full design application.[7]

A patent "protects" only when the patent holder enforces his rights to exclude others from using the patented invention or technology.[8,9]

A patent does not give the owner the right to make, use, or sell your invention. A US patent only gives the right *to exclude others*—except the US government—in the United States and its territories from making, using, and selling or importing your invention. Suppose you create a widget that is different from other widgets that received a patent. An owner of an enforceable prior patent on an older widget that is broader in its approach than yours (as provided for in the claims of their original patent) and which reads on your invention can stop you, various laws can stop you, and the government can stop you from making, using, and selling your own invention within the United States. Your US patent has no effect outside the United States or its territories.[10] Thus, any profits that accrue would be directed to the original widget owner, not you.

The bottom line is that a patent is a valuable business tool *only when it can be used to protect a profit stream.* As the White House publication *International Crime Threat Assessment* states:

Patent violations involve the illegal manufacture of products using production processes, designs, or materials that are protected by patents giving the holder the right to exclude others from making, using, or selling an invention for a specified period of time. The 1995 Agreement on Trade-Related Aspects of Intellectual Property Rights (TRIPS) requires that members of the World Trade Organization protect most inventions for a period of 20 years and that their domestic laws permit effective action against patent infringement.[1]

TRADEMARK AND SERVICE MARKS

The federal law of trademarks and service marks is designed to protect a commercial identity or brand used to identify a product or service to consumers. The Lanham Act (15 U.S.C. §§ 1051–1127) prohibits the unauthorized use of a trademark, which is defined as "any word, name, symbol, or device" used by a person "to identify and distinguish his or her goods, including a unique product, from those manufactured or sold by others and to indicate the source of the goods." By registering trademarks and service marks with the USPTO, the owner is granted the exclusive right to use the marks in commerce in the United States. They can likewise exclude others from using the mark (or similar/comparable mark), in a way likely to cause confusion in the marketplace.[11,12]

The benefits of owning a federal trademark registration on the USPTO Principal Register, according to the USPTO document *Basic Facts About Trademarks*, include the following:

- Public notice of your claim of ownership of the mark
- A legal presumption of your ownership of the mark and your exclusive right to use the mark nationwide on or in connection with the goods/services listed in the registration
- The ability to bring an action concerning the mark in federal court
- The use of the US registration as a basis to obtain registration in foreign countries
- The ability to record the US registration with the US Customs and Border Protection Service to prevent importation of infringing foreign goods
- The right to use the federal registration symbol®
- Listing in the USPTO's online databases[13]

The legal protection for trademarks and service marks ultimately helps protect the goodwill and reputation of the trademark or service mark owner but, by extension, helps promote better and more competition in the market, while at the same time protecting the consumer by helping to ensure they know the origin of products and services, for example, the manufacturer of the product.

Federal criminal law has long prohibited trafficking in goods or services that bear a counterfeit mark.

In March 2006, the criminal trademark statute was amended to also prohibit trafficking in labels or packaging bearing a counterfeit mark, even when the label or packaging is unattached to the underlying good. Individuals convicted of § 2320 offenses face up to 10 years' imprisonment and a $2,000,000 fine.[14]

A trademark (™) is a name, phrase, sound, or symbol used in association with services or products. It connects a brand with a level of quality on which companies have built their reputation. Trademark protection lasts for 10 years after registration and, like patents, can be renewed. But trademarks don't have to be registered. If a company creates a symbol or name it wishes to use exclusively, it can simply attach the ™ symbol, which effectively marks the territory and gives the company room to prosecute if other companies attempt to use the same symbol for their own purposes.[11]

- A **trademark** is a word, phrase, symbol, or design, or a combination of words, phrases, symbols, or designs, that identifies and distinguishes the source of the goods of one party from those of others.
- A **service mark** is the same as a trademark, except that it identifies and distinguishes the source of a service rather than a product.

A trademark can be varied in how it is seen and perceived. It can be words, a graphic image (picture or drawn), a unique design, sounds, even distinctive colors or a combination of colors, or smells (and combinations of those elements), anything that will identify and distinguish it from all others in terms of the products or goods of a given party from any other similar parties. A service mark (SM) is the same as a trademark, except that it identifies and distinguishes the source of a service rather than a product. To establish a trademark, it has to be used publicly, as being "attached" to a product of a type of business activity within a clearly defined or specific geographic location.[15]

Trademarks can be registered (®) by or nationally with the US Trademark Office. The mark must be deemed to be distinctive and not of a type that might be considered by many as generic, in which case any protection for it would be denied. As with copyrights being established when an author creates a book in tangible form, basic trademark protections accrue immediately upon the use of the mark in commerce. However, additional protections/rights are added through the registration process.[15]

US Trademark Act and Trade Dress

"Trade Dress" is somewhat unusual and not a term heard by the general public. It is the form, shape, or look of a product or service-distinctive packaging and presentation. Elements of trade dress are treated, by IP law, in ways similar to trademarks and service marks. Think of the big red K on yellow for a camera film package. You know exactly what company it relates to; you identify with the product's quality and an implied guarantee that it is the best; after all, it has been around for over a century.[16]

The USPTO Trademark Manual of Examining Procedure, Section 1202.02, states that trade dress constitutes a "symbol" or "device" within the meaning of §2 of the Trademark Act, 15 U.S.C. §1052. Trade dress originally included only the packaging or "dressing" of a product, but in recent years, it has been expanded to encompass the design of a product. It is usually defined as the "total image and overall appearance" of a product, or the totality of the elements, and "may include features such as size, shape, color or color combinations, texture, graphics."[16]

Thus, trade dress includes the design of a product (i.e., the product shape or configuration), the packaging in which a product is sold (i.e., the "dressing" of a product), the color of a product or of the packaging in which a product is sold, and the flavor of a product. The case of *Wal-Mart,* 529 US at 205, 54 USPQ2d at 1065 discussed the design of children's outfits as constituting product design; the *Two Pesos,* 505 US at 763, 23 USPQ2d at 1081 was somewhat unique in the determination that an interior of a restaurant is akin to product packaging; and the *Qualitex Co. v. Jacobson Prods. Co.,* 514 US 159, 34 USPQ2d 1161 (1995) seemed unusual in that the case revolved around whether color alone may be protectable. These several cases are only typical of what may be considered as trade dress since almost anything that is determined by someone to be capable of carrying some form of meaning could be used as a "symbol" or a "device," thus constituting a form of trade dress wherein it would identify the source or origin of a product. When it becomes difficult to determine whether a proposed mark is product packaging or product design, such "ambiguous" trade dress would be treated as product design. In essence, then, trade dress marks may be used in connection with goods and services.[16]

In some cases, it has been found that the nature of a potential trade dress mark may not be readily apparent. A determination of whether the mark constitutes trade dress would have to be provided by the applicant for a trademark to include a drawing, a description of the mark, the identification of goods or services the mark would be placed upon, and the specimen example, if any.[16]

In general terms, trade dress is functional, and cannot serve as a trademark, if there is a feature of the trade dress that is "essential to the use or purpose of the article or if it affects the cost or quality of the article."[16]

COPYRIGHT

Copyright is a form of protection grounded in the US Constitution and granted by law (Title 17, US Code) for original works of authorship fixed in a tangible medium of expression. Copyright covers both published and unpublished works.

As a form of IP law, copyright protects original works of authorship including literary, dramatic, musical, and artistic works, such as poetry, novels, movies, songs, computer software, and architecture. Copyright does not protect facts, ideas, systems, or methods of operation, although it may protect the way these things are expressed.[17,18]

A copyright protects original works of authorship, while a patent protects inventions or discoveries. Ideas and discoveries are not protected by the copyright law, although the way in which they are expressed may be. A trademark protects words, phrases, symbols, or designs identifying the source of the goods or services of one party and distinguishing them from those of others. US copyright laws have been created to protect written or artistic expressions fixed in some form of a tangible medium: books (novel or non-fiction), cartoons books, painting and lithographs, poems, songs, moves, DVDs, and CDs. *A copyright protects the expression of an idea but not the idea itself.* The owner of a copyrighted work has the right to reproduce it, to make derivative works from it (such as making a movie based on a book), or to sell, perform, or display the work to the public. It isn't necessary to register the material since current law provides for "copyright" immediately upon creation. But copyright registration is really prerequisite if it becomes necessary to sue for copyright infringement. A copyright lasts for the life of the author plus another 50 years.[17,18]

Subject to sections 107 through 122 of the Copyright law, the owner of copyright has the exclusive rights to do and to authorize any of the following:

- To reproduce the copyrighted work in copies or phonorecords
- To prepare derivative works based upon the copyrighted work
- To distribute copies or phonorecords of the copyrighted work to the public by sale or other transfer of ownership, or by rental, lease, or lending
- In the case of literary, musical, dramatic, and choreographic works, pantomimes, and motion pictures and other audiovisual works, to perform the copyrighted work publicly
- In the case of literary, musical, dramatic, and choreographic works, pantomimes, and pictorial, graphic, or sculptural works, including the individual images of a motion picture or other audiovisual work, to display the copyrighted work publicly
- In the case of sound recordings, to perform the copyrighted work publicly by means of a digital audio transmission

A copyright protects original works of authorship be they literary, dramatic, musical, or artistic. A copyright also gives the rights holder preference for the performance, distribution, display/performance, and reworking (derivative works) of the creative production. Copyright protection is in place whenever the material is fixed into a tangible medium of expression. For authors, these rights are secured for their lifetime plus 70 years. For a corporate author, the rights are secured for the shorter of 95 years from publication or 120 years from creation. An individual's standing in legal cases adjudicating copyright issues can be improved/augmented by displaying the copyright symbol © with the work. To ensure full protection under the law within the United States, the work should be formally registered with the US Copyright Office.[19]

A copyright protects the particular way authors have expressed themselves. It does not extend to any ideas, systems, or factual information that may be included and/or conveyed in a work.[20] Copyright protection is sometimes suspended due to "fair use." Fair use is established, in section 107

FAIR USE

The following is taken from the US Copyright Office's publication *Fair Use*.[21]

One of the rights accorded to the owner of copyright is the right to reproduce or to authorize others to reproduce the work in copies or phonorecords. This right is subject to certain limitations found in sections 107 through 118 Title 17, US Code, of the copyright law. One of the more important limitations is the doctrine of "fair use." The doctrine of fair use has developed through a substantial number of court decisions over the years and has been codified and can be found in section 107 of the copyright law.

Section 107 contains a list of the various purposes for which the reproduction of a particular work may be considered fair, such as criticism, comment, news reporting, teaching, scholarship, and research. Section 107 also sets out four factors to be considered in determining whether or not a particular use is fair:

- The purpose and character of the use, including whether such use is of commercial nature or is for nonprofit educational purposes
- The nature of the copyrighted work
- The amount and substantiality of the portion used in relation to the copyrighted work as a whole
- The effect of the use upon the potential market for, or value of, the copyrighted work

The distinction between fair use and infringement may be unclear and not easily defined. There is no specific number of words, lines, or notes that may safely be taken without permission. Acknowledging the source of the copyrighted material does not substitute for obtaining permission.

The 1961 *Report of the Register of Copyrights on the General Revision of the U.S. Copyright Law*[22] cites examples of activities that courts have regarded as fair use: "quotation of excerpts in a review or criticism for purposes of illustration or comment; quotation of short passages in a scholarly or technical work, for illustration or clarification of the author's observations; use in a parody of some of the content of the work parodied; summary of an address or article, with brief quotations, in a news report; reproduction by a library of a portion of a work to replace part of a damaged copy; reproduction by a teacher or student of a small part of a work to illustrate a lesson; reproduction of a work in legislative or judicial proceedings or reports; incidental and fortuitous reproduction, in a newsreel or broadcast, of a work located in the scene of an event being reported."

of the Copyright Act, in order to protect the reproduction of works for purposes such as criticism, comment, news reporting, teaching, scholarship, and research.[20]

What Does a Copyright Protect?

Copyright law has two goals: to protect the rights of authors, and, thereby, to foster development of more creative works for the benefit of the public. When the Constitution granted (in Article I, § 8, cl. 8) Congress the power to enact IP laws, it described both these goals and the means to achieve it: "To promote the Progress of Science and useful Arts, by securing for limited Times to Authors and Inventors the exclusive Right to their respective Writings and Discoveries." It has been found over time that maintaining an appropriate balance between protecting works and incentives for creators of works, on the one hand, and disseminating knowledge and information to the public, on the other, is a constant theme throughout the history of copyright law.[18,23]

An important limitation of copyright is that it protects *only the creative expression of an idea, but not the idea itself.* Novel ideas, methods, and processes may enjoy protection under patent law (or other areas of law, such as trade secret protection), but are not copyrightable. For example, consider a microbiologist who invents a new technique for modifying particular genes in a cell, then writes an article for a magazine that describes the technique. The article may be protected by copyright as the author's original expression of his or her ideas regarding this new technique. The technique itself, however, would not be copyrightable, although it may be patentable.

TRADE SECRETS

In their publication *State-Sponsored Crime: The Futility of the Economic Espionage from 2006,* Susan W. Brenner and Anthony C. Crescenzi offer a great account of the Economic Espionage Act and guidelines regarding trade secrets:

> The EEA takes a traditional approach to economic espionage by treating the misappropriation of proprietary economic information as theft and criminalizing it.[24] The premise is that by prosecuting and sanctioning those who unlawfully appropriate proprietary information, others will be deterred from engaging in such conduct.
>
> Under 18 U.S.C., section 1839(3), a trade secret "includes ... all types of information, however stored or maintained, which the owner has taken reasonable measures to keep secret and which has independent economic value."[25] The EEA encompasses intangible property, including "information stolen in electronic form or merely memorized."[26]
>
> Unlike patents, trade secrets need only be "minimally novel."[25] This means "a trade secret must contain some element that is not known and sets it apart from what is generally known."[27] The key attribute of a trade secret under the EEA is that it is information which "is not ... generally known to, and not being readily ascertainable through proper means by, (sic) the public."[25] It is not necessary that every aspect of the information be confidential; a trade secret can consist of a "combination of elements that are in the public domain," if the trade secret itself constitutes "a unique, effective, successful and valuable integration of the public domain elements."[28]
>
> To qualify as a trade secret, information must also derive independent economic value from not being generally known to the public.[29] ... According to the U.S. Department of Justice, the value of the trade secret need not be established.
>
> The final requirement for bringing information within the EEA's definition of a "trade secret" is that the owner(s) of the **information must have taken reasonable measures to keep the information secret.**[29] ... In this respect, trade secret law differs fundamentally from the laws that protect other types of property; theft and other statutes do not impose a similar requirement.[25,30]

All of the above is interesting and must be considered in protecting trade secrets and also when any legal action is taken against someone who steals it. When the theft is by a person representing the PRC, the individual caught suffers initially, and the trade secret owner suffers in the long run, because China has the trade secret and will use it. US law does not extend to China, and they well know it. In the past, China has stated that individuals acted on their own, not under the guidance and direction of the PRC. Individuals prosecuted have gone to jail and have been fined, but the PRC stands back and disavows them. For the United States to prove beyond a reasonable doubt that China specifically directed one or more individuals to steal the trade secret is not an easy task because there are no specific lines that can be traced back to the Chinese government. No money traded hands, and no documentation was found that specifically linked individuals within the government or one of their state agencies to the theft. Where documentation has been found, it has usually been from a non-government (directly) connected private sector company.

TRADE SECRET PROTECTION

Everything that qualifies for a patent can normally also qualify as a trade secret. But it cannot be both a patent and a trade secret; it must be one or the other! As a patent, the information will, at some point after the application is made, be made public and available to anyone who looks at patent office files. If it is patentable, there will have to be a determination made as to whether it is better to seek its protection via a patent or to maintain it and its subsequent continued protection as a trade secret.

According to the USPTO's *Small Business FAQ*:

> The first step in protecting your business from intellectual property (IP) theft is to protect your IP in both the United States and in any other country where you do business and source products. Most IP rights are territorial, meaning, for example, a U.S. patent or trademark only provides protection in the United States. To receive IP protection in other countries, you need to apply for protection in those countries.[31]

It is necessary that a company identifies its trade secrets. Proprietary information comes in many forms, so this should be coordinated with both the legal and the security departments. The legal department, for the protection that certain laws may afford a level of protection in court, in dealing with people who have access to or could in the future learn about it, and the security department, to receive their views and how they would protect it through physical measures, education, and training of employees. Also, every business enterprise should consider performing a cost/benefit analysis (CBA) or a comprehensive risk assessment (RA) and analysis to determine which IP protection measures make sense for both your individual IP and for your business. For some people, a CBA and a RA are the same. In a sense they are, but each takes a somewhat different approach and methodology to determine the results. If you must perform just one, then the RA is the way to go. The CBA can work, but as its name implies, it can be more of a monetary issue than a true protection issue for IP in all forms.

Again, it is important to note—not gloss over—that both the security and legal departments must be consulted. Different types of IP require different types and levels of protection. In an overseas environment, or any such area where there is a possibility of the IP being stolen, increased measures will become necessary.

By their very definition, trade secrets are *not* disclosed to the world at large. Owners of trade secrets protect trade secret information by implementing special procedures for handling it, in addition to technological and legal security measures. Such protections can include, but are not limited to, non-compete clauses and non-disclosure agreements (NDAs).[32]

The protection of a trade secret can extend indefinitely. This provides a definite advantage over patent protection, which only lasts for a specified period. As long as the trade secret is protected using a level of reasonable care to ensure, to that extent possible, that it will not be disclosed outside a small circle of people who must know the trade secret, it can extend over many decades. Consider the Coca-Cola formula as a prime example, wherein it is kept inside a locked vault under stringent protection and only three people have access to it.

Reasonable steps can mean different things to different people. In the case of trade secrets, it means that reasonable steps must be taken to prevent unauthorized disclosure. The first step is physically protecting the information. It may be put in a safe, a bank deposit box, or stored somewhere else where only a limited number of people may have access. In terms of access, consider a safe with two combination dials. One person has the combination to the first dial; the second person, the combination to the second dial. Both must be present to open the safe to access the trade secret.

In addition to physically securing the trade secret data, other reasonable measures are necessary. A company policy should state how trade secrets are to be protected, who may have access, what measures to be taken if the trade secret must be imparted to another person, what restrictions are to be placed on the knowledge obtained by another person, and so on. All these should be spelled out; hence, a lawyer who is versed in trade secrets should be used. It only takes one small misstep in documentation and protection procedures for the trade secret to become public, or to be stolen.

You have a subcontractor who will take the trade secret and use it to make a specific product to sell. Your company will receive a percentage of each sale and perhaps a royalty as well, depending upon the contract. A common tool for controlling the disclosure of this company trade secret is the use of an NDA. It might also be called a secrecy agreement. In either case, the NDA will delineate what disclosure limits are being placed on the subcontractor who signs it and lays out their responsibilities for protecting the trade secret while it is in their possession and, after the contract has run its course and is completed, it would state how the trade secret information they now possess will be destroyed, or if it will be returned to you (various paperwork pieces, for instance), and that they and any of their employees who had access to one part or all of the trade secret are still bound by the NDA and can't use that information anywhere down the road without your express consent.

The NDA is in your best interest, but the problem that arises is that China really doesn't care about an NDA or other type of agreement. They would gladly sign one to get the information, but then, since they now have what they wanted in the first place, they would go ahead and use it, regardless of the signed NDA. The limits, restrictions, and ability to prosecute only work where the individual/company who obtained it is in the United States. US laws do not extend to mainland China, and they know it.

China may be a member of the World Trade Organization (WTO) and, thus, a party to the Agreement on Trade-Related Aspects of Intellectual Property Rights (TRIPS), meaning they will take certain steps to protect trade secret information. Article 39 paragraph 2 of TRIPS requires that all member nations provide a means for protecting information that is commercially valuable information because it is a secret, and that the information is subject to reasonable steps to keep it protected. In the United States, this obligation can and is fulfilled by offering trade secret protection under various state laws. Note that while various state laws differ in the specificity of how it will be protected, there is an overall similarity between them as most states have adopted some form of the Uniform Trade Secrets Act.

The need to protect trade secret information is essential since the trade secret owner/holder must maintain secrecy of the information. If it is independently discovered through other means, or is accidentally (or deliberately) released to the general public, or in some other fashion becomes generally known, the protection afforded the information as a trade secret is lost. Since trade secrets do not have a "cutoff" date, their protection continues indefinitely or until discovery or loss.

According to the USPTO web site:

> Trade secret protection is an alternative to patent protection. Patents require the inventor to provide a detailed and enabling disclosure about the invention in exchange for the right to exclude others from practicing the invention for a limited period of time. Patents do expire and when that happens, the information contained within is no longer protected. Unlike trade secrets, patents protect against independent discovery. Patent protection also eliminates the need to maintain secrecy. While most anything can be kept secret, there are limitations on what can be protected by a patent. If a given invention is eligible for either patent or trade secret protection, then the decision on how to protect that invention depends on business considerations and weighing of the relative benefits of each type of intellectual property.[33]

CHINA'S IPR ENFORCEMENT SYSTEM

China has made overt efforts, some would term it window dressing, to enforce IPRs. According to the web site of the International Trade Administration within the Department of Commerce:

> In 1998, China established the State Intellectual Property Office (SIPO), with the vision that it would coordinate China's IP enforcement efforts by merging the patent, trademark and copyright offices under one authority.[34]

The Chinese law reads well, but there are grave consequences of formally handing over any of your IP and expect the same legal levels of protection that would be afforded the same in the United States. Because the PRC has this grandiose desire to economically rule the world, when you provide the appropriate information required under Chinese law, you are essentially handing it over to them on a silver platter; they just don't have to go all the way to the United States to obtain it.

The site goes on to say:

> If the information is somehow stolen, or is determined to be in the hands of an unauthorized individual/company, you only have the Chinese legal system to, perhaps, provide a glimmer of protection and get back what is rightfully yours. Protection of IP in China follows a two-track system. The first and most prevalent is the administrative track, whereby an IP rights holder files a complaint at the local administrative office. The second is the judicial track, whereby complaints are filed through the court system. (China has established specialized IP panels in its civil court system throughout the country.) Determining which IP agency has jurisdiction over an act of infringement can be confusing. Jurisdiction of IP protection is diffused throughout a number of government agencies and offices, with each typically responsible for the protection afforded by one statute or one specific area of IP-related law. There may be geographical limits or conflicts posed by one administrative agency taking a case, involving piracy or counterfeiting that also occurs in another region. China's courts also have rules regarding jurisdiction over infringing or counterfeit activities, and the scope of potential orders.
>
> For administrative enforcement actions, the following is a list of the major players. Again this list is not exhaustive, as other agencies, such as State Drug Administration (for pharmaceutical counterfeits) or the Ministry of Culture (for copyright materials and markets) may also play a role in the enforcement process. In most cases, administrative agencies cannot award compensation to a rights holder. They can, however, fine the infringer, seize goods or equipment used in manufacturing products, and/or obtain information about the source of goods being distributed.[34]

In researching this section, the author noted on the official China web site a couple of articles with pictures that illustrated China's enforcement of IPR. In one case, counterfeit music and other CDs were confiscated and destroyed. A very nice picture was included. What made it a mockery was that with several security people, a photographer, and a large piece of equipment to crush the confiscated material, all that was being destroyed could have fit in the trunk of a car. Publicity was the point of the picture and article to show that IP enforcement was being taken seriously, but the amount of material being destroyed was a farce.

IP protection in the Chinese environment can be tricky. The US government has created an "IPR Toolkit," which describes the IP environment in China and provides information about how to obtain and enforce IPRs in China. It can be found at the Department of Commerce's web site. You also need to be aware of some of the various offices in China that will consider your IP data. These include the following:

- The China Trademark Office maintains authority over trademark registration and administrative enforcement of trademark rights.
- The State Intellectual Property Office (China's patent office) is responsible for granting patents.
- The Quality Brands Protection Committee (QBPC), a private right holders organization, comprises more than 100 multinational companies in China that work cooperatively with the Chinese government to combat counterfeiting.
- The US government publishes an annual report, called the Special 301 Report, analyzing the situation in countries with inadequate IPRs protection and enforcement. The 2005 Special 301 Report, issued by the Office of the US Trade Representative (www.ustr.gov), is available and should be read and studied.
- The Small Business Administration web site relating to stopping fake products, found at www.stopfakes.gov/smallbusiness, is also a helpful resource.

WHAT THE US GOVERNMENT CAN DO IN IPR INFRINGEMENT CASES

The following is taken from the Department of Commerce's International Trade Administration online article, *Protecting Your Intellectual Property Rights (IPR) in China: A Practical Guide for U.S. Companies.*[35]

Many companies, particularly small- and medium-sized enterprises that discover their products are being infringed in China, will contact the Department of Commerce for assistance. Because IPRs are private rights, the Department of Commerce can provide only very limited direct assistance. In many cases, the US government can provide companies with information in navigating China's legal system, including lists of local investigative firms and attorneys, and share our government's experience and expertise in China. However, the Department of Commerce cannot provide American companies with legal advice or advocate on a company's behalf without the company first taking legal action.

When a company encounters blatant infringement of its IPR, the rightful owner of the IP will probably end up having to hire local legal counsel and pursue a preliminary investigation on their own or through a contracted professional firm, keeping in mind that US companies should ensure compliance with Chinese law, which restricts private investigation to certain forms of "market research" investigations. Once an initial investigation is complete, the company and its legal department would have to determine if further action and possible costs related with such actions are worth pursuing. IPR holders will have the option to initiate actions or seek redress through either the judicial or administrative system. Foreign IPR holders have had considerably less success in encouraging criminal prosecution of IPR violations, particularly when copyright infringements are involved.

Once a company decides to pursue a remedy, the Department of Commerce, either through the Washington, D.C.-based or through the China-based office, can monitor the case, if requested to do so by the rightful IPR owner/company. The US government cannot intervene in the case but can inquire about its status or contact government officials about concerns related to the effective administration of legal remedies available to IP holders. The Department of Commerce is most likely to become involved in a case where evidence indicates China is not complying with its enforcement under the WTO TRIPS Agreement. As with other types of commercial disputes, the Department's efforts in assisting with IPR disputes are aimed at achieving a fair and timely resolution in accordance with international commitments and Chinese laws and in advancing adequate legal and judicial protection for all parties.

The information provided here above by no means constitutes any form of legal advice and should not be substituted as that of advice from the company's legal department. Its sole intended purpose is only to provide an overview of China's IPR environment, available enforcement mechanisms, and Chinese government offices sharing jurisdiction over IPR protection and enforcement. It is recommended that US companies seeking to do business in China or are facing IPR infringement issues retain qualified US and Chinese legal counsel and pursue their rights through China's IPR enforcement regime.[34]

REFERENCES

1. White House, *International Crime Threat Assessment*, December 15, 2000, found at: http://whitehouse.gov/WH/EOP/NSC/html/documents/pub45270/pub45270index.html.
2. General Information Concerning Patents, United States patent and Trademark Office, Alexandria, VA, November 2011, found at: http://uspto.gov/patents/resources.
3. 35 U.S.C. 154 Contents and term of patent; provisional rights—Patent Laws.
4. U.S. Patent Office, Patents, Washington, D.C., found online at http://uspto.gov.

5. 35 U.S.C. 101 Inventions patentable – Patent Laws, found at: http://uspto.gov/web/offices/pac/mpep/documents/appxl_35_U_S_C_101.
6. 1202.02(a)(v)(A) Utility patents and design patents, utility patents, Trademark Manual of Examining Procedure [TMEP], found at: http://www.uspto.gov/inventors/patents.jsp.
7. Types of patents, found at: http://uspto.gov/web/offices/ac/ido/oeip/taf/patdesc.
8. What can and cannot be patented?, found at: http://uspto.gov/inventors/patents.
9. 35 USC § 154, Contents and term of patent: provisional rights, found at: law.cornell.edu/uscode/text/35/154. For further data check out the web site at: uspto.gov/ebc/efs/index.html.
10. Patent protection, located at http://uspto.gov/inventors/independent/chats/faq.
11. Trademarks, found at: http://uspto.gov/inventors/trademarks.
12. Basic facts about trademarks, USPPTO, Alexandria, VA, 2010.
13. Frequently asked questions about trademarks, what are the benefits of federal trademark registration?, found at: http://uspto.gov/faq/trademarks.
14. The Office of Legal Education Executive Office for United States Attorneys, *Prosecuting Intellectual Property Crimes, Third Edition*, U.S. Department of Justice, http://www.justice.gov/criminal/cybercrime/docs/ipma2006.pdf, September 2006.
15. Trademark, copyright or patent?, What is a trademark or service mark?, found at: http://uspto.gov.
16. Trade dress, Trademark Manual of Examining Procedure [TMEP], found at: http://uspto.gov.
17. Copyright in General, found at: http://copyright.gov/help/faq/faq-general.
18. Copyright basics, Circular 01, U.S. Copyright Office, Washington, D.C., located at http://copyright.gov.
19. 17 USC § 106—Exclusive rights in copyrighted works, found at: http://law.cornell.edu/uscode.
20. Fair use [of a copyright], found at: http://copyright.gov.
21. *Fair Use*. U.S. Copyright Office, Washington, D.C.
22. *Report of the Register of Copyrights on the General Revision of the U.S. Copyright Law*. House Judiciary Committee, 87th Congress, 1st Session, Washington, D.C., July 1961.
23. What does copyright protect?, found at: http://copyright.gov/help/faq.
24. 142 Cong. Rec. S12201, S12208 (daily ed. Oct. 2, 1996).
25. Prosecuting intellectual property crimes manual, supra note 113, [section] VIII.B.2.C.
26. Erekosima, Onimi and Koosed, Brian, Intellectual property crimes, 41 *Am. Crim. L. Rev*. 809, 813–14 (2004).
27. 104 Cong. Rec. S12201, S12212 (daily ed. Oct. 2, 1996) (Managers' statement for H.R. 3723, the Economic Espionage Bill).
28. Id. (quoting *Buffets, Inc. v. Klinke*, 73 F.3d 965, 968 (9th Cir. 1996)).
29. Prosecuting intellectual property crimes manual, supra note 119.
30. Brenner, Susan W. and Crescenzi, Anthony C., State-Sponsored Crime: The Futility of the Economic Espionage Act, 28 *Hous. J. Int'l L*. 389, 436 (2006).
31. Department of Commerce, USPTO, FAQs, How can I protect my business from IP theft?, USPTO, Alexandria, VA, found at: http://uspto.gov/smallbusiness/pdfs/USPTOSmallBusinessCampaignFAQ.pdf.
32. Criminal Division, Computer Crime and Intellectual Property Section, *Prosecuting Intellectual Property Crimes*, 3rd Edition, U.S. Department of Justice, Executive Office for U.S. Attorneys, Washington, D.C., September 2006.
33. Office of the Administrator for Policy and External Affairs: Patent trade secrets, Office of Policy and External Affairs, USPTO, found at: http://uspto.gov/ip/global/patents/ir_pat_tradesecret.
34. Department of Commerce, Protecting your intellectual property rights (IPR) in China: A practical guide for U.S. companies, found at: http://www.mac.doc.gov/China/Docs/BusinessGuides/IntellectualPropertyRights.htm, Retrieved April 2, 2013.
35. *Protecting Your Intellectual Property Rights (IPR) in China: A Practical Guide for U.S. Companies*. U.S. Department of Commerce, International Trade Administration, Washington, D.C.

15 Internet Exploitation
The Web, Your Computer, Your IT System

Critical U.S. infrastructure is vulnerable to malicious cyber activity. Chinese Military doctrine calls for exploiting these vulnerabilities in case of a conflict.

Report to Congress of the US–China Economic Security and Review Commission, 2009[1]

In August 2011, McAfee issued a report, *Revealed: Operation Shady RAT,*[2] which investigated targeted intrusions into 72 global companies, governments, and non-profit organizations during the last 5 years. Of the intruded targets, 49 were in the United States. While no specific individual, group, or country was ever mentioned, commentators across the spectrum of media outlets indicated that China was the most likely suspect. As such, it is necessary to recall (from various public reports in the press) that, over the past half-dozen years right into early 2012, China has been identified publicly as being behind almost all of the computer intrusions. Imagine your system, your neighbor's system, your company's system, various government agencies, organizations, and institutions of high learning being hacked. And the hacking is going on almost continuously. When you have a nation such as China with millions of young people who are very creative in their endeavors, all of whom searching out methods and means to intrude on your system, then any reasonable person could reasonably conclude that such a series of attacks would be directed or at least monitored by the government of any given nation. China has the people, the technology, the creative minds, and the will and the desire to know what is going on everywhere in the world. At the same time, such ventures also provide the means to an end: an opportunity to steal a massive amount of scientific, technical, mechanical, engineering, chemical, agricultural, energy, military, and political data for their own use.

Since China has been identified over and over at being at the forefront of such attacks, ask yourself, "Where did my computer and its internal electronic parts come from?" Don't say "the computer company," because the company only sold the computer to you. The computer company purchased the computer, either in whole, or portions of, or individual parts, from a foreign country. Most likely, from China. China has been at the forefront of electronic processing in terms of making various computer components and ensuring that they will work. To do so, the various bytes of data that will be created on the computer will have an algorithm to control them for proper sequencing, and will have various internal programs that will make it possible to store, retrieve, and send data, as well as receive data from other computers and systems. Is it so far-fetched to say that whoever put the computer components together and made it possible for the individual computer or system to work just might have dropped in a few extra bytes of controlling data that would allow somebody or some entity from outside the system the ability to come into the system and retrieve that data? It is not far-fetched. It is very reasonable, and that is why security firewalls were developed and added to computer systems. Individuals, companies, and entire computer systems may have one or several different firewalls. Firewalls provide differing levels of security protection against attack and intrusion into the system and the data it protects. The author, at this time, does not know of any given company that has such a high level of security that, given the time and effort, it cannot be hacked to some extent. If it was created by man, it can be defeated by man, but just how long it would take is unknown. Whether that hack would be successful will only depend upon how many internal levels of firewall protection there are, how good the firewall really is, and how diligent the information technology (IT) professionals are at detecting a hack or other unique intrusion into the system. Backdoors, those built into the system and can allow access without being found out, have been around for a long time. Finding the backdoor and closing it are immensely difficult when one considers the untold millions upon millions of lines of data that exist for a large system. Finding that one or several lines of data that make backdoor access possible is mostly pure luck!

As a sidelight, remember that your Kindle, iPad, iPhone, tablet, cell phone, or other electronic device was also from China (Figure 15.1). All of these have various items of information that could be subverted and "backdoored" for access from afar, in this case, China. Imagine your cell phone, its numbers, and any messages sent and received being obtained by China. Suppose you conduct business in the finance field, government, and research and development, and you talk about them. Most probably, you send instant messages. What then? Text messages are more specific when they deal with a specific type of information, and when that information is sensitive or innovative, or deals with a new product or a possible new product under development, imagine what someone would give to know about it in advance. Just like computers, these items can be used to obtain our sensitive information.

Essentially, getting back to your computer, be it a laptop, a full-blown system with access to the outside, or a desktop with modem access, one can conclude that your organization and its computers have been targeted. Just because an attack has not been detected or stopped does not mean that it never occurred. The most successful IT intrusions are those that are never detected.

They are also the ones that will continue into the future. When such intrusions are successfully made and not detected, the same techniques and methods will be used again and again on other organizations and computers in hopes of accomplishing the very same: the collection of data of value to the perpetrator.

Software with a backdoor or with a code can always be compromised by an intruder. As soon as the software is loaded onto a computer, it makes the computer vulnerable to attack, and when that computer is tied to a system that has Internet access, it makes the entire system vulnerable.

Computers "talk" to each other. They transmit data back and forth, provide a "handshake" to say, "Hello, I'm Computer X; if you are Computer Y, let's swap data." Once access is given, the hunt for

FIGURE 15.1 If you aren't concerned about possible "backdoor" exploits of your handheld devices, you should be!

general or specific data begins. The search will also include—for targeting purposes—such items as "bookmarks" and the identification of other computers outside the initial system, to other servers and routers, and into other systems of other companies, organizations, and even government agencies. All of this is possible because of a simple line of code that allows unfettered access or a firewall that could be hacked into from the outside.

Taking a step further, consider your own computer and the system it is on, and recall that the computer was probably purchased with the lowest cost possible, but having all the bells and whistles. The computer was probably built overseas, in a low-wage country, and that company has lower security standards than your company from which your computer was purchased.

China is one of the major high-tech exporters. They have been cranking out computers for a couple of decades, and everyone has been buying them, many under different names, but the same few companies were producing them.

The fact that the Chinese company put the authorized designated software on the computer doesn't mean that they didn't include additional, unknown, unseen, or undetermined software data that could do a whole bunch of other things. Such things can provide one or more hidden backdoors, or just a couple of lines of code that allow direct access to the computer, or several lines of code that would call up another computer during off-peak hours (when the computer is still tied to the system), or maybe insert those few lines of code into your system servers (which are running all the time) and, at an opportune moment, send a coded signal to someplace else. At any given time, then, the system could be easily entered and hacked, and data could be automatically sent to another off-site computer, perhaps one in another country. Just because you have firewalls doesn't mean these things can never happen. Firewalls only protect against known threats, against certain hack attempts, but when the software code is revised slightly, the firewall can accept an unauthorized entry attempt as legitimate, and thus data become compromised, damaged, destroyed, or altered.

The computer and the Internet changed the world—and we haven't changed with it, or at least changed enough to be prepared for everything that happens after their creation and subsequent evolution.

National competition in global markets by many countries is demonstrated by the plethora of varying products that emanate from every corner of the world. Via the collection of economic data, countries and business interests chart their current and future successes. And the Internet allows everyone to probe your computers to take a small step—or a giant stride—ahead.

FEDERAL INFORMATION SECURITY MANAGEMENT ACT

The Federal Information Security Management Act of 2002 (FISMA) clearly established new and necessary criteria to greatly improve US federal agencies' cyber security programs. FISMA established the criteria to improve federal agencies' cyber security programs through the enactment of the law on December 17, 2002. FISMA required *all* federal agencies to *protect and maintain* the confidentiality, integrity, and availability of their information and the associated information systems. It also assigned specific information security responsibilities to the Office of Management and Budget (OMB), which is the overarching organization for FISMA, and also certain responsibilities to the Department of Commerce's National Institute of Standards and Technology (NIST), agency heads, chief information officers, and inspectors general. For the OMB, those responsibilities included the development and overseeing of the implementation of specific policies, principles, standards, and guidelines on information security, as well as reviewing them on an annual basis, and also approving or disapproving agency information security programs.[3]

According to the NIST's web site (http://csrc.nist.gov/groups/SMA/fisma/overview.html), FISMA further required each agency, including especially those varied agencies with national security systems, "to develop, document, and implement agency-wide information security programs which would then provide information security protection for that agencies' information and information systems that support the operations and assets of the agency, including those provided or managed by another agency, contractor, or other source. An effective information security program should include:

- Periodic assessments of the risk and magnitude of harm that could result from the unauthorized access, use, disclosure, disruption, modification, or destruction of information or information systems;
- Risk-based policies and procedures that cost-effectively reduce information security risks to an acceptable level and ensure that information security is addressed throughout the life cycle of each information system;
- Subordinate plans for providing adequate information security for networks, facilities, and systems or groups of information systems;
- Security awareness training for agency personnel, including contractors and other users of information systems that support the operations and assets of the agency;
- Periodic testing and evaluation of the effectiveness of information security policies, procedures, and practices, performed with frequency depending on risk, but no less than annually, and that includes testing of management, operational, and technical controls for every system identified in the agency's required inventory of major information systems;
- A process for planning, implementing, evaluating, and documenting remedial action to address any deficiencies in the information security policies, procedures, and practices of the agency;
- Procedures for detecting, reporting, and responding to security incidents; and
- Plans and procedures to ensure continuity of operations for information systems that support the operations and assets of the agency.[3,4]

In 2003, the United States Computer Emergency Readiness Team (US-CERT) was created; currently, it resides under the Department of Homeland Security (DHS). Its purpose is to (1) aggregate and disseminate a wide variety of cyber security information to improve early warning about and response to various security-related incidents, (2) increase coordination of response information from various government agencies, (3) reduce vulnerabilities as much as possible, and (4) enhance prevention and protection of IT systems. The US-CERT analyzes incidents reported by the various federal civilian agencies and then coordinates across the board with national security incident response centers to enhance their response to various incidents on both classified and unclassified systems. US-CERT also provides a service through its National Cyber Alert System to identify, analyze, prioritize, and disseminate information on emerging vulnerabilities and threats.[5]

Within the FISMA document, there is the FISMA requirement that directs the NIST to establish appropriate standards, guidelines, and requirements to help agencies improve the posture of their information security programs. NIST has issued several publications relevant to assisting agencies in protecting their systems against emerging cyber security threats. For instance, Special Publication 800-61, Computer Security Incident Handling Guide,[6] advises agencies to establish an incident-response capability that includes establishing guidelines for communicating with outside parties regarding incidents, including law enforcement agencies, and also discusses handling specific types of incidents, including malicious code and unauthorized access. Additionally, NIST Special Publication 800-68 (Draft), Guidance for Securing Microsoft Windows XP Systems for IT Professionals: A NIST Security Configuration Checklist,[7] describes configuration recommendations that focus on deterring malware, countermeasures against security threats with malicious payload, and specific recommendations for addressing spyware. The FISMA and NIST web sites also provide a number of other IT-related subjects that are of great interest to the reader. Depending upon your specific requirements, you may wish to download and have them available for study, reference, and review.

Everyone realizes the fact that the government wants a better quality of security, especially for computers and, more importantly, for those that can be or are currently tied to the Internet. With the federal wake-up call in 2002, the private sector, to some extent, followed the government.

Unfortunately, it was the government that was following the private sector, and even with the FISMA, the standards and actual quality of protection levels did not increase. The author believes that one reason for this is the simple fact that neither the government nor the private industry was willing to be as creative as the hundreds of thousands of computer hackers and geeks worldwide that have an innate desire to probe the Internet and every possible Internet connection to see if individual systems can be successfully entered. Everyone is really behind the power curve. If it can be created, it can be defeated, and that is exactly what is being accomplished each and every day.

The computer really belongs not to the current generation of professional users (in both business and government) but rather to the younger generations. Our generation may have invented the computer, its games, and software, but we don't own it. Those that do are people from 10 to 30 years old. They are the most creative, the most innovative, and the most curious. They haven't read the manual that says "you do X to achieve Y" with the computer. They don't know that it can't be done, so they write various programs, and browse the Internet with those programs, testing and seeing what they can learn. They look at the computer and the Internet as part of a worldwide game of hide and seek: you hide the information and they seek it out. There are no rules or book to follow, but only the creativity of their minds. In effect, these seekers of information are the newest wave in the battle to protect or seek out information through the Internet.

As worldwide economic competition intensifies, the activities of the traditional espionage agent have changed. Of course, some will continue in their tried and true tested methods, but the acquisition of information has become more acute, and thus, the systems and methods for the protection of information have also been elevated to a greater level of concern. As the world slowly changes before our eyes, new rivalries in the economic world have shifted to the forefront. This means that economic competition is overarching and doesn't necessarily recognize the world of political alliances that can change in a heartbeat and also the changing boundaries of a nation's economic strength that can change within weeks to a downturn within money markets, stock markets, and foreign monetary exchange rates, or because of a lowering of a nation's credit rating. Some of the changes in economics are based upon foreign efforts that have allowed them to penetrate the industry, gather innovative technology, or otherwise acquire sensitive business secrets.

Understanding the collection methodology for business intelligence as an organized information system has been mastered by the Chinese. They have the resources of time, personnel, and money, and they couple it with a national desire to win economically at any cost. The system requires them to collect, analyze, and distribute all forms of business intelligence to the key players in the government and private industry.

To a great extent, China probably learned some of these techniques by studying JETRO, the Japan External Trade Organization, which, for decades, directed how the Japanese would do business. It reached into every business and coordinated information gathering at high levels of government and then, with a coordinated effort by business, went to seek out the information required to make Japan a powerful economic power. Every branch of every business endeavor would operate like a greedy vacuum cleaner in a room full of dust. Every bit was sucked up, be it specific or general items of information, statistics, brochures, and articles from scientific, technical, or specialty magazines, and the current business and government news was compiled right along with it. Any tidbit of information found, no matter how inconsequential, was saved and filed away.

China is doing the same thing, but on a much grander scale, using not just one vacuum cleaner to suck up information but hundreds of them, and the use of the Internet has only made it easier and less time-consuming.

As America and China become more closely intertwined through business, spying became the next natural step to protect the economic viability of America. They spy on us; we spy on them. But it is now done electronically. And China now has the upper hand. So much information is being stolen via the Internet that China now has probably stolen more than several terabytes of sensitive data. We can reasonably postulate that in addition to specific information, such things as user names and passwords for personal and government computers, for bank accounts, for weapons systems, and so on, have been collected. Every month, there is news that another spate of hackers have attacked US computer systems. And they show no sign of letting up. Alan Paller, director of research at the information-security training group SANS Institute, located in Washington, D.C., said that that "The attacks coming out of China are not only continuing, they are accelerating." This makes the McAfee report on computer intrusions more reliable.

The WikiLeaks publication of various US State Department cables on the Internet also indicated system breaches by the Chinese military. An April 2009 State Department cable pinpointed the attacks to a specific unit of the People's Liberation Army (PLA).

One such intrusion could be traced back to 2006 and was tagged Byzantine Hades and had a subset of the operation referred to as "Byzantine Candor," which specifically targeted operations against the US government using social engineering and malicious attachments and links in e-mail messages. The PLA Third Department deals with "reconnaissance," a fancy term that, in essence, was set up to oversee China's electronic eavesdropping. It monitors communications systems, both in China and abroad. Using extremely talented and trained individuals, they probe and seek out information via the Internet. Their continued attempts on massive scales can overwhelm government networks. For most of the past decade, the DHS's CERT has reported to have increased more than 650%. In 2006, there were 5503 incidents; by projecting such data, the author estimates that by 2012, there may well be more than 40,000 incidents occurring.[8,9]

Another WikiLeaks expose, in December 2010, showed the severity of the so-called spear-phishing technique. One released cable stated that, "Since 2002, government organizations have been targeted with social-engineering online attacks,"[10,11] and those attacks were able to gain access to hundreds of (US) government and cleared defense contractor systems. All the e-mails were evidentially aimed at the US Army, the Department of Defense, State Department, Department of Energy, and other government entities, in addition to some companies in the private sector.

In the past two years, companies in the gas, oil, financial, and technical sectors also have had their computer systems infiltrated. These and many other firms whose business requires a large amount of intellectual property have indicated that their systems are under almost a constant attack by outsiders seeking to get at their proprietary information. Some believe that China is the threat, and they are probably right. What this amounts to is that if your company or organization has any potential competition from China, it will be targeted. Whether the company does business directly with China, or if they were to directly compete with China, then hacking attempts will start and continue indefinitely.

For the most part, the public sector at large is not really cognizant of many of these attacks. Why? Simply because companies do not want to report such attacks, or especially any successful attacks because it means the company stock will drop, public confidence will go away, and the profits of the business will suffer. Further, the cost of investigating a computer attack is time-consuming and costly, and the IT people will just spend more time in developing newer and hopefully better methods to protect the system. The majority will not report such attacks to the government either, even if legally obligated to do so.

Sometimes, it is necessary to continue to use agents or get others to obtain the information, especially if it cannot be obtained over the Internet. Once such case involved a Canadian national, a US company, and software. On December 6, 2004, a Canadian national suspected of stealing proprietary software programs from a US company was apprehended in Orlando, Florida. The individual was there to attend a defense conference, but, apparently, was attempting to sell the software to the People's Republic of China (PRC). Immigration and Customs Enforcement agents coordinated with others to conduct a search of the individual and his belongings upon entering the United States. A preliminary search of the contents of his laptop revealed software that belonged to an American company.[12]

SENSITIVE US INTERNET TRAFFIC SENT TO CHINESE SERVERS

In November 2010, it was reported that highly sensitive Internet traffic from various US government and military web sites was routed through Chinese servers due to hacking. This breach occurred six months earlier, in April, and it only lasted some 18 minutes. E-mail traffic from the US Senate, Department of Defense, Department of Commerce, and NASA was rerouted to a Chinese state-owned telecommunications firm.[13] In a mere 18 minutes, probably millions upon millions of bytes of information could have been collected by China. There is no way to prove that the PRC government knew about it, and authorized or approved it, but to not consider such would be folly. Only with government direction and control could something this massive have been affected.

"The massive scale and the extensive intelligence and reconnaissance components of recent high profile, China-based computer exploitations suggest that there continues to be some level of state support for these activities," said commission vice chair Carolyn Bartholomew of the US–China Economic and Security Review Commission.[14–16] Again, this has not been proven but is a reasonably accepted conclusion based upon past experience and data concerning China.

Web security firm McAfee had warned of a rise in cyber attacks, painting China as one of the major actors launching assaults. US targets included the White House, the DHS, the US Secret Service, and the Department of Defense. In any given week, if you troll the web for news stories, you will normally find several that deal with cyber attacks, on both government and the private sector, and more than likely, China will be referenced as the source of the attack.

In February of 2010, Michael McConnell, former US intelligence chief (under former President George W. Bush) stated before a Senate panel that the United States would definitely lose a cyber war if it fought one today. "We're the most vulnerable, we're the most connected, we have the most to lose." He also said that if the United States is not able to effectively mitigate the risk, "we are going to have a catastrophic event."[17]

The reason for this is that China is focused on a larger concern—how to keep its economy, the world's second largest, growing. And the most cost-effective, easiest way to grow is to innovate through plagiarizing, that is, by stealing US intellectual property.

A couple of years ago, an e-mail was sent from an address on the unofficial US Armed Forces family welfare network called AFGIMail. Attached to the message was an Excel spreadsheet labeled "Titan Global Invitation List." When opened, the spreadsheet would install a malicious code that searches for documents on the victim's computer. The computer code could then have access to the computer data and communicate it to a web site hosting company in Orange County, California, that, not coincidentally, had additional sites in China.[18]

When you travel, be it by car, train, airplane, or ship, you assume some risk in that a collision, a crash, or a sinking may occur. But when you "travel" in cyberspace, you may anticipate a risk, but you will never see it coming until your system is attacked. Cyberspace travel necessitates each person to individually evaluate and consider his or her risk and vulnerability once connected to the Internet.

CHINA'S THINKING AND CAPABILITIES IN CYBERSPACE

China's military strategy has determined that cyber capabilities is an area that the PLA must invest in and, further, should be used on a larger scale. US Secretary of Defense Robert Gates is concerned about China's cyber advancement. Further, he and others have observed the continuing decades-long trend of cyber attacks on US systems.

China's use of asymmetric capabilities, especially when directed toward cyber warfare, can pose a serious threat to the American economy. There are some analysts who believe that China could well have the most extensive and aggressive cyber warfare capability in the world, and that this is being driven by China's desire to achieve "global power status." China does have a global power status, and its aggressive cyber capability is due to the use of thousands of hackers who are probably directed by the central government in its quest to further their political, military, and economic status. While American security experts call the US defense against cyber attacks "embarrassing" and state that it "has effectively run out of steam," China is allocating many resources to its cyber program.[19–21]

The director of the DHS has compared such attacks to those of 9/11. "(W)e take threats to the cyber world as seriously as we take threats from the material world."[22] A 2007 cyber attack on one of America's nuclear arms laboratory has only confirmed the need to take cyber threats seriously. For the general population at large, it is not really known with any great certainty how much data were downloaded from the site during the attack, but since the attack could be traced to China, all the indications were that it was carried out by state organizations. Knowing and proving are two different things, though.

In the United Kingdom, the 14-page document from MI5, *The Threat from Chinese Espionage,* was produced in 2008. The restricted report said that "(a)ny UK company might be at risk if it holds information which would benefit the Chinese."[23]

The report also covered China's cyber warfare campaign that had targeted British defense, energy, communications, and manufacturing companies, as well as public relations and international law firms. Most of these are vital segments of the United Kingdom's critical infrastructure, which would most certainly include both the nation's defense and economic sectors.

Though not directly related to the above, two statements are of interest to the reader. Both concern China's cyber abilities. The first is that "Critical U.S. infrastructure is vulnerable to malicious cyber activity. Chinese military doctrine calls for exploiting these vulnerabilities in the case of a conflict."[19] This came from the US–China Economic and Security Review Commission. Second, and again, important was the quote that "(The Chinese government) resolutely oppose(s) any crime, including hacking, that destroys the Internet or computer network (…); some people overseas with Cold War mentality are indulged in fabricating the sheer lies of the so-called cyberspies in China." This quote was from Wang Baodung, spokesman for the Chinese Embassy in Washington, in April 2009.[19]

THE DETERRENCE EFFECT ON THE UNITED STATES

Cyber capabilities have a real deterrent effect when a nation such as China shows its capabilities to the world. This happened when the United States became aware that its electricity network had been hacked into in 2009 and that parts of the network allegedly could be shut down whenever the hacker wished to do so. There were other sources who, even a little more skeptical about the scope of such intrusions, indicated that while the intruders did not cause immediate damage, they left behind software programs that could be used in the future to disrupt this critical infrastructure. This attack was traced back to China, and the chief of counterintelligence in the United States at the time stated that "(w)e have seen Chinese network operations inside certain of our electricity grids."[21,24*]

In 2009, there was a forced electronic entry into the Joint Strike Fighter program and large amounts of data were copied. According to present and former employees at the Pentagon, the attack can be traced to China. By analyzing the obtained data, it would mean that it would be much easier for China to defend itself against the aircraft. With the Joint Strike Fighter's top-notch abilities in combat, other nations would likely purchase them for their own purposes. Now, assuming China collects enough data on the fighters, they may even be able to copy parts of it. The American chief of counterintelligence, Joel Brenner, speaking to an audience of American business people in Austin, Texas, said that "our networks are being mapped" with reference to American flight traffic control, and warned about a situation in which "a fighter pilot can't trust his radar."[25]

* According to Larry Wortzel, Chinese researchers at the Institute of Systems Engineering at the Dalian University of Technology have published a paper showing how to attack a small west coast power grid. Also, testimony of Larry Wortzel Commissioner, U.S.-China Economic and Security Review Committee, "China's approach to cyber operations: implications for the United States," before the Committee on Foreign Affairs "Hearings on 'The Google predicament: transforming U.S. cyberspace policy to advance democracy, security, and trade' House of Representatives, Washington, D.C., March 10, 2010.

Just about every computer savvy person has at least one universal serial bus (USB) memory stick. USBs are small but can hold an enormous amount of data. They are easy to carry (and also easy to lose), so many people easily attach them to their key rings. The Pentagon banned them after an incident in which data were transferred to a memory stick. If you didn't know by now, China is the world's largest producer of USB memory sticks. A memory stick is just like a CD-R or a small 3.5" computer disk in that it allows an individual to easily transfer data from a laptop or office desk computer to another laptop/computer. There is no reason to not believe that such memory sticks could be developed and have a subtle collection program within them to collect more data or at least program names, among other things, from a computer when such memory stick is being used to transfer other data. At a later date, and in conjunction with the use of the stick, it might be possible to transfer data to another computer that has outside access and automatically send it to a location overseas. This might seem unbelievable (and might be attributed to paranoia), but if it can be imagined or deduced from any state-of-the-art computer program or system, and if you have a dedicated group of software engineers and programmers putting their minds to it, it could be done. In the cyber warfare and hacking world, I suspect that it is already being developed, if not actually realized and used somewhere.

Now, you have had a look into Internet concerns and what China will do to take advantage of our daily "need" for a "fix" by constantly using the computer and feeding it with information such as our trade secrets, intellectual property, and even classified government information. China will take every means and opportunity to work its way into any computer system that contains data of possible value. This alone should make you realize that just pausing and thinking about the problem will not solve it.

You have been forewarned, but unless your IT people and security personnel work closely together, and you limit the external access to your systems and computers, you might as well just hand it over. Again, YOU HAVE BEEN WARNED!

REFERENCES

1. U.S.–China Economic Security and Review Commission (USCC), 111th Congress, 1st Session, Washington D.C., November 2009.
2. Alperovitch, Dmitri, VP threat research, revealed: Operation Shady RAT, McAfee reports in a white paper, Santa Clara, CA, August 2011.
3. National Institute of Standards and Technology (NIST), Computer Security Division, Computer Resource Center, Department of Commerce, Washington, D.C., found at: http://csrc.nist.gov/groups/SMA/fisma/overview.html.
4. Federal Information Security Management Act (FISMA), [Title III of the E-Government Act Public Law107-347].
5. Information security: emerging cybersecurity issues threaten Federal Information Systems, U.S. General Accounting Office, GAO-05-231, Washington, D.C., May 2005.
6. Computer Incident Handling Guide, National Institute of Standards and Technology (NIST), Computer Security Division, Computer Resource Center, Department of Commerce, Washington, D.C., March 2008.
7. Guide to Securing Microsoft Windows XP Systems for IT Professionals, Rev. 1, National Institute of Standards and Technology (NIST), Computer Security Division, Computer Resource Center, Department of Commerce, Washington, D.C., Oct. 2008. (Numerous other publications of importance concerning IT systems, their protection, and IT risk management concerns can be found at: http://csrc.nist.gov.)
8. Roberts, Paul, Report Describes Far-Flung Chinese Cyber Espionage Against U.S. Government, found at: http://www.threatpost.com, the Kaspersky Lab Security News Service, April 15, 2001.
9. Department of Homeland Security, Computer Emergency Response Team (CERT), Washington, D.C.
10. WikiLeaks Cable about Chinese Hacking of U.S. Networks, April 18, 2011, found at: http://schneier.com/blog/archives/2011/04/wikileaks_cable.html.
11. Lemos, Robert, Byzantine Hades shows China's cyber chops, April 21, 2011, found at: csoonline.com.
12. Department of Homeland Security, Leadership Journal Archive, CBP laptop searches, Washington, D.C., June 30, 2008.

13. Homeland Security Newswire, China "hijacked" sensitive U.S. Internet traffic to Chinese servers, November 18, 2010, found at: http://www.homelandsecuritynewswire.com.
14. Beckford, Martin, Heidi Blake and Duncan Gardham, found at: http://www.telegraph.co.uk, Nov. 18, 2010.
15. 2010 US–China Economic and Security Review Commission Report, November 2010.
16. Internet traffic "hijacked" to China servers, says US report, found at: http://PHYSorg.com. November 17, 2010.
17. Ogle, Alex, Internet traffic "hijacked" to China servers, says US report, *The Associated Press*, November 10, 2010.
18. Grow, Brian and Mark Hosenball, Special report—in cyberspy vs. cyberspy, China has the edge, found at: http://us.mobile.reuters.com, April 14, 2011.
19. Hjortdal, Magnus, ChinaSec, Centre for Military Studies, University of Copenhagen, 'China's use of cyber warfare: espionage meets strategic deterrence', *The Journal of Strategic Security*, Vol IV, issue 2, 2011.
20. Maggie, Shiels, "US cybersecurity 'embarrassing,'" *BBC News*, April 29, 2009. Available at http://news.bbc.co.uk/2/hi/technology/8023793.stm.
21. Sanger, David E., John Markoff, and Thom Shanker, U.S. steps up effort on digital defenses, *New York Times*, April 28, 2009, found at: http://www.nytimes.com/2009/04/28/us/28cyber.html.
22. Chinese Industrial Espionage, Department of Homeland Security, found at: http://www.dhs.gov.
23. Gonzales, Mariano, The Overwatch Report, April 13, 2011, in discussing the MI5 restricted report 'The threat from Chinese espionage' circulated to various manufacturers and companies in 2008.
24. Electricity grid in U.S. penetrated by spies, April 8, 2009, found at: http://www.online.wsj.com.
25. Gorman, Siobhan, August Cole and Yocki Dreazen, Computer spies breach fighter-jet project, *Wall Street Journal*, April 21, 2009.

16 Protecting Your Data

The preceding chapters have, hopefully, opened your eyes to the massive and insidious threat posed by China to your intellectual property (IP), trade secrets, research and development (R&D), and other areas that you hold dear. As we jump into some areas that can help you protect all these various types of information, remember a couple of things: First, no system, policy, or security program is so good that it cannot be overcome. What has been created by man can be defeated by man. Second, the more people know about something specific, the less protection and security is offered for it in terms of being accessed or obtained by someone else who is not authorized to have that information. Third, once the information is out of the henhouse, you can't recapture it and say it never happened. Fourth, knowing and proving it was stolen are two different things, especially if the culprit was not caught red-handed taking the information. Fifth, if the information is in a computer system, and anyone other than you has access to that information, it is now in the position to be downloaded, copied, or transferred somewhere else, if not outright stolen. Sixth, tied closely to the fifth, if your system is tied to the Internet, don't consider anything on the system wholly protected. Firewalls can and will be attacked and, at some point, someone will figure out how to get past the firewall and take your data. The Internet has only made it easier and much cheaper to steal your information.

With the above in mind, herein we turn to possible solutions that can increase your level of security for information in its various forms. Some are purely administrative, others have legal implications (along with the dire consequences of prison if a person is caught taking your property), and others can help you formulate procedures and methods to further protect the information. But, all in all, if it's down on paper, publicly available in one form or another, or the knowledge of it becomes known, someone will, over time, figure out how to obtain it. All you can do is protect it as long as possible, knowing that, within reason, it will become available to someone else in the future.

Everyone must be concerned with security. By protecting the present, we can better secure the future. In this regard, protecting against the threat means having a strong security/counterintelligence office with trained personnel, a continuing security education program that highlights the espionage factor for the protection of IP and trade secrets, and the appropriate policies and procedures in place that are understood and used by everyone.

Whether at home or abroad (where more and more cases of espionage are taking place), have briefings and (upon a traveler's return) debriefings for employees. At the same time, the company should have identified those high-risk personnel who carry vast amounts of sensitive knowledge in their heads because they are prime targets for intelligence collectors.

All this is for naught if there are no checks or other reviews (at least annually, but preferably semiannually). At the same time, the security and counterintelligence offices should be conducting at least minimal preliminary inquiries into even the possibility of economic theft.

Here, also, is the opportunity to have liaison with the local offices of the Federal Bureau of Investigation (FBI). They bring a tremendous amount of professional knowledge and can advise and also provide security education on the theft of economic secrets and other sensitive company information. If you are a government department or agency, go through your local security office because they will already have liaison contacts in place.

Since the Internet is such a much used and valuable tool in the transmission and storage of critical data, there is the necessity to have strong cyber security support with user IDs and passwords being changed somewhat frequently (minimum of once a year), continual monitoring and upgrading of firewalls, and knowledge by system administrators of who is accessing what sensitive information and how frequently.

At one time, the United States was really concerned about communist espionage within the country. It could have been considered as "number one" in terms of foreign threats, but with a shrinking world and more and more businesses setting up overseas offices, as well as the transmission of technology, IP, R&D, new product testing, and the like, espionage against the US government and businesses has moved overseas also. This is not to say that the threat has been removed from US shores, but that others like China have really taken over as the threat, and that threat has been bumped by people behind that of terrorism (Figure 16.1).

In the area of espionage and the theft of national secrets, it can be seen that it is much easier to gain information overseas than within the United States. Because of this, greater efforts must be paid to educating and training employees who travel temporarily or long term to foreign countries to conduct business. Such businesses also include conferences, meetings, and symposia, as well as contacts for the initiation or further development of a business relationship, or for providing on-site advice and assistance to an overseas office, support of a joint venture, or starting or expanding a venture. In all these cases, espionage must be considered as a routine consideration from the foreign country, either by the government, competitors, a new company, or an individual.

As you move through this chapter, to make it easier, the author has reviewed numerous personal and government documents that relate to the protection of information in its varied forms. This information is the knowledge that you may have in your head, on your laptop, or on paper that might be targeted by an individual who is seeking government or non-government information, but more likely information that relates to specific work products in technology, engineering, agriculture, R&D, and so on, especially information related to patents, specific IP, and closely held corporate secrets. Hence, the author has extracted from the best sources pertinent information that can direct, remind, or provide guidance in the protection of the information in varying circumstances and situations, both in the United States and abroad.

FIGURE 16.1 With billions of dollars' worth of trade taking place with China, it is easy to forget that China is a communist nation with communist roots. Shown is a poster from the Cultural Revolution in the 1970s.

ESPIONAGE AND FOREIGN TRAVEL

Traveling to a foreign country for most is truly an extraordinary and exciting experience as you see new places, eat local and regional foods, tour historic sites, and meet new people.

Unfortunately, in virtually any region of the world, individuals can become targets for theft, kidnapping or espionage. Though the focus of this chapter is on countering espionage in its various forms, personal safety is of primary importance while traveling. As with any trips—whether domestic or abroad to foreign countries—proper planning and research are vital and will pay off later. Your awareness of the foreign travel threats and vulnerabilities can provide you with a sense of well-being and comfort during the trip.[1]

In general, many foreign collection efforts are driven by nations' military force modernization, the desire for economic growth, competition—and possible domination in a given field—and commercial modernization of their manufacturing facilities, especially those using technologies with dual-use applications.[2] Foreign individuals, businesses, government entities, and intelligence-affiliated personnel will always employ collection techniques against US targets, whether they are abroad or located in the United States. Just because the individual is from a nation considered friendly or is allied (either politically or militarily) with the United States doesn't mean he or she isn't on the lookout for information. Essentially, trust nobody in these situations when it comes to your organization's secrets.

AS A TRAVELER, WHY SHOULD YOU BE CONCERNED ABOUT ESPIONAGE?

The following, with some additional author commentary added, is taken from the Department of Energy's (DOE's) travel brochure *Espionage and Foreign Travel.*[3]

First, foremost, and most important, you probably have actual or potential access to information of value. If they are interested in you, who you work for, what your specialty is, you are perceived as a potential source of valuable information, whether you agree or not.

Second, when you travel, you are most vulnerable to the devices and machinations of the foreign government and its intelligence service. You are in *their* country; they control it (and you, if so desired). Even in countries with a long democratic tradition, the local intelligence/security services can control much of your environment—it is to their benefit to do so.

Intelligence Services may:

- "Bug" selected seats of national airlines with continuous receiving radios/tape recorders to listen in on you
- Arrange for audio or video coverage of your hotel room, a rental car or touring type bus, conference rooms and their associated dining facilities, and, in some cases, nearby local restaurants
- Download information from your laptop computer or other electronic information devices, when they are left unattended in your room or when you might put it in a room or hotel safe for "safekeeping"
- Monitor your conversations and behavior through interpreters and tour guides.
- Surreptitiously enter your hotel room or other quarters at will, to search your luggage, papers, and trash
- Surveil your movements, day and night, on foot or by vehicle
- Tap your telephone and fax machine[3]

These intrusions can be as extensive as the intelligence service's determination to learn more about you, what you are doing, and who you are associating with.

WHO IS MOST LIKELY TO BE TARGETED?

Some factors that increase the possibility that you, or any other person in your party, will be targeted and assessed include the following:

- Your access to information, people, or places of interest
- Any location(s) where foreign intelligence can gain access to you on their home turf
- You work in a position or geographic location in the United States or overseas where it is easy to gain access to you, formally or accidentally
- You have an ethnic, racial, or religious background that can be used by an intelligence operative to gain some form of "trust"[3]

It is important to note that the above factors increase the chances of you being the person that is selected for targeting and assessment via circumstances over which you may have little or no control. Most contacts that are made that have some form of interaction are perfectly legitimate and well meaning. Your ability to recognize the few that are not will help you avoid problems. In the future, also, it will also help your security office to assist others to avoid potential problems with intelligence collectors.

You should have noticed from the above that the words "China" or "Chinese" were not included. This is simply because the Chinese may use another individual, not one of Chinese or even oriental descent to approach you. While it is more likely, especially at conventions, seminars, and the like, the individual might have some oriental ancestry, the Chinese intelligence apparatus is so large, and with so many contacts around the world, it is somewhat easy for them to use another person. Thus, the occasion arises where, while you are on the lookout for someone of oriental ancestry, another person say, from Western Europe, approaches you, and to that end, you relax your vigilance.

THE RECRUITMENT CYCLE

All intelligence services follow some version of the recruitment cycle in seeking sources. It is simply a logical, systematic plan that has been used for a very long time that can allow them to find and then exploit people for information. Think of it as the spy version of marketing!

The recruitment cycle has five basic steps, starting with (1) Spotting: The identification of potential sources; (2) Assessing: Learning as much as possible about the potential source; (3) Recruitment: Actually enticing the potential source to provide information; (4) Handling: Continuing a relationship; and (5) Termination: Ceasing the relationship. This process is very flexible. It can go very quickly, or take many months or years.[3]

Let's take a look at this process using one individual who is attending a conference, either within the United States or in some other country around the world.

First, consider the topic of the conference. A very general topic, with numerous specialized sub-genre topics that will be discussed, explored, and commented on, during and after hours of the convention.

Second, who are you? Really, who are you? You are an attendee, and you attend the conference because of the subject matter. Perhaps you are a speaker on a unique sub-genre topic. Maybe you have a specialty that will be discussed, and you want to have the latest information, seek views from colleagues around the world to see what their views are, what strides they have made, or whether they have a unique product or service that you might be interested in. At this point, remember the other attendees are viewing you in the same light: what do you know or have that would be useful to them? When you registered for the conference, you provided some basic information about yourself:

your name, organization or company, title, e-mail, and other contact information. All this information went into a program listing the attendees. If you are a speaker, then a short bio was provided for the program handbook.

At this point, the information about you is out there. Anyone with an interest in the topic, your background, company, or your job/profession has now decided whether or not to target you in terms of possibly obtaining information. They may start ahead of the conference, sending you a polite e-mail in which they comment on your background and (lucky for you) they are in the same field, and would like to get together. If you are a speaker, the e-mail will talk about their interest in the topic. ("And, by the way, I'm staying at the conference hotel, so perhaps we can get together for dinner one evening.")

Don't think that is all. You're interesting to them, so they go onto the Internet, check out your company, learn everything about it that is publicly available, browse your division, and see if you are important enough to be listed and what the company web site says about you. Next, they look to various sites like a personal blog you write, Twitter, Facebook, YouTube, and so on, to see if you maintain some sort of profile on the Internet. Also, they start looking at local and national professional organizations to see which ones you belong to. What papers, books, or reports have you written, speeches made, consulted on what project, and so forth. The list can be long and varied, but with several hours' work, they have gained a good deal of information about you.

Don't think it can be done? Go on the Internet and search for anything related to you. Just type in your name and hit "search" and, voila, look what comes up. Now search these sites for further information. Make a list of all the information that is available about yourself. It is so easy to get background, and you thought maybe only your friends would know that information.

Was your company and job title listed? If so, start looking at your company, what division you work in, anything about what you might be doing, and so on.

Suddenly, as you peruse the information, think also that someone else has seen the same information and is considering how to approach you, either one time or multiple times, to seek out information from you, to make friends—even on a professional level—in order to get closer to you and gain your trust before making a move on the information and knowledge you have.

With all this information available, it is necessary to study the appropriate approach. Since it is a conference, a professional approach will be made. If you are a speaker, you are approached during or after the speech with a few questions, and then business cards are exchanged. Now, they have your telephone number, cell phone number, fax number, and anything else you have on the card.

A conversation topic is broached that will take more than a minute or two to answer, so it is suggested "lunch," which will be light hearted and relaxing with no real attempts for specific information, but rather a few probing questions of no great value. What is happening is you are being put in a position of providing miscellaneous and innocuous information of no great value, but questions that can have long-range goals of further questions. Since both of you are interested in the topic, perhaps something else is mentioned in passing. ("Oh, by the way, I wrote a short paper on the topic. Here, have a copy and tell me what you think.") You got the paper and it is good, but it also provides an opening for further discussion. You finish lunch and go on to other parts of the convention, perhaps strolling the exhibit floor together. Your newfound professional friend walks a bit with you, looks at some of the same displays and items in the trade booths, comments on various things, picks up numerous brochures and pamphlets, and then he goes his way and you, your way. But, if you stop and think about it, he now knows some more specifics about what you are interested in from the booths you stopped at and asked specific questions. Perhaps, he wandered after you, slowly, discreetly, a dozen or so yards behind you, always seeming to look at other things of interest. Actually, he is tailing you, getting a better sense of what you are really interested in. Did you spend a bit more time at one booth over another, or did you stop and speak several minutes with another attendee? If so, he will check them out, just breezing by and getting their name to check out later as another potential source that can be associated with you.

HOW ARE YOU AFFECTED BY THE RECRUITMENT CYCLE?

The following, again with some additional author commentary added, is taken from the DOE's travel brochure *Espionage and Foreign Travel.*[3]

As a traveler, especially if you have a government passport or have applied for a visa, you can assume that you have at least been spotted. Most security services review visa applications from official travelers as a matter of routine. Non-government groups may have also run your name to compute programs to see what the web says about you, where you work, or any other details that might pique their interest in you.

Those deemed interesting may then be subject to the next step, that of assessment, or to put it another way—getting to know you! An intelligence service will likely start by debriefing your foreign contacts. Certainly, some of your contacts may be talking about you to their intelligence services, and refuse their requests. But experience says that most will cooperate, for any number of reasons. And depending on the country involved, some may not have much choice.

After being spotted and assessed, if you continue to be of interest, you will become a candidate for the most delicate phase, that of recruitment. Recruitment in its simplest terms means persuading you to divulge privileged information, whether it is classified or unclassified. The key is PRIVILEGED! It can be about your work, your organization's work, or personal information about you or your colleagues.[3]

For some reason or other, you will run into him again during the multi-day convention, both attending the same presentations, eating lunch with colleagues at the same or nearby tables, and, maybe, a night on the town with him. ("Hey, let me pick up the bill; my company pays for this, and I can always use the receipts to at least show that I met some other attendees.")

The last day, you run into him again, and suddenly you find out he will be coming to your town in a few months and wants to get together. Perhaps he indicates that his company and yours might be able to do some business together, so let's stay in touch. ("And, by the way, I was thinking about the speech you made, and I started wondering if maybe, we can use that as a starting point to develop a new product. So, I'll send you an e-mail and outline something I think my company may want to work with you on, so maybe this conference can be beneficial for both of us. If it goes well in the future, I might even get a promotion or at least a raise from working closely with you.")

That is the start of a long-term relationship, or so he and you probably hope, with potential future job benefits accruing. Sounds nice, doesn't it? Unfortunately, it really only works one way, and it is not to your benefit.

At some point in the future, you will be "terminated"; that is, the relationship will cease. That will occur when you are of no further value to the information collector, or he is caught by the authorities with information obtained from you. So, consider how you will be affected by this recruitment cycle.

ELICITATION: WHAT IS IT?

According to the Naval Criminal Investigative Service (NCIS), "In the vernacular of the espionage trade, elicitation is the term applied to subtle extraction of information during an apparently normal and innocent conversation. Conducted by a well-trained and skillful intelligence professional, elicitation appears to be a normal, perhaps even mundane, social or professional discussion and can take place virtually anywhere and at any time. In actuality, though, the focus of their questions on issues of importance to their intelligence service and exploit the subject's desire to be cordial, interesting, and helpful."[4]

Everyone maintains a lot of information in their head. You know a lot of information and a skilled interrogator can use elicitation techniques to find out a whole lot about you, your work, your company, and your coworkers. Regretfully, you don't recognize the technique. It's like friends talking and getting to know each other better. It's very subtle and the interrogator is unassuming; thus, your defenses are down. Unfortunately, it can be extracted by a skilled interrogator.

Think of it as social engineering, which offers almost unlimited opportunities to "quiz" you and gain information through direct, personal contact. It probably will not be a one-time affair. Contact for purposes of elicitation can take place over days, weeks, or months. In terms of foreign travel, or even at a convention or seminar, you will run into the person (or a like-minded person who may be tied to another individual who had previously met you); various bits of information you have unknowingly provided may be the final bits of information they were looking for, and all the while, you were an unsuspecting provider of that information.

This is very true at conventions, or anywhere when like-minded people in the same field come together. Of course, there is the typical social talk, but with everyone working at least somewhat within the same field, generalities about work, work products, advances being made, and so on, the topics soon become more specialized and pointed in terms of questions and answers. The give-and-take, as it were, may be to soften you up a bit, providing just a tad of information you don't know about, and you are now more interested in continuing the conversation. This is the break your newfound "friend" is looking for. More questions, comments, give-and-take, and soon you are giving away data that you don't realize. Answering the question quickly, thoughtfully, or being slightly reticent, or providing a partial answer, or hemming and hawing over the answer also provides information and clues to what is more sensitive and shouldn't be talked about. You didn't give the answer they hoped for, but your partial or no answer told them that you have knowledge of value, and you may have just pointed them toward it. So, in essence, no answer is also helpful to them.

Personal information, information regarding your colleagues, and information not publicly available concerning your employment, for example, may be very valuable to the Chinese. Consequently, disclosures, though seemingly harmless individually, can become valuable in the aggregate and can jeopardize the safety of Americans and compromise national security.[4]

The point for you is not to give away information to someone who shouldn't have it. Skillful interrogation, under the guise of friendly conversation, business dealings, and so forth, is a surefire way to lose what valuable knowledge you have. Of course, during business, some information is passed along, but be aware that skillful probing and easily friendly questions during a discussion can get you to reveal a lot more information than you may realize. Just a hint of something, or "I can't discuss that," is enough to give another person the scent so down the road they are looking at more specific information. Maybe not from you, but from another unsuspecting colleague.[5,6]

So, in the end, when conducted by a skillful intelligence collector, elicitation appears to be normal social or professional conversation and can occur anywhere—in a restaurant, at a conference, or during a visit to one's home.

Why Elicitation and What Is Its Appeal to Today's Spy?

As an intelligence technique, elicitation exploits several fundamental aspects of human nature. Most of us want to be polite and helpful, so we answer questions even from relative strangers. We want to appear well informed about our professional specialty, so we may be tempted to say more than we should.

Americans, more than citizens of other countries, want to be appreciated, and to feel that they are doing something important and useful. As a result, people often talk more expansively in response to praise about the value or importance of any ongoing or future work. Feeling important strokes one's ego, and good elicitation can draw you out in this regard.

As open and honest people, many people are often reluctant to withhold information, lie, or be suspicious of others' motives. Americans tend to talk, to brag if you will, more about who we are and what we do. Essentially, we like to show off and puff up our self-esteem about what we know.

Anyone seeking economic or other sensitive information will play upon this in hope of getting you to tell them something they desire to know.

Because elicitation appears simply as normal, non-threatening conversation, it is the technique most likely to be used to extract information.

In many instances, consider the terms *elicitation* and *recruitment* as interchangeable since they accomplish the same objective—the acquisition of privileged information. (There are those purists who will object to equating the two terms since, strictly speaking, a recruited person knows he or she is working for a foreign government, whereas elicitation implies gaining information under the guise of innocent conversation.) Regardless of the specific term definitions, you could be pressed for information that should not be shared.[5]

If you feel uncomfortable discussing anything with a foreign contact, you have no obligation to continue the specific conversation. Change the topic, stop the conversation, or just walk away.

According to the DOE, the following are some points to remember:

- The world has changed, but the need for information has not; it will always continue.
- Spies look and act like normal people; they don't wear black hats and look sinister.
- You do not control the foreign environment—they do!
- As a traveler, you are subject to foreign intelligence scrutiny.
- Even seemingly innocuous unclassified information may require protection.
- Report suspicious situations to the nearest US diplomatic facility while overseas or to your security office upon return to the United States.[5]

Elicitation Response

Although it has been discussed somewhat above, the NCIS offers the following recommendations should you ever feel you are being drawn into a conversation that is making you uncomfortable:

- You are not obligated to tell anyone anything or provide any information they are not authorized to receive, and that includes personal information about your or your colleagues.
- You can simply ignore any questions you think are improper and change the topic.
- Deflect their questions with one of your own.
- Give a nondescript answer.
- If appropriate, simply say you do not know.
- If possible, avoid the individual.
- If all else fails, suggest you would have to clear such discussion with your security office (**Note:** such an answer, though, indicates a sensitive subject area and your response—in itself—may tell them something about the subject area).

Because elicitation is so subtle and difficult to recognize, report any suspicious conversations to your security office.[5]

Your Response

Likewise, NCIS recommends the following in your response:

- Don't be overly wary of meeting new people to such a degree that you avoid establishing contacts and friendships. When you meet people, it is because you want to know about them, what they do, and if anything beneficial can result from the meeting. Being standoffish identifies that you are a person who may have something important to hide or are overly cautious about other people, or that you are a "cold fish" and word gets around to avoid you. As such, you become a pariah to others, and meetings go downhill fast or are never held. So, it is to your benefit, even from a business point of view, to be friendly to others. You never know when that association (not necessarily friendship) might be of use in the future. In some instances, you may not be able to avoid contact with a specific person, despite your best efforts. If they really want to meet you, they will find a way. Feel free to expand your professional and personal horizons, but keep in mind that not everyone you meet has the best intentions.

- Be mindful not to draw special attention to yourself and your professional affiliation when meeting new people. Of course, if there are many people in the same field of endeavor, the professional affiliation goes by the wayside. At the same time, a guarded demeanor may actually set you apart and could highlight you as someone of particular importance, should you come in contact with an intelligence collector. An obvious or clumsy avoidance of talking about where you work and what you do during certain conversations will seem strange and could draw further and unwanted attention to you.
- Give forethought to what you will say if your employment, job duties, sometimes even the job title and where within the organization you work, or personal questions come up in conversation. Be prepared. Be ready to tactfully deflect questions that lean toward being intrusive or are too probing regarding your job, private life, and coworkers. Never feel compelled to directly answer any questions where you might feel uncomfortable.[4]

Tips on Deflecting Elicitation Attempts

- Don't allow others to control the conversation; the person that asks the questions controls the conversation.
- Listen more than you talk.
- Deflect a question with another question.
- Change the topic.
- Provide a general or a nondescript answer.
- Plead ignorance rather than share information you shouldn't.
- Don't answer. Being blunt is OK; you are not obligated to tell anyone anything they are not authorized to know.
- It is never too late to stop talking! Think before you speak![4]

ELICITATION: AN INTELLIGENCE COLLECTOR'S VIEWPOINT

Per the US Army's Publication *Counterintelligence* (FM 34-60),[7] "since elicitation is gaining information through direct communication, where one or more of the involved parties is not aware of the specific purpose of the conversation, a certain amount of planning must be made." From the collector's point of view, the elicitation process begins when you are "spotted" and considered to be a possible target for information of value. The Chinese have been at this for a very long time, and they have learned from reading many books and treatises on the subject, studied other intelligence services' methods, learned from doing, and have specialized courses available to them. So, if you have been targeted as a possible source of information, it might be that you have been considered some time ago, or you were noticed at the convention (continuing our example) and are to be approached. From the collector's viewpoint, what is necessary for them to approach a "subject," that is, you? The following, from *Counterintelligence*, provides a view of the information collector's minds and what is being done prior to actually approaching you in any venue.

1. Preparation. Always apply elicitation with a specific purpose in mind. What is the objective, or information desired? This is the key factor in determining the subject and the setting. Once the subject has been selected because of his or her access to, or knowledge of, or potential knowledge of any desired information, numerous areas of social and official dealings may provide the setting. Before the actual approach is made, the collector will review (or has been

briefed on you based on) all available intelligence files and records, personality dossiers, and knowledge possessed by others who have previously dealt with you. This helps the collector to determine your background, motivation, emotions, and psychological nature.

2. The Approach. You will typically be approached in normal surroundings. There are two basic elicitation approaches: flattery and provocation. The following variations to these approaches may be used:
   a. By appealing to the ego, self-esteem, or prominence, you may be subtly guided into a conversation on the area of interest.
   b. By soliciting your opinion and by insinuating that you are an authority on a particular topic.
   c. By adopting an unbelieving attitude, you may be subtly caused to explain in detail or to answer out of irritation. The collector won't want to provoke the subject to the point where rapport is broken.
   d. By inserting bits of factual information on a particular topic, you may be influenced to confirm and further expound on the topic. This approach is used carefully because it does not always lend itself to sudden impulse. Carelessness or overuse of this technique may give away more information than gained.
   e. By offering sincere and valid assistance without giving away what information the collector is really looking for, your specific area of interest is determined, as well as possible subspecialty areas that can be used in the future for further collection efforts.
3. Conversation. Once the approach has succeeded in opening the conversation, conversational techniques will be devised to channel and direct the conversation to the area of interest. Some common techniques include the following:
   a. An attempt to obtain more information by a vague, incomplete, or a general response.
   b. A request for additional information where your response is unclear; for example, "I agree; however, what did you mean by...?"
   c. A hypothetical situation that can be associated with a thought or idea that you expressed. Many people who would make no comment concerning an actual situation will express an opinion on hypothetical situations.[8]

HOSTING FOREIGN VISITORS

This section and the one to follow, *Host Responsibilities*, include passages and recommendations, and draw heavily from the DOE publication *Hosting Foreign Visitors*.[7] The publication states:

> Hosting foreign visitors is a critical responsibility. This is especially true when the foreign national is from a country that is directly competing against the United States militarily or economically. You need to take appropriate measures and care when dealing with foreign visitors.

The reason being, that it is the visit on your home turf. It is in your organization, perhaps in your office, and there could be examples of (1) current and future projects visible, or perhaps, a point of the facility that is seen by visitors covers (2) manufacturing, R&D, development projects, manufacturing techniques, and the like. Thus, the following is being included to:

- Enhance your understanding of risks associated with the foreign visits
- Inform you how to identify and mitigate these risks
- Remind you of your responsibilities as a host of foreign visitors[7]

In order to discover new technologies or obtain more critical insights, companies often search out or meet with individuals and programs from other countries with the desirable scientific and technical skills and to join with them in cooperative and joint ventures to achieve our goals. By engaging in such ventures, certain benefits can accrue since the development of future technologies could benefit the United States and the world. This is the perspective of your company, but China's perspective is far different; they want to get anything and everything they can and then exploit it to the fullest. So, think of what you might want to learn about another company when you visit them, and then look at it from China's viewpoint, and further, add anything else you might ever think about, and then add it all together, and that is what China will be looking for when they come on a site visit to your facility.[8]

There are inherent risks, though, with any site visit or when you have other associations with foreign nationals. Even though the Cold War is officially over, all countries still pursue their own self-interests. Today, the self-interests of foreign countries is advanced by economic, rather than by military means. In today's race for international economic strength and influence, all countries are competitors, and China ranks at the top in its greed for your information.[7]

Site visits or any short- or long-term assignment through exchange or on-site training at your facilities will provide foreign representatives with a low cost and low risk opportunity to gain access to needed technologies. Most come just for their stated purpose when they request to visit or are invited for one reason or another. However, a few visitors always will have a hidden agenda: they are at your facility collecting information, and this information doesn't have to be classified to be valuable and desirable. Unclassified, sensitive information is often targeted because it is typically more readily accessible, easier to obtain, and may not be available to them in their home country. Also, even if the visitor is not from China, such a person could be a surrogate, or work for a company indirectly owned or controlled by China.

Host Responsibilities

Before you host a foreign visitor, assignee, or delegation:

- Ensure that the benefits gained from the visit will outweigh the potential risks of the visit. Determine which areas of your work may be sensitive and might create a more than passing interest. If you deal with classified information under a government contract, look at the work that is not classified, but could still shed some light on classified work.
- Personally assess whether the discussion of selected topics of information could reveal proprietary information that is not covered during the visit. If the visitor is long term, determine how you will keep details of items not to be shared away from their presence, and how to limit their access to various computers, especially from your network that maintains a great deal of information on other work projects. Determine exactly the details that are related to cooperative research or other collaborative work at your facility.
- Working closely with the security department, carefully craft a unique security plan that addresses the visitor/delegation/long-term visitor, and the plan should take into consideration the true purpose of the visit and anything related to it within your department that needs protection from the visitor(s). The plan must cover the entire visit and should at least give some thought to other unexplained personnel that arrive for the visit, what to do when topics not covered under the visit request arise, and how to answer questions that are proposed after the visit, whether by telephone, e-mail, fax, and so on.

During the visit, be alert to indications that any of the visitors might be collecting information on the basis of intelligence tasking, or might be an intelligence officer.

The following are some indicators:

- The visitor inquires too frequently about information outside the stated subject area of the visit or seeks information and gives little in return.
- In a delegation of visitors, one individual doesn't have the same level of expertise as others in the group, does not stay focused on the agenda of the visit, or engages in incongruous behavior for the occasion.

- A "wandering" visitor who is offended when he is challenged about his presence in locations away from the normal area of the visit. For a long-term individual, he should have an identification badge that is color coded or specifically spells out the area(s) he is authorized to visit, to include his normal work space.
- The visitor is unduly curious about other employees, what they do, and other programs and areas beyond the scope of the visit.

Also, you should:

- Deflect any inquiry that seeks information that should not be shared about you, your colleagues, your employer, or a US government agency for which you may be performing classified or sensitive unclassified work, a competitor or other company, and also programs and policies that are ongoing.
- Exercise caution if you are asked to assist the visitor with mailing of packages or letters out of the United States. Prior to mailing, all items should be checked out and the contents should be reviewed before mailing. You need to know if anything from the business is being mailed, and if it has been approved to be mailed. Always question any computer disks that are included; they need to be carefully checked for what information is on the disk. If the information is in a foreign language, it is highly recommended that it not be sent. You can always hold on to it, wait for an authorized translator to look at the information, and then determine if it should be sent. If your visitor has a problem with it, the problem is because you want to know what is on the disk, and the visitor wants the disk sent without being checked.
- Monitor computer access. Often, collectors look for sensitive projects or proprietary business information on unclassified networks. Disks, thumb drives, and so on, hold a lot of information. In terms of thumb drives, there are so many out there today that don't look like a thumb drive, it is hard to spot them. One way to control any access is to provide a computer that has no drives present and also doesn't have a printer hookup. Thus, your visitor can only look at the computer screen, but can't download or print anything off it.
- Ensure that the visitor's access is restricted to information and locations approved for the visit.[7,9]

LONG-TERM FOREIGN VISITORS

This section and the one to follow, *The Technology Control Plan*, includes passages and recommendations, and draw heavily from the DOE publication *Hosting Foreign Visitors*.[7] The publication states: "Long-term foreign visits to US defense contractors, national laboratories, or to other companies or research laboratories in the private sector can pose a serious threat to security. Cleared contractors that have foreign national employees or that host long-term foreign visitors should have developed and use a technology control plan (TCP) or other comparable procedures to mitigate the vulnerabilities associated with the foreign presence." Note that in previous espionage cases, Chinese nationals have come to work for US companies, obtained naturalized status, and gone on to work their way up within companies, all for the express purpose of collecting a myriad of information over the years, and then passing such information on to China.

Given access to US scientific, technical, or other proprietary information, Chinese experts can gain for their country a lot of information that will erode the US lead in militarily critical and emerging commercial technologies. As an example, the difference between the technology used in unclassified research and a classified weapons program is only the "application" of the technology.

During joint R&D activities, foreign governments routinely request the presence of an on-site liaison officer to monitor progress and provide guidance, or to allow some of their company employees to be trained on a system program, or major project, and then with the gained knowledge, they go back to China and develop the project on their own. Several allied nations have also used such positions as cover for intelligence officers who are tasked to collect as much information about a facility as possible. These officers use their access to the facility's computer network or relationship with their US counterparts to gain unapproved access to classified or restricted data that are then sent back to their home country.

Foreign scientists and engineers sometimes offer their services to research facilities, academic institutions, or defense contractors, many times as a "learning" process so the individuals can gain appropriate knowledge. Essentially, though, the individual may know much more than you imagine. (Think back to the old Soviet regime; they had "students" come over to attend college in the engineering and science fields. They also worked at various commercial facilities under the guise of being a student. Some of them were in their 30s and 40s.) All this can be an effort to place a person inside the facility to collect information on the technology available there. Some prominent foreign scientists who obtained employment with US companies have *immediately* began to send acquired information via fax transmissions back to their home country, using their native language so the US company could not monitor what was being sent.

As part of a joint venture, one cleared government contractor had a number of foreign representatives working on unclassified projects. One was caught hacking into an unclassified, but proprietary local area network system. This person accessed company proprietary source code information. He was expelled, but the computer intrusions continued a few days later. The later suspects were the remaining representatives from the same country. What made the whole case interesting is that since the start of the joint venture, the foreign representatives had stated their desire for the source codes.

In some instances, Chinese undergraduate and graduate students in the United States have been asked by their government or a private-sector company to serve as "assistants" at no cost to professors doing research in a targeted field. The student then has access to the professor's research and learns the applications of the technology.

One can be pretty well assured (but not proven) that China routinely tasks their graduate students in the United States to acquire information on a variety of economic and technical subjects. In some instances, the students are contacted and recruited before they come to the United States to study. Others are approached after arriving and are recruited or pressured based upon a sense of loyalty or fear of the Chinese government or intelligence service. An example, though not from China, is one where the security officer of a cleared US defense contractor reported the company's desire to employ the son of a prominent foreign scientist from a European country. A name check of the scientist revealed he had previously cooperated with his country's foreign intelligence service.

France has an organized program to send interns abroad as an alternative to compulsory military service. In return for exemption from military service, the intern has the specific task of collecting foreign business and technological information. A student who offers to work "free" for a US company that has a US government contract for classified work is a student to be very wary of, for the saying goes that "nothing is truly free." In the end, if accepted, you would get a person who works for no pay, but France would get everything the intern could obtain.

The following indicators should trigger security concern:

- The applicant has a scientific background in a specialty for which his country is known or suspected to have a collection requirement or has indicated an interest in the subject area or one close to it.
- The technology the individual wants to conduct research on may have classified applications (dual-use technology), be on the militarily critical technology list, or be export-controlled technology.
- An intern (typically a student working on masters or doctorate degree) offers to work under a knowledgeable individual for free, usually for a period of 2–3 years. A question in your mind should arise of who is paying the expenses of the individual, and what do they expect to gain from paying these expenses. ("Hey, it's free labor on the project. Who cares who is paying his expenses.")

Without sustained security and counterintelligence awareness training programs, assimilation of foreign personnel into the work environment will usually result in a relaxation of security awareness among US employees. This is because after a while, nobody takes notice of the individual, he makes friends and, over a period of time, starts to gain just a bit of access and knowledge in areas that should be off-limits. Security compromise is a frequent result in such situations.[10–13]

THE TECHNOLOGY CONTROL PLAN

Cleared contractors with foreign national employees or long-term foreign visitors are required to have an approved TCP or comparable procedures. There is no reason why the private-sector companies shouldn't have a TCP also. In fact, it can be recognized that more information will probably be stolen from the private sector than from government organizations and government contractor facilities. Thus, a TCP is really essential. The TCP identifies the specific information that has been authorized for release to the foreign visitors or employees as well as what classified, export-controlled, other sensitive or proprietary information needs to be protected from the visitors or employees. Note that any discussion of export-controlled information with a foreign national in the United States is an "export" of that information and is subject to all the export control procedures.

Whether government or the private sector, a TCP should have the following elements:

- All information that needs to be protected must be appropriately indicated prominently or otherwise identifiable to all personnel, and the penalties for noncompliance or negligence should be well known. Even within a large division of a corporation, there should be limits. Nobody needs to know everything, especially when it is very sensitive information. Such information may be a trade secret, propriety to a given project, program, or specific item. (Under the Economic Espionage Act of 1996, information is not considered a trade secret unless the owner of the information has taken reasonable measures to protect it.)
- All employees should be briefed prior to the arrival of a visitor (whether an identifiable foreign national or not) on the access limitations, potential collection techniques that could be used, recognizing indicators of economic espionage, and to whom to report any relevant security information.
- All employees who have frequent contact with visiting personnel should be interviewed periodically to check for indicators of economic espionage.
- Foreign nationals and long-term foreign visitors should be briefed on their obligations and responsibilities, including limitations on access and any limitations on their use of computers, copiers, or fax machines. They should be asked to sign a legally binding agreement that they will comply with security requirements. The agreement should state what the consequences are for not complying with the security requirements. (The agreement should include all legal ramifications involved.) If the foreign national is later caught doing something wrong, the written agreement eliminates the "I didn't know" excuse.
- In anticipation of gaining access to an organizations' computer network, some visitors are well trained in hacking techniques. Good risk management means reducing any vulnerabilities to the technologies or information you are trying to protect. It may mean providing long-term visitors with a "stand-alone" computer instead of access to your entire network. At a minimum, it must include regular checking of computer audit logs to detect any effort by the visiting employee to exceed his or her approved computer access.
- Foreign visitors should not be given access to company fax machines unless you have some means to read and review all documents being sent, including those written in a foreign language. Fax machines make it possible for someone who is stealing information to compromise documents without having to take the riskier step of physically removing them from the building.[10–13]

Security Reporting Responsibilities

If you suspect a visitor has a hidden agenda, or if you observe any suspicious behavior, contact your security office. Also report any attempts to probe for information, efforts to put you in a compromising situation, and any other anomalous behaviors.

Most foreign contacts are perfectly legitimate and well meaning. Your ability to recognize the few who are not will help you avoid problems. It will also help your security officer help others avoid problems.

As the DOE publication *Hosting Foreign Visitors* states: "As a host in the visit of a foreign national, you should maintain awareness before the visit, diligence during the visit and take caution in any subsequent interactions with the visitor. As a visit progresses, permanent employees often forget that the visitor is a foreigner who is there only temporarily. Security restrictions can be forgotten or overlooked."[14] You must consider yourself personally responsible for maintaining the security of the visit and for precluding the inadvertent or unintentional passage of unauthorized information.

Remember, in today's global economic competition, knowledge has value. IP is the key to America's continued success.

As the DOE publication *CounterIntelligence in our World* recommends, other considerations include the following:

- Unofficial contacts within or outside the United States (social, personal, or other unreported professional settings, such as conferences, where there is significant contact).
- Any attempted elicitation of information or contact (official or unofficial that would indicate a foreign intelligence presence).
- Any contact involving inappropriate efforts to obtain information about a sensitive subject, classified information, or any counterintelligence-related incidents. This may include perceived efforts to obtain sensitive or proprietary data.
- Any contact via telephone, facsimile machine, e-mail, Internet, or other electronic means (usually only the initial contact, official or unofficial).
- Anomalies, that is, any activity or knowledge, inconsistent with the expected norm, which suggests they have some knowledge of information, processes or capabilities that wouldn't be known by an outsider.[14]

Espionage Indicators

If a person, especially a regular employee, is working covertly for China, note that while they may be an American, an American of Chinese descent (second or third generation), another foreigner, or someone else, there are certain "red flag" indicators that something could be amiss. As the DOE publication *CounterIntelligence in our World* suggests, "individuals involved in espionage each have unique motivators for the betrayal of their country and each has displayed questionable but identifiable behavior in the following:

- Any attempt to obtain information for which an individual does not have a proper access and need-to-know in the performance of their assigned duties and job responsibilities.
- Unauthorized removal of any information (classified, sensitive unclassified, company proprietary, research notes and agendas, etc.) from the work area.
- Using copying equipment in another office to reproduce material when equipment is available in the individual's own office. In this regard also, consider that when people go to lunch the visitor "needs to work through the lunch hour" without any other supervision being present.
- Obtaining witness signatures on any unclassified sensitive or classified document destruction forms when the witness did not observe the destruction.

- Sudden purchase of high value items where no logical income source exists.
- Free spending or lavish display of cash or wealth that appears to be beyond the normal income level of the individual.
- Sudden repayment of loans.
- Foreign travel that does not appear to justify the expense involved.
- Recurring, unexplained weekend trips not associated with recreation or family.
- Patterns of unreported foreign travel.
- Relatives and friends who have known connections with persons residing overseas, whether or not in designated countries that may have commercial, military or political interests that are contrary to those of the United States.
- Requests from "relatives or friends" in foreign countries to provide assistance or information that relates to any organizational projects or programs."[7]

A good rule is to report to your security office anything, however minor or insignificant it may seem, that makes you "feel uncomfortable" or out of place from the individual requesting such information or assistance.

PROTECTING YOUR IP RIGHTS (IPR) IN CHINA

The information in this section and the following subsections are taken from the US Department of Commerce's publication *Protecting Your Intellectual Property Rights (IPR) in China, A Practical Guide for U.S. Companies*, which provides an introduction to China's IPR environment, describing methods for safeguarding and protecting IPR, outlining possible enforcement actions available in China's IPR enforcement regime, and explaining the limited role of the US government in IPR infringement cases.

In 1999, more than 80% of all US firms that exported to China were composed of small- and medium-sized enterprises (SMEs), generating more than a quarter of US exports to China. As China's World Trade Organization (WTO) accession promises them greater market access and a more predictable commercial environment, new entrants will be encouraged to enter China's market. Though companies are finding commercial opportunities in China, there are many potential pitfalls companies should be aware of, including issues related to the protection of IP. Remember, in this regard, that our laws do not equate to China's laws or are not enforceable in China. Thus said, a US firm considering entering the Chinese market must perform significant, specific due diligence, of which this guide is only the first step.[15]

CHINA'S CURRENT IPR ENVIRONMENT

Since joining the WTO, China has strengthened its legal framework and amended its IPR and related laws and regulations to comply with the WTO Agreement on Trade-Related Aspect of Intellectual Property Rights (TRIPS). Despite stronger statutory protection, China continues to be a haven for counterfeiters and pirates. According to one report, the piracy rate in China remains one of the highest in the world (over 90%) and US companies lose over $1 billion in legitimate business each year to piracy. On average, 20% of all consumer products in the Chinese market are counterfeit. If a product sells, it is likely to be illegally duplicated. US companies are not alone, as pirates and counterfeiters target both foreign and domestic companies.[15]

Though Chinese government officials may, to some extent, tackle the problem, enforcement measures taken are not sufficient to deter massive IPR infringements. There are several factors that undermine enforcement measures, including China's reliance on administrative instead of criminal measures to combat IPR infringements, corruption and local protectionism at the provincial levels, limited resources and training available to enforcement officials, and lack of public education regarding the economic and social impact of counterfeiting and piracy.[15]

There have been instances of China enforcing illegal product manufacture of counterfeit products through crackdowns of pirated and other products developed with stolen IP. But when you look at the pictures that are shown on China's web site, you would notice that very few products are really being confiscated or destroyed. Further, it seems all the crackdowns are of much, much smaller companies, and there just happens to be a photographer present to take the appropriate pictures. In reality, only when it benefits the government, and makes the government look good because of the publicity, can you expect to see any crackdowns. Again, think about it; you never see a major Chinese company have its doors shuttered and all its products destroyed by the millions, and you probably never will, because it would cost too much money to be lost in the economy.

The Best Protection Is Prevention

Though China is a party to international agreements to protect IP (including WIPO, the Bern Convention, and the Paris Convention, among others), a company must register its patents and trademarks with the appropriate Chinese agencies and authorities for those rights to be enforceable in China. Copyrights do not need to be registered but registration may be helpful in enforcement actions.

Patent Law. China's first patent law was enacted in 1984 and has been amended twice (1992 and 2000) to extend the scope of protection. To comply with TRIPS, the latest amendment extended the duration of patent protection to 20 years from the date of filing a patent application. Chemical and pharmaceutical products, as well as food, beverages, and flavorings are all now patentable. *China follows a first-to-file system for patents*, which means patents are granted to those that file first even if the filers are not the original inventors. This system is unlike the United States, which recognizes the "first-to-invent" rule, but is consistent with the practice in other parts of the world, including the European Union. Under China's patent law, a foreign patent application filed by a person or firm without a business office in China must apply through an authorized patent agent, while initial preparation may be done by anyone. Patents are filed with China's State Intellectual Property Office (SIPO) in Beijing, while SIPO offices at the provincial and municipal level are responsible for administrative enforcement.[15]

Trademark Law. China's trademark law was first adopted in 1982 and subsequently revised in 1993 and 2001. The new trademark law extended registration to collective marks, certification marks, and three-dimensional symbols, as required by TRIPS. China joined the Madrid Protocol in 1989, which requires reciprocal trademark registration for member countries, which now include the United States. *China has a "first-to-register" system* that requires no evidence of prior use or ownership, leaving registration of popular foreign marks open to third party. However, the Chinese Trademark Office has cancelled Chinese trademarks that were unfairly registered by local Chinese agents or customers of foreign companies. Foreign companies seeking to distribute their products in China are advised to register their marks or logos with the Trademark Office. Further, any Chinese language translations and appropriate Internet domains should also be registered. As with patent registration, foreign parties must use the services of approved Chinese agents when submitting the trademark application; however, foreign attorneys or the Chinese agents may prepare the application.[15]

Copyright Law. China's copyright law was established in 1990 and amended in 2001. The new implementing rules came into force in 2002. Unlike the patent and trademark protection, copyrighted works do not require registration for protection. Protection is granted to individuals from countries belonging to the copyright international conventions or bilateral agreements of which China is a member. However, copyright owners may wish to voluntarily register with China's National Copyright Administration (NCA) to establish evidence of ownership, should enforcement actions become necessary.[15] Even though copyrighted, from just about any street vendor, you can obtain copies of the latest videos, DVDs, and books for a fraction of what they would cost anywhere else in the world. There is so much piracy and copyright infringement going on in China, that it would take a large force, working full time to shut down the vendors, and to a lesser extent, find and shut down all the small entrepreneurs who are creating the products.

Unfair Competition. China's Unfair Competition Law provides *some* protection for unregistered trademarks, packaging, trade dress, and trade secrets. The Fair Trade Bureau, under the State Administration for Industry and Commerce (SAIC), has responsibilities over the interpretation and implementation of the Unfair Competition Law. Protection of company names is also provided by SAIC. According to the TRIPS Agreement, China is required to protect undisclosed information submitted to Chinese agencies in obtaining regulatory approval for pharmaceutical and chemical entities from disclosure or unfair commercial use. China's State Drug Administration and Ministry of Agriculture oversee the marketing approval of pharmaceuticals and agricultural chemicals, respectively.[15]

China's IPR Enforcement System

In 1998, China established the SIPO, with the vision that it would coordinate China's IP enforcement efforts by merging the patent, trademark, and copyright offices under one authority. SIPO is responsible for granting patents (national office), registering semiconductor layout designs (at a National level office), and enforcing patents (local SIPO offices), as well as coordinating domestic foreign-related IPR issues involving copyrights, trademarks, and patents.[15]

Protection of IP in China follows a two-track system. The first and most prevalent is the administrative track, whereby an IPR holder files a complaint at the local administrative office. The second is the judicial track, whereby complaints are filed through the court system. (China has established specialized IP panels in its civil court system throughout the country.) Determining which IP agency has jurisdiction over an act of infringement can be confusing. Jurisdiction of IP protection is diffused throughout a number of government agencies and offices, with each typically responsible for the protection afforded by one statute or one specific area of IP-related law.[15]

For administrative enforcement actions, the following lists the major players. Other agencies, such as the State Drug Administration (for pharmaceutical counterfeits) or the Ministry of Culture (for copyright materials and markets) may also play a role in the enforcement process. In most cases, administrative agencies cannot award compensation to a rights holder. They can, however, fine the infringer, seize goods or equipment used in manufacturing products, or obtain information about the source of goods being distributed.

- Administration for Quality Supervision, Inspection and Quarantine. China's standard setting agency, is primarily tasked with ensuring Chinese product quality and standards and also handles infringements of registered trademarks, when the infringing products are inferior or shoddy quality goods.[15]
- SAIC, Trademark Office. The Trademark Office, under the SAIC, maintains authority over trademark registration, administrative recognition of well-known marks, and enforcement of trademark protection. The Fair Trade Bureau handles disputes arising under the Law to Counter Unfair Competition, including trade secret matters. In enforcement efforts, SAIC has the power to investigate the case. When an infringement is determined, SAIC has the power to cease the sale of infringing items and to stop further infringement, order the destruction of infringing marks or products, impose fines, and remove machines used to produce counterfeit goods.[15]
- SIPO at the national level is responsible for the examination of foreign and domestic patents and supervision of local SIPO bureaus. Provincial offices generally handle the administrative enforcement of patent complaints.[15]
- NCA is responsible for copyright administration and enforcement. NCA is also responsible for nationwide copyright issues, including investigating infringement cases, administering foreign-related copyright issues, developing foreign-related arbitration rules, and

supervising administrative authorities. Though administrative remedies are available, NCA generally encourages complainants to use the court system due to lack of personnel.[15]

- General Administration of Customs. The Customs Regulations ban the import/export of IPR infringing goods. In order for Customs to exercise this right, the IP holder must record its IP with Customs. The certificate issued by Customs is valid for seven years and is renewable for seven-year periods. When a rights holder suspects infringing goods are about to enter or exit China, he or she may submit a written application to Customs at the suspected point of entry or exist where protection is sought. When Customs' investigation reveals a case of infringement, it has the authority to confiscate the goods, and may destroy or remove the infringing goods, and impose a fine.[15]
- Public Security Bureau (police)/Procuratorate (prosecutors). Under enforcement provisions of TRIPS, China must provide IP remedies through criminal enforcement for commercial scale piracy and counterfeiting. China's laws and regulations stipulate that IP administrative authorities and Customs may transfer egregious IP infringement cases to police and prosecutors (procuratorate) for initiating criminal investigation. Despite these criminal provisions, most IP cases continued to be handled through the administrative system. Under Chinese law, individuals also have the right to prosecute criminal cases, which has rarely been used.[15]

What the US Government Can Do in IPR Infringement Cases

Many companies, particularly SMEs that discover their products are being infringed in China, contact the US Department of Commerce for assistance. Because IPR are private rights, the Department of Commerce can provide only some limited direct assistance. In many cases, the US government can provide companies with information in navigating China's legal system, including lists of local investigative firms and attorneys, and share our experience and expertise in China. However, the Department of Commerce cannot provide American companies with legal advice or advocate on a company's behalf without the company first taking legal action.[15]

When a company encounters blatant infringement of its IPR, the rights holder should hire local counsel and pursue a preliminary investigation on one's own or through a contracted professional firm, keeping in mind that US companies should ensure compliance with Chinese law, which restricts private investigation to certain forms of "market research" investigations. Once the initial investigation is complete, the company should determine if further action and possible costs related with such actions are worth pursuing. Rights holders will have the option to initiate actions or seek redress through either the judicial or administrative system. Foreign rights holders have had considerably less success in encouraging criminal prosecution of IPR violations, particularly when copyright infringements are involved.[15]

Once a company decides to pursue a remedy, the Department of Commerce, through the Washington D.C.- or China-based offices, will monitor the case, if requested to do so by the company. The US government cannot intervene in the case; however, the US government can inquire about its status or contact government officials about concerns related to the effective administration of legal remedies available to IP holders. The Department of Commerce is most likely to become involved in a case where evidence indicates China is not complying with its enforcement under the WTO TRIPS Agreement. As with other types of commercial disputes, the Department's efforts in assisting with IPR disputes are aimed at achieving a fair and timely resolution in accordance with international commitments and Chinese laws and in advancing adequate legal and judicial protection for all parties.[15]

ABOUT TRADE SECRETS IN CHINA

Nearly all businesses in all industries and sectors possess trade secrets, which are a valuable and highly useful form of IPR. Unlike registrable IP such as patents and copyrights that have a finite term, trade secrets can theoretically enjoy an infinite term of protection as long as the trade secret remains just that—a secret. On the other hand, once the information becomes public, it no longer enjoys any legal protection. As a result, prevention is the golden rule when it comes to trade secrets.

STRATEGY TARGETING ORGANIZED PIRACY

The US Department of Commerce has established the Strategy Targeting Organized Piracy (STOP!) Program to deter and prevent the trade of counterfeit and pirated goods both domestically and globally. According to its publication *Protect Your Intellectual Property: Stop Trade in Fakes!*:

> Intellectual property rights (IPR) encourage the innovation and creativity that is fundamental to sustained economic growth. Unfortunately, the growing global trade in pirated and counterfeit goods threatens innovation, workers' livelihoods, health, and safety. Fake products—such as CDs, DVDs, software, electronic equipment, clothing, pharmaceutical products, and auto parts—account for an estimated 5 to 7 percent of global trade. This trade costs legitimate rights holders around the world billions of dollars annually. The U.S. Department of Commerce's Strategy Targeting Organized Piracy (STOP!) is a comprehensive program to stop trade in pirated and counterfeit goods. Through STOP!, the U.S. government is working to make it easier for rights holders to obtain and enforce their intellectual property rights at home and abroad. The U.S. government has also leveraged its law enforcement resources and is establishing international cooperation to dismantle the criminal networks that manufacture and distribute fake goods. STOP! underscores the U.S. government's continuing commitment to level the playing field for American businesses and workers. Owners of intellectual property also need to act to obtain intellectual property rights, thereby securing the economic benefits of their intellectual property and laying the foundation for curbing the trade in fake goods.[16]

The Department of Commerce has a hotline (1-866-999-HALT) for further assistance. The hotline allows US businesses to speak with IPR specialists and obtain practical information on how to protect IP. The US government web site, www.StopFakes.gov, can provide you with information about obtaining and enforcing IPR.

GETTING HELP TO PROTECT YOUR RIGHTS

Regarding Market Access and Compliance, The Department of Commerce's Market Access and Compliance (MAC) unit, according to them, is set up "to help U.S. businesses to overcome trade barriers and ensure that China in this case complies with their trade agreement and treaty commitments to the United States. MAC's Intellectual Property Rights Office and country experts—both within MAC and at U.S. embassies—are ready to work with U.S. companies to enforce their intellectual property rights. MAC experts can suggest strategies to evaluate IPR problems encountered abroad and will work with embassies to pursue a course of action for resolution of problems. MAC has established a special telephone line and web site designed specifically to deal with companies' international intellectual property concerns."[16]

Companies can contact MAC about IPR problems abroad at: US Department of Commerce, Intellectual Property Rights Office, 1401 Constitution Avenue, N.W., Washington, DC 20230; telephone: toll free, (866) 999-HALT (866-999-4258) or go to the web site, http://www.StopFakes.gov.

YOUR KNOWLEDGE OF METHODS USED IN ECONOMIC ESPIONAGE

With everything else going on in your mind, you should be aware of various areas Chinese collectors will use to obtain information. You may wish to extract the following for security education purposes, making an employee handout for their future reference.

Several well-known modus operandi (MO) are used when attempting to acquire sensitive corporate or proprietary information through economic espionage. These activities serve as indicators of economic espionage. While these do not always mean there is an actual foreign collection threat, they can serve as a signal. Several indicators occurring in a given situation might warrant further examination.

Unsolicited Requests for Proprietary Information

Occasionally, your company or agency may receive unsolicited, outside requests—in the guise of marketing surveys—for proprietary or sensitive government unclassified and classified information. Requests may include phoning, faxing, e-mailing, or mailing individuals. The requests may involve surveys or questionnaires and are frequently sent over the Internet.

Marketing surveys can elicit sensitive technological and business information. With this particular method, it is important to consider who (a company or individual) is the end user of the information and who is completing the survey. Increasing use of the Internet provides a method of direct communication with government and the private sector for collection purposes. Internet access to a company's bulletin board, home page, and employees provides a foreign collector many avenues to broaden collection efforts.[17]

ESPIONAGE INDICATORS

The following bullet lists in this section are compiled from the Defense Security Service publication *Suspicious Indicators and Security Countermeasures for Foreign Collection Activities Directed Against the U.S. Defense Industry.* Though a few of these issues have been noted previously in this chapter, they are provided to give you a fairly complete list of intelligence collection indicators.[17]

- The Internet address is in a foreign country.
- The recipient has never met the sender.
- Information on the technology requested is classified, is export controlled, or has both commercial and military applications (dual-use technologies).
- The requester identifies his or her status as a student or consultant.
- The requester identifies his or her employer as a foreign government or the work is being done for a foreign government or program.
- The requester asks about a defense-related program, project, or contract.
- The requester asks questions about defense-related program or an emerging technology program using acronyms specific to the program.
- The requester admits he or she could not get the information elsewhere because it was classified or controlled.
- The requester advises the recipient to disregard the request if it causes a security problem or if it is for information the recipient cannot provide due to security classification, export controls, and so forth.
- The requester advises the recipient not to worry about security concerns.
- The requester assures the recipient that export licenses are not required or are not a problem.
- Marketing surveys may be faxed or mailed to an individual via the company marketing office.
- Marketing surveys may be sent by foreign consortiums or consulting companies. Companies with intelligence involvement are likely to be a consortium of officials, military officers, or private interests.
- Marketing surveys often may exceed generally accepted terms of marketing information.
- Strong suspicions that the "surveyor" is employed by a competing foreign company.
- Surveys may solicit proprietary information concerning corporate affiliations, market projections, pricing policies, program or technology director's names, company personnel

working on the program, purchasing practices, and types and dollar amounts of Canadian government contracts.
- Customer and supplier bases for a company may also be sent marketing surveys that exceed accepted terms of marketing information.

Inappropriate Conduct during Visits

Foreign visits can present potential security risks if sound risk management is not practiced and appropriate security measures are not implemented. Major indicators[17] include the following:

- Visitors are escorted by a diplomatic or embassy official who attempts to conceal their official identities during a supposedly commercial visit.
- Hidden agendas, as opposed to the stated purpose of the visit; that is, visitors arrive to discuss program X but do everything to discuss and meet with personnel who work with program Y.
- Last minute and unannounced persons added to the visiting party.
- "Wandering" visitors, who act offended when confronted.
- Using alternate mechanisms. For example, if a classified visit request is not approved, the foreign entity may attempt a commercial visit.
- Visitors ask questions outside the scope of the approved visit, hoping to get a courteous or spontaneous response.

Suspicious Work Offers

Foreign scientists and engineers will offer their services to research facilities, academic institutions, and defense contractors. This may be an MO to place a foreign national inside the facility to collect information on a desired technology. Here, there are only a few indicators[17] to consider:

- The foreign applicant has a scientific background in a specialty for which his country has been identified as having a collection requirement.
- The foreign applicant offers services for free. The foreign government or the corporation associated with the government is paying expenses.
- Foreign interns (students working on masters or doctorate degrees) offer to work under a knowledgeable individual for free, usually for a period of two to three years.

Exploitation of Joint Ventures and Joint Research

Co-production, joint ventures, and various exchange agreements potentially offer significant collection opportunities for foreign interests to target restricted or proprietary technology. In these instances, be on the lookout for the following indicators:[17]

- The foreign representative wants to access the local area network.
- The foreign representative wants unrestricted access to the facility.
- Enticing contractors to provide large amounts of technical data as part of the bidding process, only to have the contract cancelled.
- Potential technology-sharing agreements during the joint venture are one sided.
- The foreign organization sends more foreign representatives than are necessary for the project.
- The foreign representatives single out various company personnel to elicit information outside the scope of the project.

Acquisitions of Technology and Companies

There are always attempts by a foreign company to gain access to sensitive technologies by purchasing companies or technologies. The main indicator is that new employees hired from the foreign partner's company, or its foreign partners, wish to immediately access sensitive corporate or proprietary information.

Co-Opting of Former Employees

Former employees who had access to sensitive, proprietary, or classified program information remain a potential counterintelligence concern. Targeting cultural commonalities to establish rapport is often associated with the collection attempt. Former employees may be viewed as excellent prospects for collection operations and considered less likely to feel obligated to comply with export controls or company security requirements.[17] Look at such employees carefully for the following:

- The former employee took a job with a foreign company working on the same technology.
- The former employee maintains contact with former company and employees.
- Employee alternates working with companies and foreign companies every few years.

Targeting Cultural Commonalities

Foreign entities exploit the cultural background of company personnel in order to elicit information.[17]

- Employees receive unsolicited greetings or other correspondence from the embassy of the country of origin.
- Employees receive invitations to visit the country of family origin for the purpose of providing lecture or receiving an award.
- Company personnel are singled out by foreign visitors of the same cultural background to socialize.

THE BOTTOM LINE FOR PROTECTING AGAINST THREATS

Whether at home or abroad, how can your company protect against these threats?

There are some simple steps to help prevent information leakage.

First, it is necessary to gauge what information is sensitive and how it will be protected. To what extent will it be available to others outside the area where it is being used is also necessary to know. Though some information such as technological innovations, state-of-the-art emerging technologies, or new market strategies may be easily identified, other information, such as that found in customer/public relations, sales and marketing, pricing structure, subcontractors and suppliers of certain electronic or mechanical items, may be just as valuable.[18]

Second, conduct a complete risk assessment of a given area of the organization, or the entire organization, to determine vulnerability.[18] Your information technology systems' individual computers and certain fax machines may send off various levels of electronic emanations when used. As such, with the appropriate equipment, such emanations can "be read" from a distance. Collectors are then able to access the information as it is being entered into a computer or when being transmitted via the fax machine. Whenever emanations are given off by electronic devices, there is always the possibility that others will seek to exploit those vulnerabilities. Many people use laptops with WiFi, so they needn't hook up to a company computer with outside access to transmit and receive information. The risk assessment survey should address this issue and ban such laptops from sensitive areas, or ban them completely unless the laptop is company provided and has restrictions on what information may be on its hard drive.

Third, you must have in place a realistic and workable security policy that addresses various concerns that could arise in the future due to R&D, new technologies, or products under development. The procedures of the security policy must be realistic, must be easily identifiable, and must require no interpretation or misinterpretation by employees. Everyone directly involved and also those outside a program should be briefed (at least in general for employees outside a given area) that many items of information require protection, and how to best protect it. Easily understandable procedures should be laid out. When all employees and staff are clearly informed on what information is to be protected, a giant step toward securing the information is taken. But don't do this just once. Annually, or every six months, or when there is a major change to the policy, procedures, or implementing instructions, security education presentations should be made. Whenever possible, use the most current true cases that can be gleaned from newspapers and other reports to provide illustrations of what is actually happening because these are the most helpful and drive home the point of properly protecting the information of your organization. If someone suspects that information is being solicited, stolen, or used in a manner not consistent with security procedures, a specific person or office should be notified. In this way, also, all employees become part of the security protection system, being additional "eyes and ears" for the company.

Last, security policies must be routinely examined and adjusted regularly to reflect changes in the information and competitive landscape.[18]

SECURITY PRECAUTIONS AS A BUSINESS ENABLER

Information breaches of sensitive company and government information are always taking place. They cost everyone, from the company to individual taxpayers' money, and, in one manner or another, can degrade national security. The risk of losing information to China is only enhanced by the current recession. Because of the slight downturn in economic conditions, companies are likely to cut back on items that do not "show a profit," and security education can be one of the first to be reduced. Security education is one of a series of countermeasures a company uses to protect it assets, tangible and intangible. "Security education" is often quick to be cut or abolished since it is an expense that shows no viable return for the company "bottom line." This is a risky move, as security is only as strong as its weakest link. Ultimately, security measures must be deemed as business enablers and return on investment rather than simply a cost item.[18]

The Awareness of National Security Issues and Response Program of the FBI is the "public voice" of the FBI for espionage, counterintelligence, counterterrorism, economic espionage, cyber and physical infrastructure protection, and all national security issues. The FBI has some great training presentations in the security education field for companies who may need or require an update on economic espionage. The FBI is actually here to help you; take advantage of their expertise. When in doubt, contact your local or regional FBI office. You can also go to their web site at http://www.fbi.gov.

REFERENCES

1. U.S. Department of Energy, Hanford (WA) site, Foreign travel, found at: http://www.hanford.gov.
2. National Counterintelligence Center, Annual report to Congress on foreign economic collection and industrial espionage, Washington, D.C., 1998.
3. U.S. Department of Energy, Chicago Regional Office, Espionage and foreign travel, found at: ch.doe.gov/offices/OCI/EspionageTravel.
4. Naval Criminal Investigative Service (NCIS), Elicitation: The enemy is listening, Washington, D.C., found at: ncis.navy.mil.
5. U.S. Department of Energy, Chicago Regional Office, Elicitation, found at: http://ch.doe.gov/offices.
6. Defense Security Service, Elicitation: Can you recognize it? DSS, Washington, D.C.
7. U.S. Department of Energy, Chicago office, Hosting foreign visitors, found at: DOE web site: http://ch.doe.gov/offices/OCI.

8. Department of the Army, Field Manual 34-60, Counterintelligence, HQDA, Washington, D.C., October 1995.
9. U.S. Department of Energy, Hanford (WA), Hosting and escorting foreign national visits, found at: http://www.hanford.gov.
10. United States Department of Agriculture, Personnel and Document Security Division, Long-term foreign visitors, Washington, D.C., found at: http://dm.usda.gov/ocpm.
11. Long-term foreign visitors threaten security, *Counterintelligence News and Developments*, March 1997, National Counterintelligence Center.
12. National Counterintelligence Center, Annual report to Congress on foreign intelligence collection and industrial espionage, July 1995.
13. Norvell, James, Assessing foreign collection trends, *Security Awareness Bulletin*, No. 1-98 (Richmond, VA: Department of Defense Security Institute, 1998).
14. U.S. Department of Energy, Chicago office, brochure: Counterintelligence in our changing world, found at: DOE web site: http://ch.doe.gov/offices/OCI.
15. U.S. Department of Commerce, International Trade Administration, Protecting your Intellectual Property Rights (IPR) in China, a practical guide for U.S. companies, Washington, D.C., found at: http://mac.doc.gov/china, January 2003.
16. Department of Commerce, Intellectual Property Rights Office, Protect your intellectual property: Stop trade in fakes!, Washington, D.C., 2005, found at: http://stopfakes.gov.
17. Defense Security Service, brochure: Suspicious indicators and security countermeasures for foreign collection activities directed against the U.S. Defense Industry, Washington, D.C., May 1997, found at: dss.mil. Although the brochure was created in 1997, the data contained is still current and very relevant in 2012.
18. Naef, Wanja E., Economic and industrial espionage: A threat to Corporate America, *Infocon Magazine*, issue 1, October 2003.

17 Source Documents and Other Resources

Research for a book such as this involves an inordinate amount of research and evaluation. Fortunately, in this day and age, the Internet allows for a vast accumulation of data that, once downloaded, provides a myriad of data readily at hand. The following provides you with the basic source materials so you can determine for yourself the extent to which China has gone (or will do so in the future) to obtain trade, military, intellectual, and technological secrets.

Source documents include basic background, specific sources used, and other related reference materials that bolster the initial data. While every document reviewed was used for this book, the importance of the information could not be discounted as the methods used by other collectors apply also to China. Some data confirmed other sources, while further data in a given subject area supported or provided alternative views or interpretative versions of the baseline information.

Since a majority come from the Internet, they do not necessarily give the author of the article, paper, or report, but only have an indicator of who "owns" the material in terms of copyright, thus becoming a reference source. Where appropriate, the specific web address for the article has been indicated.

A&E Television Network, Special Report: Espionage with Chinese characteristics, March 24, 2010, A&E Television.

Acronym Institute, FBI reassesses China espionage evidence, Issue No. 52, November 2000, The Acronym Institute.

Allen, Ian, Analysis: Canada becoming a heaven for spies claims ex-CSIS agent, April 9, 2010, found at: IntelligenceNews.org.

Alperovitch, Demitri, Revealed: Operation Shady RAT, 2011, McAfee.

American Manufacturing, ITC releases Study on Chinese intellectual property theft, found at: http://www.americanmanufacturing.org/blog, December 14, 2010, Posted by jeckert, found at: http://www.americanmanufacturing.org/blog.

Becker, Peter, Eyes and ears of the Dragon: Chinese intelligence services organisation and activities, September 26–27, 2008, Netherlands Intelligence Studies Association (NISA) Conference, The Hague, Netherlands.

Best Mobile Mart, Chinese defector reveals that China has Over 1000 spies in Canada alone, February 2, 2010, found at: http://www.BestMobileMart.com.

bizinformer.com, Stop intellectual property theft in China.

British Broadcasting Company, China spying 'biggest U.S. threat', November 2007, BBC.

British Broadcasting Company, Cyber criminals step up the pace, November 18, 2004, bbc.co.uk.

British Broadcasting Company, Secret world of industrial espionage, May 31, 2005, BBC.

British Broadcasting Company, Spy charges for US computer duo, September 27, 2007, found at: http://www.bbc.co.uk.

British Broadcasting Company, The spies watching while you type Cash and keyboard, BBC/Corbis, March 17, 2005, BBC.

British Broadcasting Company, The spy in your computer, July 4, 2004, found at: bbc.co.uk.

British Broadcasting Company, UK 'spied on UN's Kofi Annan', found at: http://www.abc.net.au.

British Broadcasting Company, US Group wants China 'spy' probe, March 27, 2006, BBC.

British Broadcasting Company, Viruses, Trojans and other malicious programs sent on to the net to catch you out are undergoing a subtle change, January 25, 2005, BBC.

British Broadcasting Company, Threats on the net, December 6, 2004, found at: http://www.news.bbc.co.uk/2/hi/programmes/click_online/4154917.arm.

British Broadcasting Company, Threats on the net, January 7, 2005.

Brookes, Peter, The spies among us, (opinion), found at: http://www.Military.com.

Burke, Jessica, Kloppers feared Chinese espionage but offered secrets to US: WikiLeaks, February 15, 2011, found at: http://www.miningaustralia.com.au.

Burrone, Esteban, Intellectual property rights and exports: avoiding common pitfalls, found at: http://www.winnt\apsdoc\nettemp\576\$asqip and exports.doc.

Canada Free Press, Foreign companies concerned over intellectual property theft in China, *Epoch Times*, January 21, 2010, found at: http://www.canadafreepress.com.

Canadian Security Intelligence Service and International Development Research Centre, World Watch: Expert Notes Series publication No 2010-02-01, China and its New Place in the world, (a jointly sponsored conference of the CSIS and the IDRC) found at: http://www.mi5.gov.uk/output.

Canadian Security Intelligence Service, 2008–2009 Public Report, http://www.csis-scrs.gc.ca.

Canadian Security Intelligence Service (CSIS), Overview of the Canadian Security Intelligence Service, July 28, 2011, CSIS, Ottawa ON, Canada.

Cave, Andrew, Intellectual property in China, June 16, 2010, Telegraph Media Group Ltd, found at: http://www.telegrtaph.co.uk.

Changqing, Cao, China: The world's worst employer for spies, found at: theepochtimes.com.

Channelnewsasia.com, Chinese woman admits to helping Pentagon-linked spying, May 29, 2008.

Cheng-China Huang, A brief chronology of China's intellectual property protection, found at: http://www1.American.edu.

China and Intellectual Property, December 23, 2010 (a version of this editorial appeared in print on December 24, 2010, on page A22 of the New York edition, *The New York Times*).

China beefs up punishment for intellectual property theft, January 12, 2011 (posted by WebmasterWorld), found at: http://www.hostmds.com/blog.

China Law Blog, China intellectual property theft. The statistics are damn lies. Posted by Dan on June 23, 2010, found at: http://www.chinalawblog.com.

China Law Blog, Chinese companies buying U.S. companies/names in bankruptcy, Posted by Dan on April 03, 2011, found at: http://www.chinalawblog.com.

China Law Blog, How to protect your China IP. Don't go there?, Posted by Dan on April 3, 2011, found at: http://www.chinalawblog.com.

China Law Blog, Is China cracking down on foreigners? Again, Posted by Dan on March 31, 2011, found at: http://www.chinalawblog.com.

China Law Blog, Is this China contract valid? Posted by Dan on April 5, 2011, found at: http://www.chinalawblog.com.

China Law Blog, Who's stealing your China trade secrets?, Posted by Dan on December 28, 2010, found at: http://www.Chinalawblog.com.

China spying on three key Canadian government departments, February 20, 2011, found at: Goldfizz.com, Ottawa, Canada.

Christusrex.org, PRC acquisition of U.S. technology, no date, found at: http://www.cyber-crime.gov/reporting.htm.

Codija, Marquis, Special Report: The art of economic espionage: why China is crushing America's global supremacy, February 5, 2010, found at: http://www.EzineArticles.com/?expert=Marquis_Codjia,marquisc.wordpress.com.

Collins, Steven, Russia and China enemy status becomes more evident, November 7, 2007, found at: http://www.stevenmcollins.com/wordpress.

Commercial Business Intelligence, White papers and industry articles on various subjects relating to business intelligence and security, no date, found at: http://www.cbintel.com/WPcompetintel.htm.

Completosec Channel (blog), Chinese cyber spying and intellectual property theft, October 23, 2009, found at: http://www.completosec.wordpress.com.

Connolly, Kate, Germany accuses China of industrial espionage, July 22, 2009, found at: http://www.guardian.co.uk/world/2009/jul/22.

Constitution of the People's Republic of China, esp. Articles 2, 3 and 29.

Cooper, Simon, China stealing sensitive military secrets, 2011, found at: http://www.popularmechanics.com.

CTV, China is top espionage risk to Canada: CSIS, Canadian Press, April 30, 2007, found at: http://www.ctv.ca.

CTV, Government 'concerned' about Chinese espionage, April 14, 2006, found at: http://www.ctv.ca.

CTV, Spies target natural resource sector, CSIS says, June 22, 2006, found at: http://www.ctv.ca.

Cui Ning, Hi-tech projects highlight five areas, *China Daily*, April 3, 1996.

Davis, Anthony M., China: taking small steps leading to global control, April 20, 2006, found at: CTV.ca News Staff.

Davis, Anthony M., How Boeing engineer spied for Chinese for 30 years … and stole secret space shuttle designs, July 17, 2009, found at: http://www.Daily Mail.co.uk.

Defense Security Service Academy (DSSA), Procedural guidance for conducting DoD classified conferences, July 2008, DSSA, Baltimore, MD.

Defense Security Service, Targeting U.S. Technologies: a trend analysis of reporting from Defense Industry—2008, Washington, D.C.

Defense Security Service, Targeting U.S. Technologies: a trend analysis of reporting from Defense Industry—2009, Washington, D.C.

Defense Security Service, Targeting U.S. technologies: a trend analysis of reporting from Defense Industry—2010 report, Washington, D.C.

Dening, Dorothy E., Who's stealing your information? Extract from book: Information Warfare and Security, 1999, found at: http://www.buscalegis.ufsc.br.

Department of Commerce, International Trade Administration, intellectual property rights, includes: China's current IPR environment, The best protection is prevention, China's IPR enforcement system, U.S. Government role in IPR infringement cases, January 2003, U.S. Department of Commerce, International Trade Administration, Washington, D.C. (specific data on these subject available at the Department of Commerce web site).

Department of Justice, Former Chinese national convicted for committing economic espionage to benefit China Navy Research Center in Beijing and for violating the Arms Export Control Act, press release 07-572, August 2, 2007, Washington, D.C.

Department of Defense (DOD) Directive 5205.2, DoD Operations Security Program, July 7, 1983.

DOD Directive 5240.3, Counterintelligence and operations security support program for the Defense Nuclear Agency, January 25, 1983, ASD(C3I), and change 1, August 7, 1992.

Drew, Christopher, New spy game: firms' secrets sold overseas, October 17, 2010, *New York Times*.

Dublin, Thomas, Women and the early industrial revolution in the United States, December 2006, found at: http://www.gilderlehrman.org/historynow/12_2006/print/historian4.php.

Dumitrescu, Octavian, Considerations about the Chinese Intelligence Services (II), July 16, 2010, World Security Network.

Economic Espionage Act of 1996, Title 18 U.S.C.

Economic espionage, found at: fbi.gov/about-us/investigate/counterintelligence/counterintelligence. FBI.gov is an official site of the U.S. Federal Government, U.S. Department of Justice.

Eftimiades, Nicholas, Statement before the Joint Economic Committee United States Congress, May 20, 1998.

Epoch Times, Stop intellectual property theft, *Epoch Times*, January 20, 2010, found at: http://www.theepochtimes.com/n2/business/foreign-companies-concerned-over-intellectual-property-theft-in-china.

Federal Bureau of Investigation, *CI Strategic Partnership Newsletter*, vol 3, issue 7, July 1, 2011, Federal Bureau of Investigation Tampa, FL.

Federal Bureau of Investigation, Counterintelligence Division, Economic espionage, undated, Washington, D.C.

Federal Bureau of Investigation, Counterintelligence Division, Intellectual property protection: safeguard your company's trade secrets, proprietary information and research, undated, Washington, D.C.

Federal Bureau of Investigation, Counterintelligence Division, The insider threat: an introduction to detecting and deterring an insider spy, undated, Washington, D.C.

Federal Bureau of Investigation, Office of Public Affairs, Chinese national charged with economic espionage involving theft of trade secrets from leading agricultural company based in Indianapolis, August 31, 2010, Indianapolis, IN.

Federal Bureau of Investigation, Office of Public Affairs, Chinese national pleads guilty to economic espionage and theft of trade secrets, October 18, 2011, Indianapolis, IN.

Federal Bureau of Investigation, U.S. Attorney's Office, Chinese national sentenced for stealing Ford trade secrets, April 12, 2011, Eastern District of Michigan.

Fernandez, Dennis, and Weinstein, Veronica, found at: http://www.edn.com/article/479737, Will China enforce your intellectual property rights? Note a few facts before jumping into the biggest untapped market By Dennis Fernandez and Veronica Weinstein—EDN, January 1, 2004 © 2010 UBM Canon.

Fife, Robert, http://www.orwelltoday.com/chinaspy.shtml China spying on us: CSIS, National Post, December 29, 2004, found at: http://www.canada.com/national/nationalpost.

Fishman, Ted C., How to stop intellectual property theft in China, June 1, 2006, Inc. Newsletter.

Fitz-Gerald, Keith, By putting real teeth into its intellectual-property-rights rules, China moves a step closer to superpower status, found at: http://www.moneymorning.com, June 4, 2009.

Foreign companies concerned over intellectual property theft in China (SOURCE). Epoch Times Staff. Created on web site January 20, 2010, found at: http://www.theepochtimes.com/n2/business/foreign-companies-concerned-over-intellectual-property-theft-in-china

Foreign Confidential (formerly China Confidential), Chinese defector presents evidence, found at: http://www.Chinaconfidential.blogspot.com, June 21, 2005.

Frankenstein, John and Gill, Bates, Current and future challenges facing Chinese defense industries, *China Quarterly*, June 1996.

Freeh, Louis J., Director, FBI, Statement of Louis J. Freeh Before the House Judiciary Committee Subcommittee on Crime Hearing on Economic Espionage, May 9, 1996, Washington, D.C.

Gardner, Richard, China continues espionage against the USA, November 6, 2005, found at: http://www.outsidethebeltway.com.

Gaylord, James E., FBI, Affidavit, October 2005.

General Accounting Office (GAO), Defense inventory: action needed to avoid inappropriate sales of surplus parts, August 1998, Washington, D.C.

Gertz, Bill, China removed as top priority for spies, January 20, 2010, *Washington Times*.

Global Security, Chinese intellectual property violations, 2011, found at: http://www.globalsecurity.org/intell/world/china/mss-ops (site maintained by John Pike).

Global Security, Ministry of State Security (MSS), (site maintained by John Pike), page last modified: October 24, 2007.

Goldfizz.com, China spying on three key Canadian government departments but denied, undated, found at: http://www.goliath.ecnext.com.

Grace, Kevin Michael, *The Sidewinder scandal* Report November 6, 2000, found at: http://www.telusplanet.net.

Gross, Grant, US panel looks at intellectual property violations in China, June 15, 2010, IDG News, found at: http://www.pcworld.com.

Gu, Wei, Winning the copyright battle in China, October 28, 2009, found at: http://www.blogs.reuters.com.

Ha, K. Oanh, 'Hotbed' of economic espionage—Silicon Valley: Chinese front companies stealing secrets, FBI says, *Mercury News*, September 27, 2006.

Halligan, R. Mark. Esq., Recent decisions in Trade Secrets Law—Year 2000, found at: http://rmarkhalligan.com, 1994–2007 (this is considered by many as the best site around for case information on trade secret law).

Hapsakis, Rosalind Hurst (editor), *FBI Counterintelligence Newsletter*, July 7, 2010, Washington, D.C. (The CI Strategic Partnership Newsletter is a product of the Counterintelligence Program Coordination Section's CD-6A Unit,. National Security Higher Education Advisory Board (NSHEAB), FBIHQ, Washington, D.C.)

Hays, Jeffrey, Chinese espionage, Katrina Leuk, Chi Mak and other Chinese spies in the U.S., 2008, found at: http://www.factsanddetails.com.

Hecker, Jay Etta, Challenges and opportunities for U.S. businesses in China, testimony of GAO before the Committee on Banking and Financial Services, U.S. House of Representatives, July 29, 1996, Washington, D.C.

Hidden Harmonies Org. (blog), China denies 'Cold War Ghost' computer espionage, March 31, 2009, found at: http://www.blog.hiddenharmonies.org.

Hill, John, Defections reveal extent of China's espionage operations, Jane's Intelligence Review, October 11, 2005, found at: freerepublic.com/focus/f-news/1502969/posts.

Homeland security news wire, U.S. worried about China industrial espionage activities during World's Expo, May 3, 2010.

Homick, John F., The impact of the Economic Espionage Act of 1996, *AIPLA Trade Secret News*, February 1999, Finnegan, Henderson, Farabow, Garrett & Dunner, LLP.

Infosecisland.com/clog, Chinese spies may have spear-fished U.S. diplomats, February 2, 2011, found at: source: http://www.net-security.org/secworld.php?id=10526, Infosec Island, LLC.

Institute for Global Ethics, Counterfeiting and intellectual property theft hurting U.S. economy and posing safety concerns, September 20, 2010, found at: http://www.globalethics.org/newsline.

Intelligence search, era of espionage not over, CSIS says, 2006 (Intelligence Search is the web's only search engine to exclusively index underground espionage web sites and geopolitical intelligence sources).

Intelligencesearch.com, Chinese spy exposes CCP espionage network in Europe, July 5, 2005, found at: http://www.InfoBureau.netCo.

Interagency OPSEC Support Staff (IOSS), Intelligence Threat Handbook, undated, found at: http://www.ioss.gov, Washington, D.C.

Interagency OPSEC Support Staff (IOSS), Operations Security Intelligence Threat Handbook, April 1996, revised May 1996, Washington, D.C.

Invictis Risk Intelligence Service (IRIS) Report, Commercial espionage: the threat from Chinese cyber attacks—executive summary, March 17, 2011, Invictis Information Security, Ltd., UK.

Ivy, Himfr, Another version of Chinese silk history, undated, found at: popsarts.com.

Ivy, Himfr, The history of silk, undated, found at: http://www.silk.org.uk/history.

Jackson, David and Sun, Lena H., Liu's deals with Chung: an intercontinental puzzle, Washington Post, May 24, 1998.

James, Geoffrey, Protecting your intellectual property in China, June 6, 2008, found at: http://www.bnet.com.

Jawa Report, The, China accused of computer espionage, August 28, 2007, found at: http://www.mypetjawa.mu.nu/archives.

Joint Security Commission, Redefining security: a report by the Joint Security Commission, February 28, 1994, Washington, D.C.

Jones, Gary L., Fenzel, William F., Brack, David, Schulze, John R., Charlifue, James, and Waterous, Frank B., DOE needs to improve controls over foreign visitors to weapons laboratories (GAO/RCED-97-229, September 25, 1997), Washington, D.C.

Kabay, Michel E., Industrial security, found at: undated, http://www.mekabay.com.

Karns, Jack E., McIntyre, Roger P., and Uhr, Ernest B., Corporate espionage in the global market: the Federal Government's role in the protection of private sector trade secrets, 1999, Ohio Northern University Law Review.

Kellingley, Nick, China's 5 year plan—the overall impact on clean technology, 2011, found at: http://www.EzineArticles.com.

Kennedy, Tim, U.S. military technology sold by Israel to China upsets Asian power balance, Washington Report on Mideast Affairs, pgs. 12, 96. January 1996.

Knight, Judson, Satellite technology exports to the People's Republic of China (PRC), 2011, Advameg, Inc., found at: http://www.faqs.org/espionage/Ec-Ep/Economic-Espionage.html.

Knowles, William, Chinese espionage handbook details ease of swiping secrets William, December 26, 2000 (Information Security News mailing list archives as initially written by Bill Gertz), Washington, D.C.

Koninklijke Philips Electronics, Intellectual property and standards in China, 2006, found at: http://www.ip.philips.com/articles/backgrounders.

Kouri, Jim, Chinese spies infiltrating U.S. businesses, March 3, 2009, Accuracy in Media, aim.org.

Kremmer, Janaki, Chinese defector details country's espionage agenda, *The Christian Science Monitor*, June 30, 2005.

Minieri, Michael W., Protecting corporate secrets, a Kroll White Paper, 2004, Kroll Schiff and Associates, Reston, Virginia.

Levin, Sen. Mark, We need to stop China's intellectual property theft, press release, October 15, 2010, U.S. Senate, Washington, D.C.

Lewis, James Andrew, Does China's new J-20 stealth fighter have American technology?, January 26, 2011, Center for Strategic and International Studies.

Lockley, Peter, Chinese spy who defected tells all, March 19, 2009, *The Washington Times*.

Lynch, David J., FBI goes on offensive against China's tech spies, July 23, 2007 (updated 7/25), *USA Today*.

Lynch, David J., Law enforcement struggles to combat Chinese spying, July 23, 2007, found at: http://www.myusatoday.com.

MacLean, Pamela A., Frustrations abound for corporate spycatchers, *The National Law Journal*, May 31, 2006.

Mai Lee, Currency and intellectual property theft may cause a trade war between the US and China, Wednesday, January 12, 2011, found at: http://www.ewireinformer.com.

Malakoff, David, Nuclear espionage report details spying on touring scientists, March 14, 2011, found at: http://www.maoxian.com.

Mattis, Peter, Shriver case highlights traditional Chinese espionage, Close Protection World, *China Brief*, vol 10, issue 22, November 5, 2010, U.K., found at: http://www.closeprotectionworld.co.uk/forum.

McDonald, Hamish, Spying the Chinese way: millions of snippets from all over the world, June 6, 2005, *The Sydney Morning Herald*.

McTigue, Lynette, China and your intellectual property Risk, April 17, 2008, found at: http://www.manufacturingindustry.blogs.xerox.com.

Mears, Pat, ITC details widespread theft of intellectual property in China, December 14, 2010, National Association of Manufacturers, found at: http://www.shopfloor.org.

Milhollin, Gary, and Richie, Jordan, What China didn't need to steal, *The New York Times*, May 5, 1999.

Milhollin, Gary, China cheats (what a surprise!), *The New York Times*, April 24, 1997.

Milhollin, Gary, Testimony on nuclear arms control before the U.S.–China Security Review Commission, January 17, 2002, Washington, D.C., found at: http://www.wisconsinproject.org/pubs/reports.

Mills, Elinor, Report: U.S. vulnerable to Chinese cyber espionage, November 24, 2008, found at: http://www.news.cnet.com.

Moore, Andrew P., Cappelli, Dawn M., Caron, Thomas C., Shaw, Eric, and Trzeciak, Randall, Insider theft of intellectual property for business advantage: a preliminary model, CERT®3 Software Engineering Institute and CyLab, Carnegie Mellon University, Pittsburgh, PA, 2009.

Mossinghoff, Hon. Gerald J., Mason, J. Derek, and Oblon, David A., The Economic Espionage Act: federal protection for corporate trade secrets, March 1999, *The Computer Lawyer*, vol 16, March 1999.

Moynihan, Maura, Big Brother in a Mao cap, January 13, 2009, undated, found at: http://www.Phayul.com.

Mulvenon, Mames, Testimony of James Mulvenon, RAND, before the Select Committee, October 15, 1998, Washington, D.C.

Naef, Wanja Eric, Economic and industrial espionage: a threat to Corporate America, October 2003, *Infocom Magazine*, issue 1.

National Defense Industrial Association, *FBI Counterintelligence Newsletter*, July 7, 2010, found at: http://www.ndiastl.org/blog/fbi-counterintelligence-newsletter.

National Security Decision Memorandum (NSDD) 298, National Operations Security Program, January 22, 1988, White House, Washington, D.C.

Nevins, Jess, Victorian women: industrial espionage and you!, September 22, 2010, found at: http://www.nofearofthefuture.blogspot.com.

Newman, Alex, Chinese spying in the United States, April 27, 2010, *The New American Magazine*.

New York Times, editorial, China and intellectual property, December 23, 2010.

Noonan, Sean, Examination of Chinese espionage, January 20, 2011, 5195, found at: http://www.darkgovernment.com (via STRATFOR).

O'Connell, Kelly, U.S. Congress: Chinese Internet espionage biggest net threat, December 03, 2007, Internew Business Law Services, found at: http://www.ibls.com/internew_law_new_portal_view.

Office of Technology Assessment (OTA), Other approaches to civil-military integration: the Chinese and Japanese arms industries, OTA, Congress of the United States, March, 1995.

Office of the National Counterintelligence Executive (ONCIX), Annual Report to Congress on Foreign Economic Collection and Industrial Espionage—1995, Washington, D.C.

Office of the National Counterintelligence Executive (ONCIX), Annual Report to Congress on Foreign Economic Collection and Industrial Espionage—July 1995, Washington, D.C.

Office of the National Counterintelligence Executive (ONCIX) Annual Report to Congress on Foreign Collection and Industrial Espionage—1996, Washington, D.C.

Office of the National Counterintelligence Executive (ONCIX) Annual Report to Congress on Foreign Collection and Industrial Espionage—1997, Washington, D.C.

Office of the National Counterintelligence Executive (ONCIX), Annual Report to Congress on Foreign Economic Collection and Industrial Espionage—1998, Washington, D.C.

Office of the National Counterintelligence Executive (ONCIX), Annual Report to Congress on Foreign Economic Collection and Industrial Espionage—1999, Washington, D.C.

Office of the National Counterintelligence Executive (ONCIX), Annual Report to Congress on Foreign Economic Collection and Industrial Espionage—2001, Washington, D.C.
Office of the National Counterintelligence Executive (ONCIX), Annual Report to Congress on Foreign Economic Collection and Industrial Espionage—2002, Washington, D.C.
Office of the National Counterintelligence Executive (ONCIX), Annual Report to Congress on Foreign Economic Collection and Industrial Espionage—2003, Washington, D.C.
Office of the National Counterintelligence Executive (ONCIX), Annual Report to Congress on Foreign Economic Collection and Industrial Espionage—2004, Washington, D.C.
Office of the National Counterintelligence Executive (ONCIX), Annual Report to Congress on Foreign Economic Collection and Industrial Espionage—2007, Washington, D.C.
Office of the National Counterintelligence Executive (ONCIX), Annual Report to Congress on Foreign Economic Collection and Industrial Espionage—2008, Washington, D.C.
Office of the National Counterintelligence Executive (ONCIX), Annual Report to Congress on Foreign Economic Collection and Industrial Espionage—2011, Washington, D.C.
Office of the National Counterintelligence Executive (ONCIX), Foreign Spies Stealing U.S. Economic Secrets in Cyberspace: Report to Congress on Foreign Economic Collection and Industrial Espionage, 2009–2011, Washington, D.C.
Osnos, Evan, Chinese espionage, October 26, 2010, Letter from China dispatches, found at: http://www.newyorker.com/online/blogs.
Pandey, Dr. Sheo Nandan, China's economic espionage prowess, ISPSW Institute for Strategic, Political, Security and Economic Consultancy, Berlin, Germany, November 4, 2010.
Paradise, James F., The intellectual property conundrum in China, November 21, 2005, found at: http://www.asiamedia.ucla.edu.
Pentland, William, Entrepreneurial espionage—made in China, January 22, 2011, found at: Forbes.com, http://www.blogs.forbes.com.
People's Republic of China, Information Office, China's National Defense, Information Office, PRC State Council, July 27, 1998.
People's Republic of China, Supreme People's Court, Intellectual property protection by Chinese Courts in 2009, April 2010, Beijing, China.
Pillsbury, Dr. Michael, Testimony before the Senate Select Committee on Intelligence, September 18, 1997, Washington, D.C.
Piraino, A. Scott, Chasing the Dragon: Clinton's China Policy, undated, found at: http://www.artistmarket.com/writers/piraino.
Porteous, Holly, Cybersecurity and intelligence: the US approach, February 8, 2010, Library of Parliament, Ottawa, Canada.
Porteous, Samuel, Commentary No. 32: Economic espionage, May 1993, CSIS, Ottawa, Canada, found at: http://www.csis-scrs/gc/ca/pblctns.
Porteous, Samuel, Commentary No. 46: Economic espionage (II), July 1994, CSIS, Ottawa, Canada.
Ragan, Steve, DoD official charged with espionage, May 14, 2009, found at: TechHerald.com.
Raman, B., Chinese espionage in U.S., paper no. 300, South Asia Analysis Group, August 28, 2001.
RCMP-CSIS Joint Review Committee, Sidewinder: Chinese intelligence services and triads financial links in Canada, draft submitted to the RCMP-CSIS Joint Review Committee, June 24, 1997, Ottawa, Canada.
Reimer, Jeremy, China: 'aggressive and large-scale' espionage against US, updated November 18, 2007, found at: http://www.keznews.com.
Reisman, Arnold, Illegal transfer of technologies: a taxonomic view, Reisman and Associates, September 8, 2004.
Reynolds, Paul, The world's second oldest profession, BBC News Online, February 28, 2004.

Rishikof, Harvey, Economic and industrial espionage: a question of counterintelligence or law enforcement?, NSF Review/Spring Summer 2009 NSFR Online Journal, found at: http://www.nationalstrategy.com.

Slate, Robert, Competing with intelligence: new directions in China's quest for intangible property and implications for Homeland Security, Homeland Security Affairs, vol. V, no. 1, January 2009, found at: http://www.hsaj.org.

Smale, Will, Industrial espionage 'real and out there', *BBC News*, February 26, 2004.

Smith, Charles R., China's economic war—stealing jobs and technology from America, September 14, 2004, found at: http://www.archive.newsmax.com/archives.

Smith, Charles R., Clinton gave China chips for nuclear war, October 1, 2003, found at: http://www.archive.newsmax.com/archives.

Smith, Charles R., Defector confirms Chinese army spying on U.S., March 27, 2001, found at: http://www.archive.newsmax.com/archives.

Spybusters (blog), Industrial espionage in the 1700 and 1800s shapes the world, August 2010, found at: http://www.spybusters.blogspot.com.

Starkin, Pete, On the introduction of The Arms Surplus Reform Act of 1997, statement by Rep. Pete Stark in the U.S. House of Representatives, October 1, 1997.

Su, Kuoshan, Road of hope—reviewing the accomplishment of the '863 Project on the 10th Anniversary of its implementation, April 5, 1996, (reproduced in Foreign Broadcast Information Service, Daily Report, May 8, 1996, FBIS-CHI-96-089).

survivingtheworkday.blogspot.com, No China diet: intellectual property theft, June 20, 2007.

Taipei Times, Book lists China's spy techniques, December 29, 1999, found at: http://www.taipeitimes.com.

Taiwan News, China's spy techniques, December 23, 1999.

The Guardian, Intellectual property we can't afford to lose, August 9, 2005, found at: http://www.guardian.co.uk.

Thomas, Randall, Affidavit of Randall Thomas, Special Agent (SA), Federal Bureau of Investigation.

Thome, Jennifer, Corporate espionage in China—an interview with counterespionage specialist Bruce Wimmer, *Agenda* March 10, 2011, found at: http://www.agendabeijing.com.

Thompson, Sen. Fred., Handling of the espionage investigation into the compromise of design information on the W-88 Warhead, statement by Sen. Thompson of the Senate Governmental Affairs Committee, August 5, 1999, Washington, D.C.

Thorpe, Simon, More intellectual property theft, GM lose $40M of hybrid vehicles trade secrets to China industry, July 22, 2010, found at: http://www.blog.oracle.com/irm.

U.S. Army, AR530-1, Operations Security (OPSEC).

U.S. Congress, House of Representatives, PRC Acquisition of U.S. Technology, Government Reform and Oversight Committee ("HGROC Report"), Government Printing Office, 1999, found at: http://www.access.gpo.gov/congress/house/hr105851.

U.S. Customs, briefing to Select Committee Staff, October 28, 1998. (In response to this situation, in October 1997, Representative Pete Stark introduced H.R. 2602, the Arms Surplus Reform Act of 1997, to place a moratorium on all surplus arms sales until DOD certified to Congress that steps had been taken to correct weaknesses in the surplus sales program. The Act did not pass, but a section was added to the Defense Authorization Act for Fiscal Year 1998, Pub. L. 105-85, Sec. 1067, requiring similar steps. The DOD submitted its report to Congress in June, 1998, identifying problem areas and steps taken to address them.)

U.S. Department of Agriculture, Economic espionage forced Ellery Systems, Inc. out of business and robbed the U.S. of a competitive advantage in an emerging high-tech industry, undated on web site, found at: http://www.dm.usda.gov/ocpm/Security%20Guide/Spystory/Ellery.htm.

U.S. Department of Energy, Espionage and foreign travel; counterintelligence in our changing world, undated brochures, found at: http://www.doe.gov/offices/OCI/Brochures.

U.S. Department of Justice, Economic Espionage Act of 1996 (18 U.S.C. §§ 1831–1837)—Prosecutive Policy, 1999 25 Ohio N.U.L. Rev. 331, Washington, D.C., 2009.

U.S. Department of Justice, Executive Office for United States Attorneys, Prosecuting Intellectual Property Crimes (third edition, September 2006), Computer Crime and Intellectual Property Section, Criminal Division, pub by the Office of Legal Education Executive Office for United States Attorneys.

U.S. Department of Justice, Higher Education and National Security: The targeting of sensitive, proprietary and classified information on campuses of higher education, April 2011, U.S. Department of Justice Federal Bureau of Investigation.

U.S. Department of Justice, Office of Public Affairs nbr. 07-807, Major U.S. export enforcement actions in the past year, October 11, 2007, Department of Justice, National security Division (fact sheet), Washington, D.C. 07-807.

U.S. Department of Justice, Office of Public Affairs nbr. 09-1033, Jury convicts Defense Department official of unlawful communication of classified information and making false statements, September 25, 2009, Department of Justice, Washington, D.C.

U.S. Department of Justice, Office of Public Affairs nbr. 09-688, Former Boeing engineer convicted of economic espionage in theft of space shuttle secrets for China, July 16, 2009, Department of Justice, Washington, D.C.

U.S. Department of Justice, Office of Public Affairs, Department of Justice, Office of Public Affairs, nbr. 97-368. Taiwanese businessman and daughter arrested on industrial espionage charges, September 5, 1997, Department of Justice, Washington, D.C.

U.S. Department of Justice, Report to Congress on Chinese espionage activities against the United States: intellectual property theft in China and Russia hearings before the Subcommittee on Courts, the Internet, and Intellectual Property, report to the Committee on the Judiciary of the House of Representatives, *109th Congress, First Session*, May 17, 2005 (serial no. 109-34) found at: http://www.commdocs.house.gov/committees/judiciary/hju21217.000/hju21217_0f.htm.

U.S. House of Representatives, Sources and methods of foreign nationals engaged in economic and military espionage, hearing before the Subcommittee on Immigration, Border Security, and claims of the Committee on the Judiciary, House of Representatives, *109th Congress, First Session*, September15, 2005 (Serial No. 109–58), found at: http://www.house.gov/committees/judiciary/hju23433.000/hju23433_0f.htm.

U.S. International Trade Commission, China; intellectual property infringement, indigenous innovation policies, and frameworks for measuring the effects on the U.S. economy, Investigation No. 332-514, USITC Publication 4199 (amended), November 2010, USITC, Washington, D.C.

U.S. Office of Science and Technology, The National Security Science and Technology Strategy, U.S. Office of Science and Technology Policy, 1996, Washington, D.C.

U.S. Senate, Commercial Activities of China's People's Liberation Army (PLA), Hearing Before the Committee on Foreign Relations, November 6, 1997, Washington, D.C.

U.S. Senate Judiciary Subcommittee on Administrative Oversight and the Courts. Department of Defense Disposition of Government Surplus Items, Hearing before the Senate, July 8, 1997, Washington, D.C.

U.S.-China Economic and Security Review Commission, Report to Congress of the U.S.-China Economic and Security Review Commission, 2009, Washington, D.C.

United States Government Accountability Office (GAO), Export controls: agencies should assess vulnerabilities and improve guidance for protecting export-controlled information at companies, GAO-07-69, 2006, GAO, December 2006, Washington, D.C.

Vijayan, Jaikumar, FBI sees big threat from Chinese spies, *The Wall Street Journal*, 12 August 2005.
Wallis, Paul, Op-Ed: Chinese espionage threat to US, but Congress told nothing new, undated on web site, found at: http://www.digitaljournal.com.
Walters, Jason S., China—economic growth, development and world history (undated on web site), Global Sherpa, found at: article source: http://www.http://EzineArticles.com/?expert=Jason_S_Walters.
Westerman, Toby, Ex-foreign espionage operative reveals how people are recruited to undermine U.S. (commentary), June 10, 2009, Post Chronicle Corp.
Wheeler, Scott L., China makes spying a company policy, November 12, 2002, CBS Interactive, found at: http://www.findarticles.com.
White House, Message to the Congress on the China National Aero-Technology Import and Export Corporation Divestiture of MAMCO Manufacturing, Incorporated, The White House, February 1, 1990, Washington, D.C.
Wikipedia, Chinese intelligence activity in other countries, found at: http://www.en.wikipedia.org/wiki.
Wikipedia, Chinese intelligence operations in the United States, found at: http://www.wikipedia.org.
Wikipedia, Canadian Security Intelligence, found at: http://www.en.wikipedia.orgn.
Wikipedia, Intellectual property in the People's Republic of China, no date, found at: http://www.en.wikipedia.org.
Wikipedia, Intelligence collection management, no date, found at: http://www.wikipedia.org.
Wikipedia, Katrina Leung, page last modified June 25, 2011, found at: http://www.wikipedia.org.
Wikipedia, List of intelligence gathering disciplines, no date, found at: http://www.wikipedia.org.
Wikipedia, Ministry of State Security of the People's Republic of China, November 26, 1997, found at: http://www.wikipedia.org.
Wikipedia, Technical intelligence, no date, found at: http://www.wikipedia.org.
Wilke, John R., Two Silicon Valley cases raise fears of Chinese espionage, January 15, 2003, *The Wall Street Journal.*
Wisconsin Project on Nuclear Army Control, U.S. Exports to China 1988–1998: fueling proliferation, April 1999, The Wisconsin Project on Nuclear Arms Control, Washington, D.C.
Wittman, George H., Chinese rules, 2008, April 14, 2010, *The American Spectator.*
Worthington, Peter, China's boom: fueled by spies?, February 10, 2011, found at: http://www.frumforum.com.
Zhongwen, Huo and Zongxiao, Wang, Sources and techniques of obtaining National Defense Science and Technology Intelligence, Kexue Jishu Wenxuan Publishing Co., Beijing, China, 1991, found at: http://www.www.fas.org/irp/world/china/docs/sources.html.

Appendix A: The Dongfan "Gregg" Chung and Chi Mak Economic Espionage Cases

We have reiterated many times that allegations that China stole U.S. military secrets are groundless and made out of ulterior motives.

Chinese Foreign Ministry spokesman Qin Gang at a news conference
March 2007, Beijing, PRC

"Long term" can almost be a buzz phrase for the continued collection of information. China does not take a short-term view of its own progress. It looks not to the next rice harvest or to next year, but a decade or two, or more, into the future, while the rest of the world views long term as within the next few years. In terms of the collection of intellectual property and trade secrets, China has, and will always have, a long-term outlook because it is in their interests to see beyond the distant future and grasp the potential that will arise at any given point in time.

Before discussing this major case, we must first consider how it came about. Dongfan "Gregg" Chung, 73, a native of China and a naturalized citizen, was employed by Rockwell International from 1973 until its defense and space unit was acquired by Boeing in 1996. He held a US government–issued "secret" level security clearance when he worked at Rockwell and Boeing on the Space Shuttle program. He retired from the company in 2002, but the next year he returned to Boeing as a contractor, a position he held until September 2006.[1] At that point, his clearance, because he had been gone merely a year, would have been reinstated with little effort.

During his 30 years of employment, Chung had been very, very busy. Chung took and concealed Boeing trade secrets relating to the Space Shuttle program and the Delta IV rocket, materials that he had acquired for the benefit of the People's Republic of China (PRC). Acting as an agent of China, he stole these restricted technologies and many other Boeing trade secrets.[1]

As early as 1979, individuals within the Chinese aviation industry began sending Chung "tasking" letters about what they were interested in so as to rapidly expand and build aircraft and other items. Over the years, the various letters that were sent directed Chung to collect specific technological information, including data related to the Space Shuttle and various military and civilian aircraft. Allegedly, Chung responded in one undated letter that "I would like to make an effort to contribute to the Four Modernizations of China."[2]

In various letters to his handlers in the PRC over the years, Chung referenced engineering manuals he had collected and sent to the PRC, including 24 manuals relating to the B-1 Bomber that Rockwell had prohibited from disclosure outside of the company and "selected federal agencies."[2]

Between 1985 and 2003, Chung was able to make a number of trips to the PRC to deliver lectures on technology involving the Space Shuttle and other programs. While in the PRC, Chung had meetings with PRC government officials and agents that were associated with the People's Liberation Army.

Chung and PRC officials also exchanged letters that discussed Chung's travel agenda to China, and these letters made various recommendations for the use of several methods for passing information, including suggestions that Chung use Chik Mak and his wife Rebecca to transmit information.

In a letter dated May 2, 1987, from Gu Weihao, who was an official in the Ministry of Aviation and China Aviation Industry Corporation, there was a discussion about the possibility of inviting Chung's wife, an artist, to visit an art institute so that Chung could use her trip as an excuse to travel to the PRC. Note that this is a mere two years after Chung is insinuated himself so as to obtain information of value to China. This letter also suggested that if he passed the information to the PRC through Chik Mak, it would be "faster and safer." The letter concluded with the statement: "It is your honor and China's fortune that you are able to realize your wish of dedicating yourself to the service of your country."[1,2]

A report of a Federal Bureau of Investigation (FBI)–monitored telephone conversation between Chik and his older sister indicated that she had just returned from the PRC and had taken care of matters for Tai and Chik and had both of their deeds. The FBI's understanding of this call was that Chik and Tai owned property in the PRC.

This tied in to a report of another monitored phone call between Chik and a person in Hong Kong in which Chik asked about housing prices in Hong Kong and said that he wanted to purchase a house or condominium in Hong Kong to live in. Other electronic surveillance indicated that Chik was planning to retire in March 2006.[3]

At that time, Tai and his wife, Fuk, owned a house in Alhambra, California. From a trash search (dumpster diving, if you will), it was learned that Tai was the Broadcast and Engineering Director for Phoenix North American Chinese Channel ("Phoenix"). An immigration records check indicated that he was a Chinese citizen who had entered the United States at Los Angeles on May 22, 2001, and later became a permanent resident of the United States.

Rebecca, Chik's wife, was formerly a Chinese citizen and was naturalized in Los Angeles on June 20, 1985. In her naturalization application, Rebecca stated that she had worked as an electrical engineer. Surveillance showed that she was apparently unemployed at the time of the FBI check.

Tai's wife, Fuk, was a citizen of the PRC and had entered the United States in 2001 and then also became a lawful permanent resident.

David Kris, Assistant Attorney General for National Security, said that "For years, Mr. Chung stole critical trade secrets from Boeing relating to the Space Shuttle and the Delta IV rocket, all for the benefit of the government of China." He also stated that "the stolen technology compromised not only the American company that developed and owned the trade secrets, but national security as well because the secrets could be used by the PRC to develop its own military technology." Chung willingly compromised "America's economic and national security to assist (a) foreign government."[4]

Salvador Hernandez, the Assistant Director in Charge of the FBI in Los Angeles, stated: "The cost of Mr. Chung's traitorous actions to American security and the economy cannot be quantified, but have now been exposed, and his ability to exploit critical technology has come to an end."[5] In the end, Mr. Chung received a 24-year sentence for his espionage activities.

During the FBI investigation into Chung, it was discovered that another engineer was also heavy into economic espionage along with several other people. The details of that case follow with verbatim excerpts taken from the sworn affidavit of FBI Special Agent James E. Gaylord.

In a detailed affidavit[4] relating to this case, Special Agent James E. Gaylord, a 20-year veteran of the FBI, who spent over 15 years conducting counterintelligence investigations, obtained arrest and search warrants charging the individuals with violations of 18 U.S.C. § 641 (theft of government property), 18 U.S.C. § 371 (conspiracy), 18 U.S.C. § 2314 (transportation of stolen goods), and 18 U.S.C. § 2 (aiding and abetting) against Chik Mak, aka Jack Mak, aka Tai Chik Mak, aka Dai Chik; Mak, aka Dazhi Mai ("Chik"); Tai Wang Mak, aka Taihong Mak, aka Daihong Mak, aka Dahong Mai ("Tai"); Rebecca Laiwah Chik U, aka Rebecca Mak, aka Laiwa Chu, aka Lihua Zhao, aka Meihua Zhao ("Rebecca"); and Fuk Heung Li, aka Fuk Heung Li Mak, aka Flora Mak, aka Flora Li ("Fuk").

As part of the ensuing arrest procedures, FBI agents conducted searches of a variety of properties owned by the individuals and also various business premises to ascertain information relating to espionage, the theft of trade secrets, and the transmission of such to China.

Special Agent Gaylord's affidavit also stated "there is probable cause to believe that Chik, Tai, Rebecca, and Fuk had engaged in the theft of government property, in violation of 18 U.S.C. §§ 641 and 2, and had conspired to transport stolen goods, in violation of 18 U.S.C. § 371 and 18 U.S.C. § 2314."[4] As such, there was probable cause to believe that evidence relating to those crimes would be found. In the final analysis, it all was exceedingly true.

A roster of employees and a schematic of their workstations from L-3/SPD Technologies/Power Systems Group verified that Chik was employed as a Principal Support Engineer by Power Paragon, a subsidiary of L-3/SPD Technologies/Power Systems Group.

As one of the major espionage cases in the last decade, this one has numerous details of interest to the reader in terms of what the FBI was looking for.

The FBI used applicable statutes in developing this affidavit for search warrants, which included the following:

a. Section 641 of Title 18 provides, in pertinent part: "Whoever embezzles, steals, purloins, or knowingly converts to his use or the use of another, or without authority, sells, conveys or disposes of any record, voucher, money, or thing of value of the United States or of any department or agency thereof, or any property made or being made under contract for the United States or any department or agency thereof... Shall be fined under this title or imprisoned not more than ten years, or both...."[4]
b. Section 2 of Title 18 provides that whoever aids, abets, counsel, and induces the commission of an offense is punishable as a principal.[4]
c. Section 371, which provided criminal penalties for individuals who would conspire to commit an offense against the United States, provided *that one or more of such persons acted to effect the object of the conspiracy.*
d. Section 2314 provided in pertinent part: "Whoever transports, transmits, or transfers in interstate or foreign commerce any goods, wares, merchandise, securities or money, of the value of $5,000 or more, knowing the same to have been stolen, converted or taken by fraud (shall be fined or imprisoned or both)."[4]

Since search warrants require probable cause, the FBI laid out in great detail their reasoning.

In the affidavit overview for probable cause, the FBI stated that Chik was employed as a Principal Support Engineer by Power Paragon, a subsidiary of L-3/SPD Technologies/Power Systems Group ("Power Paragon"). In 1996, Chik was granted a secret clearance that provided him legitimate access to classified Navy technology through his Power Paragon employment. As part of his employment, Chik was the lead project engineer on a research project involving Quiet Electric Drive ("QED") propulsion, which would be used on United States Navy warships.[4]

QED was an extremely sensitive project. According to the Office of Naval Research, Department of the Navy, the technology developed in the QED program was considered "significant military equipment" and therefore would be banned from export to those countries specifically designated by the US State Department, including the PRC. The very sensitive technological information was also covered by the security caveat "NOFORN, Distribution Schedule D." NOFORN is an additional marking applied to US documents to indicate that the information within the document will restrict its dissemination to foreign entities, agents, or interests, and the material can be released to and must be maintained only to Department of Defense contractors and their employees who may access it in the performance of their daily duties under a given government contract. QED technology was being developed by Power Paragon under a contract with the US Navy, which owned the technology.[4]

By virtue of his employment, Chik also had access to other valuable material belonging to the government such as technical records, schematics, and various other documents bearing a stamp or notation restricting dissemination of the information. The sensitive technical material, including research and development information and the QED technology referenced herein, was extremely valuable.

The continuing investigation plainly showed that Chik had transferred vital information concerning the QED and other projects belonging to the government from his workplace to his home. Ensconced in his home, Chik copied the information onto CDs and delivered them to his brother, Tai. Tai then encrypted the information with the assistance of another person. Tai had also made arrangements to travel, with the encrypted CDs, to China. Tai and Fuk had planned to leave the United States with the information on the encrypted CDs on October 28, 2005, for Hong Kong, then continuing on to Guangzhou in the PRC. In a monitored phone call between Tai and a person he planned to meet in the PRC, Tai and his recipient contact used what appear to be code words when speaking. During all this time, Rebecca assisted Chik in copying the information onto CDs and delivering them to Tai.[4]

Fuk, Tai's wife, discussed with Tai the encrypting of the CDs and would travel with him to China to deliver the CDs.

BACKGROUND OF THE INVESTIGATION

At a certain point in time, suspicions were raised within the industry that indicated economic espionage might be taking place. The FBI began collecting information that Chik Mak, Tai Mak, and Rebecca Chik were possibly stealing sensitive government-owned information from Power Paragon. Based on that information, the FBI opened a formal investigation of the three individuals and their associates. As part of the investigation, numerous surveillance techniques were employed, including court-authorized electronic surveillance. As a result of these surveillance and other investigative techniques that were used, the FBI learned of Chik Mak's theft of government property and the plans to deliver the material to China.[4]

THEFT OF GOVERNMENT PROPERTY

Around February 7, 2005, two lists were recovered from the trash of Chik's residence. It should be noted that trash, when placed out for pickup and off a person's property is "up for grabs" and that anyone could take it. The two lists had been torn up into small pieces. The FBI reassembled and translated the two lists. Translations indicated that one document was machine printed in Chinese and contained instructions to join more associations and participate in more seminars with special subject matters. The document contained a directive to compile the special conference material on a disk, which would later produce meaningful research. The document then listed a number of military technologies that were sought, including space-based electromagnetic intercept system, space-launched magnetic levitational platform, electromagnetic artillery system, submarine torpedoes, electromagnetic launch system, and aircraft carrier electronic systems, among others. The second document was hand printed in Chinese and identified nine related technologies: water jet propulsion; ship submarine propulsion technology, non-air reliant; power system configuration technology, weapons standardization, modularization; early warning technologies, command and control systems technology, defense against nuclear attack technology; permanent electromagnetic motor, overall solution for shipboard power system; shipboard internal and external communications systems; establishment of high frequency, self-linking, satellite communications; submarine: HF transient launch technology; and DDX (next-generation destroyer). Surreptitious searches of Chik's residence showed that the documents pertained to a number of the technologies listed on both documents that were found in the residence.[4]

In October of 2005, Fuk told Tai that she had made travel arrangements and that they both would be leaving on October 28th for China and returning on November 12th. Fuk also told Tai that she had booked airline tickets and that the return date would be November 9th. Tai then called a person in the PRC to tell him of Tai's arrival date in the PRC. In that phone call, Tai advised that he would be traveling with his wife and an "assistant." Based on the fact that only two tickets had been purchased, the reference to an "assistant" was probably a code word that means that Tai would be bringing desired information to an individual in the PRC.[4]

On October 25, 2005, the FBI recovered a document discarded from the Alhambra residence of Tai and Fuk. The document contained a flight number for Cathay Pacific Airlines departing Los Angeles International at 11:59 p.m. on October 28, 2005. The ultimate destination for the traveler was listed as Guangzhou (in the PRC). Tai would be met in Guangzhou at the airport.

Around a week prior to their departure, Tai told Fuk that Chik was definitely nervous. Fuk instructed Tai not to "carry them" because "those are kind of heavy." Tai replied that he knew and that "it" was "only disks." Fuk asked "doesn't he know how to do it?" Tai explained, "He has to give it to me to do it; it's on my (computer) notebook; he definitely has to give it to me; he can't do it." Fuk reminded that "he has to give us the papers." Tai corrected, "No, he has to give me a disk, but I still have to take his disk and then have it encrypted on… (my notebook)… They don't have… over there…. Only the IBM… which I took from the second floor can do it. But he must give me the disk." Tai went on to discuss how in the past Chik would separate reporting by tearing off a couple of pages at a time. Fuk observed that the pages were non-consecutive and that he "can't just give one half of it and not giving *[sic]* the other half." Fuk then commented "Don't bother with him (Chik), he's just doing/reporting his job." During the conversation, Tai repeated several times that Chik and Rebecca were "very nervous."[4] These surveillance excerpts, when studied and analyzed by the FBI, along with all the other information they had accumulated, clearly indicated that the trip would probably be a real highlight of a long espionage venture and that very important and critical US defense classified information was about to be lost to the PRC.

While at work at Power Paragon on October 21, 2005, surveillance was able to determine that Chik placed numerous items, including what appeared to be computer disks, into his briefcase and departed.

The next day or so, Chik told Tai that he had been busy and that his project at work was moving smoothly. Tai told Chik that he (Tai) would be going to Hong Kong the next week. Chik asked what date he would be leaving. Tai indicated the 28th. Tai said that he would "swing by" mainland China. Upon hearing this, Chik said, "Good. It will be beneficial to meet," (this evidentially meaning he would meet up with Tai). In discussing the reason for the trip, Tai had spoken to Chik in a somewhat hesitant manner, stating that it was for business and other reasons. Tai reiterated that he had earlier tried to reach Chik. Both Chik and Tai then finally agreed to meet around 11:30 or at noon on Sunday, October 23rd. At the end of the phone conversation, Chik said he would be there, and "perhaps I will bring you something."[4]

On the 22nd, Chik worked on his laptop at home. On the 23rd, Chik said "the stuff is from 2005," and Rebecca replied "it'll take a long time to read it… We haven't read it yet." Chik advised Rebecca that "The original is in my office. I can take it home and then take it back." Chik then mentioned to Rebecca about "three CDs" and to "make copies of them." Chik indicated that he will take "them to him/her." Rebecca reminded Chik that the "things" that Chik is asking him (Tai) to take "are certainly against the law."[4] This simple statement clearly indicated that everyone knew that the information that had been stolen and was about to be transferred to China was in direct violation of US espionage laws, but evidentially they were not greatly concerned about that fact.

FBI Special Agent James Gaylord believed that "the stuff from 2005" referred to the most current QED research information in Chik's possession and that Rebecca expressed concern that they would be unable to read the information before giving it to Tai. Agent Gaylord believed that Chik's reference to taking "it" home and "back" referred to Chik's ability to retrieve the QED and other sensitive information from work at any time and to return it without detection. Later in the conversation, Chik mentioned that the first presenter was from the Navy Academy and this probably referred to material presented by a naval officer at a conference Chik attended in 2005. This conference was probably from a professional organization of engineers in Philadelphia.

On or around October 23, 2005, Chik told Rebecca that "Everything is in it" (meaning a disc). Chik stated, "P is a protection document" and Chik explained that other people cannot open a PDF file.[4]

On October 23, while loading computer files, Chik told Rebecca that he and a fellow engineer from Power Paragon had given a presentation to the American Society of Naval Engineers in Philadelphia in July 2005. Rebecca said that the recipients of the CDs could read the entire paper. Chik advised that it would take a lot of writing and time to prepare these "three pieces" (referring to the three CDs). Rebecca replied "Of course. Do you think it's easy? Those who receive them would have to spend a lot of time. Otherwise they can't handle them." Rebecca was probably referring to the large amount of information on the CDs that they were preparing to send to China.[4]

On October 23rd, Chik had a very busy morning. During a two-hour period, he inserted a number of compact disks into his laptop computer, downloaded information from the CDs, then removed the original CDs, inserted new CDs, and copied information onto the blank CDs. These would have been the copies of the initial CDs he had been instructed to make. This activity took place between approximately 9:00 and 11:00 a.m. and was observed secretly by FBI surveillance personnel. Rebecca asked Chik about the disks he was copying. As she asked the question, a hidden closed circuit television showed Rebecca standing behind Chik and pointing to the laptop. Chik told Rebecca that "these CDs are all about Department of Defense programs." (Author's note: I know from my experience in the national security arena wherein major government programs are at stake that in the defense contracting industry, the term "program" refers to a major Department of Defense project and will involve many people and an exceptionally vast amount of classified data.) In further conversation, Chik indicated to Rebecca that one of the CDs contained material written by Paragon staff and concerns the programs. Chik advised that a particular CD probably is a P (protected) disk that contains QED. A reference was also made to "the most recent one… the carrier program."[4]

Around 11:13 a.m., less than a quarter hour after the data had been copied, Chik and Rebecca arrived at Tai's Alhambra residence. Twenty minutes later, Chik and Rebecca, along with Tai and his family (Fuk, his son and daughter), departed Tai's residence.

The next day, Tai had someone go to buy three or four CDs that could be recorded. He said "I need to do something when I get home tonight." That day, Chik asked Tai if everything was ready to go. Tai replied, "Not quite."[4]

On the 25th, someone (who was not further identified by the FBI) indicated to Tai that he was helping him work on the disks, but needed the small disk to do it. The person asked where Tai had put the small disk. Tai replied that it was in a white envelope, which was inside the first drawer of his night stand, that being the night stand near where he sleeps. The person said he didn't see the envelope, but saw a disk that wasn't inside an envelope. Tai advised that was the disk. (The "small disk" referred to above was likely a device used to unlock the computer or encrypt the data. Both are used as security features.)[4]

Later that day, Tai asked the person where he was, and the person indicated he was on his way back (possibly home). Tai said "I saw that your computer up there kept on spinning." Tai was probably referring to an IBM notebook he told Fuk was on the second floor and is the only one that could be used to encrypt his CDs. (This statement was interpreted to mean that the computer was either still copying information or experiencing a writing error.) The person said it was because he was burning a disk for Tai. Tai said he knew that he needed to click "OK" or something. The person said he would come back and take care of it.[4]

There it was, then, the probable cause to believe that Chik, Tai, Rebecca, and Fuk had committed violations of 18 U.S.C. § 641 (theft of government property), 18 U.S.C. § 2 (aiding and abetting), 18 U.S.C. § 371 (conspiracy), and 18 U.S.C. § 2314 (transportation of stolen goods in interstate and foreign commerce).

Based on the various discussions between Tai and Fuk in which Fuk told Tai that she had made plane reservations to depart on October 28 for China, Tai's phone call to a PRC contact person informing him of Tai's arrival date in Guangzhou, PRC, on October 30, Tai's discussion with Chik telling him that they had made the travel arrangements, and the discovery of the travel itinerary to China found in the trash search of Tai's residence, the FBI believed that Tai and Fuk were planning to leave the United States with the encrypted CDs on the night of October 28, 2005.

PROBABLE CAUSE BY VARIOUS SEARCH LOCATIONS

The FBI is nothing but meticulous and scrupulously detailed in ferreting out every detail and would ensure that all the places the various individuals worked, lived, and moved about in, wherein they would have reason to believe they were relatively safe, would have to be carefully searched and any further potentially incriminating or related information should be discovered and analyzed to further buttress their case.

A careful search of the home of Chik and Rebecca contained evidence of the theft of government property. In particular, FBI surveillance had shown Chik taking computer disks from Power Paragon when he was leaving work. In addition, surveillance of Chik's e-mail traffic showed he had e-mailed documents from his computer at Power Paragon to his computer at his home. Some of the e-mails intercepted contained photographs of the QED system and reports concerning the QED system. Also, additional surreptitious searches of his house revealed stacks of documents pertaining to defense programs and documents bearing notations restricting dissemination were being stored in the house.[4]

The home of Tai and Fuk was also found to contain evidence of the theft of government property. In particular, surveillance showed that Tai encrypted the CDs at his home. Other various surveillance reports indicated that Fuk questioned Tai as to why Chik could not encrypt the CDs himself, and Tai had explained to Fuk, in essence, that he must use his IBM computer notebook to encrypt the disks that Chik would provide to Tai. Conversations further indicated that the actual encryption occurred at Tai's home. Based on these statements, the FBI found there was probable cause to believe that evidence pertaining to the theft of government property would be found in their home.[4]

Chik's workplace at Power Paragon revealed that Chik used his employment to obtain QED technology and other sensitive national security information. Chik uses his workstation at Power Paragon to collect the information he has been tasked to provide to the PRC. In one intercepted conversation, Chik advised Rebecca that he would take certain material from his office to his home and return the material to his workplace. Furthermore, Chik used his work computer to transmit sensitive information by e-mail to his home. In addition, recorded telephone conversations showed that Chik placed "recruitment calls" from his work telephone at Power Paragon. In these "recruitment calls," Chik attempted to gather information from contacts in fields related to his tasking. Essentially, he was using social engineering in attempts to gain even peripheral information that would be of value. Chik's workstation contained stacks of technical documents, including reports, schematics, and conference papers.

NIGHTTIME SEARCHES

In criminal procedure, good cause must exist for execution of the arrest and search warrants at night. Since the targets of this investigation were foreign intelligence operatives, it would seem very probable that they had received some form of training in avoiding arrest and establishing preplanned escape routes in the event their operations are discovered. Such plans could be put in place by a signal, such as a simple word or telephone call, or even an agreement made in advance that if one member, such as a courier, was discovered, the other operatives would immediately execute their escape plans. In this particular case, the arrest of one or more of the targets could or would alert the others, leading to their flight. Discussions among Chik, Tai, and their wives showed both the knowledge of the illegality of their plan, as well as the fact that they are extremely nervous about being caught.[4]

If word of the arrest of one of the targets became known to the others, that could lead to the swift destruction of evidence and possibly their escape. In this case, that evidence would include electronically stored data on CDs and computers, as well as encryption devices. That type of evidence could be destroyed or made otherwise irretrievable without detection by agents posted outside the subject's residences.

The FBI determined that the arrests of Tai and Fuk must take place at LAX before their departure (currently scheduled for 11:59 p.m.) on Friday, October 28, to ensure that the disks containing the government property were retrieved before they could leave the country. Because the arrests of Tai and Fuk had to take place at night, an unreasonable risk existed that word would reach the other targets, who might then flee or destroy evidence, before search warrants could be executed on Saturday morning.

A Federal Rule provided that warrants shall be served during the daytime (6:00 a.m. to 10:00 p.m.), *unless good cause exists* to execute the warrants at night. In this particular case, because the targets were foreign intelligence agents who would likely have one or more escape plans in place, and who are already worried about being caught, good cause existed to authorize the nighttime execution of various arrest warrants to avoid the destruction of evidence and the escape of the targets.

COMPUTER DATA

We all live in an era of virtual electronics. Just about everything we do is recorded electronically, from getting gasoline, theater tickets, or groceries. Also, we almost live on the Internet. Everyone has a desktop or laptop computer, for use at work or at home, or both. And we use these electronic devices to record everything from the mundane, to chat rooms to blogs, and also to have a lot of research data stored so it can be worked on anywhere. It is almost inconceivable for a person to lug around a briefcase full of several hundred pages or more of data when it can much more easily be loaded electronically on a computer and carried with ease.

Computer data can be stored on a variety of systems and storage devices including hard disk drives, floppy disks, compact disks, magnetic tapes, thumb drives, and memory chips. During any search of a given premises, it is not always possible to search computer equipment and storage devices. There are a number of reasons for this, according to the Department of Justice, including the following:

a. Searching computer systems is a highly technical process that requires specific expertise and specialized equipment. There are so many types of computer hardware and software in use today that it is impossible to bring to the search site all of the necessary technical manuals and specialized equipment necessary to conduct a thorough search. In addition, it may also be necessary to consult with computer personnel who have specific expertise in the type of computer, software application, or operating system that is being searched.[4]
b. Searching computer systems requires the use of precise, scientific procedures that are designed to maintain the integrity of the evidence and to recover "hidden," erased, compressed, encrypted, or password-protected data. Computer hardware and storage devices may contain "booby traps" that destroy or alter data if certain procedures are not scrupulously followed. Since computer data are particularly vulnerable to inadvertent or intentional modification or destruction, a controlled environment, such as a law enforcement laboratory, is essential to conducting a complete and accurate analysis of the equipment and storage devices from which the data will be extracted.[4]
c. The volume of data stored on many computer systems and storage devices will typically be so large that it will be highly impractical to search for data during the execution of the physical search of the premises. A single megabyte of storage space is the equivalent of 500 double-spaced pages of text. A single gigabyte of storage space, or 1000 megabytes, is the equivalent of 500,000 double-spaced pages of text. Storage devices capable of storing

15 gigabytes of data are now commonplace in desktop computers. Consequently, each non-networked, desktop computer found during a search can easily contain the equivalent of 7.5 million pages of data, which, if printed out, would completely fill a 10′ × 12′ × 10′ room to the ceiling.[4]

d. Computer users can attempt to conceal data within computer equipment and storage devices through a number of methods, including the use of innocuous or misleading file names and extensions. For example, files with the extension ".jpg" often are image files; however, a user can easily change the extension to ".txt" to conceal the image and make it appear that the file contains text. Computer users can also attempt to conceal data by using encryption, which means that a password or device, such as a "dongle" or "keycard," is necessary to decrypt the data into readable form. In addition, computer users can conceal data within another seemingly unrelated and innocuous file in a process called "steganography." For example, by using steganography, a computer user can conceal text in an image file that cannot be viewed when the image file is opened. Therefore, a substantial amount of time is necessary to extract and sort through data that are concealed or encrypted to determine whether it is evidence, contraband or instrumentalities of a crime.[4]

Based on the ongoing FBI investigation, to include surreptitious entries into residences, electronic monitoring, and visual surveillance, it was believed, and rightly so, that Mak, Rebecca, Chik, and Fuk Li were in violation of US law and their residences contained evidence of such criminal violations.

During the entire time, FBI counterintelligence agents and NASA received the full cooperation of the Boeing Company in building this three-year investigation, the successful outcome of which marked the first true major conviction by trial under the Economic Espionage Act of 1996.

One person stated later that "I'm confident this milestone conviction will serve as a deterrent to would-be spies contemplating theft of precious U.S. secrets." The case against Chung resulted from an investigation into another engineer (again a long-term undercover agent) who worked in the United States and obtained sensitive military information for the PRC. That engineer, Chik Mak, and several of his family members were convicted of providing defense articles to the PRC. Chik Mak was sentenced to more than 24 years in federal prison.[4]

The Justice Deparment's Office of Public Affairs press release states:

> On Sept. 11, 2006, when FBI and NASA agents searched Chung's house, they found more than 250,000 pages of documents from Boeing, Rockwell and other defense contractors inside the house and in a crawl space underneath the house. Among the documents found in the crawl space were scores of binders containing decades worth of stress analysis reports, test results and design information for the Space Shuttle.
>
> Each charge of economic espionage carried a maximum possible penalty of 15 years in federal prison and a $500,000 fine. The charge of acting as an agent of a foreign government carries a maximum penalty of 10 years imprisonment and a $250,000 fine. The charges of conspiracy to commit economic espionage and making false statements to federal investigators each carry a maximum possible penalty of five years imprisonment and a $250,000 fine.[4]

The FBI went aggressively on the offensive against the people involved in this case. The arrests capped a long probe that demonstrated the difficulty to combat what the FBI saw as a very Chinese espionage campaign to scoop up a myriad of advanced US technology secrets from defense and civilian companies.

REFERENCES

1. Abdollah, Tami and Goffard, Christopher, Chinese-born engineer convicted of espionage, *Los Angeles Times*, July 17, 2009.
2. United States Attorney's Office, Central District of California, Former Boeing engineer sentenced to nearly 16 years in prison for stealing aerospace secrets for China, Public Affairs release 10-027, February 8, 2010.

3. Gaylord, James E., FBI Special Agent, Affidavit sworn before a US Magistrate Judge, October 2005.
4. Department of Justice, Office of Public Affairs, Former Boeing engineer convicted of economic espionage in theft of space shuttle secrets for China, OPA release 09-688, July 16, 2009, http://www.justice.gov/opa/pr/2009/July/09-nsd-688.html, Retrieved March 3, 2013.
5. United States Attorney's Office, Former Boeing engineer convicted of economic espionage in theft of space shuttle secrets for China, Central District of California, release No. 09-084, July 16, 2009, Santa Ana, California.

Appendix B: Economic Espionage Killed the Company, The Four Pillars Enterprise Case

This case involves two companies, a half a world apart. First is the Four Pillars Enterprise Co., Ltd., a Taiwanese company that manufactures and sells pressure-sensitive tapes.[1] The company under attack from economic espionage is the Avery Dennison Inc., an American company that competed with Four Pillars in the manufacturing of adhesive tapes and labels.[1]

Prior to this case, the United States lost its competitive advantage in a strategically important emerging industry when a Chinese citizen employee of Ellery Systems, Inc., resigned and took with him computer software source codes. The codes had cost $950,000 to produce and had a potential market value of tens of billions of dollars.[2,3]

As a direct result of this loss, Ellery Systems, Inc., went out of business and 25 employees lost their jobs. Man-centuries of incredibly complex and hard work and millions of dollars of investment were lost to a foreign country.[3]

Despite the arrest, a lot of evidence, and a confession, the case ended up being dropped because the United States did not have an effective espionage law at the time. Since this case, the Economic Espionage Act (EEA) was passed by Congress and went into law. The first case that was successfully prosecuted was against Four Pillars Enterprise Co., Ltd., for their massive theft of trade secrets from Avery Dennison. Below lays out the case and what happened over a period of time.

THE PLAYERS

Four Pillars is a Taiwanese company owned (at the time of this case) by P.Y. (Pat) Yang, employing more than 900 people and had annual revenues of more than $150 million.[2]

P.Y. Yang was the president of Four Pillars Enterprise Co., Ltd., of Taiwan, which manufactured and sold pressure-sensitive products, mainly in Taiwan, Malaysia, Singapore, the United States, and the People's Republic of China.[2]

Hwei Chen (Sally) Yang of Taiwan was his daughter and was a corporate officer of Four Pillars. Sally Yang had a PhD in analytical chemistry from New Mexico State University and was also employed by Four Pillars as an Applied Research Group Leader.[4]

The Avery Dennison Company (ADC), based on Pasadena, California, was one of the largest manufacturers of adhesive products in the world with more than 16,000 employees worldwide. It is one of the largest US manufacturers (if not the largest) of adhesive products, including adhesives for such things as postage stamps, mailing labels, and even diaper tape. ADC was one of Four Pillars' chief manufacturing and distribution competitors. One of the ADC plants was located in Concord, Ohio, where Dr. Victor Lee worked.[4]

Dr. Ten Hong (Victor) Lee, a native of Taiwan and a US citizen, had been employed by ADC since 1986 as a research engineer where he performed scientific research into adhesives. Dr. Lee held advanced degrees in chemistry and physics from Texas Tech University and also the University of Akron. At all times relevant to this case, Lee was an employee of ADC.[5]

THE CASE

In 1989, Dr. Lee went to Taiwan (on vacation?) and made a presentation about adhesives to a local group. He was later asked to make the same presentation to a small private group of businessmen who were affiliated with Four Pillars. C.K. Kao, Four Pillars vice president at the time, introduced Dr. Lee to Pat Yang and his daughter, Sally Yang. Yang asked Dr. Lee to serve as a "consultant" to Four Pillars and offered him a compensation of $25,000 for a year of consultation. In the orient, if one doesn't disagree, or makes no comment, it is typically assumed the individual agrees. Dr. Lee said nothing, essentially agreeing. The parties agreed that they would keep the arrangement secret. Lee received his first check, made out to his sister-in-law, from Four Pillars shortly thereafter.[6] By making the check out to a relative in Taiwan, people in the United States would be unaware of his involvement since none of the money would show up or be spent in the United States, essentially concealing the fact that as a consultant, Dr. Lee was becoming involved in economic espionage.

Dr. Lee, over approximately eight years' time, would go on to receive between $150,000 and $160,000 from Four Pillars/Pin Yen Yang for his involvement in the illegal transfer of ADC's proprietary manufacturing information and research data.[5]

After his return to the United States, Lee corresponded with Yang and Sally, wherein he described, probably in considerable detail, the information he would provide them. In his correspondence, Dr. Lee indicated that some of the information he intended to provide to the Yangs and Four Pillars was confidential to Avery. In August 1989, Lee sent two confidential Avery rheology reports to the Yangs. The Yangs responded that the information was very helpful.[7] Such confidential papers would be proprietary to Avery and contain sensitive details about their adhesives. As an ADC employee, Dr. Lee would have signed a confidential statement, in addition to papers covering legal ethics and conflict of interests. In doing so, these documents would have clearly informed Dr. Lee that what he eventually did would be illegal and could be a basis for legal action against him. The author suspects that Dr. Lee had no qualms about his entry into economic espionage since, within days of his return to the United States, he was already getting items ready to transmit to Four Pillars concerning sensitive details about Avery adhesives.

Dr. Lee continued to supply the Yangs/Four Pillars with sensitive confidential information from Avery including information that Four Pillars could use in making a new acrylic adhesive recently developed by Avery. The Yangs even sent Dr. Lee samples of the adhesives they had created using information he had supplied; Lee then used Avery laboratories to test the samples and offered comparisons with Avery's products derived from the same adhesive formula.[7]

IT ALL STARTED TO UNRAVEL ...

The entire case started innocuously when ADC learned from an individual who had sought employment (and was from Taiwan) suddenly reversed a decision to work for Avery. When Avery pursued his reason as to turning down employment, it became known that Four Pillars already had an individual working within the company as a consultant. Recall that employees signed confidential agreements, legal ethics, and conflict of interest forms. Hence, at this point, ADC knew they might have a problem. But how big of a problem would they eventually have? And would it affect ADC's proprietary information? Only time would tell.

Companies like Avery Dennison normally perform, on a somewhat continuing basis, internal personnel security audits, reviewing employee behavior and attitudes, or conducting general security surveys relating to protecting its products and the associated trade secrets. Such companies continuously monitor computer usage, and check on researchers, scientists, and engineers to ensure they maintain the integrity of the work being performed. At the point ADC first learned of the possibility that a consultant was within their organization, the possibility of espionage probably popped into their mind, and an internal investigation was begun at the Ohio facility. Based upon what they learned, in November 1986 they contacted the Federal Bureau of Investigation (FBI). From then until the arrest of the Four Pillars people, and throughout the entire period, ADC continued to provide extensive assistance to the FBI.[5]

For the next several years, Dr. Lee provided confidential information, including formulas for adhesives and reports about rheology (the study of adhesives), to the Yangs/Four Pillars. In addition, Dr. Lee took advantage of his position at ADC and used Avery machines to test various Four Pillars' adhesives and then provided Four Pillars/Yangs with reports comparing and analyzing those products to Avery products.[6]

The FBI confronted Dr. Lee after learning of his industrial espionage. Dr. Lee admitted his relationship with the Yangs and Four Pillars and provided the government with materials documenting his activities. Dr. Lee also agreed to cooperate with the government in a sting operation to arrest and prosecute the Yangs.[6]

According to published reports, Dr. Victor Lee, an Avery Dennison researcher at Avery's manufacturing complex in Concord Township, Ohio, confessed to giving Four Pillars "highly sensitive and valuable proprietary manufacturing information and research data" since 1989 and was paid over $150,000 (over eight years) by Four Pillars as a consultant. To conceal the scheme, arrangements for payment were made through Lee family members in Taiwan.[5,8]

As a sidelight, note that Dr. Lee first sent data to the Yang/Four Pillars only days after he became a consultant, so the possibility exists that he was ready to conduct espionage immediately, probably having a wide variety of technical papers and other data at his residence or immediately available in his office that could be provided to the Yangs and Four Pillars.

In an earlier FBI sting operation, Ten Hong "Victor" Lee attended a meeting at Avery Dennison where he and others were told of a binder containing confidential information on Avery's plans for the Far East. A closed-circuit TV recording reviewed later showed Dr. Lee several times gaining access to the file drawer where the binder was kept, once wearing gloves when he removed it from the office for a few minutes. Confronted by FBI agents in March 1997, Lee admitted he had been providing confidential information to Four Pillars. Thereafter, Lee pleaded guilty to wire fraud and turned over to the FBI a virtual treasure trove of Avery Dennison documents. Dr. Lee then worked with federal agents, cooperating in an undercover capacity with the FBI leading to the arrest of the Yangs on September 4, 1997.[5]

Early in 1997, after agents with the FBI suspected that Dr. Lee was providing confidential information and confronted him with their suspicions, he quickly agreed to cooperate and assisted in taping several telephone conversations with Yang and Sally Yang. During those conversations, including at least one initiated by Yang, she continued to ask for Lee's help in solving Four Pillars' production problems.[6]

During one of the telephone conversations, Yang told Dr. Lee that he would be visiting the United States during the summer of 1997, and Lee informed Yang that he (Dr. Lee) had information about a new emulsion coating that he would provide Yang during his visit. He also asked Yang whether he was interested in information on Avery's plans in the Far East, and Yang stated that he was.[6]

On September 4, 1997, at a Holiday Inn hotel room in Westlake, Ohio, Dr. Lee met with Pat and Sally Yang. Dr. Lee had consented to FBI agents videotaping the meeting. Prior to the meeting, the FBI would covertly prepare the hotel room with audio and video feeds, probably to a motel room adjacent to the actual meeting room. In the course of the meeting, Dr. Lee showed the Yangs, among other things, a mock document created with help from ADC and provided Dr. Lee by the FBI that included an Avery patent application relating to a new adhesive product. The various documents was clearly marked with "confidential" and "Property of Avery Dennison Corp" stamps, which Dr. Lee emphasized to the Yangs that the information was the confidential property of Avery. He gave the materials to Yang, emphasizing that the patent application was a confidential Avery document relating to a new adhesive product. Yang pointed to the "confidential" stamp on the document and instructed Sally Yang to remove the various stamp markings. The three also discussed the "treasure box" of materials that Lee had provided petitioners over the years. Yang and Sally Yang were arrested shortly after the meeting. In their luggage were the various documents Dr. Lee had provided to them at the meeting. Yang had in his suitcase the patent application and other Avery documents that he had obtained from Lee, with the "confidential" markings removed.[6]

The Yangs' conspiracy to steal the trade secrets was in violation of §1832(a)(5) and was completed when, with the intent to steal the trade secrets, they agreed to meet with Lee in the hotel room and they took an overt act toward the completion of the crime, that is, when the Yangs went to the hotel room. The fact that the information they conspired to obtain was not what they believed it to be does not matter because the objective of the Yangs' agreement was to steal trade secrets, and they took an overt step toward achieving that objective. Conspiracy is nothing more than the parties to the conspiracy coming to a mutual understanding to try to accomplish a common and unlawful plan.[6]

Pat Yang and his daughter Sally Yang were arrested by FBI agents while at Hopkins International Airport in Cleveland.[8]

They were arrested for the theft of trade secrets under the EEA. Also charged was the Four Pillars Enterprise Co., Ltd., which had its offices in Taiwan. It also had a registered agent in El Campo, Texas.

In various court papers, the arrests (and the reason behind them) were spelled out in greater detail. The Four Pillars, Pat Yang (CEO of Four Pillars), daughter Sally Yang, and Dr. Ten Hong (Victor) Lee were conspirators involving the illegal transfer of very sensitive and valuable trade secrets and other proprietary information. They were charged with mail and wire fraud, conspiracy to steal trade secrets, money laundering and receipt of stolen goods from the Avery Dennison Corporation facility in Concord, Ohio, and the transfer of that information to the Four Pillars Company in Taiwan.[6]

A Federal Grand Jury returned a 21-count indictment charging Four Pillars, Pin Yen Yang, and Sally Yang with attempted theft of trade secrets, mail fraud, wire fraud, money laundering, and receipt of stolen property. During the same period, Dr. Lee pled guilty to one count of wire fraud in exchange for his full cooperation in the US government's case against the accused. The economic losses to ADC were estimated to be about $50–60 million.[9]

The *Cleveland Plain Dealer* newspaper of April 24, 1999, noted that the prosecution bolstered its arguments that the Yangs and their company intentionally stole Avery Dennison's proprietary information by playing portions of a tape that clearly showed the Yangs removing "confidential" stamps and "Avery Dennison" identification data off the papers delivered by Lee to the hotel room in September of 1997.[5]

The Yangs did not testify at the trial and their lawyers argued that their clients never asked Lee to steal his employer's trade secrets and that the engineer took them on his own. Be that as it may, the Yangs had no compunction about clipping ADC identifying data and retaining the documents for their (and Four Pillars) own use.

Federal prosecutors estimated that the research and development costs expended by Avery Dennison to develop the information obtained by the Yangs and Four Pillars exceed $50 million.

In closing arguments before the Federal District Court in Cleveland on April 23, 1999, US Assistant Attorney Marc Zwillinger argued to the jury that Pat Yang and his daughter Sally "knew Avery Dennison was a world leader in the adhesive industry" and paid an Avery Dennison Corporation employee, Victor Lee, to steal Avery Dennison's confidential and proprietary information.[8]

Deliberations in the case were extended to about 18 hours spread over three days, and the jury found the Yangs guilty of economic espionage for attempting to steal trade secrets. Four Pillars itself was also convicted on the espionage charges. The Yangs were acquitted of mail fraud charges.

On April 28, 1999, the jury in the Northern District of Ohio convicted the Yangs and their closely held corporation, Four Pillars, for attempt and conspiracy to steal trade secrets from Avery Dennison Corporation in violation of the EEA of 1996.

On January 5, 2000, US District Judge Peter C. Economus fined Four Pillars Enterprise Co., Ltd., $5 million and sentenced Pat Yang to six months of home confinement and a $250,000 fine. His daughter, Sally, was fined $5,000 and received one year of probation.

In February 2000, a jury verdict in US District Court, Cleveland, ruled in favor of ADC in a civil case against Four Pillars and the judge awarded $80 million in damages.[10]

Shortly after the verdict, Avery Dennison issued a statement that "There was never any doubt in our minds that the evidence of illegal activity by Four Pillars was overwhelming."[8]

Later on, FBI Director Freeh said that the investigation and conviction demonstrate "The importance and value of law enforcement and industry working in partnership under the EEA to combat the theft of American trade secrets and jobs by foreign business interests. It is essential that this partnership continue to adequately combat a crime which has such an impact on the economic well-being of this nation." FBI Director Freeh also stated that "This case marks one of the first convictions of foreign individuals under the Economic Espionage Act of 1996 which has gone to trial. It is also the first case in which a foreign company was charged and found guilty of an Economic Espionage violation."[11]

Pat Yang did apologize at his sentencing and said it was not his intention to steal trade secrets. "I'm deeply sorry for what I've done," Yang said. Federal prosecutors objected that no prison time was imposed. Assistant US Attorney David Green said to the court, "Is the message, if you steal information from your competitor, you'll be given a probationary term?"[8]

CORPORATE AMERICA INTELLECTUAL PROPERTY THEFT SUMMARY

The potential loss to corporate America from the theft of intellectual properties was estimated to be more than $250–300 billion a year and thousands of jobs, according to various surveys conducted by the FBI, the intelligence community, and the private industry. These numbers are just estimates because in many cases businesses are reluctant to admit either committing or being victimized by espionage. Still, with these high stakes, industrial espionage will continue to grow for many years to come.[12–14]

Corporations, unlike government, have less recourse against employees that violate established rules. Corporate security must therefore allow collectors the opportunity to "succeed" when the tipping point has been reached: the point at which the cost of safeguarding information outweighs the intrinsic value of the said information. As a result, it would seem that the threat of espionage will continue to be a real and present threat for the foreseeable future.[15]

REFERENCES

1. Department of Justice Press Release, Taiwanese firm, its president and his daughter indicted in industrial espionage case, October 1, 1997.
2. Technology for self-adhesive products; November 28, 2001; Department of Commerce, Western Region Security Office, NOAA; wrc.noaa.gov/wrso.
3. Espionage killed the company; November 28, 2001; Department of Commerce, Western Region Security Office, NOAA; wrc.noaa.gov/wrso.
4. Department of Justice, Press Release 97-414, Taiwanese firm, its president and his daughter indicted in industrial espionage case; October 1, 2007.
5. Robenault, James D., Thompson Hine, LLP; Report, Avery Dennison: a case study in trade secret theft; hanford.gov/files.cfm/fourpillars; September 17, 2001.
6. The Supreme Court of the United States, Pin Yen Yang, Four Pillars Enterprise Co., Ltd., and Hwei-Chen Yang, Petitioners v. United States of America, On Petition for a Writ of Certiorari to the United States Court of appeals for the Sixth Circuit, Brief for the United States; No. 02-136, October 2002.
7. *United States v. Yang, United States of America, Plaintiff-Appellee/Cross-Appellant, v. Pin Yen Yang,* a/k/a P.Y. Yang, a/k/a P.Y. Young; Four Pillars Enterprise Company, Ltd.; Hwei Chen Yang, a/k/a Huen Chan Yang, a/k/a Sally Yang, a/k/a Sally Young, Defendants-Appellants/Cross-Appellees, Nos. 00-3125, 00-3126, 00-3150. United States Court of Appeals, Sixth Circuit Court, argued June 5, 2001–February 20, 2002.
8. Reported Criminal Arrests and Convictions under the Economic Espionage Act of 1996 [updated 2/17/03], R. Mark Halligan, Esq., tradesecretshomepage.com.

9. National Counterintelligence Center, Annual report to Congress on economic collection and industrial espionage: 1988; Washington, D.C.
10. United States Court of Appeals, Ninth Circuit. Four Pillars Enterprises Co., Ltd, *Petitioner-Appellant, v. Avery Dennison Corporation*, Respondent, Appellee. No. 01-55639. Argued and Submitted May 9, 2002. Decided October 24, 2002. Located on web at: openjurist.org/308/f3d/1075/four-pillars-enterprises-co-ltd-v-avery-dennison-corporation.
11. US Department of Justice, Federal Bureau of Investigation, FBI National Press Office press release, Four Pillars, P. Y. Yang and Sally Yang Convicted of Violating the Economic Espionage Act of 1996; Washington, D.C., April 28, 1999.
12. Statement of Judiciary Committee Chairman Lamar Smith Hearing on H.R. 3261, the "Stop Online Piracy Act," US House of Representatives, Committee on the Judiciary, Washington, D.C., November 16, 2011.
13. A.E. Feldman Blog, U. S. firms paying high price for global IP theft, blog.aefeldman.com/2009/08/04/.
14. National Crime Prevention Council, Intellectual Property Theft: Get Real, found at: www.ncpc.org/top ics, Arlington, VA, 2012.
15. Wallace, William A., Industrial espionage experts, The University of New Haven—California Campus: Student Papers; retrieved from: all.net/CID/Threat/papers/IndustrialEspionage.html.

Appendix C: Summary of Major US Export Enforcement, Economic Espionage, Trade Secret, and Embargo-Related Criminal Cases, 2007 to the Present

The National Security Division of the Department of Justice (DOJ) maintains a fact sheet that provides snapshots of the major criminal prosecutions over the years related to US export enforcement and embargo-related cases. To follow are summary snapshots of a variety of major export and embargo-related criminal prosecutions that are directly attributable to China; these cases are reproduced verbatim from the DOJ document, entitled *Summary of Major U.S. Export Enforcement, Economic Espionage, Trade Secret and Embargo-Related Criminal Cases: 2007 to the Present.* These cases were taken from a much longer listing of over 200 cases that were delineated in the February 2012 fact sheet. While the list is somewhat lengthy, it should be noted that the entire list is not exhaustive and only represents selected cases.

In essence, these cases are most indicative of China's desire to obtain US technological secrets in their myriad forms. The data show that 22.12% of all the identified prosecutions during this period involved China. All of these cases resulted from investigations by the Department of Homeland Security's US Immigration and Customs Enforcement (ICE), the Federal Bureau of Investigation (FBI), the Department of Commerce's Bureau of Industry and Security (BIS), the Pentagon's Defense Criminal Investigative Service (DCIS), and other law enforcement agencies.

These are just a sampling of what the United States has discovered and was able to prosecute. Imagine for yourself what hasn't been found about our economic, military, technological, and trade secrets, and other intellectual property that is being stolen by China, much the less other nations.

Provided here is a summary from the DOJ document listing many identified high-profile cases involving China during this period, where they emanated from, and the type(s) of information targeted. A summary of cases involving countries other than China concludes the appendix.

Trade Secrets to China—On Jan. 25, 2013, Ji Li Huang, a Chinese business owner, and his employee, Xiao Guang Qi, pleaded guilty and were sentenced in the Western District of Missouri for conspiring to steal trade secrets from Pittsburgh Corning Corporation, which produces FOAMGLAS insulation. Huang is the CEO of Ningbo Oriental Crafts Ltd., which employs 200 factory workers to manufacture promotional products for export to the United States and Europe. Qi was his employee. Huang was sentenced to 18 months in prison and ordered to pay a fine of $250,000. Qi was sentenced to time and ordered to pay a fine of $20,000. Pittsburgh Corning, headquartered in Pittsburgh, Pennsylvania, manufactures various grades or densities of cellular glass insulation sold under the trade name FOAMGLAS. That material is used to insulate buildings, industrial piping systems, and liquefied natural gas storage tank bases. Pittsburgh Corning considers the product formula and manufacturing process for FOAMGLAS proprietary and trade secrets. By pleading guilty, Huang and Qi admitted that they attempted to illegally purchase trade secrets of Pittsburgh Corning for the purpose of opening a plant in China to compete with Pittsburgh Corning. The court ruled that the intended loss to Pittsburgh Corning exceeded

$7 million, based on the company's investment of time and resources to research, develop, and protect the proprietary information the defendants attempted to steal. Huang and Qi were arrested when they met with an individual they believed to be an employee of Pittsburgh Corning who had stolen documents that contained trade secret information and was willing to sell it to them for $100,000. That employee, however, was cooperating with law enforcement and the meetings in Kansas City were a sting operation that led to their arrests on Sept. 2, 2012. The case was investigated by the FBI.

Sensitive Microwave Amplifiers to China and India—On Jan. 17, 2013, Timothy Gormley was sentenced to 42 months in prison, three years supervised release, and a $1000 fine in the Eastern District of Pennsylvania for five counts of violating the International Emergency Economic Powers Act (IEEPA). On Oct. 17, 2012, Gormley, the former export control manager of AR Worldwide/ Amplifier Research in Souderton, Pennsylvania, pleaded guilty in connection with the illegal export of over 57 microwave amplifiers, which are controlled for National Security reasons due to their applications in military systems, including radar jamming and weapons guidance systems. The Aug. 9, 2012, information alleged that between 2007 and 2011, Gormley failed to obtain the required licenses on behalf of the company for shipments sent to destinations requiring such licenses for the shipment of these goods. The information cited specific shipments of amplifiers from the United States to customers in India and China that Gormley caused without the required export license. This investigation was conducted by the Department of Commerce.

Dual-Use Programmable Logic Devices to China—On Dec. 18, 2012, federal prosecutors in the District of Oregon unsealed a 12-count indictment charging Wan Li Yuan, aka "Nicholas Bush," a resident of China, and another Chinese resident known as "Jason Jiang" with export and money laundering violations in connection with their alleged efforts to obtain dual-use programmable logic devices (PLDs) from the United States for export to China. According to the indictment, while operating from China, Yuan and Jiang created a sophisticated scheme to conceal their true identity and location in order to mislead US companies into believing they were dealing with American customers so they could procure and send sensitive technologies to China without the required export licenses. Yuan and Jiang allegedly sought to procure PLDs made by Lattice Semiconductor Corporation in Oregon, which are designed to operate at extreme temperature ranges and which can have military applications such as in missiles and radar systems. To further his efforts, the indictment alleges that Yuan created a fake web site and e-mail addresses using the name of a legitimate New York-based company. Yuan requested US companies to ship the desired parts to the address of a freight forwarder in New York, which he also falsely represented as being associated with the New York company whose business name Yuan had stolen. Through the investigation and use of an undercover operation, the FBI and Department of Commerce were able to seize approximately $414,000 in funds sent by Yuan as down payments for the Lattice PLDs. Lattice Semiconductor cooperated with the government in the investigation, which was conducted by the FBI and Department of Commerce's BIS.

Coatings for Rocket Nozzles and Other Goods to Taiwan and China—On Dec. 6, 2012, Mark Henry, a US citizen and resident of Queens, New York, who operated a company called Dahua Electronics Corporation, was arrested on an indictment in the Southern District of New York charging him with conspiracy to violate and violating the Arms Export Control Act and violating the IEEPA. According to the indictment, from April 2009 through September 2012, Henry purchased ablative materials that are used for protective coating for rocket nozzles from a Colorado company and caused 294 kilograms of these materials to be exported to a company in Taiwan. These particular materials are controlled under the US Munitions List and may not be exported without a State Department license. Henry also purchased from a company in Pennsylvania microwave amplifiers that are controlled by the Commerce Department and have potential military uses and falsely stated that the goods were for an educational institution in New York. Henry allegedly attempted to ship the microwave amplifiers to China without a Commerce license. This investigation was conducted by the Department of Commerce and the FBI.

Carbon Fiber and Other Materials to Iran and China—On Dec. 5, 2012, prosecutors in the Southern District of New York unsealed charges against four individuals for exporting various goods to Iran and to China, including carbon fiber (which has nuclear applications in uranium enrichment as well applications in missiles) and helicopter components. Hamid Reza Hashemi, an Iranian national, and Murat Taskiran, a Turkish citizen, were charged in one indictment with conspiracy to violate and violating the IEEPA by working to arrange the illegal export of carbon fiber from the United States to Hashemi's company in Iran via Europe and the United Arab Emirates. Hashemi was arrested upon arrival in New York City on Dec. 1, 2012. Taskiran remains a fugitive. Peter Gromacki, a US citizen and resident of Orange County, New York, is charged in another indictment with violating IEEPA by using his New York company to illegally export carbon fiber from the United States to China. According to the indictment, in June 2007, Gromacki arranged for the illegal export of more than 6000 pounds of carbon fiber from the United States to Belgium, which was then shipped to China. He allegedly made a variety of false statements on shipper's export declaration forms. Gromacki was arrested at his home on Dec. 5, 2012. Amir Abbas Tamimi, an Iranian citizen, was charged in a separate indictment with violating IEEPA by working to export helicopter component parts from the United States to Iran, via South Korea. The components were for a particular type of helicopter that can be used for military purposes. Tamimi was arrested upon arrival in New York City on Oct. 5, 2012. None of the defendants obtained the requisite approval from the Department of Treasury for such exports. This investigation was conducted by the FBI, ICE, and Department of Commerce.

Restricted Microwave Amplifier Technology to China—On Oct. 31, 2012, Fu-Tain Lu was sentenced in the Northern District of California to 15 months in prison. On Nov. 17, 2011, Lu pleaded guilty to selling sensitive microwave amplifiers to the People's Republic of China (PRC) without the required license. Lu was the owner and founder of Fushine Technology, Inc., a corporation formerly located in Cupertino, California. Fushine was an exporter of electronic components used in communications, radar, and other applications. At the time of the offense, Fushine had a sales representative agreement with Miteq Components, Inc., a New York-based manufacturer of microwave and satellite communications components and subsystems. Lu admitted that, on March 1, 2004, Fushine submitted a purchase order to Miteq for one microwave amplifier and requested that Miteq notify Fushine immediately if an export license was required. Miteq responded that the part was controlled for export to China. Nonetheless, on April 2, 2004, Fushine exported the amplifier to co-defendant Everjet Science and Technology Corporation (Everjet), located in China, without a license from the Department of Commerce. Lu further admitted that the amplifier he shipped was restricted for export to China for reasons of national security. Lu and the two corporate defendants, Fushine and Everjet, were first indicted on April 1, 2009. A superseding indictment was returned on Feb. 17, 2010. In addition to the count of conviction, the indictment also charged him with conspiring to violate US export regulations and lying to federal agents who were investigating that conduct. The superseding indictment quoted from an internal company e-mail in which an Everjet employee told a Fushine employee, "Since these products are a little bit sensitive, in case the maker ask [*sic*] you where the location of the end user is, please do not mention it is in China." As part of the plea agreement, Lu also agreed to forfeit 36 additional microwave amplifiers seized on March 24, 2010, but those were not included in the superseding indictment. This investigation was conducted by the Department of Commerce (BIS), the FBI, ICE, and the US Customs and Border Protection (CBP).

Firearms to China—On Oct. 4, 2012, Zhifu Lin, a Chinese national and resident of West Virginia, pleaded guilty in the Eastern District of New York to violating the Arms Export Control Act and to illegal weapons trafficking. Lin's plea came after Joseph Debose, a resident of North Carolina and former Staff Sergeant in a US Special Forces National Guard Unit, pleaded guilty on Sept. 6, 2012, to violating the Arms Export Control Act. Lin, Debose, and others exported multiple shipments of firearms from the United States to China by secreting them in packages and transporting them to shipping companies, including one in Queens, New York, to be sent to China.

The weapons included numerous semiautomatic handguns, rifles, and shotguns. The smuggling scheme came to light after authorities in China seized a package containing firearms with defaced serial numbers shipped from Queens, New York Thereafter, US agents traveled to China and examined the firearms. Using forensic techniques, agents learned that one of the seized weapons had originally been purchased in North Carolina. Among the weapons seized in China were those Debose provided to his associates for export. On May 20, 2012, Debose was arrested in Smithfield, North Carolina, pursuant to a May 17, 2012, criminal complaint charging him with illegally exporting firearms to China without the required licenses. Lin and another Chinese national, Lila Li, were also arrested and charged in connection with the case in an April 16, 2012, indictment in the Eastern District of New York. This investigation was conducted by ICE; The Bureau of Alcohol, Tobacco, Firearms and Explosives (ATF); the Internal Revenue Service (IRS); and BIS.

Military Technical Data and Trade Secrets to China—On Sept. 26, 2012, Sixing Liu, aka "Steve Liu," a native of China with a PhD in electrical engineering who worked as a senior staff engineer for Space and Navigation, a New Jersey-based division of L-3 Communications, was convicted in the District of New Jersey of exporting sensitive US military technology to China, stealing trade secrets, and lying to federal agents. The jury convicted Liu of 9 of 11 counts of an April 5, 2012, second superseding indictment, specifically six counts of violating the Arms Export Control Act, one count of possessing stolen trade secrets in violation of the Economic Espionage Act, one count of transporting stolen property, and one count of lying to federal agents. The jury acquitted Liu on two counts of lying to federal agents. According to documents filed in the case and evidence presented at trial, in 2010, Liu stole thousands of electronic files from his employer, L-3 Communications, Space and Navigation Division. The stolen files detailed the performance and design of guidance systems for missiles, rockets, target locators, and unmanned aerial vehicles (UAVs). Liu stole the files to position and prepare himself for future employment in China. As part of that plan, Liu delivered presentations about the technology at several Chinese universities, the Chinese Academy of Sciences, and conferences organized by Chinese government entities. However, Liu was not charged with any crimes related to those presentations. On Nov. 12, 2010, Liu boarded a flight from Newark to China. Upon his return to the United States on Nov. 29, 2010, agents found Liu in possession of a non-work-issued computer found to contain the stolen material. The following day, Liu lied to ICE agents about the extent of his work on US defense technology. The State Department later verified that several of the stolen files on Liu's computer contained technical data that relate to defense items listed on the US Munitions List. The jury also heard testimony that Liu's company trained him about the United States' export control laws and told him that most of the company's products were covered by those laws. Liu was first arrested on March 8, 2011, in Chicago on a complaint in the District of New Jersey charging him with one count of exporting defense-related technical data without a license. The investigation was conducted by the FBI, ICE, and the CBP.

Aerospace-Grade Carbon Fiber to China—On Sept. 26, 2012, a criminal complaint was unsealed in the Eastern District of New York charging Ming Suan Zhang with attempting to illegally export thousands of pounds of aerospace-grade carbon fiber from the United States to China. According to the complaint, Zhang was arrested in the United States after trying to negotiate a deal to acquire the specialized carbon fiber, a high-tech material used frequently in the military, defense, and aerospace industries, and which is therefore closely regulated by the US Department of Commerce to combat nuclear proliferation and terrorism. The complaint alleges that Zhang came to the attention of federal authorities earlier this year after two Taiwanese accomplices attempted to locate large quantities of the specialized carbon fiber via remote Internet contacts. In July 2012, Zhang allegedly told an accomplice: "When I place the order, I place one to two tons. However, the first shipment will be for 100 kg [kilograms]." Shortly thereafter, Zhang contacted an undercover law enforcement agent in an effort to finalize the deal to export the carbon fiber from New York to China. In one recorded conversation, Zhang stated that he had an urgent need for the carbon fiber in connection with the scheduled test flight of a Chinese fighter plane. Zhang then arranged a meeting with an undercover agent to take possession of a carbon fiber sample, which was to be shipped to China and analyzed to verify its authenticity. Zhang was subsequently placed under arrest. This investigation was conducted by ICE and BIS.

Theft of Trade Secrets for Potential Use in China—On Sept. 19, 2012, Chunlai Yang, a former senior software engineer for Chicago-based CME Group, Inc., pleaded guilty in the Northern District of Illinois to two counts of theft of trade secrets for stealing source code and other proprietary information while at the same time pursuing plans to improve an electronic trading exchange in China. Yang admitted that he downloaded more than 10,000 files containing CME computer source code that made up a substantial part of the operating systems for the Globex electronic trading platform. The government maintains that the potential loss was between $50 million and $100 million. Yang began working for CME Group in 2000 and was a senior software engineer at the time of his arrest. Between late 2010 and June 30, 2011, Yang downloaded more than 10,000 computer files containing CME computer source code from CME's secure internal computer system to his CME-issued work computer. He then transferred many of these files from his work computer to his personal USB flash drives and then transferred many of these files from his flash drives to his personal computers and hard drives at his home. Yang also admitted that he downloaded thousands of others CME files. Yang admitted that he and two unnamed business partners developed plans to form a business referred to as the Tongmei (Gateway to America) Futures Exchange Software Technology Company (Gateway), whose purpose was to increase the trading volume at the Zhangjiagang, China, chemical electronic trading exchange (the Zhangjiagang Exchange). The Zhangjiagang Exchange was to become a transfer station to China for advanced technologies companies around the world. Yang expected that Gateway would provide the exchange with technology through written source code to allow for high trading volume, high trading speeds, and multiple trading functions. Yang was indicted on Sept. 28, 2011. This investigation was conducted by the FBI.

Motorola Trade Secrets to China—On Aug. 29, 2012, Hanjuan Jin, a former software engineer for Motorola, was sentenced in the Northern District of Illinois to four years in prison for stealing trade secrets from Motorola, specifically Motorola's proprietary iDEN telecommunications technology, for herself and for Sun Kaisens, a company that developed products for the Chinese military. According to court documents filed in the case, Motorola spent more than $400 million researching and developing iDEN technology in just a matter of years. On Feb. 8, 2012, Jin was found guilty of three counts of stealing trade secrets. Jin, a naturalized US citizen born in China, possessed more than 1000 electronic and paper Motorola proprietary documents when she was stopped by US authorities at Chicago's O'Hare International Airport as she attempted to travel to China on Feb. 28, 2007. The judge presiding over the case found her not guilty of three counts of economic espionage for the benefit of the government of China and its military. According to the evidence at trial, Jin began working for Motorola in 1998 and took medical leave in February 2006. Between June and November 2006, while still on sick leave, Jin pursued employment in China with Sun Kaisens, a Chinese telecommunications firm that developed products for the Chinese military. Between November 2006 and February 2007, Jin returned to China and did work for Sun Kaisens on projects for the Chinese military. On Feb. 15, 2007, Jin returned to the United States from China and reserved a flight to China scheduled to depart on Feb. 28, 2007. Jin advised Motorola that she was ready to return to work at Motorola, without informing Motorola that she planned to return to China to work for Sun Kaisens. On Feb. 26, 2007, she returned to Motorola and accessed hundreds of technical documents belonging to Motorola on its secure internal computer network. As she attempted to depart from Chicago to China, authorities seized numerous materials, some of which provided a description of communication feature that Motorola incorporates into its telecommunications products. Authorities also recovered classified Chinese documents describing telecommunication projects for the Chinese military. Jin was charged with theft of trade secrets in an April 1, 2008, indictment. A superseding indictment returned on Dec. 9, 2008, charged her with economic espionage. The investigation was conducted by the FBI, with assistance from the CBP.

Sensitive Military Encryption Technology to China—On July 31, 2012, Chi Tong Kuok, a resident of Macau, China, pleaded guilty in the Southern District of California to one count of conspiracy to illegally export defense articles and to smuggle goods from the United States. According to the guilty plea, Kuok and others conspired to purchase and export from the United States defense articles, including communication, precision location, and cryptographic equipment, without a license from the State Department. Kuok also caused $1700 to be sent to the United States for the purchase and unlicensed export of a KG-175 Taclane Encryptor. According to court documents, the KG-175 Taclane Encryptor was developed by General Dynamics under a contract with the National Security Agency for use by the US military to encrypt Internet Protocol communications. Kuok was first arrested on June 17, 2009, in Atlanta, Georgia, after he arrived from Paris to catch a connecting flight to Panama in order to meet with undercover federal agents to take possession of controlled US technology. A criminal complaint was filed on June 23, 2009, and an indictment returned on July 7, 2009. On May 11, 2010, Kuok was convicted at trial of conspiracy to export defense articles without a license and to smuggle goods to Macau and Hong Kong, China; smuggling goods; attempting to export defense articles without a license; and money laundering. On Sept. 13, 2012, Kuok was sentenced to 96 months in prison. Kuok appealed, and in January 2012, the 9th US Circuit Court of Appeals vacated Kuok's convictions on counts three and four and remanded to the district court for a new trial on counts one and two. The appeals court ruled that Kuok should have been allowed to put on a defense that he was forced into trying to procure the equipment by the Chinese government. Kuok pleaded guilty before the second trial. This investigation was conducted by ICE and DCIS.

Military Gyroscopes to China—On July 30, 2012, Kevin Zhang, aka Zhao Wei Zhang, was arrested as he attempted to enter the United States from Canada at a port of entry in Washington state. Zhang had been charged on Jan. 14, 2011, in a sealed indictment in the Southern District of California with one count of conspiracy to export defense articles (specifically G-200 Dynamically Tuned Gyroscopes) from the United States to China without a license or approval from the State Department. According to the indictment, these particular gyroscopes may be used in tactical missile guidance and unmanned aircraft systems. Zhang allegedly instructed individuals in the United States to obtain and export defense articles, including the gyroscopes, to China and allegedly sought to use a courier to smuggle the gyroscopes out of the United States. The indictment alleges that Zhang, acting on behalf of a client in China, sought to purchase three gyroscopes for $21,000 from an individual in the United States as a prelude to future purchases of gyroscopes. This investigation was conducted by ICE.

Military Software Used for China's First Modern Attack Helicopter—On June 28, 2012, in the District of Connecticut, Pratt & Whitney Canada Corp. (PWC), a Canadian subsidiary of Connecticut-based defense contractor United Technologies Corp. (UTC), pleaded guilty to violating the Arms Export Control Act and making false statements in connection with its illegal export to China of US-origin military software that was used in the development of China's first modern military attack helicopter, the Z-10. In addition, UTC, its US-based subsidiary Hamilton Sundstrand Corp. (HSC), and PWC all agreed to pay more than $75 million as part of a global settlement with the Justice Department and the State Department in connection with various export violations, including those related to the Z-10, and for making false and belated disclosures to the US government about the illegal exports for the Z-10. A three-count criminal information was filed against the companies. Count one charged PWC with violating the Arms Export Control Act for the illegal export of defense articles to China for the Z-10 helicopter. Specifically, in 2002 and 2003, PWC knowingly and willfully caused HSC military software used to test and operate PWC engines to be exported to China for the Z-10 without any US export license. PWC knew from the start of the Z-10 project in 2000 that the Chinese were developing an attack helicopter and that supplying it with US-origin components would be illegal. According to court documents, PWC's illegal conduct was driven by profit. PWC anticipated that its work on the Z-10 attack helicopter in China would open the door to a far more lucrative civilian helicopter market in China potentially worth as much as $2 billion to PWC. Count two of the information charged PWC, UTC, and HSC with making false statements about these illegal exports to the State Department in their belated disclosures, which did not begin until 2006. Count three charged PWC and HSC for their failure to timely inform the State Department of the unlawful export of defense articles to China, an embargoed nation, as required by US export regulations. This is the first case in which the provisions in count three have been enforced criminally. While PWC pleaded guilty to counts one and two, prosecution of PWC, UTC, and HSC on the other charges is deferred for two years, provided that the companies abide by the terms of a deferred prosecution agreement with the Justice Department. In addition to the resolution of the criminal charges, as part of a global settlement, UTC also resolved over 500 additional administrative charges with the State Department. Those charges involved more than 800 exports in violation of the Arms Export Control Act from the mid-1990s to 2011. In connection with the global settlement with the Justice and State Departments, PWC, UTC, and HSC agreed to pay more than $75 million in penalties, subject themselves to independent monitoring for several years, and be required to comply with an extensive training and remedial action program to strengthen their export compliance. This investigation was conducted by ICE, the DCIS, the FBI, the Department of Commerce, and the State Department.

Trade Secrets to Competitors in China—On May 7, 2012, an indictment returned in the District of Utah in April 2012 was unsealed charging two people and two companies with theft of trade secrets, wire fraud, and conspiracy to commit wire fraud in connection with the alleged theft of trade secrets from Orbit Irrigation Products, an irrigation company headquartered in Utah. The defendants are Janice Kuang Capener and Luo Jun, both citizens of China, as well as Sunhills International LLC, a California company established by Capener, and Zhejiang Hongchen Irrigation Equipment Co., LTD, a Chinese company under contract with Orbit. According to court documents, Capener worked at Orbit from June 2003 through Nov. 1, 2009, including serving chief of operations at Orbit's manufacturing plant in Ningbo, China. Capener allegedly stole Orbit trade secrets relating to sales and pricing and used that information for herself and others to the detriment of Orbit. Capener also allegedly worked with Jun, Sunhills International, and Zhejiang Hongchen Irrigation Equipment to devise a scheme to undermine Orbit's position in the marketplace using illegally obtained proprietary pricing information. Capener and Jun were arrested on May 4, 2012. This case was investigated by the FBI.

Drone, Missile, and Stealth Technology to China—On April 25, 2012, an amended criminal complaint was unsealed in the District of New Jersey charging Hui Sheng Shen, aka "Charlie," and Huan Ling Chang, aka, "Alice," both Taiwanese nationals, with conspiracy to violate the Arms Export Control Act. Both had previously been arrested on Feb. 25, 2012, in New York in connection with a complaint in New Jersey charging them with conspiring to import and importing crystal methamphetamine from Taiwan to the United States. According to the amended complaint, during negotiations with undercover FBI agents over the meth deal, the defendants asked FBI undercover agents if they could obtain an E-2 Hawkeye reconnaissance aircraft for a customer in China. In subsequent conversations, Shen and Chang allegedly indicated they were also interested in stealth technology for the F-22 fighter jet, as well missile engine technology, and various UAVs, including the RQ-11b Raven, a small, hand-launched UAV used by the US Armed Forces. Shen and Chang allegedly stated that their clients were connected to the Chinese government and its intelligence service. According to the complaint, they sent undercover agents a code book to facilitate communications relating to the proposed arms exports and opened a bank account in Hong Kong to receive and disburse funds related to the transactions. On a visit to New York in February 2012, the defendants allegedly examined a Raven RQ-11b UAV and manuals relating to the RQ-4 Global Hawk UAV (provided by undercover FBI agents) that they allegedly intended to export to China. Shen and Chang were arrested shortly thereafter. The export investigation was conducted by the FBI, while ICE was responsible for a parallel investigation into the import of counterfeit goods from China involving other defendants.

Thermal Imaging Cameras to China—On April 23, 2012, Jason Jian Liang, the owner and operator of Sanwave International Corporation in Huntington Beach, California, was sentenced to

46 months in prison and three years' supervised release after pleading guilty on July 18, 2011, in the Central District of California to violations stemming from his illegal exports of thermal imaging cameras to Hong Kong and China. Lian was first indicted on June 2, 2010. An Aug. 18, 2010, superseding indictment charged Liang with illegally exporting more thermal imaging cameras to China without first having obtained the required licenses. The cameras in question were manufactured by L-3 Communications Infrared Products and were designated by the Commerce Department as an export-controlled item that could not be exported to China for national security and regional stability reasons. Ultimately, Lian admitted making seven illegal exports of 300-D thermal imaging cameras over a 31-month period. All told, he exported 63 cameras.

DuPont Trade Secrets to China—On March 2, 2012, former DuPont scientist Tze Chao pleaded guilty in the Northern District of California to conspiracy to commit economic espionage, admitting that he provided trade secrets concerning DuPont's proprietary titanium dioxide manufacturing process to companies he knew were controlled by the government of the PRC. On Feb. 7, 2012, a grand jury in San Francisco returned a superseding indictment charging Chao and four other individuals, as well as five companies, with economic espionage and theft of trade secrets for their roles in a long-running effort to obtain US trade secrets from DuPont for the benefit of companies controlled by the PRC. The five individuals named in the indictment were Walter Liew, his wife Christina Liew, Hou Shengdong, Robert Maegerle, and Tze Chao. The five companies named as defendants are Pangang Group Company Ltd., Pangang Group Steel Vanadium Industry Company Ltd., Pangang Group Titanium Industry Company Ltd., Pangang Group International Economic & Trading Co., and USA Performance Technology, Inc. (USAPTI). According to the superseding indictment, the PRC government identified as a priority the development of chloride-route titanium dioxide (TiO_2) production capabilities. TiO_2 is a commercially valuable white pigment with numerous uses, including coloring paint, plastics, and paper. To achieve that goal, companies controlled by the PRC government, specifically the Pangang Group companies named in the indictment, and employees of those companies conspired and attempted to illegally obtain TiO_2 technology that had been developed over many years of research and development by DuPont. The Pangang Group companies were aided in their efforts by individuals in the United States who had obtained TiO_2 trade secrets and were willing to sell those secrets for significant sums of money. Defendants Walter Liew, Christina Liew, Hou Shengdong, Robert Maegerle, and Tze Chao allegedly obtained and possessed TiO_2 trade secrets belonging to DuPont. Each of these individuals allegedly sold information containing DuPont TiO_2 trade secrets to the Pangang Group companies for the purpose of helping those companies develop large-scale chloride-route TiO_2 production capability in the PRC, including a planned 100,000-ton TiO_2 factory at Chongqing, PRC. The Liews, USAPTI, and one of its predecessor companies, Performance Group, entered into contracts worth in excess of $20 million to convey TiO_2 trade secret technology to Pangang Group companies. The Liews allegedly received millions of dollars of proceeds from these contracts. The proceeds were wired through the United States, Singapore, and ultimately back into several bank accounts in the PRC in the names of relatives of Christina Liew. The object of the defendants' conspiracy was to convey DuPont's secret chloride-route technology to the PRC companies for the purpose of building modern TiO_2 production facilities in the PRC without investing in time-consuming and expensive research and development. DuPont invented the chloride-route process for manufacturing TiO_2 in the late 1940s and since then has invested heavily in research and development to improve that production process. The global TiO_2 market has been valued at roughly $12 billion, and DuPont has the largest share of that market. This investigation was conducted by the FBI.

Dow Trade Secrets to China—On Jan. 12, 2012, Wen Chyu Liu, aka David W. Liou, a former research scientist at Dow Chemical Company in Louisiana, was sentenced in the Middle District of Louisiana to 60 months in prison and two years' supervised release, and was ordered to pay a $25,000 fine and to forfeit $600,000. Liu was convicted on Feb. 7, 2011, of one count of conspiracy to commit trade secret theft for stealing trade secrets from Dow and selling them to companies in China, and he was also convicted of one count of perjury. According to the evidence presented in court, Liou came to the United States from China for graduate work. He began working for Dow in 1965 and retired in 1992. Dow is a leading producer of the elastomeric polymer, chlorinated polyethylene (CPE). Dow's Tyrin CPE is used in a number of applications worldwide, such as automotive and industrial hoses, electrical cable jackets, and vinyl siding. While employed at Dow, Liou worked as a research scientist on various aspects of the development and manufacture of Dow elastomers, including Tyrin CPE. The evidence at trial established that Liou conspired with at least four current and former employees of Dow's facilities in Plaquemine, Louisiana, and in Stade, Germany, who had worked in Tyrin CPE production, to misappropriate those trade secrets in an effort to develop and market CPE process design packages to Chinese companies. Liou traveled throughout China to market the stolen information, and he paid current and former Dow employees for Dow's CPE-related material and information. In one instance, Liou bribed a then-employee at the Plaquemine facility with $50,000 in cash to provide Dow's process manual and other CPE-related information. The investigation was conducted by the FBI.

Military Accelerometers to China—On Jan. 4, 2012, Bulgarian authorities in Sofia, Bulgaria, arrested Bin Yang, aka "Raymond Yang," a citizen and resident of China, pursuant to a US provisional arrest warrant. A Dec. 7, 2011, criminal complaint filed in the Southern District of California charged Yang with smuggling goods from the United States and attempted illegal export to China of defense articles—specifically accelerometers used in aircraft, missiles, "smart" munitions, and measuring explosions. According to the complaint, Yang, operating out of Changsha Harsay Industry Co., Ltd., in Hunan, China, posted a request for Honeywell accelerometers in an online business-to-business forum in August 2010. An undercover federal agent responded to the request and agreed to supply the requested accelerometers. After nearly a year of negotiations, with no deal finalized, Yang allegedly asked for Endevco 7270-200K accelerometers, which are used for "smart" munitions, bunker-busting bombs, and measuring ground motions caused by nuclear and chemical explosions, among other things. In August and October 2011, Yang allegedly caused two payments totaling $4875 to be sent to the undercover agent as a down payment for the accelerometers. According to the complaint, Yang subsequently agreed to meet with the undercover agent in Bulgaria so the undercover agent could hand deliver two Endevco accelerometers to him. After his arrest in Bulgaria, Yang was charged on Jan. 13, 2012, in a five-count indictment returned in the Southern District of California. This investigation was conducted by ICE.

Dow Trade Secrets to China—On Dec. 21, 2011, Kexue Huang, a Chinese national and former resident of Indiana, was sentenced to 87 months in prison and three years' supervised release on charges of economic espionage to benefit a foreign university tied to the PRC and theft of trade secrets. On Oct. 18, 2011, Huang pleaded guilty in the Southern District of Indiana to these charges. In July 2010, Huang was charged in the Southern District of Indiana with misappropriating and transporting trade secrets to the PRC while working as a research scientist at Dow AgroSciences LLC. On Oct. 18, 2011, a separate indictment in the District of Minnesota charging Huang with stealing a trade secret from a second company, Cargill Inc., was unsealed. From January 2003 until February 2008, Huang was employed as a research scientist at Dow. In 2005, he became a research leader for Dow in strain development related to unique, proprietary organic insecticides marketed worldwide. Huang admitted that during his employment at Dow, he misappropriated several Dow trade secrets. According to plea documents, from 2007 to 2010, Huang transferred and delivered the stolen Dow trade secrets to individuals in Germany and the PRC. With the assistance of these individuals, Huang used the stolen materials to conduct unauthorized research to benefit foreign universities tied to the PRC. Huang also admitted that he pursued steps to develop and produce the misappropriated Dow trade secrets in the PRC. After Huang left Dow, he was hired in March 2008 by Cargill, an international producer and marketer of food, agricultural, financial, and industrial products and services. Huang worked as a biotechnologist for Cargill until July 2009. Huang admitted that during his employment with Cargill, he stole one of the company's trade secrets—a key component in the manufacture of a new food product, which he later disseminated to another person, specifically a student at Hunan Normal University in the PRC. According to the plea agreement, the aggregated loss from Huang's conduct exceeds $7 million but is less than $20 million. This investigation was conducted by the FBI.

Stolen US Military Night Vision and Optics to China and England—On Nov. 4, 2011, Phillip Andro Jamison, a former Gunner's Mate Petty Officer First Class in the US Navy stationed aboard Naval Amphibious Base Coronado, was sentenced to serve 30 months in prison for violating the Arms Export Control Act. Jamison pleaded guilty on April 28, 2011. On Sept. 9, 2010, he was indicted for trafficking in stolen government property, interstate transportation of stolen goods, and exporting defense articles without a license. The indictment alleged that Jamison, while assigned to work at his unit's armory, stole more than 280 items from the US Navy between October 2008 and September 2009 and then sold these items to customers via eBay, an Internet auction and shopping web site. The indictment further alleged that Jameson illegally exported to Hong Kong and England combat-grade night vision devices, riflescopes, and laser aiming devices without first obtaining the required export licenses from the State Department. Jamison admitted stealing the items and illegally exporting some of the technology to Hong Kong. The investigation was conducted by ICE and the Naval Criminal Investigative Service (NCIS).

Radiation-Hardened Defense and Aerospace Technology to China—On Oct. 27, 2011, Lian Yang, a resident of Woodinville, Washington, was sentenced in the Western District of Washington to 18 months in prison and a $10,000 fine. On March 24, 2011, Yang pleaded guilty to conspiring to violate the Arms Export Control Act by trying to sell radiation-hardened military and aerospace technology to China. Yang was arrested on Dec. 3, 2010, pursuant to a criminal complaint filed charging him with conspiracy to violate the Arms Export Control Act. According to the complaint, Yang attempted to purchase and export from the United States to China 300 radiation-hardened, programmable semiconductor devices that are used in satellites and are also classified as defense articles under the US Munitions List. The complaint alleges that Yang contemplated creating a shell company in the United States that would appear to be purchasing the parts, concealing the fact that the parts were to be shipped to China. Yang allegedly planned that false purchasing orders would be created indicating that parts that could be legally exported were being purchased, not restricted parts. It is believed that Yang and his co-conspirators allegedly wire-transferred $60,000 to undercover agents as partial payment for a sample of five devices. As part of the conspiracy, Yang allegedly negotiated a payment schedule with the undercover agents for the purchase and delivery of the remaining 300 devices in exchange for a total of $620,000. This investigation was conducted by the FBI, ICE, and the CBP.

Radiation-Hardened Aerospace Technology to China—On Sept. 30, 2011, defendants Hong Wei Xian, aka "Harry Zan," and Li Li, aka "Lea Li," were sentenced in the Eastern District of Virginia to 24 months in prison for conspiracy to violate the Arms Export Control Act and conspiracy to smuggle goods unlawfully from the United States, in connection with their efforts to export to China radiation-hardened microchips that are used in satellite systems and are classified as defense articles. Both defendants pleaded guilty to the charges on June 1, 2011. The defendants were arrested on Sept. 1, 2010, in Budapest by Hungarian authorities pursuant to a US provisional arrest warrant. On April 4, 2011, they made their initial court appearances in federal court in the Eastern District of Virginia after being extradited from Hungary. According to court documents, Zan and Li operated a company in China called Beijing Starcreates Space Science and Technology Development Company Limited. This firm was allegedly in the business of selling technology to China Aerospace and Technology Corporation, a Chinese government-controlled entity involved in the production and design of missile systems and launch vehicles. According to court documents, from April 2009 to Sept. 1, 2010, the defendants contacted a Virginia company seeking to purchase and export thousands of Programmable Read-Only Microchips (PROMs). The defendants ultimately attempted to purchase 40 PROMs from the Virginia firm and indicated to undercover agents that the PROMs were intended for China Aerospace and Technology Corporation. The investigation was conducted by ICE and the DCIS.

Outsourced Manufacture of Military Items—On Sept. 13, 2011, Staff Gasket Manufacturing Corporation, a defense contracting company in New Jersey, was sentenced in the District of New Jersey to five years' probation and ordered to pay $751,091 in restitution and an $800 special assessment. Eric Helf, Staff Gasket's president, was sentenced to three years' probation and was ordered to pay a $500 fine, and a final order of forfeiture was entered for $49,926. On April 19, 2011, Staff Gasket pleaded guilty to Arms Export Control Act and wire fraud violations, while Helf pleaded guilty to one count of wire fraud. From August 2004 to March 2006, Staff Gasket entered into contracts with the Department of Defense to provide replacement parts for use in military operations. Many of the parts to be supplied were critical application items and were thus required to be manufactured in the United States. Nonetheless, Staff Gasket contracted with foreign manufacturers and many of the parts ultimately supplied to the Defense Department, including lock pins for helicopters, were made overseas, were substandard, and failed in the field. As a result, Staff Gasket caused the Defense Department to sustain losses of some $751,091 in connection with the fraudulent contracts. This investigation was conducted by the DCIS and ICE.

Fighter Jet Parts to Singapore—On August 22, 2011, Russell Marshall was sentenced in the Southern District of Florida to three years' probation, while his Boynton Beach, Florida, company, Universal Industries Limited, Inc., was sentenced to one year probation and a $1000 fine in connection with an effort to illegally export J-85 engine blades for F-5 fighter jets to Singapore. Both defendants pleaded guilty on June 3, 2011. On April 21, 2011, Marshall and Universal Industries Limited, Inc., were charged with making false statements and violating the Arms Export Control Act. According to court documents, Marshall illegally attempted to export 200 J-85 engine blades for F-5 fighter jets to Singapore. Marshall allegedly failed to obtain the required State Department license for such exports and recorded the value of the parts as $2000 in invoices, when in fact the shipment of military parts was valued at more than $105,000. This investigation was conducted by ICE.

Holographic Weapons Sights and Firearms Parts to China and Japan—On Aug. 3, 2011, Andrew Vincent O'Donnell, of Georgia, was sentenced in the Northern District of Georgia to 37 months in prison and three years' supervised release for conspiracy to violate and violating the Arms Export Control Act and possessing short barrel rifles. O'Donnell operated an eBay online store called "LRA Tactical Gear" through which he sold various weapons parts and accessories, including military holographic weapons sights and gun parts. O'Donnell sold more than 50 export-controlled military holographic weapons sights to a customer in Hong Kong without the required export license, falsely labeling the shipments as toys. He also sold gun parts used to assemble an AR15/M16/M4 rifle to a customer in Japan after routing the parts through a third country to conceal the illegal nature of the exports. This investigation was conducted by ICE.

Machine Gun Specifications and Components to China—On July 12, 2011, Swiss Technology (Swiss Tech), Inc., a company in Clifton, New Jersey, that makes equipment for the US military, pleaded guilty in the District of New Jersey to a one-count criminal information charging the firm with conspiracy to violate the Arms Export Control Act from August 2004 to about July 2009. Swiss Tech also consented to pay restitution in the amount of $1.1 million to the Defense Department in connection with fraudulent contracts. Swiss Tech was under contract with the Department of Defense to manufacture components for the M249 machine gun. In order to lower its manufacturing costs, Swiss Tech sent defense articles, including specification drawings and parts samples, to a company in the PRC so that the Chinese company could make these machine gun components for Swiss Tech. Swiss Tech did not have the required State Department license for exports of these munitions to China. After receiving the components from the Chinese company, Swiss Tech then shipped the defense articles and other parts to the Department of Defense, purporting that the defense articles were made by Swiss Tech in conformance with its contract. Among other things, Swiss Tech illegally exported to China specifications for the production of M249 machine gun parts, as well as components for the M249 machine gun, and M16 or M4 rifle. This investigation was conducted by the DCIS and ICE.

Illegal Exports of Military Night Vision Technology to China, Singapore, and United Kingdom—On April 12, 2011, the Justice Department announced that a government motion to dismiss the remaining deferred criminal charge against ITT Corporation, the leading manufacturer of military night vision equipment for the US Armed Forces, was granted by the court. On March 27, 2007, ITT Corporation pleaded guilty in the Western District of Virginia to two criminal counts of violating the Arms Export Control act stemming from its illegal exports of restricted military night vision data to China, Singapore, and the United Kingdom and omission of statements of material fact in required arms exports reports. As part of the plea agreement, ITT Corporation agreed to invest $50 million toward the development of the most advanced night vision systems in the world for the US Armed Forces. The Justice Department agreed to dismiss the remaining criminal charge against ITT Corporation after ITT Corporation implemented an extensive remedial plan overseen by an independent monitor to prevent future Arms Export Control Act violations. ITT Corporation and the Justice Department will continue to work together to utilize resources set aside by the deferred prosecution agreement to further the development and fielding of the most advanced night vision technology. This investigation was conducted by the DCIS and ICE.

Military Technical Data to China—On March 8, 2011, Sixing Liu, aka "Steve Liu," of Deerfield, Illinois, was arrested in Chicago on a criminal complaint filed in the District of New Jersey charging him with one count of exporting defense-related technical data without a license. Liu, a native of China with a doctorate degree in electrical engineering, worked as a senior staff engineer for Space & Navigation, a New Jersey-based division of L-3 Communications, from March 2009 through November 2010. He was part of a team that worked on precision navigation devices and other innovative components for the US Department of Defense. Liu was never issued a company laptop or approved to possess the company's work product outside the firm's New Jersey facility. In November 2010, he traveled to China and, upon his return to the United States later that month, CBP inspectors found him to be in possession of a computer that contained hundreds of documents related to the company's projects, as well as images of Liu making a presentation at a technology conference sponsored by the PRC government. Many of the documents on his computer were marked as containing sensitive proprietary company information or export-controlled technical data. The State Department verified that information on Liu's computer was export-controlled technical data that relate to defense items on the US Munitions List. The investigation was conducted by the FBI and ICE.

Electronics Used in Military Radar and Electronic Warfare to China—On Jan. 27, 2011, Yufeing Wei was sentenced in the District of Massachusetts to 36 months in prison, while on Jan. 26, 2011, her co-defendant, Zhen Zhou Wu, was sentenced to 97 months in prison. Their company, Chitron Electronics, Inc., was fined $15.5 million. Wei, Wu, and Chitron Electronics, Inc., were convicted at trial on May 17, 2010, of conspiring for a period of more than 10 years to illegally export to the PRC military electronics components and sensitive electronics used in military phased array radar, electronic warfare, and missile systems. Several Chinese military entities were among those receiving the exported equipment. Wu and Wei were also both convicted of filing false shipping documents with the US government. As proven at trial, defendants illegally exported military electronic components to China through Hong Kong. The electronics exported are primarily used in military phased array radar, electronic warfare, military guidance systems, and military satellite communications. The defendants also illegally exported Commerce Department–controlled electronics components to China with military applications such as electronic warfare, military radar, and satellite communications systems. Wu founded and controlled Chitron, with headquarters in Shenzhen, China, and a US office located in Waltham, Massachusetts, where defendant Wei served as Manager. Wu and Chitron sold electronics from the US to Chinese military factories and military research institutes, including numerous institutes of the China Electronics Technology Group Corporation, which is responsible for the procurement, development, and manufacture of electronics for the Chinese military. Since as early as 2002, Wu referred to Chinese military entities as Chitron's major customer and employed an engineer at Chitron's Shenzhen office to work with Chinese military customers. By 2007, 25% of Chitron's sales were to Chinese military entities. Shenzhen Chitron Electronics Company Limited, Wu's Chinese company through which US electronics were delivered to the Chinese military and other end users, was also indicted. On Feb. 9, 2011, Chitron–Shenzhen received a fine of $1.9 million for refusing to appear for trial. Co-defendant Bo Li, aka Eric Lee, previously pled guilty to making false statements on shipping documents. The case was investigated by BIS, ICE, the FBI, and the DCIS.

Stealth Missile Exhaust Designs and Military Technical Data to China—On Jan. 24, 2011, a federal judge in the District of Hawaii sentenced Noshir Gowadia, 66, of Maui to 32 years in prison for communicating classified national defense information to the PRC, illegally exporting military technical data, as well as money laundering, filing false tax returns, and other offenses. On Aug. 9, 2010, a federal jury in the District of Hawaii found Gowadia guilty of 14 criminal violations after six days of deliberation and a 40-day trial. These included five criminal offenses relating to his design for the PRC of a low-signature cruise missile exhaust system capable of rendering a PRC cruise missile resistant to detection by infrared missiles. The jury also convicted Gowadia of three counts of illegally communicating classified information regarding lock-on range for infrared missiles against the US B-2 bomber to persons not authorized to receive such information. Gowadia was also convicted of unlawfully exporting classified information about the B-2, illegally retaining information related to US national defense at his home, money laundering, and filing false tax returns for the years 2001 and 2002. Gowadia was an engineer with Northrop Grumman Corporation from 1968 to 1986, during which time he contributed to the development of the unique propulsion system and low observable capabilities of the B-2 bomber. Gowadia continued to work on classified matters as a contractor with the US government until 1997, when his security clearance was terminated. Evidence at trial revealed that from July 2003 to June 2005, Gowadia took six trips to the PRC to provide defense services in the form of design, test support, and test data analysis of technologies for the purpose of assisting the PRC with its cruise missile system by developing a stealthy exhaust nozzle and was paid at least $110,000 by the PRC. The jury convicted Gowadia of two specific transmissions of classified information: a PowerPoint presentation on the exhaust nozzle of a PRC cruise missile project and an evaluation of the effectiveness of a redesigned nozzle, and a computer file providing his signature prediction of a PRC cruise missile outfitted with his modified exhaust nozzle and associated predictions in relation to a US air-to-air missile. The prosecution also produced evidence that documented Gowadia's use of three foreign entities he controlled, including a Liechtenstein charity purportedly for the benefit of children, to disguise the income he received from foreign countries. This case was investigated by the FBI, the US Air Force Office of Special Investigations, the IRS, the CBP, and ICE.

Restricted Electronics to China—On Oct. 11, 2010, York Yuan Chang, known as David Zhang, and his wife, Leping Huang, were arrested on charges in the Central District of California of conspiring to export restricted electronics technology to the PRC without a license and making false statements. According to the Oct. 9, 2010, criminal complaint, the defendants are the owners of General Technology Systems Integration, Inc., (GTSI), a California company involved in the export of technology to the PRC. GTSI allegedly entered into contracts with the 24th Research Institute of the China Electronics Technology Corporation Group in China to design and transfer to the PRC technology for the development of two types of high-performance analog-to-digital converters (ADCs). The defendants allegedly hired two engineers to design the technology and provide training to individuals in the PRC. Twice in 2009, CBP officials stopped the engineers upon their return to the United States and allegedly found computer files and documents indicating illegal technology transfer involving GTSI and China. According to the complaint, Chang and Huang allegedly sought to cover up the project after authorities contacted the engineers. The ADCs that the defendants allegedly attempted to export to the PRC are subject to export controls for national security and anti-terrorism reasons. This investigation was conducted by the FBI, BIS, ICE, the IRS, and the DCIS.

Thermal Imaging Cameras to China—On May 14, 2010, Sam Ching Sheng Lee, part-owner and chief operations manager of Multimillion Business Associate Corporation ("MBA"), pleaded guilty in the Central District of California to conspiracy to violate the International Emergency Economic Powers for illegally exporting national security–controlled thermal imaging cameras to China. His nephew, Charles Yu Hsu Lee, pleaded guilty the same day to misprision of a felony for the same activity. The Lees were arrested on Dec. 30, 2008, in Hacienda Heights, California, pursuant to a Dec. 16, 2008, indictment charging them with conspiracy to export and exporting national security–controlled items without a license in violation of the IEEPA. The indictment alleged that the defendants, doing business as MBA, an import/export business located in Hacienda Heights, assisted persons in China to illegally procure export-controlled thermal imaging cameras. During the period between April 2002 and July 2007, defendants allegedly exported a total of 10 thermal imaging cameras to China in circumvention of export laws. After being advised of strict export restrictions, Charles Lee allegedly purchased the cameras from US suppliers for approximately $9500 a piece by withholding the fact that the devices were destined to China. His uncle, Sam Lee, then received the devices and, through his company, arranged for their shipment to Shanghai, China, without obtaining proper licenses. One of the recipients is alleged to be an employee of a company in Shanghai engaged in the development of infrared technology. The thermal imaging cameras are controlled for export to China by the Department of Commerce for national security and regional stability reasons because of their use in a wide variety of military and civilian applications. This investigation was conducted by the Export and Anti-proliferation Global Law Enforcement (EAGLE) Task Force in the Central District of California.

Economic Espionage/Theft of Space Shuttle and Rocket Secrets for China—On Feb. 11, 2010, former Rockwell and Boeing engineer Dongfan "Greg" Chung was sentenced to 188 months' imprisonment and three years' supervised release after his July 16, 2009, conviction in the Central District of California. Chung was convicted of charges of economic espionage and acting as an illegal agent of the PRC, for whom he stole restricted technology and Boeing trade secrets, including information related to the Space Shuttle program and the Delta IV rocket. According to the judge's ruling, Chung served as an illegal agent of China for more than 30 years and kept more than 300,000 pages of documents reflecting Boeing trade secrets stashed in his home as part of his mission of stealing aerospace and military trade secrets from Boeing to assist the Chinese government. Chung sent Boeing trade secrets to the PRC via the mail, via sea freight, via the Chinese consulate in San Francisco, and via a Chinese agent named Chi Mak. On several occasions, Chung also used the trade secrets that he misappropriated from Boeing to prepare detailed briefings that he later presented to Chinese officials in the PRC. Chung was originally arrested on Feb. 11, 2008, in Southern California after being indicted on eight counts of economic espionage, one count of conspiracy to commit economic espionage, one count of acting as an unregistered foreign agent, one count of obstruction of justice, and three counts of making false statements to the FBI. The investigation was conducted by the FBI and NASA.

Carbon Fiber Material with Rocket and Spacecraft Applications to China—On Oct. 8, 2009, three individuals were sentenced in the District of Minnesota for illegally exporting high modulus carbon fiber material to the China Academy of Space Technology. Jian Wei Ding was sentenced to 46 months in prison. Kok Tong Lim was sentenced to just over one year of confinement because of his cooperation in the case, while Ping Cheng was sentenced to one year probation due to his cooperation. On March 20, 2009, Ding pleaded guilty to one count of conspiracy to violate the Export Administration Regulations. Cheng entered his plea on Feb. 13, 2009, and Lim entered his plea on March 9, 2009. All three men were indicted on Oct. 28, 2008, for conspiring to illegally export to China controlled carbon fiber material with applications in aircraft, rockets, spacecraft, and uranium enrichment process. The intended destination for some of the materials was the China Academy of Space Technology, which oversees research institutes working on spacecraft systems for the PRC government. For national security, nuclear proliferation, and antiterrorism reasons, the US government requires a license to export these carbon fiber materials. Jian Wei Ding was a resident of Singapore and owned or was affiliated with various Singaporean import/export companies, including Jowa Globaltech Pte Ltd., FirmSpace Pte Ltd., and Far Eastron Co. Pte Ltd. Kok Tong Lim was a resident of Singapore and once was affiliated with FirmSpace, Pte Ltd. Ping Cheng was a resident of New York and the sole shareholder of Prime Technology Corporation. This investigation was conducted by ICE and BIS.

Restricted Integrated Circuits with Military Applications to China—On Aug. 3, 2009, William Chai-Wai Tsu, an employee of a Beijing-based military contracting company called Dimigit Science & Technology Co. Ltd., and the vice president of a Hacienda Heights, California, front company called Cheerway, Inc., was sentenced in the Central District of California to 40 months in prison. Tsu illegally exported more than 400 restricted integrated circuits with applications in military radar systems to China over a 10-month period, according to court documents. These dual-use items are restricted for export for national security reasons. Tsu purchased many of the items from US distributors after falsely telling these US companies that he was not exporting the circuits abroad. According to court documents, Tsu supplied restricted US technology to several customers in China, including the "704 Research Institute," which is known as the "Aerospace Long March Rocket Technology Company" and is affiliated with the state-owned China Aerospace Science & Technology Corporation. Tsu's employer in China, Dimigit, boasted in brochures that its mission was "providing the motherland with safe, reliable and advanced electronic technical support in the revitalization of our national military industry." Tsu was indicted in the Central District of California on Feb. 6, 2009, on charges of violating the IEEPA. He later pleaded guilty to two federal counts of the indictment on March 13, 2009. This case was the product of an investigation by the EAGLE Task Force in the Central District of California, which includes BIS, ICE, the FBI, the CBP, the Diplomatic Security Service (DSS), and the Transportation Security Administration (TSA).

Restricted Thermal Imaging Technology to China—On July 27, 2009, Zhi Yong Guo, a resident of Beijing, was sentenced in the Central District of California to 60 months in prison, while Tah Wei Chao, also a resident of Beijing, was sentenced to 20 months in prison. Both were sentenced in connection with a plot to procure and illegally export thermal imaging cameras to the PRC without obtaining the required export licenses. Guo and Chao were indicted on federal charges on July 17, 2008. Chao pleaded guilty to three federal counts in July 2008. On Feb. 23, 2009, following a one-week trial, Guo was convicted of two federal counts. The case was related to 10 cameras concealed in luggage destined for China in April 2008. The export of these thermal imaging cameras to China is controlled by the Department of Commerce for national security and regional stability reasons because of their use in a wide variety of civilian and military applications. In March 2008, Chao ordered 10 thermal imaging cameras from FLIR Systems, Inc. for $53,000. Representatives from FLIR Systems repeatedly warned Chao that the cameras could not be exported without a license. Both Chao and Guo were arrested at the Los Angeles International Airport in April 2008 after authorities recovered the 10 cameras that had been hidden in their suitcases. In addition to the 10 cameras intercepted by federal authorities, Chao admitted that, acting at the behest of Guo, he shipped three cameras to China in October 2007. The evidence at trial showed that Guo, an engineer and a managing director of a technology development company in Beijing, directed Chao to obtain the cameras for Guo's clients, the Chinese Special Police and the Special Armed Police. This case was the product of an investigation by the EAGLE Task Force in the Central District of California, including BIS, ICE, the FBI, the CBP, the DSS, and the TSA.

Military Technical Data on Unmanned Aerial Vehicles to China—On July 1, 2009, Dr. John Reece Roth was sentenced in the Eastern District of Tennessee to 48 months in prison and two years' supervised release and was ordered to pay a $1700 assessment fee for illegally exporting sensitive military technical data related to a US Air Force contract. Roth, a former Professor Emeritus at the University of Tennessee, was convicted on Sept. 2, 2008, of 15 counts of violating the Arms Export Control Act, one count of conspiracy, and one count of wire fraud. Roth had illegally exported military technical data relating to plasma technology designed to be deployed on the wings of UAVs or "drones" operating as a weapons or surveillance systems. The illegal exports involved technical data related to an Air Force research contract that Roth provided to foreign nationals from China and Iran. In addition, Roth carried multiple documents containing controlled military data with him on a trip to China and caused other controlled military data to be e-mailed to an individual in China. On Aug. 20, 2008, Atmospheric Glow Technologies, Inc. (AGT), a privately held plasma technology company in Tennessee, also pleaded guilty to charges of illegally exporting US military data about drones to a citizen of China in violation of the Arms Export Control Act. AGT was sentenced on Feb. 12, 2010, and was ordered to pay a $4000 assessment fee and a $25,000 fine. Roth and AGT were first charged on May 20, 2008. In a related case, on April 15, 2008, Daniel Max Sherman, a physicist who formerly worked at AGT, pleaded guilty to an information charging him with conspiracy to violate the Arms Export Control Act in connection with this investigation. Sherman was later sentenced to 14 months in prison on Aug. 10, 2009, after cooperating in the investigation. The investigation was conducted by the FBI, ICE, the US Air Force Office of Special Investigations, the DCIS, and BIS.

Military Night Vision Technology to China—On July 1, 2009, Bing Xu, of Nanjing, China, was sentenced in the District of New Jersey to 22 months in prison followed by two years of supervised release after pleading guilty on Feb. 24, 2009, to conspiracy to illegally export military-grade night vision technology to China. Xu, a manager at Everbright Science and Technology, Ltd., a company in Nanjing, China, admitted that he conspired with others at Everbright to purchase certain night vision technology from a company in the United States, which required a license from the State Department for export. Xu admitted that he and others at Everbright first attempted to obtain the necessary export license for the night vision equipment. When the license application was denied by the Department of State, Xu agreed with others at Everbright to take steps to export the night vision optical equipment illegally. Xu has been in custody since his arrest in on October 2007 pursuant to a criminal complaint. Xu arrived in New York on Oct. 26, 2007, from China a day after his Chinese employer wire transferred $14,080 to agents as payment for the purchase of the equipment. The investigation was conducted by ICE and the DCIS.

Thermal Imaging Cameras to China—On June 9, 2009, a federal grand jury in the Southern District of Ohio indicted Hing Shing Lau, also known as Victor Lau, a foreign national living in Hong Kong, PRC, on charges of trying to buy 12 infrared thermal imaging cameras from a Dayton-area company in order to illegally export the cameras to Hong Kong and China. The indictment alleges that Lau tried to buy 12 thermal imaging cameras manufactured in Texas by contacting a company in the Dayton area. On three occasions, he wire transferred a total of $39,514 from Hong Kong to the United States as partial payment for the cameras. The indictment charges Lau with two counts of violating export control laws and four counts of money laundering. Canadian authorities arrested Lau on June 3, 2009, at the Toronto International Airport pursuant to a provisional arrest warrant issued by US authorities. The investigation was conducted by the FBI and BIS, with the assistance of the US Department of State.

Amplifiers and Missile Target Acquisition Technology to China—On May 14, 2009, Joseph Piquet, the owner and President of AlphaTronX, a company in Port St. Lucie, Florida, that produces electronic components, was sentenced in the Southern District of Florida to 60 months in prison followed by two years' supervised release. On March 5, 2009, he was convicted of seven counts arising from a conspiracy to purchase military electronic components from Northrop Grumman Corporation and to ship them to Hong Kong and the PRC without first obtaining required export licenses under the Arms Export Control Act and the IEEPA. Among those items involved in the conspiracy were high-power amplifiers designed for use by the US military in early warning radar and missile target acquisition systems, as well as low-noise amplifiers that have both commercial and military use. Piquet was first indicted on June 5, 2008, along with his company, AlphaTronX, Inc., as well as Thompson Tam, and Ontime Electronics Technology Limited. Tam is a director of Ontime Electronics, an electronics company in China. On March 2, 2009, the Court ordered the dismissal of the indictment against AlphaTronX. This investigation was conducted by BIS and ICE.

Trade Secrets to China—On April 10, 2009, Yan Zhu, a Chinese citizen in the United States on a work visa, was arrested in the District of New Jersey on charges of theft of trade secrets, conspiracy, wire fraud, and theft of honest services fraud in connection with a plot to steal software from his former US employer and sell a modified version to the Chinese government after he was fired. Zhu was employed as a senior environmental engineer from May 2006 until his termination in July 2008. Zhu worked for a comprehensive multimedia environmental information management portal that developed a proprietary software program for the Chinese market that allows users to manage air emissions, ambient water quality, and groundwater quality. This investigation was conducted by the FBI.

Restricted Technology to China—On April 7, 2009, Fu-Tain Lu was arrested in San Francisco pursuant to an April 1, 2009, indictment in the Northern District of California charging him with lying to federal agents and conspiring to illegally export restricted microwave amplifier technology to China. According to the indictment, Lu, and the two companies he founded, Fushine Technology, Inc., of Cupertino, California, and Everjet Science and Technology Corporation, based in China, conspired to export sensitive microwave amplifier technology that was restricted for national security reasons to China without first obtaining a Commerce Department license. On Feb. 17, 2010, a superseding indictment was returned charging Fu-Tain Lu, Fushine Technology, Inc., and Everjet Science and Technology Corporation with conspiracy to violate export regulations and making false statements. This investigation was conducted by the Department of Commerce (BIS), the FBI, ICE, and the CBP.

Rocket/Space Launch Technical Data to China—On April 7, 2009, Shu Quan-Sheng, a native of China, naturalized US citizen, and PhD physicist, was sentenced to 51 months in prison for illegally exporting space launch technical data and defense services to the PRC and offering bribes to Chinese government officials. Shu pleaded guilty on Nov. 17, 2008, in the Eastern District of Virginia to a three-count criminal information. He was arrested on Sept. 24, 2008. He was the President, Secretary, and Treasurer of AMAC International, a high-tech company located in Newport News, Virginia, and with an office in Beijing, China. Shu provided the PRC with assistance in the design and development of a cryogenic fueling system for space launch vehicles to be used at the heavy payload launch facility located in the southern island province of Hainan, PRC. The Hainan facility will house launch vehicles designed to send space stations and satellites into orbit, as well as provide support for manned space flight and future lunar missions. Shu also illegally exported to the PRC technical data related to the design and manufacture of a "Standard 100 M3 Liquid Hydrogen (LH) 2 Tank." In addition, Shu offered approximately $189,300 in bribes to government officials with the PRC's 101 Institute to induce the award of a hydrogen liquefier project to a French company he represented. In January 2007, the $4 million hydrogen liquefier project was awarded to the French company that Shu represented. This investigation was conducted by the FBI, ICE, BIS, and the DCIS.

Miniature Unmanned Aerial Vehicle Components to China—On March 12, 2009, a federal grand jury in the District of Columbia returned an indictment charging Yaming Nina Qi Hanson, her husband Harold Dewitt Hanson (an employee at Walter Reed Army Medical Center), and a Maryland company, Arc International, LLC, with illegally exporting miniature UAV Autopilots to a company in the PRC. The UAV components are controlled for export to China for national security reasons. According to court documents, beginning in 2007, the Hansons began attempting to acquire the autopilots from a Canadian manufacturer in order to re-export them to Xi'an Xiangyu Aviation Technical Group in China. Qi Hanson initially represented that the autopilots would be used for a model airplane civilian flying club in China. When Canadian company officials questioned the utility of autopilots—designed for use on unmanned aircraft—for flying club hobbyists, Qi Hanson claimed that autopilots would be used on US aircraft to record thunderstorm and tornado developments and ice-pack melting rates in the arctic. On or about August 7, 2008, after having fraudulently taken delivery of 20 of these autopilots (valued at $90,000), Qi Hanson boarded a plane in the United States bound for Shanghai, and hand delivered the items to the Xi'an

Xiangyu Aviation Technical Group in China. Both Hansons ultimately pleaded guilty on Nov. 13, 2009, to felony false statement violations. On Feb. 3, 2010, Harold Dewitt Hanson was sentenced to 24 months' imprisonment, while his wife, Yaming Nina Qi Hanson, was sentenced to time served. The investigation was conducted by BIS and the FBI.

Restricted Electronic Components to China—On Jan. 20, 2009, Michael Ming Zhang and Policarpo Coronado Gamboa were arrested pursuant to indictments in the Central District of California charging them with separate schemes involving the illegal export of controlled US electronic items to China and the illegal trafficking of counterfeit electronic components from China into the United States. Zhang was the president of J.J. Electronics, a Rancho Cucamonga, California, business, while Gamboa owned and operated Sereton Technology, Inc., a Foothill Ranch, California, business. Zhang allegedly exported to China dual-use electronic items that have uses in US Army battle tanks. He also allegedly imported and sold in the United States roughly 4300 Cisco electronic components bearing counterfeit marks from China. Gamboa is charged with conspiring with Zhang to import Sony electronic components with counterfeit marks from China for distribution in the United States. On July 9, 2009, Gamboa pleaded guilty to one count of the indictment and was later sentenced to five years' probation and was ordered to pay $13,600 restitution to Sony Electronics. On July 6, 2009, Zhang pleaded guilty to count one in each of the indictments. The case was investigated by the FBI, BIS, the DCIS, ICE, the US Postal Inspection Service, and the Orange County Sheriff's Department, in conjunction with the EAGLE Task Force in the Central District of California.

Trade Secrets to China—On Dec. 9, 2008, in the Northern District of Illinois, Hanjuan Jin was charged in a superseding indictment that added three counts of economic espionage in violation of 18 U.S.C. § 1831. The charges were added to an April 1, 2008, indictment that charged Jin with theft of trade secrets under 18 U.S.C. § 1832. Jin is a former Motorola employee who started with the company in 1998. On February 28, 2007, one day after quitting Motorola, Jin was stopped at O'Hare airport with over 1000 Motorola documents in her possession, both in hard copy and electronic format. A review of Motorola computer records showed that Jin accessed a large number of Motorola documents late at night. At the time she was stopped, Jin was traveling on a one-way ticket to China. The section 1831 charges are based on evidence that Jin intended that the trade secrets she stole from Motorola would benefit the Chinese military. Motorola had spent hundreds of millions of dollars on research and development for the proprietary data that Jin allegedly stole. The investigation was conducted by the FBI, with assistance from the CBP.

Stolen Trade Secrets to Chinese Nationals—On Nov. 21, 2008, Fei Ye and Ming Zhong were sentenced in the Northern District of California to one year in prison each, based in part on their cooperation, after pleading guilty on Dec. 14, 2006, to charges of economic espionage for possessing trade secrets stolen from two Silicon Valley technology companies. The pair admitted that their company was to have provided a share of any profits made on sales of the stolen chips to Chinese entities. The case marked the first convictions in the nation for economic espionage. They were first indicted on Dec. 4, 2002. The investigation was conducted by ICE, the FBI, and the CBP.

Military Accelerometers to China—On Sept. 26, 2008, Qing Li was sentenced in the Southern District of California to 12 months and one day in custody, followed by three years of supervised release, and was ordered to pay $7500 for conspiracy to smuggle military-grade accelerometers from the United States to the PRC. Li pleaded guilty on June 9, 2008, to violating Title 18, USC Section 554. She was indicted for the offense on Oct. 18, 2007. According to court papers, Li conspired with an individual in China to locate and procure as many as 30 Endevco 7270A-200K accelerometers for what her co-conspirator described as a "special" scientific agency in China. This accelerometer has military applications in "smart" bombs and missile development and in calibrating the g-forces of nuclear and chemical explosions. The investigation was conducted by ICE and the DCIS.

Military Aircraft Components to China and Iran—On Aug. 28, 2008, Desmond Dinesh Frank, a citizen and resident of Malaysia, was sentenced to 23 months in prison after pleading guilty on May 16, 2008, to several felonies in the District of Massachusetts in connection with a plot to illegally export military items to China and Iran. A six-count indictment returned on Nov. 15, 2007, charged Frank, the operator of Asian Sky Support, Sdn., Bhd., in Malaysia, with conspiring to illegally export items to Iran, conspiring to illegally export C-130 military aircraft training equipment to China, illegally exporting defense articles, smuggling, and two counts of money laundering. Frank was arrested in Hawaii on Oct. 8, 2007, by ICE agents. Frank conspired with others to illegally export and cause the re-export of goods, technology, and services to Iran without first obtaining the required authorization from the Treasury Department. He also conspired with others to illegally export 10 indicators, servo driven tachometers—which are military training components used in C-130 military flight simulators—from the United States to Malaysia and, ultimately, to Hong Kong, China, without the required license from the State Department. This investigation was conducted by ICE, BIS, and the DCIS.

Military Laser Aiming Devices and Fighter Pilot Cueing Systems to Taiwan—On Aug. 18, 2008, Yen Ching Peng was arraigned in the Southern District of New York on Arms Export Control Act violations, as well as money laundering and smuggling violations after being extradited from Hong Kong. Among other things, Peng allegedly attempted to illegally export to Taiwan infrared laser aiming devices, thermal weapons sights, and a Joint Helmet Mounted Cueing System. On occasion, Peng requested that military items be delivered to his associate, Peter Liu, in New York for delivery in Taiwan. On Dec. 11, 2007, Peng was arrested in Hong Kong, while Liu was arrested in New York. Liu later pleaded guilty and was sentenced to 30 months in prison on Aug. 7, 2008. On Dec. 12, 2008, Peng pleaded guilty to five counts of the indictment against him. The investigation was conducted by ICE and the DCIS.

US Military Source Code and Trade Secrets to China—On June 18, 2008, Xiaodong Sheldon Meng was sentenced in the Northern District of California to 24 months in prison and three years of supervised release, and was ordered to pay a $10,000 fine for committing economic espionage and violating the Arms Export Control Act. Meng pleaded guilty in August 2007 to violating the Economic Espionage Act by misappropriating a trade secret used to simulate motion for military training and other purposes, with the intent to benefit China's Navy Research Center in Beijing. He also pleaded guilty to violating the Arms Export Control Act for illegally exporting military source code involving a program used for training military fighter pilots. Meng was the first defendant in the country to be convicted of exporting military source code pursuant to the Arms Export Control Act. He was also the first defendant to be sentenced under the Economic Espionage Act. Meng was charged in a superseding indictment on Dec. 13, 2006. The investigation was conducted by the FBI and ICE.

Controlled Amplifiers to China—On June 6, 2008, WaveLab, Inc. of Reston, Virginia, was sentenced in the Eastern District of Virginia to one year of supervised probation and was ordered to pay a $15,000 fine, together with $85,000 in forfeiture previously ordered, for the unlawful export of hundreds of controlled power amplifiers to China. The exported items, which have potential military applications, are controlled and listed on the Commerce Control List for national security reasons. WaveLab purchased these items from a US company and assured the company that the products would not be exported from the United States, but would be sold domestically. WaveLab pleaded guilty on March 7, 2008, to a criminal information filed the same day. The investigation was conducted by BIS and ICE.

US Naval Warship Data to China—On March 24, 2008, Chi Mak, a former engineer with a US Navy contractor, was sentenced in the Central District of California to 293 months (more than 24 years) in prison for orchestrating a conspiracy to obtain US naval warship technology and to illegally export this material to China. Mak was found guilty at trial in May 2007 of conspiracy, two counts of attempting to violate export control laws, acting as an unregistered agent of the Chinese government, and making false statements. The investigation found that Mak had been given lists from co-conspirators in China that requested US Naval research related to nuclear submarines and other information. Mak gathered technical data about the Navy's current and future warship technology and conspired to illegally export these data to China. Mak's four co-defendants (and family members) also pleaded guilty in connection with the case. On April 21, 2008, Chi Mak's brother, Tai Mak, was sentenced to 10 years' imprisonment pursuant to a June 4, 2007, plea agreement in which he pleaded guilty to one count of conspiracy to export defense articles. On Oct. 2, 2008, Chi Mak's wife, Rebecca Chiu, was sentenced to 3 years in prison for her role in the plot. On Oct. 1, 2008, Fuk Heung Li was sentenced to three years' probation. On Sept. 24, 2007, Yui Mak was sentenced to 11 months' imprisonment. The investigation was conducted by the FBI, NCIS, and ICE.

Military Amplifiers to China—On Dec. 19, 2007, Ding Zhengxing, Su Yang, and Peter Zhu were indicted in the Western District of Texas for Arms Export Control Act violations in connection with an alleged plot to purchase and illegally export to China amplifiers that are controlled for military purposes. The amplifiers are used in digital radios and wireless area networks. Zhengxing and Yang were arrested in January 2008 after they traveled to Saipan to take possession of the amplifiers. Peter Zhu, of Shanghai Meuro Electronics Company Ltd., in China, remains at large. On July 1, 2009, Zhengxing was sentenced to 46 months' imprisonment. He pled guilty on October 17, 2008, to count 1 of the second superseding indictment. The case was investigated by ICE.

Military Night Vision Technology to China—On Dec. 3, 2007, Philip Cheng was sentenced in the Northern District of California to two years in prison and ordered to pay a $50,000 fine for his role in brokering the illegal export of a night vision camera and its accompanying technology to China in violation of federal laws and regulations. Mr. Cheng pleaded guilty on Oct. 31, 2006, to brokering the illegal export of Panther-series infrared camera, a device that makes use of "night vision" technology. He was indicted on June 3, 2004. The technology used in the device was controlled for national security reasons by the United States Department of State. The case was the result of a joint investigation by ICE, the FBI, the Department of Commerce, and the IRS.

Restricted Technology to China—On Aug. 1, 2007, Fung Yang, the president of Excellence Engineering Electronics, Inc., pleaded guilty in the Northern District of California to a charge of illegally exporting controlled microwave integrated circuits to China without the required authorization from the Department of Commerce. Yang was charged by information on July 31, 2007. The investigation was conducted by BIS and the FBI.

Telecommunications Equipment from China to Iraq—On April 10, 2007, Andrew Huang, the owner of McAndrew's, Inc., an international export company, pleaded guilty in the District of Connecticut to one count of making false statements to the FBI. Huang was charged in 2006 with operating as a representative for the Chinese Electronic System Engineering Corporation, the technology procurement arm of the government of China. According to court documents, Huang allegedly helped broker the illegal sale and transfer of millions of dollars worth of telecommunications equipment from China to Iraq between 1999 and 2001. Huang was sentenced to two years' probation and a $5000 fine. The investigation was conducted by the FBI, ICE, NCIS, the IRS, and BIS. China aside, many other countries were involved in the theft of trade secrets, weapons, sensitive electronics, military-related items, and the like during the years 2007 to early 2012. While not the subject of this book, the cases below reveal a continuing threat to the United States by many other nations that seek our high technology and various types of trade secrets for their own use. The other countries seeking such sensitive information and what secrets were targeted are as follows:

Thermal Imaging Scopes and Cameras to Belarus—Feb. 14, 2013
Hawk Air Defense Missile Batteries to Iran—Jan. 9, 2013
Specialty Coatings to Pakistani Nuclear Facility—December 2012
Missiles, Aviation Equipment, and Submarine Design Information to Tamil Tigers Terrorist Organization in Sri Lanka—Dec. 27, 2012
Inertial Navigation Units to the UAE and Turkey—Nov. 28, 2012
Military Aircraft Parts to Iran—Nov. 15, 2012
Military Aircraft Engines and Components to Venezuelan Air Force—Oct. 26, 2012
Military-Sensitive Parts to Iran—Oct. 24, 2012

Military Flight Helmets and Night Vision Goggles to Panama—Oct. 23, 2012
Trade Secrets to South Korea—Oct. 18, 2012
Controlled Microelectronics to Russian Military and Intelligence Agencies—October 3, 2012
Anti-Aircraft Missile, Anti-Tank Weapons, and Machine Guns to Mexican Drug Cartel—Aug. 22, 2012
TOW Missile Components to Iran—July 26, 2012
Materials for Gas Centrifuges and Other Nuclear-Related Goods to Iran—July 12, 2012
Firearms to Nigeria—May 3, 2012
Ballistic Vests, Ammunition, and Night Vision Devices to Mexico—April 23, 2012
Military Lasers to Canada—March 22, 2012
Defense Items to the United Arab Emirates—Feb. 24, 2012
Hawk Missile Batteries to Iran—February 2012
Computer-Related Technology to Iran—February 2012
Components for IEDs to Iran and Iraq—February 2012
Aircraft Components and Other Materials to Iran—February 2012
Military-Grade Thermal Weapon Sight and Rifle Scopes to Eastern Europe—February 2012
Military Antennae to Hong Kong and Singapore—January 2012
Carbon Fiber Material to Iran—January 2012
Handguns to the United Kingdom—January 2012
Infrared Military Technology to South Korea—December 2011
Fighter Jet Engines to Iran—December 2011
Laboratory and Radiation Detection Equipment to Iran—December 2011
Defense Items to the United Arab Emirates—December 2011
Defense Items to the Philippines—December 2011
Military-Grade Riflescopes Overseas—December 2011 [offered items for sale on eBay]
Trade Secrets to India—November 2011
Assault Rifles to Mexico—November 2011
Arms to Colombian Terrorists to Kill Americans—November 2011
Exports of Hazardous Materials to Saudi Arabia—November 2011
Military Night Vision Scopes to Russia—October 2011
Military Flight Simulation Technology to Iran—September 2011
F-5 Fighter Jet and Other Military Items to Iran—September 2011
US Technology to Pakistani Nuclear Facilities—September 2011
Assault Rifles to Mexico—August 2011
Trade Secrets to Foreign Government—August 2011 [provided data to undercover FBI officer posing as an Israeli intelligence officer]
Assault Rifles to Mexico—August 2011
Military Night Vision Overseas—August 2011
Fighter Jet Parts to Singapore—August 2011
TOW Missile Components to Iran—August 2011
Automatic Rifles and Plastic Explosives to the FARC—August 2011
Export/Import of Unmanned Aerial Vehicle—July 2011 [undercover ICE agents]
Assault Rifles to Mexico—July 2011
Firearms to Nigeria—July 2011
Vacuum Pumps with Potential Nuclear Applications to Iran—July 2011
Military Aircraft Components to Iran—June 2011
Scientific Research Equipment and Technology to Iran—June 2011
Machine Guns and Grenades to Mexico—May 2011
US Aircraft Components to Iran—May 2011
Military Technical Data to South Korea—May 2011
Machine Guns and Grenades to Mexico—April 2011

Anti-Aircraft Missile and Machine Guns to Mexican Drug Cartel—April 2011
Firearms Components to the United Kingdom—March 2011
Assault Rifles and Explosives for Export—March 2011 [undercover operation]
Semi-Automatic Assault Rifles to Mexico—March 2011
Firearms and Ammunition to Mexico—March 2011
Firearms to Colombia—March 2011
Firearms and Ammunition to Mexico—February 2011
Assault Weapon Parts and Gun Sights to Philippines—February 2011
Tactical SUVs Armed with M 134 Mini-Guns to Turkmenistan—February 2011
Specialized Metals for Iranian Missile Program—February 2011
AK-47s and Other Firearms to Mexico—January 2011
Bulletproof Vest Inserts to Colombia—January 2011
Iran Embargo Violations—January 2011
US Military Equipment to Yemen—January 2011
Assault Weapons to Mexico—January 2011
Weapons and Ammunition to Nigeria—January 2011
Arms Exports to Russia—December 2010
Digital Microwave Radios to Iran—November 2010
Fully Automatic AK-47 Machine Guns to Drug Cartels in Mexico—November 2010
Firearms to Kosovo and Austria—November 2010
Military Aircraft Engines to Venezuela—October 2010
Rocket Propulsion Systems, Engines, and Technology to South Korea—October 2010
Missiles, Grenade Launchers, and Other Weapons to Sri Lankan Terrorists—October 2010
AK-47s Assault Rifles to Somalia—October 2010
US Fighter Jet Engines and Parts to Iran—September 2010
$4 Million Arms Shipment to Cote d'Ivoire—September 2010
Iran Embargo Violations—August 2010
Nuclear-Related Equipment to Iran—July 2010
Combat Riflescopes Overseas—July 2010 [various overseas locations]
F-5 Fighter Jet Components to Iran—July 2010
Oil Field Equipment to the Sudan—June 2010
Military Optics Technology to China, Russia, Turkey, and South Korea—June 2010
Illegal Oil Transaction with Iraq—June 2010
Fighter Jet Components to Iran—June 2010
Satellite Hardware and Technology to Iran—June 2010
US Missile Components to Iran—May 2010
Commercial 747 Aircraft to Iran—May 2010
$500 Million Forfeiture for Iran Embargo Violations and Other Charges—May 2010
US-Origin Tools to Libya—March 2010
BAE Systems PLC Pleads Guilty and Ordered to Pay $400 Million—March 2010 [Foreign Corrupt Practices Act, violation of Arms Export Control Act and International Traffic in Army Regulation]
Semi-Automatic Pistols to Cayman Islands—February 2010
Electronics to Designated Terror Entity in Paraguay—February 2010
Chemical Purchasing Software to Iran—January 2010
Military Equipment to Yemen, Libya, and Other Locations—January 2010
Firearms to Mexico—January 2010
Firearms to Canada—December 2009
Restricted Components to Iran—December 2009
Military Electronics for Radar, Fighter Jets, and Missiles to Iran—December 2009
Anti-Aircraft Missiles and Machine Guns to Syria—November 2009

Military and Commercial Aircraft Components to Iran—November 2009
Sensitive Aircraft Components to Iran—September 2009
Sighting Devices to Afghanistan and Taiwan—September 2009
Missiles and Other Arms to Colombian Terror Organization—July 2009
Military Night Vision Technology to China—July 2009
Restricted Nuclear Materials to Foreign Government—June 2009 [FBI undercover operation]
Fighter Jet and Military Helicopter Components to Iran—June 2009
Stolen Military Optics Sold to Hong Kong, Taiwan, and Japan via Internet—June 2009
Military Night Vision Goggles to Italy—May 2009
Military Aircraft Components to Iran—April 2009
Military Aircraft Parts to Israel—April 2009
Thermal Imaging Cameras to South Korea—March 2009
Aircraft Engines and Components to Iranian Military—March 2009
Sensitive US Technology to Iranian Missile and Nuclear Entities—March 2009
Aircraft Engines and Advanced Surveillance Cameras to Iranian Military—March 2009
3500 Military Night Vision Goggles to Iranian Military—March 2009
Pump Components to Iran—February 2009
Night Vision Technology to Singapore—January 2009
Military Night Vision Systems to Vietnam—December 2008
Software Stolen From Nuclear Plant to Iran—December 2008
Guns to Canada—December 2008
Military Night Vision Equipment to Hizballah—December 2008
Stolen Military Night Vision Systems to Hong Kong—October 2008
Violation of Trade Embargo with Iran—October 2008
Telecommunications Equipment to Iraq—October 2008
Missile Technology to Iran—September 2008
Electronics and IED Components to Iran—September 2008
Rifle Scopes to Russia—September 2008
Controlled Technology to Indian Missile and Space Facility—September 2008
Fighter Jet Components to Iran—September 2008
Ammunition to Mexico—September 2008
Forklift Parts to Iran—August 2008
Military Laser Aiming Devices and Fighter Pilot Cueing Systems to Taiwan—August 2008
Missile Technology to Indian Government Entities—August 2008
Equipment to Iran—August 2008
Engineering Software to Iran—August 2008
Telecommunications Systems to Iran—July 2008
Night Vision Firearm Sights to Japan—July 2008
Combat Gun Sights to Sweden and Canada—July 2008
Cryogenic Pumps to Iran—July 2008
Military Aircraft Components to UAE and Thailand—July 2008
Computer Software to Cuba—July 2008
Military Night Vision Systems to Lebanon—July 2008
Illegal Export of F-5 and F-14 Fighter Jet Components to Malaysia—June 2008 [parts may have ended up in Iran]
Valves to Iran—June 2008
Firearms Components to Sudan—June 2008
Theft of Military Trade Secrets to Sell to Foreign Governments—May 2008
Controlled Computers to Iran—May 2008
Controlled Radiographic Equipment to Iran—May 2008
Ammunition to Jamaica, Defense Training to UAE—May 2008

Test Tube and Microplate Coating Systems to Iran—May 2008
Controlled Computer Equipment to Iran—April 2008
Military Night Vision Systems to Iran—April 2008
Russian Attack Helicopters to Zimbabwe—April 2008
Specialty Alloy Pipes to Iran—March 2008
Nuclear Testing Equipment to India—March 2008
100,000 Uzi Submachine Guns to Iran—March 2008
Controlled Computers to Syria—February 2008
Military Weapons Sight to Germany—February 2008
Two Sentenced in Iranian Embargo Case—February 2008
Military Night Vision Systems Overseas—January 2008
Firearms to Canada—January 2008
Petrochemical Valves to Iran and Iraq—December 2007
Military Night Vision Goggles Illegally Exported Overseas—December 2007
Fighter Jet Components to Germany—November 2007
F-14 Fighter Jet Components and Other Military Items to Iran—November 2007
Pipe Cutting Machines to Iran—October 2007
Nickel Powder to Taiwan—October 2007
Tractor Parts to Iran—October 2007
Illegal Exports of F-4 and F-14 Fighter Jet Components—October 2007
Products with Nuclear and Missile Applications to Pakistan—October 2007
Radios, Ammunition Magazines, Scopes to Designated Terrorist in Philippines—Aug. 1, 2007
Aircraft Components to Iran—July 2007
Ballistic Helmets to Suriname—March 2007
Machine Guns, Arms to Indonesia—January 2007
Sensitive Technology to Prohibited Facility in India—July 2007
F-14 Fighter Jet Components to Iran—May 2007
Controlled Telecommunications Equipment to Cuba—April 2007
Military Night Vision Components to India—April 2007

REFERENCE

Department of Justice, Summary of Major US export enforcement, economic espionage, trade secret, and embargo-related criminal cases: 2007 to present, updated February 14, 2013, Washington, D.C. Found at http://www.justice.gov/nsd/docs/export-case-fact-sheet.pdf, Retrieved October 1, 1997.

Appendix D: Special 301 Report, China

Piracy and counterfeiting undermine the innovation and creativity that is vital to our global competitiveness. These notorious markets not only hurt American workers and businesses, but are threats to entrepreneurs and industries around the world.

Ron Kirk, United States Trade Representative[1]

The United States Trade Representative (USTR), under the Executive Office of the President, issues a variety of reports, and the one considered by many to be the most important is called the Special 301 Report. The US Trade Representative is Ambassador Michael Froman, who deals with the World Trade Organization (WTO), which is made up of many countries interested in maintaining fair trade policies throughout the world. The Special 301 Report is an annual review of the state of intellectual property rights (IPR) protection and enforcement.

The latest 301 Report, issued in April 2012, brought into the light some real concerns about China. Although China has been mentioned frequently in previous reports and noted in various newspapers and television reports regarding its policies, this latest report really laid out what is going on relative to the global economy and China's willingness to do anything to get ahead.

China has an indigenous innovation policy, one that benefits only China, to the immense detriment of any company that wishes to develop or produce products in the People's Republic of China (PRC). This policy, in addition to the physical marketplaces that deal with counterfeiting and piracy, has kept China at the top of a USTR list of notorious nations in terms of economic theft and IPR infringements. "Piracy and counterfeiting undermine the innovation and creativity that is vital to our global competitiveness. These notorious markets not only hurt American workers and businesses, but are threats to entrepreneurs and industries around the world," said United States Trade Representative Ron Kirk on February 2011.[1]

The February 2011 data, located at the USTR web site, also stated that the markets included, for example, the web site Baidu, which recently ranked as the number one most visited site in China, and among the top 10 in the world. Baidu has exemplified the problem of online services engaged in "deep linking," which provide links to online locations containing "allegedly" infringed materials. The list also includes numerous examples of web sites involved in BitTorrent tracking and indexing, which facilitate the high-speed transfer of infringing materials between users, as well as Internet markets involved in specific activities such as piracy of sports telecasts, smartphone software, and physical products. Key physical markets listed include, for example, Beijing's notorious Silk Market, as well as numerous other markets from a wide range of countries and regions.

In July 2011, the USTR announced that the WTO dispute settlement panel has agreed with the United States, finding that export restraints imposed by China on several important industrial raw materials were inconsistent with China's WTO obligations. China's actions were not justified as conservation measures, environmental protection measures, or short supply measures. The raw materials at issue include various forms of bauxite, coke, fluorspar, magnesium, manganese, silicon carbide, silicon metal, yellow phosphorus, and zinc, and are used in a multitude of downstream applications in the steel, aluminum, and chemical industries. Kirk stated that "China's extensive use of export restraints for protectionist economic gain is deeply troubling.[2,3] China's policies provide substantial competitive advantages for downstream Chinese industries at the expense of non-Chinese users of these materials."

The export restraints challenged in this dispute include export quotas and export duties, as well as related minimum export price, export licensing, and export quota administration requirements. These types of export restraints skew the playing field against the United States and other countries in the production and export of numerous processed steel, aluminum, and chemical products and a wide range of further processed products. The export restraints can artificially increase world prices for these raw material inputs while *artificially lowering prices for Chinese producers*. This enables China's domestic downstream producers to produce lower-priced products from the raw materials and thereby creates significant advantages for China's producers when competing against US and other producers both in China's market and other countries' markets. The export restraints can also create substantial pressure on foreign downstream producers to move their operations and, as a result, their technologies to China.

The highlights of this 2012 Special 301 Report can be found verbatim to follow in the remainder of this Appendix. The 2012 Special 301 Report can be read in its entirety at http://www.ustr.gov.[4]

TRADE SECRETS AND FORCED TECHNOLOGY TRANSFER

Companies in a wide variety of industry sectors—including information and communication technologies, services, biopharmaceuticals, manufacturing, and environmental technologies—rely on the ability to protect their trade secrets and other proprietary information. Indeed, trade secrets are often among a company's core business assets, and a company's competitiveness may depend on its capacity to protect such assets.

The theft of trade secrets and other forms of economic espionage results in significant costs to US companies and threatens the economic security of the United States. If a company's trade secrets are stolen, its past investments in research and development, and its future profits, may be lost.

US companies are experiencing an increase in the theft of their trade secrets outside of the United States. The United States urges its trading partners to ensure that they have robust systems for protecting trade secrets, including deterrent penalties for criminal trade secret theft.

Another troubling trend involving trade secrets and other IPR is an increasing tendency of governments to adopt trade-distortive policies, which are sometimes designed to promote "indigenous innovation." These policies include the following:

- Requiring the transfer of technology as a condition for allowing access to a market, or for allowing a company to continue to do business in the market
- Directing state-owned enterprises in innovative sectors to seek non-commercial terms from their foreign business partners, including with respect to the acquisition and licensing of IPR
- Failing to effectively enforce IPR, including patents, trademarks, trade secrets, and copyrights, thereby allowing firms to gain competitive advantages from their misappropriation or infringement of another's IPR
- Failing to take meaningful measures to prevent or deter cyber-espionage
- Requiring use of, or providing preferences to, products or services in which IPR is either developed or owned locally, including with respect to government procurement
- Manipulating the standards development process to create unfair advantages for domestic firms, including with respect to the terms on which IPR is licensed
- Requiring unnecessary disclosure of confidential business information for regulatory approval, or failing to protect that information

China remains on the USTR Priority Watch List and is subject to monitoring. A wide spectrum of US rights holders reports serious obstacles to effective protection and enforcement of all forms of IPR in China, including patents, trademarks, copyrights, trade secrets, and protection of pharmaceutical test data. Compounding these obstacles is the troubling direction that China's policies in the IPR area have taken recently. These policies include China's efforts to link eligibility for government preferences to the national origin of the IPR in products. In addition, many companies are concerned that Chinese government agencies are inappropriately using market access and investment approvals as a means to compel foreign firms to license or sell their IPR to domestic Chinese entities. Further, for many industries, sales of IP-intensive goods and services in China remain disproportionately low when compared to sales in similar markets that provide stronger environments for IPR protection and more open market access. These concerns, coupled with the size of China both as a consumer marketplace and a globally significant producer of a wide array of products, mean that China's protection and enforcement of IPR must remain key priorities for US trade policy.

It is important to recognize that there were some improvements in China's IPR situation in 2011. Specifically, the Chinese government continued to carry out the Special IPR Enforcement Campaign that was begun in 2010, which resulted in some improvements in targeted sectors. In November 2011, Premier Wen Jiabao announced that this campaign would be made permanent, through the creation of a National Leading Group on IPR Enforcement. In addition, in a significant shift, Chinese Internet giant Baidu reached a landmark agreement with international music rights holders to ensure that its online music platform transmits legal content. Following that agreement, USTR removed Baidu from the Notorious Markets list. The United States is encouraged that on April 22, 2012, China's Supreme People's Court issued a draft Judicial Interpretation entitled *Regulations for the Applicability of Laws in Hearing Cases Regarding Civil Disputes Concerning Infringement on Information Network Broadcasting Rights.* This draft measure is intended to clarify, among other issues, legal standards surrounding inducement of infringement. The United States looks forward to the adoption of a Judicial Interpretation consistent with China's past Joint Commission on Commerce and Trade (JCCT) commitments. [Author's note: This is a draft judicial interpretation, and may not become a final ruling, or set into law.]

Despite these signs of progress, IPR protection and enforcement in China remain a significant challenge. Significant concerns persist in light of continuing high levels of trademark counterfeiting and copyright piracy, including over the Internet, the persistence of notorious physical and online markets selling IPR infringing goods, the manufacture and availability of counterfeit pharmaceuticals, the lack of effective means to protect pharmaceutical test and other data against unfair commercial use, as well as disclosure, and the export of counterfeit goods of all sorts, including products posing significant risks to the environment and human health and safety. Many knowledge-based industries remain concerned that the Chinese government is using certain policies intended to promote "indigenous innovation" to disadvantage foreign enterprises through measures or actions that effectively coerce the transfer of IPR from foreign rights holders to domestic entities.

A recent alarming increase in cases involving the theft of trade secrets in China, as well as cases of trade secret theft that occur outside China for the benefit of Chinese entities, also demonstrates that there is a systemic lack of effective protection and enforcement of IPR. The failure to impose deterrent penalties that are sufficient to change behavior is another continuing concern that affects all forms of IPR.

SPECIAL CAMPAIGN/LEADING GROUP

In March 2011, the PRC State Council extended through June 2011 the Special IPR Campaign begun in October 2010. The Special IPR Campaign continued targeting a broad range of IPR violations including copyright piracy and trademark counterfeiting over the Internet, distribution of infringing optical discs and publications, counterfeit cell phones, counterfeit pharmaceuticals, counterfeit seeds, and counterfeit bulk commodities for export.

US industry reported positive enforcement developments in several of the sectors that the Special IPR Campaign targeted. During the Campaign, the National Copyright Administration of China

(NCAC) identified key copyright infringement cases for special investigation and supervision. NCAC also named 18 popular video web sites for close supervision and follow-up (including web site shutdown when appropriate) for allegedly providing a wide variety of pirated material, including UUsee, Sina, Letv, Youku, Sohu, Baidu, Ku6.com, Joy.com, PPStream, verycd, Tudou, QQ.com, 56.com, Xunlei, Baofeng, Funshion, PPTV, and pipi.cn. US industry reported significant progress in online licensing agreements involving audiovisual products, particularly movies and TV series. As noted above, Baidu signed contracts with three international record companies—Universal Music, Warner Music, and Sony Music—that, through Baidu's joint venture online music portal, One Stop China, authorized Baidu to upload an entire catalogue of music available for paid user legal downloads and streaming.

Chinese authorities also targeted online sales of counterfeit hard goods during the Special Campaign, focusing on audiovisual products, electronic appliances, apparel, cosmetics, foods, fake or adulterated medicines, and mother and baby products. Numerous enforcement raids and other activities were carried out in key areas of Zhejiang, Shanghai, Guangdong, and Beijing. The State Administration for Industry and Commerce (SAIC) also issued Order 49, which addresses some of the enforcement issues that pertain to online counterfeit offerings and sales/payment platforms, but its implementing regulations are still being developed. Numerous web sites and online stores were closed down, and notable sales sites including Taobao, eBay, and Paipai worked with authorities in an *apparent* effort to improve their IPR enforcement practices.

In sum, US rights holders in the trademark and copyright sectors have reported that enforcement agencies in China were markedly more active in conducting raids, seizures, and arrests during the Special Campaign. It also appears that during the Special Campaign, the Chinese government focused its efforts with respect to infringement that occurs online in a manner that was meant to ensure that online entities were more responsive to requests from rights holders to remove infringing materials. At least one industry submission commented positively that the Chinese government's efforts during the Special Campaign "generated goodwill" among rights holders and sparked some cautious optimism that a recognition of the need for IPR protection and enforcement in China may finally be starting to take root.

SOFTWARE LEGALIZATION

Another key component of the Special Campaign was a software legalization initiative designed to ensure that government agencies use only legitimate, licensed copies of software. Central authorities announced they had completed software legalization in central-level government offices in May 2011 and would continue provincial-level legalization through October 2011. Because the legalization efforts were not completed at the provincial level, the government extended the process into 2012. As a result of these efforts, US software companies have seen a modest increase in sales to the government. However, much work remains to be done with respect to the state-owned enterprise (SOE) sector, which reportedly *continues to suffer from high piracy rates* and which, according to the World Bank, accounts for 27% of China's industrial output. Software piracy by SOEs is particularly pernicious, because it not only results in lost sales for software producers but also provides an unfair commercial advantage to such SOEs. Many SOEs compete directly with US businesses, and to the degree that these SOEs do not pay for the software that runs many of their operations, they obtain an advantage relative to their US and other competitors, who pay to acquire software lawfully.

ONLINE PIRACY

In 2011, China reportedly sanctioned 14 web sites for providing illegal music downloads, requiring those web sites to remove links to offending files, which had been identified by the government (in addition to the 18 mentioned above). Nevertheless, illegal downloads account for an estimated 99%

of all music downloads in China, and piracy of copyrighted material over the Internet thus continues to be a major problem. China's Internet users are increasingly turning to streaming media to watch foreign television shows and movies. While it appears that a number of user-generated content sites have eliminated most of their pirated content, these streaming sites have become the preferred method to watch for illegal content.

Industry submissions detail the improvements as a result of the Special Campaign and the increased emphasis on ensuring that IPR is protected in the digital environment. However, despite many "Special Campaigns" in China over the years to combat IPR infringement, and despite repeated bilateral commitments to increase IPR enforcement in China, the US government is concerned that sales of IP-intensive goods and services to China from US companies remain substantially below levels in other markets, measured in a variety of ways, ranging from spending on legitimate music as a percentage of GDP to software sales per personal computer. For example, total music revenue (which includes both legitimate physical and digital sales) in China for 2010 was only $64.3 million. This compares to almost $4.2 billion in the United States, $178.4 million in South Korea, and $68.9 million in Thailand—a country with less than 5% of China's population and with roughly the same per capita GDP. If Chinese sales were equivalent to Thailand's on a per capita basis, music sales would be almost $1.4 billion.

COUNTERFEITING

As we noted in last year's report, China's manufacturing capacity also extends to all phases of the production and global distribution of counterfeit goods. The list of goods that are counterfeited includes apparel and footwear, mobile phones, pharmaceuticals and medical equipment, herbal remedies, agricultural chemicals, computer and networking equipment, software and related products, batteries, cigarettes, cosmetics, home appliances, cement, auto parts, and merchandise based on copyrighted works. This year, the USTR received lengthy submissions concerning the impact that counterfeiting was having on US agricultural industries including the fruit and vegetable industry and the wine industry. Of particular concern was the submission of the Semiconductor Industry Association that warned of counterfeit semiconductors entering the supply chain, noting the risks of installing fake and shoddy semiconductor components in electronic equipment, including in equipment used for critical functions related to safety and security.

Where counterfeiting manufacturing and sales are concerned, attitudes regarding IPR infringement vary greatly by province and locality. For instance, administrative authorities in Shenzhen have lowered the criminal case thresholds for bringing cases against optical disc pirates, and those authorities regularly transfer cases for investigation to the Public Security Bureau. In one case, those authorities followed up regularly with online sales platform Tencent to discuss the company's enforcement efforts. By contrast, rights holders have expressed concerns that local Administrations for Industry and Commerce (AIC) in Guangdong and Fujian have refused to refer cases for criminal prosecution even when thresholds are met. Even more worrisome are reports that in Fujian and Guangdong, local protectionism has impeded rights holders who have investigated and provided clear evidence of counterfeiting operations (including, in one case, evidence of an entire supply chain to support massive counterfeiting of children's toys and accessories, from design to manufacturing to packaging) only to be stymied by provincial officials who have turned a blind eye to the evidence and have failed to act.

On a positive note, trademark rights holders are beginning to report that there has been a noticeable reduction in the *visibility* of counterfeit goods for sale in some of the notorious physical markets. This appears to be the result of intensified criminal enforcement and more proactive intervention by landlords. This may be attributable to steps taken by national and local AICs to target landlords of physical markets as part of a wider effort to promote enforcement of IPR rights, as well as court decisions that have found landlords liable for infringement they knew or should have known was taking place on their premises. However, guidelines regarding landlord liability are not legally binding, and court decisions in China's civil law system are not precedential.

Furthermore, there remain many markets that continue to trade in counterfeit and pirated merchandise. In particular, there are still many markets that serve as wholesalers for counterfeits distributed around the world. These include the notorious Yiwu market where all types of products can be copied and exported throughout the world or the night market in Putian that specializes in counterfeit athletic shoes, sports equipment, handbags, and watches, and where most products are being sold for export to US, European, and African markets. The United States will examine markets such as these during the Out-of-Cycle Notorious Markets review in autumn 2012.

Counterfeit goods are also prevalent in online markets and auction sites, including those listed in the 2011 USTR Notorious Markets Report, as well as others such as DHGate, TradeMe, HC360, and Global Sources. Rights holders, however, are encouraged that the Chinese government appears committed to intensifying efforts to address online counterfeiting, including through the issuance of SAIC Order 49 and through civil court decisions that have imposed liability on the operators of online sales web sites similar to those that have been imposed on the landlords of physical markets.

The consumer shift to online sales has also changed the pattern of export trade; previously, counterfeits were shipped in large containers, which resulted in large value and capacity seizures at the US border. However, increasingly, goods are sold by online traders in China (and elsewhere) and delivered to consumers by mail and express delivery service. This phenomenon is confirmed by the continued reduction in the level of seizures of wholesale quantities by customs officials in China and abroad.

TRADE SECRETS

The United States is concerned about a growing number of cases in which important trade secrets of US firms have been stolen by, or for the benefit of, Chinese companies. It has been difficult for some US companies to obtain relief against those who have benefited from this misappropriation, despite compelling evidence demonstrating misappropriation or theft. The United States is concerned that many more trade secrets cases involving US companies and Chinese competitors go unreported because US firms fear the cost and likelihood of failure of pursuing these cases through legal channels, as well as the possible commercial repercussions for bringing such cases to light. Although US firms have recently seen some improvement in enforcement of other types of IPR-related cases, as described above, protecting trade secrets in China remains a significant challenge and is of growing concern. The United States and China have increased their bilateral exchanges on this important issue, including in the JCCT IPR Working Group and through senior-level government engagements. Ensuring that companies are able to effectively protect and enforce their IPR in China, including trade secrets, is essential to promoting successful commercial relationships between US and Chinese firms.

MARKET ACCESS AND TECHNOLOGY USE

In addition to the risks of IPR infringement, including trade secret theft, and the difficulties discussed above regarding effective enforcement, many companies remain very concerned that the Chinese government has adopted policies or practices that systematically disadvantage foreign rights holders, by inappropriately conditioning market access and investment approvals, and other government benefits on the sale or licensing of IPR and other proprietary information to domestic Chinese entities.

While the United States welcomed China's commitment, reiterated in the joint fact sheet issued during Vice President Xi Jinping's visit to Washington on February 14, 2012, "that technology transfer and technological cooperation shall be decided by businesses independently and will not be used by the Chinese government as a pre-condition for market access,"[4] the United States will continue to work with China to develop a mechanism designed to resolve, in an expeditious manner, any concerns regarding the implementation of this commitment.

IPR AND INNOVATION

Chinese government agencies, including those at the national, provincial, and local levels, frequently release documents, including regulations, rules, and regulatory documents (e.g., opinions, notices, circulars) that seek to promote China's development into an innovative, IP-intensive economy. The United States recognizes the critical role of innovation in development and in improving living standards in the United States and China. However, the United States has expressed concerns to China regarding China's innovation-related policies and other industrial policies that may discriminate against or otherwise disadvantage US exports or US investors and their investments. Chinese regulations, rules, and regulatory documents frequently call for technology transfer and, in certain cases, require, or propose to require, that eligibility for government benefits or preferences is contingent upon IPR being developed in China, or being owned by or licensed, in some cases exclusively, to a Chinese party. Such government-imposed conditions or incentives may distort licensing and other arrangements, resulting in commercial outcomes that are not optimal for the firms involved or for promoting innovation. Government intervention in the commercial decisions that enterprises make regarding the ownership, development, registration, or licensing of IPR is not consistent with international practice and may raise concerns relative to China's implementation of its WTO obligations.

In November 2009, the Ministry of Science and Technology (MOST), the National Development and Reform Commission (NDRC), and the Ministry of Finance (MOF) issued the *Circular on Launching the 2009 National Indigenous Innovation Product Accreditation Work*, requiring companies to file applications by December 2009 for their products to be considered for accreditation as "indigenous innovation products." This measure provides for preferential treatment in government procurement to any products that are granted this accreditation, which is based on criteria such as the ownership or development of a product's IPR in China. Subsequently, the United States and US industry, along with the governments and industries of many of China's other trading partners, expressed serious concerns to China about this measure, as it appears to establish a system designed to provide preferential treatment in government procurement to products developed by Chinese enterprises.

In April 2010, MOST, NDRC, and MOF issued a draft measure for public comment, the *Circular on Launching 2010 National Innovation Product Accreditation Work*. The draft measure would amend some of the product accreditation criteria set forth in the November 2009 measure, but would leave other problematic criteria intact, along with the accreditation principles, application form, and link to government procurement. In addition, the draft measure originally was to become effective the day after comments were due. The United States submitted comments in May 2010, in which it asked China to suspend the implementation of the indigenous innovation accreditation system and to engage in consultations with the United States to address US concerns about the system. This draft measure was not finalized. At the May 2010 meeting, China agreed that its innovation policies would be consistent with the following principles: nondiscrimination; support for market competition and open international trade and investment; strong enforcement of IPR; and, consistent with WTO rules, leaving the terms and conditions of technology transfer, production processes, and other proprietary information to agreement between individual enterprises.

At the December 2010 JCCT meeting, China took important steps to address US concerns about its indigenous innovation policies. China agreed not to maintain any measures that provide government procurement preferences for goods or services based on the location where the intellectual property is owned or was developed. China also agreed to take into account US views on its *Draft Regulations Implementing the Government Procurement Law*, which provide for government procurement preferences for indigenous innovation products. During President Hu Jintao's January 2011 state visit, China further committed to delink its innovation policies from the provision of government procurement preferences. To implement President Hu's commitment, at the May 2011 S&ED, China agreed to eliminate all of its government procurement product accreditation catalogues and revise the *Draft Regulations Implementing the Government Procurement Law* to eliminate the provision requiring government procurement preferences for indigenous innovation products. During the 2011 JCCT meeting, China announced that the State Council had issued a measure requiring provincial, municipal, and autonomous regional governments to eliminate by December 1, 2011, any catalogues or other measures linking innovation policies to government procurement preferences. The United States is carefully monitoring China's commitments in this area.

INDIGENOUS INNOVATION AND PLACE OF INTELLECTUAL PROPERTY OWNERSHIP OR DEVELOPMENT

During the 2010 JCCT process, including at a meeting of the JCCT IPR Working Group and at the JCCT plenary meeting, the United States requested that China not condition government preferences on the location of intellectual property ownership and development. The United States recognized that the requirement for "Chinese intellectual property and proprietary brands" in the Indigenous Innovation Product Accreditation System was also a factor referenced in important Chinese government statements and other Chinese measures. For example, the October 2010 State Council *Decision on Accelerating the Cultivation and Development of Strategic Emerging Industries* states that, "China shall boost the cultivation and development of strategic emerging industry and hold the core technologies and intellectual property as well as enhance independent growth capability."[4] In addition, the *Measures for Administration of Recognition of Innovative and High-Tech Enterprises, Guo Ke Fa Huo [2008] No. 172*, adopted in final form, without opportunity for public comment, by MOST, MOF, and the State Administration of Taxation, provide for certain tax benefits for qualifying enterprises. One of the eligibility criteria is that "Enterprises registered in China... have independent intellectual property rights over the core technology of major products through independent research and development, transfer, recipient, mergers and acquisitions within three years or through exclusive licensing over five years."

At the 2010 JCCT, China agreed not to "adopt or maintain measures that make the location of the development or ownership of intellectual property a direct or indirect condition for eligibility for government procurement preferences for products and services. China and the United States will continue to discuss whether this principle applies to other government measures."

During the 2011 JCCT, China and the United States agreed, building on the previous years' commitment, and the innovation principles agreed to in the APEC 2011 Leaders' Declaration, to study other measures, including investment and tax-related measures in 2012, to determine whether the receipt of government benefits is linked to where intellectual property is owned or developed, or to the licensing of technology by foreign investors to host country entities.

COMPULSORY LICENSING

In 2011, China's State Intellectual Property Office (SIPO) issued "Draft Measures for Compulsory Licensing of Patents" for public comments. These measures are intended to provide greater guidance to SIPO, patent holders, and individuals and entities that seek the grant of a compulsory license under China's Patent Law. The United States appreciates that SIPO provided an opportunity for interested stakeholders to comment upon the draft. A number of companies and governments, including the United States, provided comments on these measures, raising concerns ranging from the length of time provided for certain procedural steps, to substantive concerns regarding the scope and grounds for the application of a compulsory license. On March 19, SIPO issued a slightly revised document, dated March 15, 2012, with indications that the document will go into effect on May 1, 2012. The United States is concerned that many stakeholder concerns were not reflected in the final document.

PATENTS USED IN CHINESE NATIONAL STANDARDS

China has prioritized the development of Chinese national standards, as evidenced by its Outline for the National Medium to Long-Term Science and Technology Development Plan (2006–2020), issued by the State Council in February 2006, and amplified shortly thereafter in the 11th Five Year Plan (2006–2010) for Standardization Development, issued by the Standardization Administration of China. More recently, China has announced that when it develops standards, it will rely on either non-patented technology or patented technology with prices lower than those that patent owners would otherwise seek to charge. As a result, China's treatment of patents in the standard setting process has garnered increasing attention and concern around the world, including in the United States. These concerns have been reported in depth in previous editions of this Report, as well as in USTR's 2012 Report on Technical Barriers to Trade (TBT Report).

IPR PROTECTION FOR PHARMACEUTICAL PRODUCTS

The United States continues to encourage China to provide an effective system to expeditiously address patent issues in connection with applications to market pharmaceutical products. In addition, the United States continues to have concerns about the extent to which China provides effective protection against unfair commercial use, as well as unauthorized disclosure, of undisclosed test or other data generated to obtain marketing approval for pharmaceutical products. China's law, and its commitment during WTO accession, requires China to ensure that no subsequent applicant may rely on the undisclosed test or other data submitted in support of an application for marketing approval of new pharmaceutical products for a period of at least six years from the date of marketing approval in China. However, there is evidence that generic manufactures have, in fact, been granted marketing approvals by the PRC State Food and Drug Administration prior to the expiration of this period, and in some cases, even before the originator's product has been approved.

More information about the above material and other USTR and WTO concerns can be found at the USTR web site: ustr.gov/about-us/press-office/press-releases.

REFERENCES

1. U.S. Trade Representative Office Press Release, 'USTR Announces Results of Special 301 Review of Notorious Markets,' Washington, D.C., February 2011.
2. Dan Ikenson, "WTO Slap at China Export Restrictions Belied by U.S. Import Curbs" found at Forbes.com, July 7, 2011.
3. Stephen Castle, "WTO Says Chinese Restrictions on Raw Materials Break Rules," NY Times, July 5, 2011.
4. 2012 Special 301 Report. Office of the U.S. Trade Representative, Executive Office of the President, Washington, D.C., April 2012. http://www.ustr.gov/sites/default/files/2012%20Special%20301%20Report_0.pdf. Retrieved March 28, 2013.

Index

Page numbers followed by f and t indicate figures and tables, respectively.

F

J

K

L

M

N

V

W

Z